The

Web Usability & Navigation:
A Beginner's Guide

Web Usability & Navigation:
A Beginner's Guide

Merlyn Holmes

McGraw-Hill/Osborne

New York   Chicago   San Francisco
Lisbon   London   Madrid   Mexico City   Milan
New Delhi   San Juan   Seoul   Singapore   Sydney   Toronto

McGraw-Hill/Osborne
2600 Tenth Street
Berkeley, California 94710
U.S.A.

To arrange bulk purchase discounts for sales promotions, premiums, or fund-raisers, please contact McGraw-Hill/Osborne at the above address. For information on translations or book distributors outside the U.S.A., please see the International Contact Information page immediately following the index of this book.

Web Usability & Navigation: A Beginner's Guide

1234567890 FGR FGR 01987654322

ISBN 0-07-219261-5

Publisher   Brandon A. Nordin
Vice President & Associate Publisher   Scott Rogers
Acquisitions Editor   Jim Schachterle
Project Editor   Jennifer Malnick
Acquisitions Coordinator   Timothy Madrid
Technical Editor   Wendy Willard
Copy Editor   Robert Campbell
Proofreader   Susie Elkind
Indexer   Claire Splan
Computer Designers   Jean Butterfield, George Toma Charbak
Illustrators   Michael Mueller, Lyssa Wald
Series Design   Gary Corrigan
Cover Design   Greg Scott
Cover Illustration   Kevin Curry

This book was composed with Corel VENTURA™ Publisher.

This book is dedicated to you, dear readers. It gave me great joy while writing the manuscript to know that there was a body of you out there in the world keenly interested in improving the state of Web usability. I thoroughly enjoyed imagining how you might take the information in this book and run with it, finding new ways to make the Web a better place. I look forward to seeing the Web sites you will design, and perhaps even reading the books you will write.

About the Author

Merlyn Holmes is a founding partner of Hot Tea Productions, and is a Web design consultant, educator, and writer. Recently, she has been a subject matter expert and the lead author on Web design and production courses that are being offered at training centers internationally. She also teaches and conducts train-the-trainers across the United States and Europe.

Merlyn has been the Gallery Director and/or judge for the Macromedia People's Choice Awards and the NewMedia Invision Awards since 1996 and as such has—sometimes with delight and sometimes with despondency—reviewed more than 3,500 Web and multimedia entries. She is propelled by those moments when she finds herself looking at her monitor and seeing an absolute gem, an example of a Web site or CD-ROM or some other new media that takes its medium to a higher level.

Merlyn also adores photography and is inspired in her own work by the beauty of the natural world and the way in which we humans move through it. She is currently exhibiting two series, *Wind in the Blue Leaves*, a nature photography series, and *dancEssences*, an attempt to capture some of the spirit of dance in still photography. For her next book project, she plans on combining her passions and writing a guide to the Web specifically for artists and nonprofit organizations. It will cover both ends of the usability spectrum: how to fully utilize the Web as a resource and how to create Web sites to effectively further a mission.

For more information on Merlyn's Web work and photography, or to suggest sites she could use as examples in her next book, visit the Hot Tea Productions Web site at www.hottea.com or contact her directly at merlyn@hottea.com.

Pronunciation guide   For no particularly valid reason other than family tradition, "Merlyn" is pronounced like mare + lynn, *not* like Merlin the magician, although she doesn't mind the connection. She's also a she and not a he, as some people mistakenly assume. She admits her name is not very user-friendly and requires something of a learning curve. Perhaps this constant exposure to usability issues since birth has contributed to her dedication to increasing the usability of other things in the world around her.

Contents at a Glance

PART III
Appendices

Contents

ix

Appendices

Acknowledgements

As with the design and development of a good Web site, the creation of this book was a team effort. The bastion of the effort was a group of dedicated readers. I could think of no better way to ensure that the content of the book would truly be useful to the public than following a user-centric writing process, and I am deeply appreciative of all the suggestions and comments given to me throughout the writing stage. My heartfelt thanks go to my editor Jim Schachterle; to those readers who perused every chapter of the manuscript, Steve Aulenbach, Jen Oxelson, and tech editor Wendy Willard; as well as to those who read and gave me important feedback on select chapters, Theresa Thomas, Gaylynn Potemkin, Georgeanne Nelson; and my beloved husband, Chris Holmes.

Thanks also to the editorial and production teams at McGraw-Hill/Osborne, especially Tim Madrid, Jenny Malnick, and Bob Campbell; their great senses of humor and expertise provided a lively fuel to spur me on past the never-ending series of deadlines. Thanks are due also to Lyssa Wald and Michael Mueller, who created all of the cartoon-like illustrations from my rather dubious sketches.

Much appreciation, thanks, and respect also go to the dozens of Web site designers and producers who gave me permission to reproduce screen grabs of their sites in this book. I will not list them all here, for you will see their work in these pages. Designing Web sites is a brave feat in any circumstances, but maintaining the open spirit of cooperation in word as well as deed and granting permission for their Web sites to be discussed in the context of finding ways to create even better, more useable sites is honorable indeed. These are the best role models available for anyone just beginning to undertake the task of creating usable Web sites.

My greatest thanks of all go to the love of my life: my husband, partner in Hot Tea Productions, and fellow accomplice in life, Chris Holmes. He not only provided practical help with the content of the book but also kept firm sight on the big picture and helped me navigate toward it with vision, purpose, and meaning.

Introduction

Usability is the lifeblood of the Web. Without it, as many Internet companies have discovered in recent months, there's no way to secure a dedicated user base and the consequent success for a Web site. Don't get me wrong; it is not the *only* factor in determining success—there are a number of business and content issues that also highly influence how likely a site is to succeed—but usability is a key building block. And whereas members of a Web site development team often cannot influence the business model or core content of a Web site, they can have a great deal of influence over how that material is presented via the Web and how easily Web site visitors can interact with it to accomplish whatever they have set out to do. In fact, that's why people hire them.

Conversely, understanding how to achieve good usability on the Web can also help create more successful business plans. Effective usability is essentially the net result of understanding three things: the market (a.k.a. the Web site users), the product or content, the delivery medium, and designing appropriately for all three.

As an interactive medium, the Web is inherently a user's medium. Web site "visitors" are not passive "viewers"; they demand more of a Web site than, say, a printed brochure or a television show. They expect to be able to *use* the Web to achieve some purpose in their lives, whether it be to find information, compare products, buy goods and have them delivered to their door, interact with other people, or even just to engage in an entertaining activity. As such, it is necessary for anyone who is involved in creating Web sites to develop a method of listening to these users, observing them, doing whatever it takes to learn what it is they want and need in a Web site—how they could best use a Web site. That's what user-centric design, and this book, are all about.

If there's one thing the first generation of Web designers has learned it is that usability cannot be taken for granted and that it must be addressed directly in order to achieve maximum effectiveness. Too many designers fell into the trap of believing that if they built a beautiful or cool Web site, visitors would come.

Learning how to create usable Web sites is a bit like magic. Essentially, you have to learn how to cast an invisibility spell. Like most components of good design, truly effective usability is transparent. In fact, the more a Web site's usability improves, the less visitors will even notice it. Instead, they can get on with their business of using a Web site to achieve some purpose.

Fortunately, the very best place to start learning about Web site usability is at the beginning: as a user, not as a designer or developer. Thus, this Beginner's Guide starts at the beginning and progresses through the necessary steps to learn about creating usable Web sites. It never forgets that point of origination, and it constantly ties all the steps back to that perspective.

Who Should Read this Book

Unlike every other arena within the field of Web development, *being a beginner is a real advantage* when it comes to identifying and understanding usability issues, so welcome, all you beginners—you are at the right door. This is not a closed party by any means; anyone who is involved in the conception, planning, design, or development of Web sites may find this book helpful, and I welcome you as well. I will ask you to remove some of your accolades, however, and tread barefoot for a while. As Marcel Proust said so well:

> *"The real voyage of discovery consists not in seeing new landscapes but in having new eyes."*

This book is for anyone who is capable of having those "new eyes," for that is what is required in adopting a truly user-centric design process. You will need new eyes to perceive the Web, to look at it through the eyes of its users, and to imagine new designs that will better unite the content, the medium, and the user.

What this Book Covers

Web Usability & Navigation: A Beginner's Guide is divided into three sections:
Seeing Through the Users' Eyes, Designing Web Sites for Their Users, and
Appendices.

Part I: Seeing Through the Users' Eyes

Part I introduces the essential concepts of a user-centric design process for the
Web in five modules, laying the foundation for the more pragmatic tasks of
designing usable Web sites later in the book.

- **Module 1: You as a Preeminent User: Put on Your Usability Spectacles**
  emphasizes the importance of approaching the Web as a user first and a
  designer second, and gives practical tips on how to tap into the usability
  experience first-hand.

- **Module 2: Swap Out Your Spectacles: Seeing from Other Perspectives**
  helps you expand your reach by observing, identifying with, and imagining
  the perspective of other users. It introduces the concept of developing Web
  site usage scenarios and explains the role they play in creating more user-
  centric Web sites.

- **Module 3: Get to Know Your Users: Creating User Profiles** introduces
  the more scientific method of collecting and interpreting user data to develop
  user profiles that can be used as a basis for a Web site's design. It explains
  the basic methods of user analysis and the all-important aspect of how to
  ask the right questions of your users.

- **Module 4: Get to Know Your Users' Computer Constraints** identifies the
  primary hardware and software constraints affecting Web site usability and
  how to best work around them in designing Web sites that will be accessible
  and usable on a wide range of systems.

- **Module 5: Know the Web Even Better Than Your Users Do** addresses the
  importance of understanding the full limitations and potential of the Web
  and provides a framework for doing so.

Part II: Designing Web Sites for Their Users

Part II outlines the practical steps necessary within a user-centric Web design process. It also presents a number of case studies of current Web sites undergoing a revision process and takes a peek at what lies ahead in the future of Web site design.

- **Module 6: Stick to a User-Centric Design Process** addresses the logistics of enlisting the whole Web team's support of a user-centric design process. It discusses an ideal Web team composite, the typical phases of Web site design and key phases of user involvement within it, and some common usability-related mistakes that can be avoided.

- **Module 7: Site Design, First Steps: Getting Users to Your Site** explains how to facilitate users' discovery of and recognition of your Web site. It covers such things as establishing good domain names and URLs, making your site findable through search engines, and distinguishing between core and supplemental content.

- **Module 8: Information Architecture: Organizing Your Web Site** presents a key step in creating usable Web sites. It identifies the classification systems available to you for organizing the content of a Web site and explains ways of organizing that content from the users' point of view instead of the designer's or client's. It also helps you determine how to choose effective labels and metaphors and gives you a chance to practice organizing content for a site.

- **Module 9: Navigation Design** shows how to design the navigation for your Web site to support and enhance the information architecture. It couches the discussion within a framework of the relative importance of aesthetics and functionality in Web site design, and provides an opportunity to practice creating part of a site's navigation design.

- **Module 10: Site Design Usability Dilemmas** addresses a number of common design dilemmas and how they can be resolved. It also outlines how to evaluate the advantages and disadvantages of proposed solutions to such dilemmas and gives you an opportunity to practice identifying ways of improving an existing Web site.

● **Module 11: Screen Design for Usability** outlines the elements of screen design that affect usability and how to establish design guidelines that will ensure a Web site's usability. It covers such things as screen size, color limitations, the amount of content to include on a screen, how to direct the user's eye, and how to secure on-screen readability.

● **Module 12: Preparing User-Friendly Content** explains what is required to provide user-friendly text, graphics, and media files for a Web site and gives you an opportunity to practice identifying appropriate content for a Web site.

● **Module 13: Case Studies: Analyzing Web Sites** analyzes two real-world Web sites in a step-by-step manner that encourages your participation. It also presents additional sites for you to practice analyzing and suggesting improvements for to give you a chance to employ everything that you have learned in the earlier modules.

● **Module 14: Testing, Testing** outlines the role of usability testing, its process and components. It helps you understand and evaluate the choices available to you and to identify the roles and responsibilities of everyone involved in a usability test. Finally, it provides you with the opportunity to participate in a usability test to experience it first-hand.

● **Module 15: Looking Ahead: Through the Users' Eyes** explores key trends in the future of the Web, in particular the evolution of Web technologies, designs, and users. It encourages participating in a conscious evolution rather than being a passive recipient in the process.

Part III: Appendices

Part III offers additional information in quick-reference format. These materials may be of use to both beginning and advanced Web site development team members.

● **Appendix A: Answers to Mastery Checks** provides the answers to the Mastery Check quizzes at the end of each module.

● **Appendix B: Print and Web Resources** lists a number of books and URLs that may be of use in continued studies, for surely if any area merits a lifetime of study, it is how to increase usability. This appendix includes materials that are specific to Web usability as well as materials beyond the topic of the Web but that may still inform your understanding of the issues involved and your design decisions.

● **Appendix C: Web Site Functionality Testing** includes an explanation and a checklist of key elements to test in order to ensure your Web site is working as intended on all of the target browsers, operating systems, bandwidths, and screen resolutions.

● **Appendix D: Web Site Usability Checklists** presents a series of handy checklists for a number of common things to test for covering a Web site's content, information architecture, navigation design, and screen design.

How to Read this Book

This book is designed so that you can read through it from cover to cover, or just work through a particular module. If you are a beginner, it is recommended that you work through the modules in order, because the content of each module builds upon the previous one.

Each module has at least one project for you to complete. You will find that your grasp of the material will increase significantly if you take the time to do the projects. It's one thing to read about designing usable Web sites; it's another thing altogether to put the steps into practice and hone your skills.

Special Features

Two kinds of self-testing features are available in every module so that you can check your own learning. *1-Minute Drills* are scattered throughout each module, giving you the opportunity for a quick "check-up" on your comprehension of the material. The answers to these appear at the bottom of their respective pages. Every module ends with a *Mastery Check* that gives you the chance to test your knowledge of the subject matter thus far. You will find the answers to the Mastery Checks in Appendix A.

Tip

Throughout this book you will find **Hints**, **Tips**, **Notes**, and words of **Caution** that will provide you with extra information or helpful ways to improve your grasp of certain points.

Ask the Expert sections provide more detailed information on related topics in an easy-to-follow question-and-answer format. One or more *Projects* are also included in every module to give you the opportunity to apply your newfound knowledge and develop hands-on skills.

Summary

I think you'll find that creating usable Web sites is not an inherently difficult process. It is just a "thought-full" one. It requires you to consider your options from a number of different perspectives and to base your design decisions on what will work best for the intended audience.

It is also an endeavor of some importance. The Web has suffered from a lack of usability and a lack of understanding of what can be done to fix it. There is a desperate need for knowledgeable, skilled, thoughtful people, and I hope this book will help you find your way to filling that niche.

Part I

Seeing Through the Users' Eyes

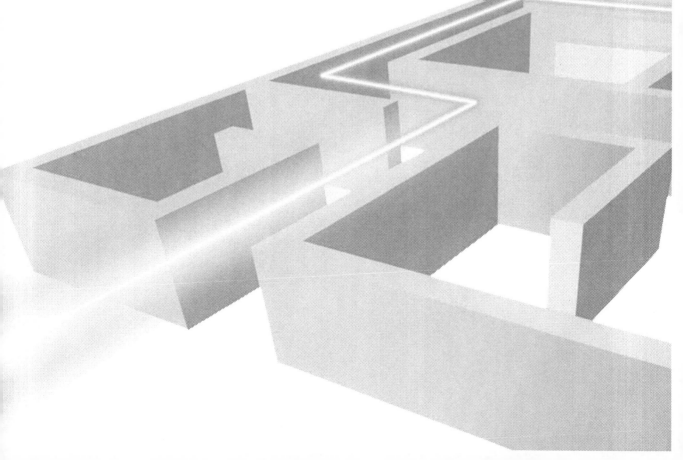

Module 1

You as a Preeminent User: Put on Your Usability Spectacles

The Goals of This Module

- Define Web site usability
- Understand the importance of user-centered Web design
- Identify your role as a user within the design and development of Web sites
- Practice how to tap into usability experiences first-hand

Web usability: This phrase is one of the most bandied-about terms in the Web industry today. In its simplest definition, a usable Web site is one that its audience can effectively *use*. Does the Web site work? Can users *easily* find the information they are looking for? Can they make transactions or be involved in their desired interactions *effortlessly*? Or do they push the off button with a snarl and pick up the telephone to conduct their business the "old-fashioned" way? Or even just blithely click the Search button in their browser and surf off to another site, leaving your site to waft into cyberspace without a bookmark to help them ever retrieve it again?

Does "usability" sound like an obvious component of Web design? It is. However, creating a usable site is not nearly so easy as recognizing it. Usability is intricately tied into the Web site design, information architecture, navigational structure, content, audience hardware and software, and the goals of whoever is creating the Web site in the first place. And, by and large, the majority of Web sites fail to be as usable as they could be. It's no easy task.

There are many contributing factors to the widespread failure of Web sites to score well on a usability scale, but by far and away the biggest, most fundamental flaw is the mental gap between being a Web site "designer" and being a Web site "user." In other contexts, you may recognize this as an "us" and "them" quandary. How can designers tell if their Web sites are usable, for example, if they are too busy designing what they think are cool site, and not actually using them?

You are not going to make that mistake. As part of a Web development team, or as a solo Web producer, you may have a wardrobe full of different hats: your programming hat, your design hat, your planning hat, your troubleshooting hat, your espresso grinding hat, and so on. But what you really need to build successful Web sites is a pair of usability spectacles. Put on a pair of these and you can see the Web through the users' eyes. And, surprise, you might find that it's not such an unnatural thing to do. After all, aren't you a Web site user anyway? Sometimes all it takes to hone usability enhancing skills is to just listen to and observe yourself, to learn to trust your own experiences as a user. That's the first step, and that's what we'll address in this first module.

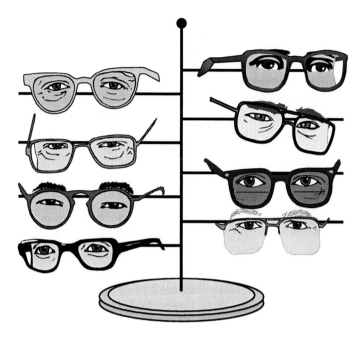

We'll begin by discussing how to experience the Web as a user, which sometimes involves forgetting all the highfalutin things you may have learned about Web site design and development. (Don't worry, these can be temporary memory lapses. Think about it as being like stashing your clothes when you go skinny-dipping. It's a little risky but well worth it, and when you need your clothes again, you know where to find them.)

We'll discuss such things as what signs to look for in good (and bad) usability, how to stay focused on examining usability issues, how to deal with distractions, and how to avoid unintentionally editing or altering your memories and experiences as a user. This last task is much easier said than done. In order to be successful at it, you need to learn how to assign the blame for bad usability where it belongs—with the design and not the user. All in all, this module should help you understand firsthand why usability is important and give you a set of analytical tools that can help you identify key aspects of usability on an ongoing basis.

In the remaining modules of Part I, we will identify more ways of seeing through other users' eyes so that you can learn from their experiences as well as your own. Part II, the bulk of this book, which encompasses Modules 6 through 15, will then address how to design user-centered Web sites today, and take a quick look at designing user-centered Web sites in the future. The medium of the Web is not standing still, so a key part of learning to design for the Web is learning to keep your eyes open so that you can assess how the medium—and its users—are evolving.

But now, on with step one!

Experience the Web as a User

Got your usability spectacles on? As when you put on any new pair of glasses, you may find that the world looks a little lopsided for a while. Let me help you get used to them. The first thing you need to remember is that you want to look at the world, or at least the Web, from a fresh perspective. Erase everything you know about the Web, all your preconceived notions, all your hard-learned experience. The goal here is to let your mind become a *tabula rasa*, a blank slate upon which new impressions can be formed. There may not be many aspects of life in which you want to be a babe in the woods, but this is one of them. Savor it. Your goal is to be a true beginner—hey, this is a beginner's guide; chances are you're way ahead of those old-time Web designers in this regard! Hang on to that advantage, and don't let any of the knowledge or experience that you accumulate obscure this vision.

Dealing with Distractions

The second thing to remember is that while it's okay to occasionally remove these usability spectacles and look at the Web with a designer's eye—after all, sometimes we can't stop ourselves—it's important to recognize when you are doing so and to keep the distinction clear in your mind. It may even help to classify your thoughts: "As a user, I think…" or "As a designer/developer, I think…"

I don't believe I am the only person in the world who sometimes gets caught up in the beauty of a design, regardless of its functionality. In my work, I've reviewed over 3500 Web sites and CD-ROMs for competitions. When I see a really fresh design, I perk up. If I were hooked up to an array of monitoring machines, I am sure you would see my brain activity spike, as well as my heart rate increase—the whole shebang. I love intriguing designs. I love puzzling through them, getting into the mind of the designer behind them, experimenting with them, letting them inform my own ideas, spark my own creativity. But... if I'm judging a category that has anything to do with creating a successful Web site, I make myself change gears, or spectacles, so that I experience the site from the viewpoint of the site's target users, and look at it again before assigning it any kind of rating.

If I can do this, you can do this.

Don't let yourself be sidetracked. Yes, you will find that these so-called spectacles occasionally slip down your nose and you will unwittingly be looking at a site from some other perspective. Sometimes it will be the content that distracts you. You may find yourself oohing and ahhing over those motorbikes, or discover that you've been absorbed for the past 20 minutes in reading salary statistics for Web development teams, or dreamily transfixed by a movie trailer, or caught up in reading about the impending release of the next, best version of whatever catches your fancy. Stop.

While many users may put up with horrible design if the content is worth it to them, many others will not. You could say that one alternative to creating good, usable Web sites is to develop content that is irresistible, but I'd vote for couching irresistible content within a good, usable Web site design. Aim to satisfy all your users. Create a site with great content and bad design, and you're just asking for someone to come along and create a better site that delivers similar content and snatches away your user base.

A User's Guide to the Usability Spectacles

The key to wearing these usability spectacles is to let yourself roam the Web doing whatever you as a user would like to do in whatever fashion you choose, following whatever path you want, while at the same time doing these two things:

- Observe your own thoughts and behaviors.

- Record the thought processes and behaviors that have to do with the functionality of the site.

Pay particular attention to the following:

- What navigation path do you follow? Do you have to backtrack at any point? If so, where did the Web site lead you astray?

- What decisions do you make along the way? Are there points at which you think something along the lines of "The information I want could be under this heading, or maybe that heading. I guess I'll try this one"? Do you take a wild guess at this juncture, or are you able to deduce which choice is probably correct from clues within the Web site?

- What clues inform your decisions? Do you have to read any text in order to navigate effectively? Does the color scheme enlighten you in any way? What about the graphics? Are there audio clues?

- What path does your eye follow within each Web site page or screen? Top to bottom? Left to right? Do you jump to the animation in the lower right then back to the heading in the upper left, or scan down the navigation bar on the left, scroll down to the navigation at the bottom, then back up to the body text in the center? Try looking at the same screen first as a general user, surfing to see what's there, and then again with the purpose of finding a specific piece of information. Does your eye follow a different path?

- Do you find any elements distracting or annoying? Never-ending animations and ad banners can be particularly annoying culprits, but there are others. Excessively busy pages top my list of Web site vexations. You can put your hand over animations and thus block them out, as many users do, but you can't block out busyness if you have to read through it to find what you want. Clashing color schemes can also make me cringe, as well as broken or missing graphics, or badly produced visuals or audio clips. This list can go on and on.

- What aspects of the site are particularly pleasing or helpful? Sometimes these elements are harder to identify than the annoying ones; we tend to take things that work well for granted. But pay attention to them; they can be valuable learning tools for what to do right.

1

When you find those usability spectacles slipping off your nose, just push them back up and start over again. There are also tools to help you refocus on what other users may perceive, including simple things like just asking them. We'll be discussing some of these tools in Module 2. But first and foremost, you need to work on becoming a critical, discerning user yourself. After all, you can be available 100 percent of the time, and you can be an invaluable assistant to that other part of yourself that may be designing or developing a Web site.

Some common usability flaws to look for include:

- Interfaces that assume the user knows how to use them or interfaces that do not *teach* the user how to use them.

- Inconsistent interfaces—including ones that establish visual metaphors on the home page, then change to text buttons on subsequent screens. Or interfaces that use color cues in some sections and not in others. Worst of all are interfaces that give one set of options for site-wide navigation on the home page, and a different set in other sections.

- Labels that use the language, or jargon, of the site's creators, not the users.

- Meaningless visual icons. A good icon should convey information about the content that will be linked to by clicking it, not just be cute or colorful or pretty.

- Reliance on a single navigation mode. Given the wide variety of *users and uses* for a Web site, it is best to offer multiple ways of finding any given piece of information on a Web site. Even the same user visiting the same site can have very different purposes at different times and require different styles of navigation. For example, I first encountered the Jimi Hendrix Web site referenced in Project 1-1 (http://www.shockwave.com/bin/shockwave/ entry.jsp?content=purplehaze) a few months ago when helping a new user explore the Web via the http://www.shockwave.com site. We stumbled, or "surfed" across it, while looking for interesting interfaces and content that he was interested in. On that luxurious, sunny afternoon, we had all the time in the world in which to play around. When I went back to look up the URL for this book earlier today, however, I went straight for shockwave.com's search function and typed in "hendrix." This time I was on a deadline and wanted that information straight away!

Remember Your Experiences Without Any Edits

The human mind is a funny thing. We have an amazing capacity to experience one thing, then edit that experience and store it away in our memory as a sequence of events that's substantially different from the original experience. You see this all the time in user studies where users will have noticeable difficulty navigating a site. If they are ultimately successful in finding what they are looking for, however, they tend to forget how difficult it was. More often than not, at the end of the study when they are asked for their overall impressions, they will smile amiably and say it was a good site and they had no problem finding what they needed. It's only when they fail to find what they were looking for that they tend to remember the difficulties they experienced (or when they go back to the site and try to find another piece of information).

The Myth about Intuitive Design

Two things are going on in these Web site usability studies. One is that we humans learn as we do things, and once we figure out how to do something, we think of it as easy within our own minds even if we initially found it confusing. Take tying your shoelaces, for example. Do you have any recollection of how hard you had to work to learn to tie your shoelaces? Most of us don't, and the process seems very easy, even intuitive. But just watch a young child attempting the same task, putting on his shoes—preferably shoes without Velcro straps! More likely than not, that's a mirror image of you puzzling over which lace goes over, or is that under, and then what do you do next? If there aren't any kids of the right age around, try French-braiding somebody's hair. If you can braid easily, try doing it backward or upside down.

The pattern is this: We learn how to do something; the process becomes easy for us, and then—and this is the death knell for designers—we assume that it's easy for everybody else, and we forget just how difficult it was for ourselves.

The idea of "intuitive design" is highly lauded in the Web industry, and yet if you really view the Web from a fresh, untainted perspective, very little about the Web is intuitive. People just learn relatively quickly, although I wouldn't say "easily," the basics of how to navigate the Web. But when you are designing most sites, the target audience typically includes complete newbies as well as much more experienced users. Every week you can read in the industry journals about the increasing number of people "on the Web." As of this writing, over 100 million people, or one-third of the American population, are nominally on the Web.

Great, the numbers are huge; a ton of users are out there ready to visit your site. But, and this is a big but, another two-thirds of the population have yet to come online. There are currently an estimated 55,000 new users every day, and that is only in the U.S. The ratios are even higher in Europe, Latin America, Africa, Asia—you know, the rest of the world—and most of those users are not native English speakers and so will have even more difficulty learning how to navigate the largely English text–based Web.

Tip

Instead of thinking about making your Web site designs *intuitive*, think about making them *learnable*. And when you are studying Web sites through your usability spectacles, pay close attention to what and how you learn whatever is necessary to successfully navigate each site. We will expand upon building learnable Web navigation in Module 9.

Assign the Blame Where It Belongs

The other useful observation from typical user studies is that users tend to blame themselves for not being able to successfully navigate a site. Statements like "How could I be so stupid?" or "Duh!" (with the appropriate slap to the forehead) are very common.

Tip

Assign the blame where it belongs. Users are not stupid, designs are. And that applies to you as well. People who know something about the Web tend to be the first to blame themselves for not figuring a site out. This is usually misplaced.

This tendency is commonplace beyond the Web as well. What will certainly be considered a classic design case in textbooks for decades to come is the infamous Palm Beach, Florida, "butterfly ballot" for the American presidential election in the year 2000. (I can hear your groans already. Sorry, we'll be reminded of this debacle for the rest of our lives, so we might as well use it as a good lesson to learn from.)

A good chunk of the world was captivated in November–December 2000 by the fallout from what was essentially a poorly designed ballot. The design made perfect sense to those who designed it, and it was reviewed and approved by members of both the Republican and Democratic parties. It did not, however, make sense to a number of the users, in this case a few thousand residents of Palm Beach County who went to the polls on November 10 to cast their vote for president. These voters were apparently confused by the butterfly ballot and unintentionally voted for a third-party candidate (Pat Buchanan) instead of a neck-and-neck front runner (Al Gore). Who could have known that the presidential election could have been determined by the ballot design in the state of Florida? Never doubt that usability issues can have a profound impact on our lives.

The members of this largely well-educated, well-to-do population of active voters, many of whom had been participating in elections for decades, were the butt of "stupidity" jokes around the world. When interviewed about the confusion regarding the ballot, their personal narratives revealed a high level of embarrassment. Account after account documented how much they initially blamed themselves for their "stupid mistakes." It was only after the story hit the press and the numbers started to add up in a way that could potentially have swayed the outcome of the presidential election that anyone seriously began to question the ballot design. That's where the real "Duh!" belongs in the history books. Remember, there are never bad users, only bad designs.

?-Ask the Expert

Question: So when I make a really dumb mistake and end up on the wrong page of a Web site, what could I say other than "Duh!" or "How could I be so stupid?"

Answer: Whenever you hear yourself say "Duh!," stop and look very closely at your whole thought process. Look at the clues given to you by the Web site design and figure out what may have led you astray or confused you in the first place. That's where the learning opportunity lies. Study it carefully and take whatever you learn with you into your next Web design. If you get tripped up over some little detail in a Web site, you can be sure that many other users will too.

In becoming a discerning user, you need to learn how to observe your own Web use carefully in a nonjudgmental way.

1-Minute Drill

● Are there ever "bad users" when you're analyzing usability issues on the Web?

● Instead of thinking about making your Web site designs intuitive, think instead about making them _____.

Another thing to look out for is what I call the "Ah hah! factor." This is the positive reinforcement side of the "Duh!" phenomenon. "Ah hahs!" usually occur when something is successfully learned. It's generally a sign of a more pleasurable learning process and, thus, a more effective design. "Ah hahs!" tend to result when users are challenged to learn something and given enough clues that they can figure it out.

Caution

One person's "Ah hah!" may often be another user's "Duh!" In these cases, it really is best to get as wide a variety of user responses as possible. We'll talk about broadening your user perspective base in Modules 2 and 3.

Once again, to get the most value from your experience as a Web user, it is necessary to

● Observe your own thoughts and behaviors.

● Record the thought processes and behaviors pertaining to the functionality of the site.

The latter step is particularly important in cases where there is faulty design. By recording your experiences, you can prevent the self-editing and the self-blame that so typically occur after the fact. Yes, recording everything can be tedious. Once you have formed really good observation habits, it may not be so necessary to record everything, but don't skimp on the learning process. Those self-editing

---

● No, there are never bad users, only bad designs. The users' so-called mistakes usually indicate a flaw in the navigation or structure of the site.

● Learnable, preferably *easily* learnable

and self-blame habits are probably more deeply ingrained than you may imagine. We all do it. I still do it, and I ought to know better by now!

Enough of all this talk. Put those usability spectacles on and try them out for yourself.

Project 1-1: Record Your Own Web Experiences

Remember that example about learning to tie your shoelaces? Well, the natural counterpart to that for Web usability studies is learning how to use the Web in the first place. In this activity, I'd like you to relive as best you can your very first experiences with the Web. We'll use a twofold approach. First off, try a simple memory recall technique. Be mindful of what self-editing you may have already introduced into your memory banks, though. Record as honestly as you can what it was like to sit down at the computer and visit your very first Web sites. Record the difficulties, the challenges, as well as the joys of discovery in learning how to use the Web.

Second, we'll try to reinitiate an experience akin to those first Web experiences by visiting some sites with rather unique, odd/wonderful (I'll leave the choice of descriptive word up to you after you've visited the sites!), but certainly fresh navigation systems. These sites are ones you can newly experience instead of having to recall your past experiences. (Use additional paper as needed to record your observations, or feel free to type them in a word processing program.)

Step-by-Step

1. Write down from memory a description of your first Web experiences: the first time you logged on, what site or sites you first visited, what difficulties you encountered, what triggered the "Ah hah!" moments or the "Duh!" moments, who or what facilitated your learning process of how to use the Web, and any other subjective or objective memories that you may have about the experience. If your only memory is that it was pretty straightforward and you've never experienced any real difficulty with it, ask someone who may have been with you at the time if they remember the same thing. If, as when learning to tie your shoelaces, you have no memory of your first experiences, try asking other users what their first experiences were. Their experiences may help you recall your own.

2. Visit one or more of the following Web sites with unusual interfaces, and try to recapture the raw feeling of being a beginner. Observe your own thoughts, actions, and learning process, and jot down notes about your experience exploring and navigating the Web site before you have a chance to "critique" or "correct" yourself. Remember, this is your chance to leave all the blame at the door; the facility or speed with which you learn how to navigate these sites is not a reflection of your abilities; it is a window into the effectiveness of the Web site design:

- http://www.thebrain.com
- http://www.lessrain.com (select the "fish" option)
- http://www.cybertown.com
- http://www.shockwave.com/bin/shockwave/entry.jsp?content= purplehaze (or go to shockwave.com and search for "Hendrix" or "Purple Haze")

3. Next, visit a more standard Web site and try to experience it as a first-time user. Leave behind everything you have learned about navigating the Web. Feel free to pick a site that you have used more than once and have taken its interface design for granted as being intuitive. Alternatively, try one or more of the following sites:

- http://www.amazon.com
- http://www.pbs.org
- http://www.si.edu
- http://www.nps.gov
- http://www.harley-davidson.com
- http://www.macromedia.com
- http://www.adobe.com
- http://www.charlesschwab.com

Assign yourself a task, whether it's finding a specific book or product or researching a fact, and so on, and then record your thought processes and the actions you take to achieve that task. Include in your notes any backtracking that you have to do—no cheating! This is time to observe and record all. Believe me, you will not be the first to have to backtrack on a site. In fact, many people backtrack all the time, but most of them just forget that was part of the process once they find what they were looking for.

4. Once you've completed your self-assigned task, go back to the home page and do it again using another method or following another path. How many ways can you find to achieve that same task? Which ways seem more effective to you and how much of that is because of habit, or the way you think, or what seem to be the established conventions of the Web?

Project Summary

Congratulations. You're on your way to becoming your own greatest asset in the Web design and development process. Sometimes all it takes to become a more mindful, self-observant user is the desire to do so and a little conscious effort. It wasn't all that hard slipping on those usability spectacles, was it?

A word of warning, though: honing your skills can go in cycles. Ironically, the more embroiled you become in Web site development, the more difficult it can become to step back and look at it from that squeaky-clean, fresh perspective. As a beginner, though, you have a great advantage. If you develop good habits now, they can last you throughout your career.

Understand First-Hand Why Usability Is Important

Hopefully, the project you just completed has given you a leg up on this section; you probably already have a good idea as to why usability is important: The less user-friendly a Web site is, the more likely that users will go elsewhere to find what they need. Which Web sites did you find yourself lingering over or bookmarking for some return visit? Generally, they are ones that have content that you're interested in and an easy-to-use interface. Yeah, yeah, you may have bookmarked a site like http://www.thebrain.com, too, just because it has such a cool interface—like I did—but chances are that was your design side controlling your actions, not your good old usability side.

What you may or may not realize from your personal experiences is the serious failings in terms of usability of many, many Web sites. Most users still cannot *easily* find the information they are looking for on most Web sites. "Easily" is the key here. Many users will put up with faulty designs for a while if they think they have a chance at succeeding; they'll grunt and growl, curse, bang on the keyboard, call themselves stupid, and sometimes call the Web site stupid— good for them! Once they've invested a certain amount of time and effort in it, though, they will sometimes stick with it through to the bitter end. Have you ever done that? I have. It's only later, after that transaction is completed, that you swear "Never again."

And before the remaining two-thirds of the population of the U.S. have even gotten online, a small but significant number of people are giving up on the Web and saying that they will never try it again. People have only a limited tolerance for poorly designed sites. Once the novelty of using the Web has worn off and its possible uses have become woven into the fabric of our lives—our work, our home, our school lives—it becomes increasingly intolerable to have to "work" at getting what we need. Conversely, it's becoming increasingly necessary to make the Web work for us—smoothly and easily.

The first major usability studies weren't conducted until the late 1990s, and the results were shocking. In 1997, the User Interface Engineering team, led by Jared M. Spool, completed one of the broadest usability studies focusing on the Web. This is what they concluded:

> The Results: Searching for information on web sites is an intensely frustrating experience. Throughout our study, we were amazed by the time and effort it took users to answer even simple questions. And repeatedly, users gave up without ever finding what they were looking for. Even in the smaller web sites, we watched users get lost or wander off the site without being aware of it....
>
> Comparing the sites to each other tells only part of the story. Even Edmund's, the best site in our study, fell far short of the highest possible score. Clearly when it comes to web site design, there is room for improvement.
>
> —Jared M. Spool, et al., *Web Site Usability: A Designer's Guide*
> (User Interface Engineering, 1997)

These results got the attention of the Web industry, and suddenly usability experts were in high demand. So here's another good point for you: Even though you may consider yourself a beginner, this usability aspect of Web site development is still quite young, and there's still great need for knowledgeable, insightful capable minds in this field.

Ask the Expert

Question: I see that the field of Web usability is pretty new, but where did it come from?

Answer: To many Web designers and developers, Web usability specialists seemed to appear out of thin air in the late 1990s. However, usability professionals have been working in related fields for several decades. The twentieth-century developments in psychology spawned the study of what is called "human factors," which typically address what factors come into play between humans, often workers, and machinery. Assembly line engineers, for example, found it useful to know how many steps an employee could easily memorize and repeat, so that they could set up the workstations accordingly.

Fortunately, the field evolved to address what environments could be most beneficial (or least detrimental) to the workers as well, and whole secondary fields like human/computer interaction (HCI) have blossomed to help reduce physical ailments such as repetitive motion injuries. The study of Web usability is yet another allied field. In designing usable Web sites, it is necessary to take into account issues revolving around the use of navigation icons, for example, as well as the standard HCI factors, such as the logistics of clicking a mouse.

Project 1-2: Begin Creating a Web Site Library

A key tool you can develop for your own use in designing usable Web sites is a Web Site Library, complete with informative, searchable details about each site. It's generally not enough just to bookmark thought-provoking sites. It takes no time at all to overload your bookmarks folder, and it's impossible to categorize each site by all the criteria that are really helpful to you on the job.

In this project, we will begin a Web Site Library. We will continue to develop it throughout the book, but I'd encourage you to think about this as the beginning of a tool that you will continue to develop throughout your career in Web site design and development.

1

Step-by-Step

1. In a program that you are comfortable with, such as MS Word or even just using HTML, create a template that allows you to make a list of Web sites with at least the following heads of information. This may take the form of a table, a spreadsheet, or just succeeding blocks of text. (Don't worry about fully understanding each of the terms at this point; we will be addressing the new terms in Modules 8 and 9.)

- URL
- Site Name (in case it's not easily determined by the URL)
- Usability
- Information Architecture
- Navigation Design
- Other Notes

The following table shows one example of how these heads can be laid out in table form. I'd suggest turning your page into landscape format and widening each of the columns as much as possible so that you have ample room to record your thoughts about each topic.

URL	Site Name	Usability	Information Architecture	Navigation Design	Other Notes

2. Feel free to add other heads that are pertinent to your interests as you see fit. These may include such things as

- Look and feel
- Use of audio/video
- HTML techniques
- JavaScript techniques
- Or other topics of your choice

3. Now, begin to build your Web Site Library. Start with a few of the sites you reviewed in Project 1-1, and jot down your notes regarding the URL, site name, and usability issues for each. Also, feel free to add anything under the "Other Notes" head or other heads that you have added. Don't worry about

the Information Architecture and Navigation Design sections right now. We will revisit those after discussing them each more fully.

Tip

To ensure the best future searchability of your library, develop a consistent vocabulary and abbreviation system. Also, use the most precise language you can. As your library grows, you will find descriptive phrases like "good use of icons and color schemes" much more helpful than "cool interface."

4. And last, but not least, take a screen shot or shots of each site and add them to your document. As wonderful a resource as the Web is, longevity is not always its strongest point. You can't rely on a site being there when you want to see it again or, even worse, when you want to show it as an example to a potential client or other member of your Web team. Screen shots obviously have limited functionality, but they are better than a 404 error message.

Tip

In addition to the fairly rudimentary capability of PCs and Macs to take screen grabs, there are a number of screen grab programs available such as Snagit or FullShot as shareware or for relatively small fees. Try searching http://www.tucows.com and http://www.downloads.com for "screen capture" programs.

Caution

It may be pretty easy to capture screen grabs of sites and even download HTML and graphic files, but keep in mind that does not give you the right to reproduce or distribute them. Always ask permission from the site's creators before distributing them—or posting them to a public Web site.

5. If you find a site that you really want to capture the functionality of, you can download the site's HTML files using a program such as WebWhacker (http://webwhacker.com). Such programs enable you to keep a working version of the site on your desktop, although keep in mind that they can not capture the more complex server-side functionality, such as database interactivity. You also cannot integrate these kinds of downloads into a word processing document with the rest of your library, so in cases like these you will need to develop a good filing system and cross-reference the files on your desktop within the text document. The storage space needed for such a filing system is, of course, a bit larger than for just text and single screen shots as well.

Project Summary

You may find when you start out that you don't have much to say about each site, but don't worry, the beauty of this kind of system is that you can always go back and fill in more details. Keep an eye out for Web site revisions, too. Analyzing the changes that a Web development team makes can be a great learning opportunity. Very often, the changes are in response to user feedback or even usability studies, so with your usability spectacles on you can trace the history of a project without ever being involved in it personally. This is not always the case, though.

You'll also soon recognize another kind of site revision, what I call "sludge creep," in which a client just keeps adding material to a site without really integrating it into the existing design. These sites tend to become less and less usable as they grow. Whatever you do, don't emulate that model!

Module Conclusion

Developing your own skills as a user is the first step toward designing usable Web sites. The next is to learn how to tap into other users' experiences as well. We'll address that in Module 2.

☑ Mastery Check

1. To get the most value from your experience of the Web as a user, what two things are necessary to do?

_____

_____

2. List four common Web site usability flaws.

_____

_____

3. Given a scenario in which 15 percent of a Web site's users accidentally click the wrong navigation button when asked to find a specific piece of information, which of the following is the appropriate action to take?

A. Discard the results because the numbers are not statistically valid.

B. Replace the entire user group and conduct the study again.

C. Revise the design of those buttons to make the information more easily accessible.

D. Revise the whole site to make all the information more easily accessible.

4. If someone starts to complain about how stupid a Web site's users are, what is a good response?

_____

_____

5. The first step in assessing a Web site's usability is to approach it through which of these perspectives? (You may pick more than one.)

A. As a babe in the woods

B. *Tabula rasa*, a blank slate

C. From a fresh perspective

D. As Mr. Hard-Core Web Designer

E. Through analyzing the source code

☑ Mastery Check

6. Who should have won the presidential election of the year 2000? (Just kidding! You can have this point for free.)

_____

_____

7. Define "Web usability."

_____

_____

8. Which of the following should you do while reviewing the Web as a user (with your usability spectacles on)? (You may select more than one.)

A. Observe your own thoughts and behaviors.

B. Observe others' reactions to you.

C. Record the thought processes and behaviors that have to do with the functionality of the site.

D. Pay particular attention to the navigation path that you follow.

E. Pay particular attention to content that interests you.

9. Once we learn how to do something, what do we usually assume about how easily others will learn how to do it?

_____

_____

Module 2

Swap Out Your Spectacles: Seeing from Other Perspectives

The Goals of This Module

- Identify ways of seeing from different users' perspectives
- Employ the power of imagination and power of observation in seeing from others' perspectives
- Practice creating Web site usage scenarios
- Understand common Web user mind-frames
- Identify Web user anxieties
- Identify key differences in learning styles
- Identify how shared physical characteristics can affect Web site design

Now that you're getting comfortable with your own usability spectacles, let me tell you that they're just one of many pairs of spectacles you have access to. As when you choose a pair of sunglasses from a rack in a store, your choices are quite broad, but in this case you get to choose whole personalities to go along with the glasses. This *can* give you a good excuse for behaving any way you want, but the benefit for our purposes here is that swapping out your spectacles will enable you to really see from the perspectives of other Web site users. This way, you can get closer to experiencing the Web as they experience it; use it as they use it.

Leave that Web designer perspective behind for a while longer; we're still trying to master the core skills needed for understanding usability. In this module, we'll explore two key techniques of seeing from perspectives other than your own, including how to leverage the use of your imagination in developing Web usage scenarios and then how to employ the power of observation to better understand your Web site's users.

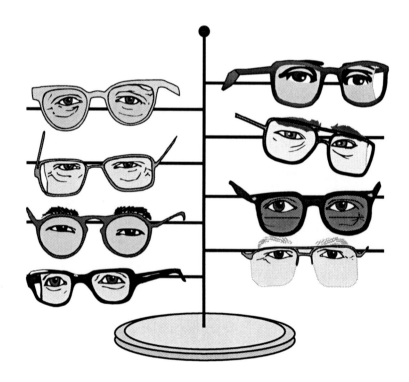

Tip

Developing your power of imagination first will give you some of the skills necessary to really understand and interpret the results of observation.

We'll conclude by stepping back and looking at some generalities about typical mind-frames of Web users, which you may or may not share in common with them, including:

- The extraordinary amount of anxiety that Web users, especially novices, experience

- Some key differences in learning styles

- Some key similarities in physical traits that impact how effective their use of the Web can be

Imagination Can Carry You a Long Way: Creating Web Usage Scenarios

Ever heard of the word "empathy"? Sure you have. It's the ability to understand or relate to how somebody else might feel. Do you need to have actually experienced the same things to be able to empathize with others? No.

Isn't that amazing? The power of human imagination is immense, and when it comes to Web site usability, it's been a vastly underutilized tool. It's cheap, too. Much, much cheaper than conducting full-scale usability tests, so it's a pity that it isn't typically used to better advantage in the early stages of Web site planning and design. You're not going to make that mistake.

Consider Emily Dickinson, the nineteenth-century poet who spent the majority of her life as a recluse in a small New England town. Despite her lack of worldly experience, she wrote poems like the following:

> I never saw a Moor—
> I never saw the Sea—
> Yet know I how the Heather looks
> And what a Billow be.

With an imagination like that, Emily Dickinson could have been a great usability expert. So get out your pen; it's time to write a little poetry....

Come back, come back. I promise you won't have to write any poetry (unless you want to, of course). I do, however, want to encourage you to write, or record on tape, or act out, or, in whatever medium you choose, *imagine* how others might use your Web site. A common vehicle for this process is called a *Web usage scenario*. Simply put, this is a record of how various people might use a Web site, what they might be looking for, how they might go about finding it, how they might be looking for a different kind of experience at different times on the same Web site. Let me explain this better with an example.

Example Site: Community Art Center

Take, for example, the case of a community art center (let's call them CAC for short). Imagine that they have decided it's time to revise their Web site. Their existing site was put together by a member volunteer a couple of years ago. It is largely what I would call "brochure-ware" and includes the CAC's background information and a schedule of upcoming exhibits at the center.

Ask the Expert

Question: What is "brochure-ware"?

Answer: Brochure-ware is essentially a brochure that has been transported to the Web without consideration as to what the medium of the Web has to offer that differs from the medium of print. You've probably seen these kinds of sites by the dozens. They are strictly informational sites with pages typically on the history of the organization, its mission, usually a calendar of events, a few nice photos (not always optimized for the Web), and a contact page. They usually offer little or no interactivity. They are often targeted to a small geographic region or membership audience but fail to come out and say so.

If, as a casual Web user, you come across this kind of site, you'll often have the feeling that you've stumbled into a conversation mid-way. The context is missing, whether it is explaining to the world (after all, this is a *World* Wide Web) just who the site's sponsors are or even what geographic range they offer services to. Some of the worst cases of brochure-ware take this to the point of leaving off the state or country from the contact address. An address of Las Vegas, for example, could be for Las Vegas, Nevada, or Las Vegas, New Mexico. London could be the metropolitan city best known in England or a fairly small town tucked away in New England in the U.S.

Question: So should I avoid creating "brochure-ware" at all costs?

Answer: Not necessarily. "Brochure-ware" isn't an inherently evil format; it just misses some of the really great opportunities of being part of the Web. There can be justifiable needs for it, especially given the limited schedules and budgets you often find in volunteer-driven organizations such as our example art center. Sometimes just having the information from a brochure readily available online can be helpful to users. If nothing else, the Web is a great filing system. Users don't need to remember where they put that brochure; they can just look up the information on the Web.

In designing sites, however, I would advise you to always ask in what ways a site could better take advantage of the medium. In many cases, your clients may assume a Web site's purpose is just an extension of their printed marketing material. It is your job to educate them as to the possibilities available to them through this new medium.

As an established nonprofit organization, the CAC has already invested the time and resources needed to establish a five-year strategic plan for their general operations. In it, they have declared their mission is "to create community through art." They plan to accomplish this mission by

- Arranging quality exhibitions of artwork by emerging, mid-career, and established artists

- Establishing education and outreach programs designed to make art accessible to people of all ages and backgrounds

- Providing affordable studio space to local artists

These goals and methods all sound reasonable, but as a Web designer you may find yourself asking what role a Web site may play in all this.

Community Art Center Web Usage Scenarios

What the Community Art Center staff has not done in their strategic plan is to envision what role their Web site can play in achieving their goals. This is where Web usage scenarios can be immensely helpful and where hiring a Web professional such as you can come in. Now, since they already have a site, there are two kinds of usage scenarios you can establish:

● Real-world accounts from their users about how and what they have actually used the site for

● Imaginary usage scenarios about how and what the site could be used for

Real-World Usage Scenarios

If the CAC were to start with their existing site and ask their members how and what they have actually used the site for, they might come up with the following real-world usage scenarios:

● Betty Surplon, one of the members of the Board, reported: "I last used the CAC site when I was trying to determine how many exhibits we had last year. I went to the home page and clicked Calendar. I then clicked Exhibits and scrolled down the list to January and counted the number of exhibits in the Main Wing and West Wing. I chose to ignore the children's exhibits, since I was focused on established artists. I wanted to see the same information for last year, but I had to go into the office and rummage around in the filing cabinets for an old newsletter that listed all the year's exhibits."

● Anthony Match, one of the studio artists, reported: "I knew Tori Morrisson's and my exhibit was coming up soon, and I just wanted to see what the other exhibits looked like on the Web. From the home page, I clicked 'Current Exhibits.' That took me to a page with the three galleries listed along with the titles of the exhibits currently on display there. I clicked the mixed media exhibit that we currently have going on in the Main Gallery and looked at the photos. Nice! Although there were only three images, I guess this serves as a preview to get people to come to the real show? I also wanted to look at the past exhibits that were in the Main Gallery as well, but I couldn't find them. I guess they get taken down after the exhibit, just like the real thing? We might think about putting up some kind of archive."

2

● Leticia Pinon, Marty Weighbret, and Kathryn Bishop, each active members and volunteers in the CAC, reported that they had not used the Web in the past six months, although they had no complaints about it. Instead, they credited the newsletter and exhibit announcements as providing everything that they needed to know. They each rely on the phone or e-mail if they need any more details on anything.

The information that can be gleaned from each of these real-world usage scenarios is valuable, even the report by the members who haven't needed to reference the Web site in the past six months. If, as a designer, you made all your revision decisions on the basis of these reports, however, you would probably do little other than beef up an archive system, both for the calendar of events and past exhibits. Thus, you might just produce enhanced brochure-ware. The site would still not be providing all that it potentially could as a Web site.

Note how the last group of members compared their Web needs to what was available via the print medium, in this case the newsletter. It seems apparent that the users in this case do not know what services the Web site could potentially provide. That's one area where the second class of usage scenarios, imaginary usage scenarios, can be really useful.

Ask the Expert

Question: Don't organizations commonly start their Web site design without developing these usage scenarios?

Answer: Unfortunately, yes, but that's also a large contributing factor to the poor design and usability of so many Web sites existing today. This book aims to teach you some fairly simple techniques to make the whole design process more focused on what the user needs and, thus, to create more successful Web sites. This approach is commonly called *user-centered design*.

Developing usage scenarios is one such technique. Once you've practiced it a bit, I think you'll find that it's a simple, inexpensive method that can supply you with a lot of valuable information that will enlighten your design.

Imaginary Usage Scenario

Let's look more closely at the CAC's mission statement "to create community through art" through the lens of the Web. Imagine for a moment how a Web site could help them achieve that goal, and jot down some of your ideas.

Yep, I can practically hear your brains whirring. There are all sorts of ways that Web sites can help build community that the print medium cannot. For one, it's an interactive communications medium. People can interact online. The challenge for the CAC might be to figure out how to do it "through art." How's this for one possible usage scenario?

CAC Scenario   Anthony Match is preparing for a joint exhibit with Tori Morrisson at the CAC. They've spent the last 12 months collaborating on a rain dance installation using a combination of recycled and renewable materials and plenty of natural pigment dyes. For the opening night, scheduled for the first day of summer, they have planned to incorporate a performance aspect with audience participation. They have been encouraged to use the CAC Web site as part of their installation, so a month before the opening night, they post a simple notice on the CAC Web site bulletin board, "Rain dancers and drummers wanted—in person and/or electronic visitors with fingers ready to drum."

Anthony and Tori also schedule periodic visits to the CAC chat room in the character of native rain dancers or crop farmers. The first time, for example, they enter together and hold a straightforward conversation about the crops and the need for rain, writing their dialogue with a mid-Western twang. Another time, they take on the characters of Native American tribesmen. This is not typical for the CAC chat room, which is usually focused on art-related topics with the obligatory bits and pieces of gossip. Each time they leave the chat room, they post a question or a solicitation, such as "We gotta have a rain dance. Can you dance? Can you rain?" They echo this sentiment in the Upcoming Events section of the home page.

The interest of the CAC members is piqued. They start to recognize these characters when they come online. They've seen the notice on the bulletin board as well, and they have perhaps read about the upcoming exhibit online or in the printed newsletter. Being a largely active group, they start to answer. "Yes, I can dance." Or "I'd like to 'rain.' Can you teach me how?"

> Anthony and Tori get a bigger response than they know what to do with. In some ways, their installation has started ahead of schedule. They decide to schedule an online rain dance workshop to help the online drumming component prepare for the opening gala event. The participants are sworn to secrecy, although they are free to discuss it among themselves and to ask other members of the CAC or arts community "We gotta have a rain dance. Can you dance? Can you rain?"
>
> They host the workshop in the Education section of the CAC Web site, which has virtual classrooms set up so that the participants can hear the instructors and see their desktops. Alternatively, to demonstrate a point or to see what the students are doing, the instructors can either look at each of the students' desktops or choose to display one of their desktops to the rest of the class. Students can also ask questions by selecting a "raise your hand" button to address the whole class, or by typing a private query to the instructor.
>
> During the workshop, Anthony and Tori give a preview of the online version of the installation and demonstrate what will be needed in terms of using the keyboards to drum during the event. In this case, the user keyboard strokes will cause visual and auditory changes in a real-time Web environment. Like an online game, the installation is structured so that each of the "players" can see all the events taking place on screen. Additionally, computer monitors and keyboards will be set up within the physical installation so that attendees can also see and participate in the online component.
>
> During the workshop, Leticia Pinon raises her hand and says, "This is fun! Couldn't we keep doing this after the opening night, sort of like a weekly jam session?"
>
> Anthony and Tori pause. "Yeah," they say. "We don't see why not."

Do you see how imagining a usage scenario can be really productive? Every scenario centers around a set of user expectations, which can ultimately be translated into design criteria. Not only can usage scenarios help prompt ideas that you might not think of "yourself" when asked what you think would be a helpful or useful addition to a Web site, they can also help you visualize ways in which users might want to use a Web site. You'll find yourself asking questions like "From this part of the site, what might Fred want to click to get ready access to this other part of the site?" Or "What sequence of events might need to happen in order for Juan to be able to make a decision about which model of a product to buy and then be able to purchase it straightaway?"

Tip

It can sometimes be helpful to consider goals that the organization may not have clearly articulated in their existing mission statements but that could be viable through the Web. For instance, with most art centers there's generally some interest in *selling* art. The Web offers all sorts of new possibilities through e-commerce that may not have been available to the members of our example, CAC. Creating usage scenarios that demonstrate how users could take advantage of opportunities for purchasing art online through either straight retail sales or other more interactive means such as live art auctions could help the staff of the art center shape their overall goals. This is definitely a two-way process.

Project 2-1: Begin a Set of Web Usage Scenarios

So now it's your turn. Create some preliminary usage scenarios for the community art center.

Step-by-Step

1. The starting point for every usage scenario you create should be reviewing the site goals; in this case, they can be gleaned from the CAC's mission statement:

To create community through art, we will

- Arrange quality exhibitions of artwork by emerging, mid-career, and established artists.

- Establish education and outreach programs designed to make art accessible to people of all ages and backgrounds.

- Provide affordable studio space to local artists.

In this case, also, let's add the goal:

- To sell art.

Note

Not all mission statements can be automatically transformed into Web site goals, but they can be an awfully good starting point. In order to establish Web site–specific goals, it is typically necessary to analyze a company's or organization's goals in terms of what might be most appropriate for a Web site. Some things really are best left for the print medium (like long, read-only documents)—or for video or television or radio or any other medium that does something particularly well and is targeted to its own user base. In the CAC case, for example, it might be difficult logistically to provide affordable studio space to local artists via the Web—unless, of course, you come up with a great idea for establishing virtual studio space.

2. Identify at least nine different distinct types of users. I'll start you off:

- Adult visual artists who are members of the CAC _____

- Kids taking art classes _____

- Casual Web users who are interested in art _____

- _____

- _____

- _____

- _____

- _____

- _____

3. Create a character from one of your user groupings. Give him/her a persona, including a name, bio, vital statistics, and so on. Really feel as though you know something about this person. In fact, if you don't care to invent somebody, pick somebody you know. How about your favorite aunt, or not-so-favorite aunt?

4. Now, create a usage scenario for how that person might use the new CAC Web site this Wednesday morning. You can, of course, write your usage scenario on a blank sheet of paper, or feel free to use a word processor or audio tape recorder. Yes, you can just imagine it, but only if you do it in exquisite detail.

If you have someone you can partner with, try telling each other usage stories. It will be best for future activities if your scenarios are in some way recorded.

Be sure to give your character a really clear purpose. Just what are they doing on that Web site? What brings them there? What do they hope to achieve? It is okay, of course, for someone to be exploring, looking for something fun to do, etc. Those are valid purposes.

If you get stymied, try visiting one or more of the following art-related sites to stimulate ideas:

- http://www.svam.org
- http://www.paperveins.org
- http://nextmonet.com
- http://www.christies.com
- http://www.artcenter.edu
- http://www.getty.edu

5. Now, using the same character, give him or her a different purpose for visiting the same Web site Sunday afternoon and develop another usage scenario. Try changing the person's mental state. If he or she was intently focused on finding a specific piece of information on Wednesday morning, think about a more leisurely way for the character to use the Web site on Sunday, or vice versa.

6. And, finally, try a different character altogether with a completely different purpose.

Project Summary

We've looked at only three usage scenarios. Just imagine how many different kinds of users there are for just this one site and how many different usage scenarios each user could have depending on that user's mind-frame and purpose of the day. While it would be impossible to write usage scenarios for every single user, it's a good idea to develop a couple of scenarios for each major type of user.

It would be a pity for a community art center site like this one to be reduced to brochure-ware. There's much more potential for taking advantage of the medium of the Web—not just for its own sake, however. Staying in line with our usability principles, the benefit of building a community art site that takes better advantage of the medium would be to benefit their user base and to help them accomplish their own goals.

The Power of Observation

I think you'll agree by now that imagination is a powerful tool. There's another tool that, like imagination, is extremely helpful, relatively inexpensive, and rather sadly underutilized in Web site design. That is the power of observation.

Observing Others' Experiences

One of the easiest ways to gain insight into other users' perspectives is to simply observe them. I can't think of any usability experts or books or articles that do not emphasize the role of observation in determining usability, and it is the linchpin upon which official usability testing relies. I place it here, after the sections on developing your own critical abilities as a user and developing your own imaginative and empathetic powers, however, because without those skills it is much more difficult to be able to understand and interpret the results of just plain observation.

It's far too easy to approach usability from an intellectual or scientific viewpoint. An impartial observer may well be able to take notes, delineating exactly what steps a user follows and how that user seems to react emotionally to his or her progress. But a passionate observer will be better able to understand the user's perspective and thus come up with better ideas for Web site designs in the first place. This is what user-centered design is all about.

In this book, I am hoping that you readers come from, or aspire to participate in, a wide range of Web design and development roles and will, thus, be able to integrate usability issues more fully throughout the entire process. Traditionally, Web usability experts have been hired to evaluate the success (or failure) of an existing Web site. It is often recommended that they *not* be part of the Web development team, primarily so that they remain unbiased and objective.

There's some logic to this argument, but it reflects something of the backward nature of this "traditional" approach to Web site design. A growing number of Web professionals, myself included, advocate starting with a usability focus and continually checking in with it throughout the design and development process. As we previously discussed, this way the design criteria can be informed by the expectations and patterns that the users bring to the Web site. This does not eliminate the need for impartial usability testing; we will cover that in Module 14. Such a process, however, will reduce the nature and quantity of usability errors that are detected during that testing stage.

Tip

As I'm sure you know, wherever a budget is concerned, doing something right the first time costs a fraction of the expense incurred by correcting it at a later stage. The purpose of user-centered design is to get it right the first time. Usability testing then becomes a confirmation of whether or not you have succeeded.

Project 2-2: Record a Beginner's Web Experiences

In the first module, we tried to recall our own experiences as a beginning Web user. Personal experience is always a good starting point, but when there's been a time lag, there's no way to ensure that you remember all the details correctly. So in this project, we want to employ that power of observation—finely tuned with the remembrance of your own experience—to record another beginner's Web experiences.

Step-by-Step

1. The first step in this activity may be the most difficult, for you have to find a few beginning Web users (or at least one), preferably absolute beginners. And you have to persuade them to let you observe them as they learn to use it. This can be tough, I know, but here are some suggestions:

- Family members can make really great suckers, I mean subjects, especially older ones who have felt for sometime that they really "ought" to learn something about this modern thingamajig. Where is that Aunt Norma when you need her, anyway?

- Kids will do in a pinch, although it's harder and harder to find ones who haven't taken over the computer from us old fogies. Sometimes, you have to get younger and younger ones—so long as they can hold the mouse and not put it in their mouth, you have a fighting chance.

- A number of institutions will love you if you offer to introduce the Web to some of their members! So if you have an ounce of goodwill in you (and aren't too shy), volunteer some time at a nearby retirement home, senior center, community center, daycare, elementary school…hey, I know of a community art center that could use your help.

One way or another, find those beginners and introduce them to the Web.

2. The rest is easy. Now all you have to do is observe them using the Web and record your observations. Feel free to use whatever recording methods you are comfortable with: taking notes, using a tape recorder, even videotaping the session so that you can review it in full detail later.

Of course, chances are that you'll have to provide some minimal explanation, but try to keep that as brief as possible, and make notes whenever you have to explain something. It can be a good idea to record their questions as well. These are the precise points that may have the weakest usability. Many of their questions may have to do with computers and/or with the operating systems or browsers. That's good information to know as well, although there's little you may be able to do to correct those issues in the role of a Web designer or developer.

Tip

Direct them to a Web site that they will be interested in. The more engaged with the content they are, the less self-conscious they will be about you watching them. Also reassure them. Let them know that you are trying to understand where the Web sites fail and where they succeed. You are not judging the user.

3. Pay close attention to the following issues and techniques:

- Navigation issues: Note when they have to backtrack, or use a search engine, or refer to a site map to find something.

- Web conventions, such as underlined links, logos that go to the home page in the upper-left corner, ad banners, navigation bars, navigation maps: Which ones make sense to them, and which ones puzzle them or require them to learn how to use them?

- Alternate between letting them explore on their own, and asking them to accomplish little tasks. You can find valuable information either way. It can be helpful to visit a few sites ahead of time to become familiar with them, but it's not essential for this project. An example might be if you asked the users to find out whether or not they could purchase some netting through the Home Depot site to help protect my friend Wendy's blueberry bushes from marauding birds. Next, ask them if they do sell it, could it be charged to my credit card but then shipped directly to her house?

Project Summary

Whew. How was that? Such experiences can be either exhilarating or debilitating, very much depending on the ease with which a new user takes to the Web. Or more accurately, depending upon the ease with which the Web initiates its new users, which is variable, to say the least. It's not a very easily usable medium, is it? But we love it anyway. Just think, you will be able to improve it.

Ask the Expert

Question: Should all Web sites be designed for this kind of brand new user to the Web?

Answer: It's difficult to make any such broad generalizations about designing Web sites. A Web site design all depends upon who the users for that particular site will be. In some cases, the primary audience is clearly more technically sophisticated than complete beginners, and you could risk alienating them if you based the design on the needs of the handful of beginners who might happen across the site.

A perfect example might be shockwave.com, an entire business and site developed to showcase and encourage the use of Macromedia's Shockwave products, including such tools as Flash and Director. Developing the site for users without any plug-ins, for example, would be foolish.

Question: So how do you account for the lowest common denominator?

Answer: First, define who the "lowest common denominator" is for your site. Too often this phrase is interpreted as the "lowest denominator," in this case complete Web beginners. If these beginners do not share the skills and tools "in common" with the majority of your audience, they do not compose the "lowest common denominator." It may be that for a site like shockwave.com the lowest common denominator consists of experienced Web users who are looking for experiences that are pushing the envelope. If this is the case, then that is who the site should be targeted at.

On the other hand, if you are developing a general interest site and want to attract users from all over the world with all levels of familiarity with the Web, the complete Web beginners will likely form a significant portion of your audience. As such, they would be your lowest common denominator, and the site should be designed for them.

Don't forget, in cases of widely divergent audience levels and needs, you do always have the option of developing separate sites or separate sections of sites to best cater to those needs. It never hurts to give your users a choice, although this will drive your costs up—for design, development, and maintenance.

Note

We will be discussing how you quantify the skill sets of your user base in Modules 3 and 4.

Common Web User Mind-Frames

To heighten your power of observation, you ought to know some generalizations about typical users. They are not by any means intended to be held as universal truths, but more as informative guidelines. There are three key areas of particular importance:

● The Web can cause a tremendous amount of anxiety in users.

● People have significantly different learning styles.

● Most users have some key similarities in physical traits that impact how effective their use of the Web can be.

Information and Navigation Anxieties

In Project 2-2, you probably witnessed first-hand some of the typical anxiety that users have about the Web, and there is a lot of it. Saul Wurman coined the term "information anxiety" in the late 1980s—well before the explosion of the Internet and then the Web. He described it as being "produced by the ever-widening gap between what we understand and what we think we should understand. It is the black hole between data and knowledge, and it happens when information doesn't tell us what we want or need to know" (Saul Wurman, *Information Anxiety*, Doubleday, 1989).

When the Web came along, it gave us greater access to even more information, thereby intensifying our information anxiety. It also presented a whole new navigational paradigm with very little instructional structure about how to use it. Thus was born what I call our "navigation anxiety."

Launching a Web site is not unlike launching a ship bound for polar exploration in the early part of the twentieth century. It is full of promise and glory, but it is also full of risk. There is no guarantee we will find what we are looking for, what kinds of problem-solving methods we will have to employ, or what kinds of problems we might encounter along the way. And there's certainly no telling how long it will take to get there, or what mental or physical state we will be in when we arrive. If we arrive.

Unfortunately, our self-identity tends to get tied up in the exploration as well. Find what you need on the Web within five minutes, make the transaction, close the deal, click away to check your e-mail in time to break for tea, and you'll be all smiles. Such prowess in getting what we need makes us feel good.

On the other hand, crash your computer three times, lose your e-mail file, fail to retrieve whatever you were looking for, and be late for your next appointment. Not such a good feeling at the end of it.

What's the solution to these information and navigation anxieties? Well, this is much easier said than done, but the most obvious solutions sound like the best ones to me:

- Provide information on an as-needed basis. Do not throw it in your user's face, expecting them to want it.

- Make the information easily accessible through the Web. (Clue: This means design usable Web sites, which are easily learnable. That's what Part II is all about.)

Learning Style Differences

Before diving into a discussion about learning style differences, I'd highly recommend that you go to one or more of the following sites and complete their learning style assessments:

- Richard M. Felder's Index of Learning Styles at
  http://www2.ncsu.edu/unity/lockers/users/f/felder/public/ILSdir/ilsweb.html

- Howard Gardner's Multiple Intelligence Inventory at
  http://surfaquarium.com/MIinvent.htm

- Canfield's Learning Style Inventory at
  http://www.tecweb.org/styles/stylesframe.html

Note

Talk about cumbersome URLs! Those three just about take the cake. The URLs themselves provide something of a usability challenge, don't they?

Just taking one of these assessments can be an eye-opening experience. One thing becomes crystal clear in the process: there are distinctly different styles of learning. Exactly how to categorize those styles, however, is quite another matter.

2

Felder breaks learning styles into eight components:

- *Active* versus *reflective* learners, where active learners learn by doing, and reflective learners learn by thinking about it.

- *Sensing* versus *intuitive* learners, where sensing learners like to learn facts, and intuitive learners like to explore relationships.

- *Visual* versus *verbal* learners, where visual learners learn best by seeing visual representations, and verbal learners, by reading or hearing explanations.

- *Sequential* versus *global* learners, where sequential learners tend to learn in linear steps, and global learners tend to need to see the big picture before being able to understand the smaller steps.

Note

For a full discussion of each of Felder's learning style, see http://www2.ncsu.edu/unity/lockers/users/f/felder/public/ILSdir/styles.htm.

These categories are not meant to be exclusionary. Most people employ multiple learning styles but tend to favor one over another.

Gardner's multiple intelligence inventory classifies learners by nine different kinds of what he calls "intelligences." The first two, verbal-linguistic and logical-mathematical, are the ones our culture and schools heavily promote. The others, he feels, are just as valid but are often underdeveloped in large part due to the same culture and schools:

- **Verbal-linguistic**   Learning through words

- **Logical-mathematical**   Learning through logical models

- **Visual-spatial**   Learning by seeing/visualizing the display of information

- **Bodily-kinesthetic**   Learning by being physically involved with the subject

- **Musical**   Learning through music, employing sound and rhythm

- **Interpersonal**   Learning by interacting with others

- **Intrapersonal**   Learning by introspection

- **Naturalist**   Learning by observing, understanding, and organizing patterns in the natural environment

- **Existentialist**   Learning through spirituality

Note

For more information on Gardner and his system, see the Resources for Howard Gardner Multiple Intelligence Web site at http://www.twblearn.com/howard_gardner_resources.htm.

Canfield's Learning Style Inventory breaks learning styles into the following much smaller components. They, in turn, could be largely grouped into the level of independence, content (numeric, qualitative, inanimate), and mode (listening, reading, iconic, direct experience).

- Peer
- Organization
- Goal setting
- Competition
- Instructor
- Detail
- Independence
- Authority

- Numeric
- Qualitative
- Inanimate
- People
- Listening
- Reading
- Iconic
- Direct experience

Tip

The TecWeb site is an excellent source of information on learning styles and has much more information on both Gardner's and Canfield's systems. It is at http://www.tecweb.org.

These three systems do not necessarily contradict each other. Rather, they are primarily different interpretations of similar phenomena. And just as teachers are able to enhance their teaching abilities by better understanding the differences between their preferred method of learning and that of each of their students, you as Web designers and developers could do the same.

Tip

Try adding the task "instructional design" to your list of things to pay attention to during the Web design process. It has been perhaps one of the most overlooked duties in the Web design field.

The Web is one big learning environment, and ideally there ought to be about as many methods of learning how to navigate each site as there are types of learners. At a minimum, such differences in learning styles validate the need for a text-based search engine as well as a visual site map as two different ways to search the same site.

When you are designing sites, I'd suggest picking one of the preceding learning style categorizations and systematically creating usage scenarios for each type of learner who might be using your site. Address both the Web site design and the treatment of the content. For example, following Feder's model, you might come up with the design ideas in Table 2-1 for a Web site that sells computer hardware.

Type of Learner	Possible Web Site Design Treatment	Possible Web Site Content Treatment
Active	Active learners would likely respond well to a straightforward navigation system that lets them get right into the site and to the information they are looking for. They could also possibly appreciate a more engaging, interactive interface. Also, typical shopping cart setups could work well for them and individualized user preferences. Let them feel involved in the experience.	They might be drawn into a game-style interface where you invite their immediate participation in a fun way—perhaps a game on how to fit the computer components together. They would probably *not* be interested in reading a heavy text intro about the company or any information they are not specifically looking for.
Reflective	Reflective learners might appreciate a description about the site and the features available on it so that they can think about it before diving in. This could be an option available from the home page but probably should not dominate the page, because it may conflict with other learners' preferences.	When it comes to making purchase decisions, they are more likely than active learners to want to print out pages of information on the products they are interested in so that they can read them carefully offline.
Sensing	Sensing learners will respond to a straightforward, no-nonsense interface that helps them get to the facts that they're interested in.	With their interest in facts, sensing learners would likely appreciate sections of the Web site that just give them the facts. Detailed product specifications, for instance, could help them make up their minds about which product to buy.

Table 2-1   Possible Design Solutions to Accommodate Different Learning Styles for a Computer Hardware Web Site

Type of Learner	Possible Web Site Design Treatment	Possible Web Site Content Treatment
Intuitive	Intuitive learners will appreciate a home page and navigational structure that convey an accurate depiction of the relationships of the site and of the computer products being sold. Image maps of the whole computer system with links to the kinds of products (CPUs, peripherals, etc.) could work well for intuitive learners.	With their interest in relationships, intuitive learners may want to learn how a whole suite of products works together before buying any individual component. They may just glance through the detailed specifications and focus instead on the marketing spiel and seeing images of the whole system connected together.
Visual	Visual learners will typically respond far better to graphical cues than will verbal learners. Icons, color coding, and image maps, as well as visual site maps, could all be used effectively for this style of learner.	They want to have images showing them how the various components will fit together. If a mouse uses a USB port, by all means show them the part of the computer with the mouse about to be plugged in.
Verbal	You may have provided navigational icons for the visual learners, but these guys would also appreciate having that little text label that confirms it is what it appears to be. They would also likely appreciate text-based search engines.	Verbal learners need text. They are likely to need full-text descriptions about each of the products in order to make purchase decisions.
Sequential	Logical navigational structure is a must for sequential learners. A hierarchical model would probably work best. Certainly provide a site map that shows each link of the hierarchy.	These guys read the directions, so when you give any installation instructions, be sure to spell it out in linear steps. First, unwrap the package. Next, attach the mouse. Third, plug in the computer.... Give them every single step and let them choose which ones they might skip over. They may gain a certain comfort in knowing that every little step is there for them if they need it.
Global	Global learners would likely appreciate the kind of navigational system suggested for intuitive learners, something that conveys the whole Web site and product line well.	Global learners may appreciate an illustration with labels showing how all of the pieces of a computer system fit together. They may then skip over all the step-by-step instructions—until they can't figure something out, that is!

Table 2-1 Possible Design Solutions to Accommodate Different Learning Styles for a Computer Hardware Web Site (*continued*)

1-Minute Drill

- What is the key difference in learning style between active and reflective learners?
- What is the key difference in learning style between interpersonal and intrapersonal learners?

Sense Differences

Two eyes, two ears, a mouth—it's easy to see certain physical things in common between us humans, isn't it? And much of the technology around us has been designed, to some extent or other, with the human body in mind. Without hands, we probably wouldn't have designed mice to click.

There are some little-known facts about our senses, particularly our sense of vision, however, that may not be so obvious but that significantly affect many of our abilities to successfully use the Web.

Visual Sense

A classic example that I just learned is that our ability to visually perceive blues decreases with age. Why, you might ask, is blue the default color for hypertext links? Good question. I don't think anybody can give you a good answer, though. It was a fairly random decision made early on in the development of the Web and has become a strong enough convention that it's best not to mess with it.

So what can you do with this information, short of changing one of the few Web conventions that has been accepted fairly universally? Two "don'ts" and one "do" come to mind:

- Do *not* override the user's settings for link and text colors. The users might have changed their preference settings for a very good reason, and it will not help to override them with a color scheme that you think may look better.

- Do *not* turn off the underlines on links, because it causes users to rely on color to indicate where to click, and in this case, unfortunately, the color is blue.

- Be strategic with the use of the color blue in your Web site designs. In particular, avoid using blue for text, or at least any text that you want to be sure everyone can read.

- Active learners learn by doing; reflective learners by thinking about it.
- Interpersonal learners like to interact with others; intrapersonal learners prefer introspection.

On the subject of color, another physical factor you might want to consider that between five and ten percent of the male population in the world suffers from some form of color blindness. That's a lot of your potential Web site users. Of course, the particulars vary quite a bit from one man to another, so you can't simply decide not to combine red and green in your design, for example. Some forms of color blindness affect the perception of red, some green, some blue, and, of course, there are ailments that affect combinations of these three colors. It's unfortunate that we are designing with an RGB (red—green—blue) color system, consisting of just the three colors that are problematic in terms of color blindness.

So how does this affect Web design? Unfortunately, it relegates the use of color to a supplemental function. Don't design anything that relies on every user being able to perceive the color information.

Quite beyond the physical component of perceiving color, keep in mind also that the interpretive meaning of color is very subjective in nature. There are, for example, significant cultural differences in color perception: white represents purity and innocence in western culture (thus we wear white wedding dresses). In China, however, white is the color of death. Red is used for weddings.

Sense of Hearing, Smelling, Tasting, and Touching

As for the other senses, I primarily want to remind you that, last time I counted, we do, typically, have at least four senses in addition to vision. Most people using

Ask the Expert

Question: Is it true that we only truly perceive color with a limited part of our eye?

Answer: As a matter of fact, yes, we perceive complete color information only from the center of the retina, which is called the fovea. This component covers only about a five-degree angle of vision, so our brain essentially takes a sample of color information, much as you would using an eyedropper tool in an image-editing program like Photoshop. It then interpolates the information to generate color for the rest of the picture. Pretty amazing, isn't it? You can credit Donald A. Norman with imparting that information. He is one of the premier cognitive scientists working in the human factors field. I'd recommend reading any of his books.

and designing for the Web seem to forget this. Granted, audio is used to a degree in Web site design, but typically as an add-on feature or to make annoying swoosh and click sounds.

Tip

Keep in mind that not all users have five fully functional senses. Ideally, a Web site should not require the use of any one particular sense. At this time, most Web sites are heavily dependent on visual elements. Try "reading" some of your favorite sites through a text-to-speech tool to get a better understanding of the challenges visually impaired users often face.

In contrast, think about how much we use audio signals to navigate the physical world. Have you tried driving lately with earplugs? Not a good idea. We get a keen sense of direction and depth through hearing in the real world. And yet, very few Web sites, in fact very few electronic media, take advantage of this ability. Ironically, electronic games, perhaps starting with the CD-ROM Myst, are one of the few examples that effectively use sound as a primary navigational device. There are notable bandwidth limitations and delays that currently limit the use of audio over the Internet, but they are slowly changing.

And then there are smell, taste, and touch. Technological developments have made the inclusion of smell and touch possible within Web site design, but adoption of the technology has been very slow. Most people have not even heard of the hardware developments and laugh at even discussing the possibilities for them. We are heavily reliant on the visual components, too heavily, I would say.

Just as there's a need to accommodate users with different learning styles, I think there's a great need to accommodate users with different levels of sense development and of reliance on particular senses. There's a bit of a chicken and egg dilemma here, though. Until enough of your user base adopts the hardware components needed for these other senses, you can't really design Web sites that utilize them. And, of course, users will hardly be inclined to adopt the new technologies until there's a use for them.

Sometimes progress is made in inches instead of leaps. This is likely one of those cases. Think about it in terms of your lifetime, however. You can be sure some of these new technologies will become common within that timeframe, and it won't hurt to start thinking about how Web sites could effectively take advantage of them sooner rather than later.

1-Minute Drill

● Why is it unfortunate that blue has become the default choice for hypertext links?

● What three things can you do to work around the faults of the color blue in Web site design?

Project 2-3: Refine and Further Develop Your Usage Scenarios

As you get to know your users better, you can expand the usage scenarios more effectively, so you'll find that we'll come back to this type of project a couple more times as we cover more related material. Usage scenarios are definitely part of an iterative process. You may be surprised at the layers of detail that you can uncover as you think more and more about how your Web site will actually be used and by whom.

In this project, we will take one of the usage scenarios you developed earlier for the CAC (community art center) and expand it in terms of Web usage anxiety, learning styles, and differences between the senses.

Step-by-Step

1. Pick one of the usage scenarios you developed earlier in this module. Or if you strongly prefer it, start afresh with a new character.

2. Expand upon the usage scenario in terms of what we have just covered: Web usage anxiety, learning styles, and sense differences. Give as much detail as you can regarding these aspects. Ask yourself questions like the following:

● What makes your character feel anxious? What might help alleviate that anxiety?

● What learning challenges is your character facing, and how would he or she most prefer to undertake them?

● What visuals does your character encounter and how can you ensure ready usability?

● If your character has visual impairments such as color blindness, how will the person navigate the site?

● How might your character choose to employ more senses than the sense of sight?

● Our ability to perceive blues decreases with age.

● Do *not* override the user's settings for link and text colors. They might have changed them for a very good reason. Also, do *not* turn off the underlines for links, since they may be the clearest indication to visually impaired users that they are links. And be strategic with the use of the color blue in your Web site designs. In particular, avoid using blue for text.

Project Summary

By now, you are probably feeling pretty intimate with the characters you invented for your Web usage scenarios. This level of depth is very helpful in designing sites that will be truly usable and useful for their visitors. But it's only the beginning. In the real world, of course, it's a bit more difficult to get to know users, and, darn it, they just aren't as susceptible to the power of suggestion as are your fictional characters.

Module Conclusion

Now that you have learned some ways to harness your power of imagination and power of observation in seeing from other perspectives, we'll focus more intently on getting to know your actual Web site users and their computer systems. In the next module, we will look at several methods of getting to know your real-world users and building what are called *user profiles*, descriptions of the basic types of users for any given Web site. Then, in Module 4, we will examine how to gather and interpret data on what hardware and software they may be using to access your Web site and how it might constrain your design.

☑ Mastery Check

1. The two types of Web usage scenarios are _____ and
_____.

2. What percentage of the male population worldwide suffers from some
form of color blindness?

_____

3. Which statement is true about the relationship between the power of
imagination and the power of observation in terms of establishing Web
site usability?

A) They are diametrically opposed.

B) They are identical.

C) They are complementary.

D) They bear no relation to one another.

4. How many different learning styles are there?

_____

5. Which of the following pairs of learning styles are essentially the same?

A) Intrapersonal and interpersonal

B) Musical and visual-spatial

C) Sensing and intuitive

D) Active and kinesthetic

E) Goal-setting and global

6. True or False: The technology now exists that make it possible to include
smell and touch in Web site design.

☑ *Mastery Check*

7. Why should we avoid the use of the color blue in Web site design?

A) It is a cold color and is off-putting to most users.

B) It causes headaches.

C) It is difficult to find complementary colors to complete the color scheme.

D) Our ability to perceive blues decreases with age.

E) It is too common in graphic design usage.

8. True or False: We should make a practice of designing all Web sites for complete Web beginners, since they will always be the lowest common denominator.

Module 3

Get to Know Your Users: Creating User Profiles

The Goals of This Module

- Understand what user profiles are
- Explore how to develop user profiles
- Identify the basic methods of prelaunch and postlaunch user analysis
- Develop a generic user questionnaire

In the first two modules, we have tried to get inside Web site users' minds, first by "putting on our usability spectacles" and becoming self-observant users ourselves and then by "swapping out our spectacles" and harnessing the power of imagination and observation to better see from other users' perspectives. In this module, we will explore a third means: getting to know the users by creating *user profiles,* a collection of statistical and descriptive information about the kinds of users who will be visiting your Web site.

One of the most basic methods for acquiring this information, of course, is to simply talk to your Web site's users, ask them questions, get to know them much as you get to know other people in your lives. There are, however, some key differences between getting to know people for the purpose of improving a Web site's usability and getting to know them as friends or colleagues. As nice as it might be to become friends with all of your Web site's users, it's not a very practical option. You'd spend years instead of days (or hours) establishing and fine-tuning the relationships. In the meantime, a number of Web sites could rise and fall before you ever got yours off the ground.

While it can be helpful to perceive the process of getting to know your Web site users as a subset of developing other relationships, it is necessary to focus your attention on discovering usability-related facts and preferences. You need to figure out how to ask the right questions and to discover what user analysis methods you can effectively employ to gather as much usability-related information as you can in the given time period. That's what we'll be focusing on in this module.

For the purposes of this book, I have separated getting to know your users, which we will address in this module, from getting to know your users' hardware and software constraints, which we will address in Module 4. In many cases, it is most efficient to pursue both avenues at the same time, using, say, different sections of a questionnaire to address each of the aspects. But a benefit of mentally separating them out (in addition to making each of the modules a more easily digestible size) is to remind ourselves that the users are, indeed, separate from the technologies.

The Web as we know it today will probably not stay in its current technological form very long. Already it is morphing out of its present desktop computer and browser form into the realm of Internet appliances, Internet-capable clothing, and other, less visible means of access and interaction through the Internet and/or Web.

This is not to imply that Web users will not also change; they will and are changing even as we speak. You as a user, for example, are likely changing in some small way with every page that you read of this book (hopefully!) or at least every time you analyze a new Web site, or design one. But one thing you can be sure of is that we will need to continue designing Web sites (or whatever they evolve into) for human users, so it is in your best interest to take a long-term approach in getting to know your users.

Tip

I'd recommend carving out a large chunk of your long-term memory and labeling it "Web User Research." This can easily be a lifetime endeavor.

Getting to know the constraints of the current hardware and software, on the other hand, could be classified as a "necessary evil." It's a bit like some of those required classes that someone arbitrarily decides every student needs to pass in order to obtain any given degree or certification. A friend of mine, for instance, recently told me that he had to pass a swimming test in order to get his high school diploma. (No, he did not live on an island or anywhere swimming would generally be construed as a necessary facet of living. This was in Ohio.... Go figure.)

In the field of Web design and development, it *is* essential to know the current state of the technology. In fact, I'd bet it's safe to say that this is probably quite a bit more important than knowing how to swim in Ohio. But a good part of the knowledge about today's technology will be relegated to the trash can tomorrow—unless, of course, you plan to write a history of the Internet someday.

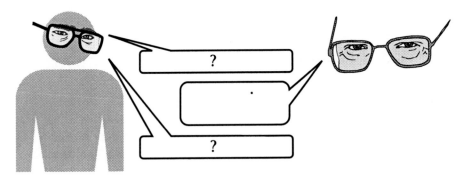

Asking the Right Questions

Questions, questions, questions. You can never have too many questions. They can be a highly cost-efficient design and development tool. It never costs money to ask a question, but it sure can make a dent in your budget if you make assumptions without asking questions and find out months into a project that you were wrong.

There are three key questions to ask regarding usability:

1. Just who are the users of this particular Web site?

2. What do these users need?

3. What do these users want?

You need to address that first question before you can proceed any further. It gives you the framework for establishing user profiles that will help ensure that you address all your other questions to the *right* people. It does you very little good, for example, to exclusively interview adults about usability issues for a kids' entertainment site. No matter how much parents or teachers or CEOs of toy companies think they understand kids, they are not going to make the same sequence of clicks on a Web site.

On the other hand, you would also not want to discard all users above age 12 from your user profiles. Parents, for example, can exert a strong influence over which sites they allow their children to visit, so their thoughts and feelings about a kidsware site are also very important. It would be important to identify their use of the site largely as previewers and/or censors, so you would want to design your site accordingly.

Ask the Expert

Question: Just what is in a "user profile"?

Answer: "User profile" is a fairly loose term that is bandied about quite a bit within the field of Web design. Essentially, a user profile is a description of the key types of users for a particular Web site. In the

3

case of a children's entertainment site, for example, you would expect there to be at least two broad categories of users: kids within some definable age bracket, perhaps of reading age through elementary school, and their parents. These groups could probably also be further broken down. For a Barbie doll–type site, there may be a very large segment of girls, for instance, and a much smaller segment of boys. The age range, as well, may extend much further, say into a group of adult collectors.

Typically, user profiles include basic demographic information such as age, race, gender, cultural background, and native language as well as more site-specific information such as level of familiarity or expertise in that site's subject matter as well as the users' hardware and software constraints (which we'll discuss in Module 4).

Question: What do "user profiles" look like?

Answer: You may encounter a number of different formats for user profiles. They can take the form of paragraphs of text, tables, or diagrams. Mark Pearrow, for example, in his *Web Site Usability Handbook* (Charles River Media, 2000) uses a table with the following column heads for his user profiles: Characteristic, Range, and % Frequency Distribution (meaning the percentage of visitors to the site that fall into that range). Here is an example of the beginning of such a table:

Characteristic	Range	% Frequency Distribution
Age	18–30	12.5
	31–40	50
	41–50	25
	51–60	12.5
Sex	Female	62.5
	Male	37.5
Education	College degree	75
	Some college	25
...	...	...

Robert W. Buchanan, Jr., and Charles Lukaszewski use diagrams to good effect to show the placement of the target audience within a continuum (see *Measuring the Impact of Your Web Site*, John Wiley

& Sons, 1997). Using the data for gender from the preceding table, for example, they might draw the following segment of a user profile:

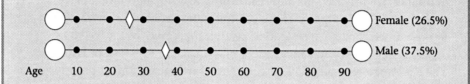

Although I find tables and diagrams helpful in assimilating information, I would recommend pulling that information into paragraph descriptions for the final user profiles. These can be a more personable and effective way to communicate information about the key user groups to the client and the development team members. It helps emphasize that these are people we are dealing with, not statistics.

Identifying Your User Base

Identifying exactly who your Web site's users are is a bit easier said than done. If there's already a version of the site up, figuring out who the current users are is one thing. There are various Web analysis tools that assimilate data that can help you identify this. (We will discuss some of these tools in the "Web Usage Analysis" section later in this module.) Figuring out who the *potential* users are is quite another. It's much more difficult to identify the users who have never visited the site or who stopped by briefly, were dissatisfied, and moved on. If you are developing the very first version of a Web site, your job is even trickier.

The best starting point is asking the client or sponsoring organization for the Web site who they think their target audience is. They generally have, or think they have, a pretty good notion of this from their business plan, market analyses, experience in other media, etc. But it is not always accurate.

Tip

Never take user information collected by a client entirely at face value. All sorts of biases can enter into the gathering and interpretation of such information. Whenever possible, verify it from a more objective stance. For example, locate some of the identified users and ask them if they do, indeed, use that Web site, if they use it in the manner that the client believes they do, or if they foresee that they would use such a site.

Consider the case of the community art center Web site we discussed in Module 2. Their usage statistics indicated very few of their members actually used their Web site. If you asked the board of directors who the audience of the site was, however, their first response would probably be their membership base. That may seem like a logical assumption to make—why else would they develop a site?—but that does not make it real. The usage statistics simply do not support that theory.

The art center's membership base is certainly full of *potential* users, however, and if you can figure out how to make the site truly useful to them, then you have a good chance of converting them from potential to actual users.

Initial user profile sketches for this site are described under the headings that follow.

Sample User Profile: Community Art Center Primary Users

These are members of the board, administrative staff, and most active members in the organization, numbering around 20 users. This group consists of 65 percent women and 35 percent men between the ages of 28 and 40 (see Figures 3-1 and 3-2). They primarily have computers at home as well as at work and consider themselves to be fairly comfortable with using the Web. Their usage ratings, however, indicate they are actually at the beginning/intermediate level. Their time spent on the current Web site is almost exclusively for organizational research.

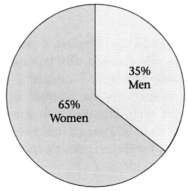

Gender Range of CAC Primary Users

Figure 3-1 Gender range of Community Art Center (CAC) primary users

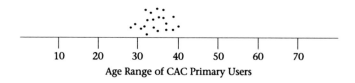

Age Range of CAC Primary Users

Figure 3-2   Age range of CAC primary users

Sample User Profile: Community Art Center Secondary Users

Three are three sizeable groups of secondary users:

- The remaining 345 members of the organization currently account for about 15 percent of the Web usage, an alarmingly low level. This group is composed of 55 percent women and 45 percent men between the ages of 14 and 70 (see Figures 3-3 and 3-4). They have widely varying computer and Internet skills, from complete novices to expert users. Across the board, however, they feel very little incentive to use the current Web site.

- Members of the public who (1) are potential members of the organization (numbering up to approximately 50 per annum) and/or (2) are merely interested in attending exhibits and art-related events (numbering up to approximately 200 per annum) account for a negligible amount of the Web usage. Again, they have widely varying computer and Internet skills. More data on this group can be gathered by attending an exhibit opening on Friday, May 20.

- Patrons of the arts and grant coordinators, a small but potentially viable target audience for this organization, also represent a negligible amount of Web usage. These individuals are estimated to have a much higher comfort level with computers and the Internet, as well as much higher bandwidth access to the Web. The executive director estimates their numbers would be less than 100 per annum but emphasizes they are a critical target audience for the art center's success.

3

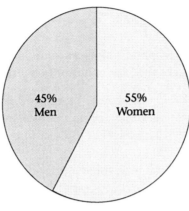

Gender Range of CAC Secondary Users

Figure 3-3   Gender range of CAC secondary users

Did you notice how in this case all of the secondary user groups are largely potential users? They are not effectively using the current site, but it is not hard to imagine how they could be served through a redesigned Web site that would more completely meet the goals set by the organizations' mission statement, as we discussed in Module 2.

Identifying who or what is missing from a Web site is not always this easy, but I hope you can see how important it is to the development of new site ideas. By including these users from the beginning of the site design or redesign, you have a much better chance of being able to develop a site that will truly be of use to them.

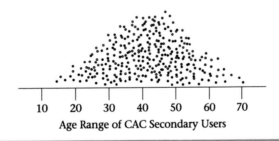

Age Range of CAC Secondary Users

Figure 3-4   Age range of CAC secondary users

Ask the Expert

Question: Identifying potential users sounds tough. Are there any groups of potential users that are commonly overlooked?

Answer: There is one huge group of untapped potential users who can be included in most Web site development plans and user profiles. They are new Web users who have an interest in that particular Web site's content.

As we discussed in Module 1, the majority of the population in the U.S. has yet to come online, and the rest of the world is lagging further behind. There are vast numbers of potential users for whom you may not be prepared if you do not make your site accessible to beginners, especially if you are creating a general-interest Web site.

In the usability-testing field, such individuals are sometimes referred to as LCUs, an acronym for "least competent users," but I prefer plain old "new Web users" or Mark Pearrow's kindlier term "ultra-novice." After all, they can play an invaluable role in helping you create the most usable, effective Web site, so give them a bit of credit.

Once you've identified your user base and gathered enough demographic information to establish user profiles, it's time to investigate the remaining key questions:

- What do the users need—in terms of basic Web site structure, as well as content and accessibility?

- What do the users want—or, what are their preferences?

This second category often overlaps the issues addressed by the first one, but the users' desires should be kept distinct in your own mind from their needs. (My friends always remind me that I should keep that distinction in my own mind, but it's much easier to do for other people!) For example, a group of users may clearly need quick access to stock market data to effectively perform their jobs, but they may state a preference for a jazzy, animation-based interface that uses a lot of beautiful but nonessential graphics. This kind of design could be at cross-purposes with their primary needs.

On the other hand, the same need for quick access to stock market data could be enhanced by a preference that a stock's history be available in the form of a visual chart as well as a text synopsis. With this kind of design, a user could have a fulfilling range of experiences that could vary with his or her pace throughout the day. In their more leisurely moments, the visual learners could take the time to load the graphics and thus more easily absorb the new information. At more hectic times, they may revert to the quick and dirty text-only version. Remember our discussion in Module 2 about catering sites to different styles of learners? This is a good example of that.

3

Level of Familiarity and Comfort with the Web

A key question to investigate of all your users is how familiar they are with the Web and how comfortable they are with it. These are not necessarily the same thing, although if you asked them in sequential questions in a questionnaire you would likely get the same answer. You try it:

1. How familiar are you with the Web?

2. How comfortable are you with the Web?

Try, instead, the following tactic:

1. How long have you been using the Web?

[ ] Less than six months [ ] One year [ ] Two years [ ] Three years
[ ] More than four years

2. How many times per week do you typically log onto the Web to do something other than check e-mail?

[ ] Less than once [ ] 2–3 times [ ] 5–10 times [ ] 10–20 times
[ ] More than 20 times

3. How long does your typical Web session last, not including e-mail?

[ ] Less than 15 minutes [ ] 15–30 minutes [ ] 30–60 minutes [ ] 1–3 hours
[ ] More than three hours

4. How comfortable do you feel in navigating most Web sites?

[ ] Uncomfortable [ ] Tolerable [ ] Just fine [ ] Comfortable
[ ] Very comfortable [ ] Pro

5. With your most recent visit to a Web site you had not visited before, how easily were you able to find the information you were looking for?

[ ] Never did find it [ ] Found it with considerable difficulty
[ ] Don't really know [ ] Found it pretty easily [ ] Piece of cake

Even better than *asking* these last questions about comfort would be watching the users find assigned bits of information on a site they had never visited before. None of our memories are perfect, and as we discussed in Module 1, we humans tend to unconsciously edit our memories. This can be especially true in an interview setting in which the user wants to give you the answer you're looking for, or wants to impress you. Facts make for reliable answers to questions; subjective impressions less so.

Collate the data you collect about your target users' comfort and familiarity with the Web and see if there are any patterns that can help you develop your user profiles. It may be, for instance, that you have three distinct user levels and they just happen to correlate with other significant characteristics.

"Hey," you might find yourself saying, "most of the high-powered Web users are interested in photography or electronic imaging. Maybe we could have a little jazzier photography section on the site." Or "Uh-oh, my ultra-novices have expressed a real interest in visiting online galleries and exhibit spaces. That idea of a surreal QuickTime VR exhibit room is really going to throw them for a loop unless I can figure out a way to easily teach them how to navigate it."

Content Needs

You might think this section should be a no-brainer, but don't ever take the content of a site for granted. Far too many companies have thought along the lines of "This is what we produce, and we will sell it over the Web to the same kinds of people we've been selling it to for the last 50 years." The Web is a different vehicle. It is in your best interest to reconsider both content and audience.

Let me give you an example. Take a business that caters to retired people, let's say the sale of burial plots. (There's a sobering example, isn't it? No more kids' entertainment sites for us!) Their typical customer is either retired or approaching retirement, and, you know, they may realize that they *should* be planning for their death but they sure as heck don't want to. Add to that the built-in disincentive of learning to use the Web and all its related technologies *and* the distrust of making purchases over the Web.

And then consider the fact that cemeteries are generally local businesses, and it's not too hard to drive out to the cemetery to see what you'd be getting. In fact, you've probably driven by it hundreds of times and already have that invaluable sense of familiarity with it that can help secure business. You might want (or need) that extra personal contact as well in having a real person help you navigate the emotional and financial obstacles involved in this particular kind of transaction. The Web—and most anything to do with computers— suffers from being a fairly cold, impersonal medium. After all, the feel of that keyboard is just not the same as a handshake. This is a business that does *not* naturally lend itself to the World Wide Web. This is not to say that you should not even consider creating such a Web site, but I would caution you that it would be inherently more difficult to create a successful site than some other kinds of sites.

On the other hand, think about the core idea behind cemeteries: Yes, they are places to put our dead bodies—we definitely have a storage issue here—but perhaps more importantly, they are "memorial centers." The service they offer to all their non-dead users is to provide a place where the memories of their loved ones can be honored and remembered and treasured.

Memories? Now that is the kind of material that the Web can house pretty darn well. And, in fact, virtual cemeteries and memorial centers have taken off on the Web and have a high level of user involvement. The audience has expanded as well to include kids and grandkids and war veteran discussion boards, the sharing of memories while people are still alive as well as honoring the memories of people after they have died. See Figure 3-5 of the World Wide Cemetery for an example of such a site.

Pet memorial centers, full of photographs and scanned in I.D. tags and cute little knitted doggie sweaters and hand-drawn illustrations, have proved successful as well. Web sites like these can perhaps appeal to people more than real-world pet cemeteries ever will. There's a fine line in there somewhere;

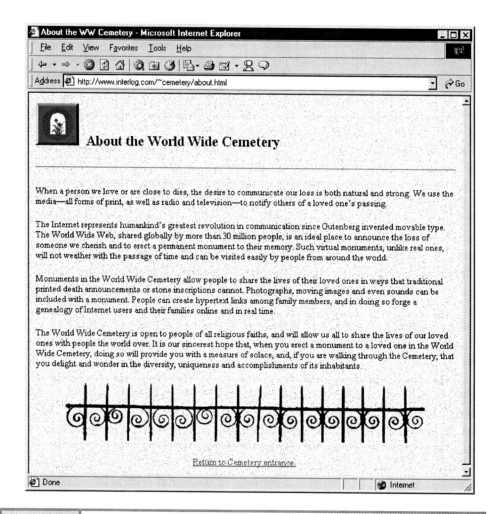

Figure 3-5 The World Wide Cemetary is a "place where Internet users, their families and friends can erect permanent memorials to the dead" (http://www.cemetery.org)

actually paying the bucks to bury your beloved pet in a formal pet cemetery can seem just silly, but, for some reason, sharing the memories of them with others over the Web does not. See Figure 3-6 of Heaven's Playground for an example.

The Virtual Pet Cemetery, at http://www.mycemetery.com/pet, is another straightforward text-only pet memorial site. At the time of this writing, it boasts that thousands of people from all over the world visit its 31-and-growing number

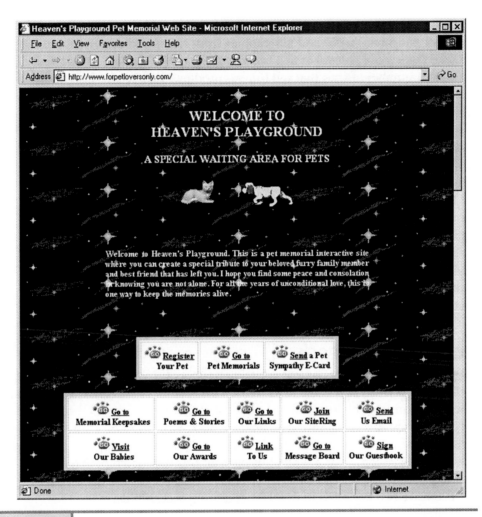

Figure 3-6   Heaven's Playground provides a place to memorialize your pet as well as share related poems or stories or post messages for other users (http://forpetloversonly.com)

of pet cemetery plots every day and the site's founders or staff are having a hard time keeping up with the user requests. Slip on your usability spectacles, though, and compare its structure and the services offered by Heaven's Playground and the World Wide Web Cemetery. Ask yourself how, for example, would you find your cousin's old dog Miffy's plot, and could you leave any remembrance of her such as flowers or a favorite Miffy story?

Other successful content models include innumerable historical Web sites that have put photographs and biographies from real-world cemeteries online to make them more accessible to a broader geographical region. Additionally, there are a number of sites that sell funeral products such as caskets and headstones. One rather unusual site called Eternal Reefs at http://www.eternalreefs.com even offers "to turn your loved one's ashes into a living coral reef to create a permanent living memorial" as an environmentally sound alternative to urns and vaults. How's that for thinking about new services to offer via a new medium? They certainly transcend the geographic constraints of traditional cemetery services.

In each of these Web sites, what started as the same business (burial and memorialization), targeting the same audience, has been transformed to significantly different content needs for the Web.

So ask your users, ask your client, ask your Web team, ask yourself or anybody else you can extract an answer from: Is this the most appropriate content *for this Web site? For this user group?* What other possibilities aren't we considering?

Accessibility Needs

Supplying the appropriate content is vital to a successful Web site, as is ensuring that content is easily accessible to its users. This becomes particularly challenging when you consider the vast range of physical abilities users across the globe may have. Yep, as a species we may typically have two legs, two arms, five senses, the ability to move and breathe fairly freely and to click away at a mouse to our heart's content, but not all of us have all this functionality in optimum working condition.

There are two key areas to consider regarding accessibility in terms of Web sites:

● The need to develop Web sites that can be viewed and otherwise fully experienced by those users in our society who are classified as "disabled" or "handicapped"

● The need to develop Web sites that cater to the particular ailments or difficulties or, more positively, the talents and dexterity of its *primary* user base

The problem I have with most accessibility discussions is that they are too often couched in negative terms. As with the figures revealing that a majority of the population comes from a "dysfunctional" family, I'd say that most of us are "disabled" in some way or another. Whether it's the 5–10 percent of the male population that has some form of color blindness or "color impairment" throughout their lives or the common loss of vision and hearing in the elderly, "disability" is awfully widespread. More accurately perhaps it ought to be called "the wide range of human abilities."

Consider, for example, the ability level of infants or toddlers. They typically do not have the dexterity or the hand-eye coordination of adults, but that's a normal part of being human in that stage of life and so, rightly, is not considered "disabled." I'd say the same line of thought could be applied to, say, the elderly where reports indicate 50 percent of people over 65 have some functional impairment. That also is just a common part of our human experience. As a rule of thumb, if we are going to design a Web site that has useful content for this target population, then it's in our best interest to design it in a way that they can access it. If they are not within the user profile, then it is not essential to make that extra effort.

It's not as easy to eliminate adults, ages 18–65, with impaired functionality from most Web site profiles, however. As Jakob Nielsen reported, in the U.S. alone there are more than 30 million people who have some condition that makes it difficult to use traditional computer input and output devices (*Designing Web Usability,* New Riders, 2000). As such, it is in our best interest to design general-interest Web sites in a way that is accessible to the vast majority of adults. That's just common sense.

The good news is that it's not all that difficult to make *most* Web sites accessible to *most* people. It can largely be accomplished by using HTML the way it was intended, to encode function rather than design. Thus, for example, you should apply first-level header HTML tags (<h1> </h1>) to content that should be designated as first-level headings, not just anything that you want to appear in a large, bold typeface. Here are a couple of additional tips:

- Don't do anything to override the user's browser settings. Users generally set their preferences for a reason, oftentimes for improved accessibility.

- Don't change the color of the hypertext links or remove their underlines. As we discussed in Module 2, this is one of the most important settings for users who have difficulty perceiving blues.

● Avoid the use of graphical text. It does not provide the necessary flexibility for the user to be able to increase the typeface, and so on.

● Always, always, use the Alternative Text attributes (<alt> </alt>) to give a text description of any visual element so that users and their Braille readers or text-to-speech conversion tools can determine what image is supposed to appear in a given place even if they can't see it. The next best thing to a picture conveying a thousand words is words conveying a description of the picture.

● Avoid creating anything that flashes on and off. The pulses can induce seizures in some people. Besides, nobody likes things that flash like that on Web sites.

● If your Web site has sound, make sure that there are enough visual clues for a user to easily use the site without it. Many users are at least partially hearing impaired and lots more either have no speakers, bad speakers, or their speakers turned off.

Tip

See the World Wide Web Consortium's Web Accessibility Initiative for more information and guidelines on making Web sites accessible. This can be found at http://www.w3.org/WAI/.

Language is another immense "disability" on the Web. The vast majority of Web sites are in English, yet the vast number of potential Web users are not native English speakers. We've definitely got a built-in accessibility problem here that's so endemic most people don't even include it under an "accessibility" heading.

Tip

The Translate-Free Web site at http://translate-free.com offers links to a wide range of foreign language translation services that are available for free on the Web. One that will translate whole Web pages is Alta Vista's Babel Fish Translations at http://babel.altavista.com/tr?.

There are a number of solutions in the works for this particular example of the "wide range of human abilities," including the development of on-the-fly translation programs. And there are a few, cumbersome solutions already in practice such as "localizing" sites whereby each site is manually translated for each linguistic user group, that is to say, for each linguistic group that is deemed important enough to merit this effort. Such sites take a lot of effort both in the initial translation and in the updating and maintenance. Suddenly, instead of just making a set of changes once, you have to make the changes several times—in several different languages.

Note

The Americans with Disabilities Act is worth paying particular attention to, since it is the U.S. government's attempt to legislate accessibility for all disabled people within the United States. It extends well beyond the parameters of the Web, however, to cover such things as requiring wheelchair accessible ramps in public places.

Ask the Expert

Question: What's this I've heard about a "Section 508"? I know it has something to do with usability.

Answer: On July 1, 2001, Section 508 of the Rehabilitation Act Congress passed in 1973 and then modified in 1998 went into effect. Among other things, it required all U.S. federal government Web sites to be accessible to *all* federal employees, regardless of any disabilities that they might have. And, apparently lawyers have interpreted the ruling to mean that any citizen could sue any government Web site that is not Section 508 compliant if they are not able to access the information properly. It took the working groups years to try to flesh out exactly what this all meant.

Even after the deadline, many government Web site designers are struggling frantically to comply with this regulation. It's one thing to make your site accessible to the vast majority of people; it's quite another to make it accessible to every single person, regardless of their type of disability.

Question: So what do you have to do to conform to Section 508?

Answer: Providing text-only sites with fully conforming HTML is perhaps the easiest sure way to provide this level of access. But of course, that isn't a good option for many sites, nor for many users. Think again of the different learning styles we covered in Module 2. Text-only sites would certainly not be ideal for, say, visual learners.

For dedicated readers, the text of Section 508 can be found at http://www.section508.gov. The final technical requirements are available at http://www.access-board.gov/news/508-final.htm. In practical terms, here is a summation of the larger fixes:

- Every graphic must also have a counterpart that can be interpreted by a screen reader for the visually impaired, such as that created with Alternative Text attributes.

- The page layout must also be interpretable by these screen readers, neatly telling the scores of tips and tricks created by Web designers to force HTML, especially tables, to make the pages look more attractive.

- Every movie or animation must be closed-captioned for the deaf and must have a text counterpart that is readable by a screen reader.

- And, any place that requires a mouse click should also be able to be activated with keystrokes.

Question: I've also heard something about Section 255. What is that?

Answer: Section 255 is a completely different accessibility requirement that has fairly recently been applied to Web sites. It is an addendum of the Communications Act dating back to 1934, and is part of the Telecommunications Act of 1996 that was created to help provide access to telecommunications service by persons with disabilities.

Its application to the Web was brought into the limelight when the American Foundation for the Blind (AFB) sued AOL for not making their "hometown" area fully accessible to the blind. They based their claim on AOL's own advertising that "hometown" was a public place. The suit expressed their concern that the disabled will suffer from a lack of access as the Internet replaces many of the existing telecommunications services and equipment—unless Web sites are made to conform with the prior accessibility legislation.

At the time of this writing, the last word was the following posting on the AFB's Web site: "AOL is looking for Beta Testers to Test New Accessibility Features," a positive sign at least that AOL is now trying to accommodate the needs of the disabled. For more information, see the AFB's Web site at http://www.afb.org.

In sum, in order to design an effective, usable site, you need to know what your users' accessibility needs are. One of the simplest ways to find out information like this is, of course, to just ask them. However, chances are they would not fully understand a question like "What are your access needs?" Just as with Web site design, it is necessary to ask the questions in language that is more natural to the users. Keep our usability jargon to ourselves.

So how do we ask them more effectively? You might try something like "Are you comfortable working with a keyboard and mouse?" "Do you have any difficulties reading small type?" and "What is your primary language?" Even better, observe them using a site that uses small type in English and that requires a keyboard and mouse and note any difficulties they have with it.

Most often, unfortunately, you can't ask all of your users all of your most pressing questions in person. It can be necessary to employ other data gathering tools. In developing Web sites, these tools can typically be separated into categories based on what's available to you before you launch a Web site, or prototype of a Web site, and what's available to you through that site once you've launched it.

If you know part of your audience has a particular kind of handicap, find out everything you can about how that handicap affects Web usage. It can be a good idea to start with organizations that have been created to help serve the needs of that particular handicap, such as the American Foundation for the Blind (http://www.afb.org). It never hurts as well to emulate that handicap as best you can so that you can get that direct personal experience with using the Web. Use a blindfold to emulate blindness, hearing plugs to emulate deafness, etc. and then try to use your site.

1-Minute Drill

● What are the two key areas to consider regarding accessibility in terms of Web sites?

● What's one of the best places to look for general guidance on usability issues for the Web?

Prelaunch User Analysis Methods

There are handfuls of ways to obtain usage information before the launch of a site. Some of the most common methods include:

● Market research

● Focus groups

● Questionnaires

● Interviews

● Heuristic evaluation

● Usability testing

● Plain old observation

● The need to develop Web sites that can be viewed and otherwise fully experienced by disabled users and the need to develop Web sites that cater to the particular abilities of its primary user base

● The World Wide Web Consortium's Web Accessibility Initiative (at http://www.w3.org/WAI/)

Let me be up-front with you, though. Of these methods, the first four (market research, focus groups, questionnaires, and interviews) are of limited value—not useless, just limited. As usability guru Jakob Nielsen recently declared in his "Alertbox" online newsletter:

> To design an easy-to-use interface, pay attention to what users do, not what they say. Self-reported claims are unreliable, as are user speculations about future behavior….

> Too frequently, I hear about companies basing their designs on user input obtained through misguided methods. A typical example? Create a few alternative designs, show them to a group of users, and ask which one they prefer. Wrong. If the users have not actually tried to use the designs, they'll base their comments on surface features. Such input often contrasts strongly with feedback based on real use.

> —Jakob Nielsen, Alertbox, August 5, 2001,
> http://www.useit.com/alertbox/20010805.html

Note

Nielsen titled this article rather dramatically "First Rule of Usability? Don't Listen to Users." But take that title with a grain of salt. It *is* important to listen to users. As he points out later in the same article, it is necessary to ask and listen discriminately; the challenge is to figure out when and how to listen. Asking the right questions is key to this process, as we have discussed earlier in this module.

Market Research

A good place to begin any inquiry is to review and analyze whatever market research information has already been gathered. Many businesses spend tens of thousands of dollars and thousands of man-hours on trying to understand their market (a.k.a. their user base) and their competitors, so they may have done a lot of the legwork for you.

Just don't rely on existing market research as being the definitive source of information, especially if the Web site you are working on is only one component of their business. There's no telling how the context of the research may have subtly influenced the results in terms of making Web design and usability decisions.

A softball manufacturer, for example, may have determined that their market consists primarily of young, active boys who really dig interactivity. Well, it may be that they really dig playing baseball with their friends—that's a pretty darn interactive activity. It does not indicate, however, how inclined they'd be to spend time online browsing softball catalogs and participating in a discussion board. They might be; they might not be. I'd say it would probably be a good idea to research this a little further.

There's also, plain and simply, good and bad market research. You don't want to base your decisions on bad market research.

Tip

One area where market research can be very helpful is in identifying business competitors. Chances are that's where some of your *potential* users are hanging out. If you can find out what those users like and don't like about the company you are developing a site for as well as its competitors, you'll have a much better chance of designing a site that will meet their needs better than anything offered before.

Focus Groups

Locate members from each of your primary user groups, put them in a room together, and ask them what they think about the ideas you have for a Web site. Do it again, with other, similar groups. That's essentially what focus groups are about. They can be fun, enlightening, dynamic, informative—and, unfortunately, the results can sometimes be misleading.

The nature of group dynamics itself is partly to blame for this failing. When you take people out of their typical environment and put them in a room together with strangers, a whole social process takes place. As much as the individuals may be interested in the topic of conversation (your Web site), they are also subconsciously interested in questions like "Who is going to dominate the conversation? Who is attracted to whom? Who is going to challenge my ideas or, even worse, my identity? What if I sound stupid? When will we break for lunch?" and "If we hurry up, could I take the rest of the afternoon off?" The group momentum can also take people away from the more mundane real-world practicality of how they would use something in their day-to-day life, so they start imagining how they might like to use something instead of reporting what they need today.

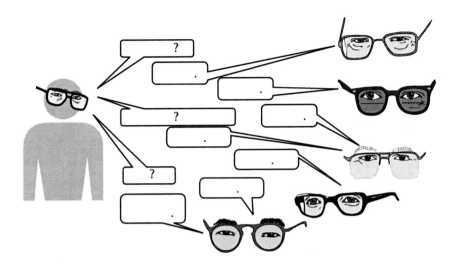

In any focus group, there's a lot more going on than coming up with real-world feedback on your ideas, and that can cloud your results. Some tips on minimizing these distractions:

● Be a strong leader of the discussion and make the procedures you'll be following very clear at the beginning. In effect, you'll be establishing the social order.

● Be prepared ahead of time. Write down exactly what you hope to explore and a list of related questions.

● Keep the discussion focused on the topic at hand. Prevent it from getting too far off-track with unrelated discussions.

● Pepper your queries with requests for real-world examples from their personal experience. It can also be very helpful if you know what each of the users does for a living and/or how they might be using the Web site, so that you can ask them very specific questions.

● Pay the participants or in some other way reward them for taking the time to help you out. Not only are they helping you out, but they will also take it more seriously if they perceive it as work instead of play. (This applies to all of these prelaunch methods.)

● Be prepared for surprises and good ideas that you hadn't thought about too!

Questionnaires

We've already covered a lot of the groundwork for developing questions under "Asking the Right Questions" earlier in this module. In developing questions, you want to be sure to do the following three things:

- Ask the right questions

- Of the right users

- In their language, without relying on industry jargon

In choosing between different ways of gathering information, you need to assess each for their pros and cons. Questionnaires, for example, can be highly efficient. Once you've decided on the questions, you can photocopy it a thousand times and distribute it willy nilly to participants all over the globe. Better yet, e-mail it or post it on a Web site. However—there always has to be a downside, doesn't there?—you won't have a chance to further explain a question if it confuses some of the users. Nor will you be able to observe the users' thinking processes and spontaneously follow up on new ideas or questions.

Questions typically fall in the following kinds of categories:

- Comfort and familiarity with the Web

- Interest and knowledge in the proposed content

- Current sources of information in the proposed content and level of satisfaction or dissatisfaction with it

- What users would like to have available on the site (features, content, etc.)

- User needs and preferences (for the content and site design)

- How they would like to access the content (interface design, learning styles, disability issues, etc.)

- What kinds of interactivity would the users be most interested in and most likely to participate in

- What kinds of media (graphics, audio, video, animation, etc.) would they find most useful

- User hardware and software constraints (which we'll cover in more depth in Module 4)

Note

You will have practice writing part of a questionnaire at the end of this module.

Interviews

One-on-one interviews, on the other hand, have opposite pros and cons to questionnaires in many regards. They are much more time- and resource-intensive. A photocopy machine doesn't even enter the picture, yet you have the benefit of the real-world interaction. For example, you can observe how long the user takes to answer a question or how certain they seem to be of their answer. And, joy of joys, you can pursue new leads that come up and get to know that user and their particular needs and desires in much more detail.

Interviews can be made over the phone or face-to-face in just about any environment. Having a computer handy with sample Web sites can be very helpful, though, to help demonstrate or confirm ideas. The simple question "Is this what you have in mind?" while pointing to an example site can help elicit an even more detailed response from the interviewee: "Yes, that's it absolutely" to "Well, not quite. What I meant to say was…." Also, having storyboards, sketches, or preliminary comps—short for comprehensive designs, also often called mock-ups—of your site can help you explain your concepts much better if you are already at that stage of development.

Caution

Showing comprehensive designs too early in the process can cause interviewees to change their focus from the broad picture to the specific. Comments like "I don't really care for that typeface" or "There's a typo in that sentence" are much less useful to you early on in a project than, say, discussing the content and accessibility needs.

In the case of either questionnaires or interviews, you still have to be careful of misleading answers. Users can try to give you the answer they think you are looking for, or they might not really know what they think. Without having the fully developed site right in front of them in their natural environment, a lot of conjecture enters the picture.

Heuristic Evaluation

A heuristic evaluation is essentially a shortcut to usability testing, introduced by Jakob Neilsen and Rolf Molich in 1990. It entails hiring a few usability experts to give you a best-guess analysis of potential usability problems. These kinds of evaluations are typically less expensive and less logistically challenging than developing a full-blown usability test, and they can do an excellent job at identifying a number of usability problems. However, if you are working on a critical project and really need to gauge full usability, it is no replacement for a formal usability test.

Heuristic evaluations can be an excellent tool during the development phase. Web usability experts understand the development process and the nature of prototypes very well, and, unlike less knowledgeable users, they tend not to be distracted by the parts of the site that have not been completed or are still in rough form. They've been wearing those usability spectacles for a really long time and can spot a usability issue right through a pile of graphics and HTML code.

Note

To stay up with the developments in the heuristics arena, I'd recommend that you check out Jakob Neilsen's archive of his "Alertbox" usability newsletters at http://www.useit.com/alertbox or sign up to have synopses of new issues e-mailed to you on a biweekly basis. Nielsen is not the only voice in this arena, but you can be sure that he will stay on top of it.

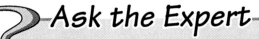

Ask the Expert

Question: Hang on a second: what the heck are heuristics?

Answer: Oops, sorry about that. Heuristics is doing something by the seat of the pants, so to speak. In this case, you hire the most knowledgeable usability gurus you can find in the field and ask them to make their best guess at what the results of a usability test would be. They follow an empirical line of reasoning and rules of thumb that have been established (although they are constantly being refined in this field). Their answers cannot be scientifically documented, but they can get pretty darn close.

A more formal definition from Webster's is:

heuristics: providing aid or direction in the solution of a problem but otherwise unjustified or incapable of justification; of or relating to exploratory problem-solving techniques that utilize self-education techniques to improve performance.

Usability Testing

If you already have a version of the site live, a great supplement to market research, focus groups, questionnaires, and interviews is to put part or all of the site in front of the users and watch them actually use it within scientifically established parameters. That's the core of Web site usability testing, which ought to be a key component of the final development and testing phase of creating Web sites in the first place. This is a big enough topic that we will devote most of our testing module (Module 14) to it.

Unfortunately, this option is not available to you during the design phase for the first version of a site, or it has limited value if you are planning a complete redesign of the site. It is also one of the most expensive methods, in terms of both development and execution. As we've discussed before, it's always better to design the site using a user-centric design process and then use formal usability testing to ensure that you have accomplished what you intended.

1-Minute Drill

● What is the key difference between a heuristic evaluation and usability testing?

● Why might it not be a good idea to rely on a company's existing market research to gain an understanding of the company's Web site user base?

Plain Old Observation

The designers at IDEO, one of the most innovative product design firms in the world, are not big fans of market research, focus groups, or even necessarily asking the users what they think they want. They give preeminent status to plain old observation. As IDEO's general manager Tom Kelly says,

> Plenty of well-meaning clients duly inform us what a new product needs to do. They already "know" how people use their products. They're so familiar with their customers and existing product line that they can rattle off half a dozen good reasons why an innovation is impractical. Of course, we listen to these concerns. Then we get in the operating room, so to speak, and see for ourselves....
>
> —Tom Kelley, *The Art of Innovation* (Random House, 2001, p. 25)

See, it's not just Web design that emphasizes the power of observation. If this technique is good enough for IDEO, then we're bound to be on the right track.

Note

Do you feel like you've been encouraged to use the "power of observation" before? Repetition is a good learning tool. I'll remind you again at the end of the next section!

● A heuristic evaluation is not a scientifically documentable process. It is an educated guess instead of a controlled study.

● The context of conducting the research for broad company-wide purposes may have subtly influenced the results in terms of making Web design and usability decisions. Also, sometimes there is just bad or inaccurate market research.

Postlaunch User Analysis Methods

Evaluating Web sites for usability issues just gets easier and easier. All of the prelaunch methods are available to you after the site is launched, as are a host of new options that you can take advantage of through the Web site itself. Count yourself lucky that interactivity is intrinsic to the Web and that its users tend to be a fairly vocal crowd who are perfectly willing to give you feedback when you ask for it—as well as when you don't!

Web Site Feedback Prompts

One of the most common links since the early days of the Web is the "Feedback" prompt. Webmasters all over the world have put such a link on their home page, often in tiny print near the bottom of the page, and sometimes much more prominently displayed.

To get open feedback, this is a great way to go. Classifying and interpreting the kinds of feedback you get may present a challenge, though. And you can be sure that you will get a lot of comments about the content and design of the site as well as its usability.

One thing you can do to try to harness this enthusiasm is to provide a series of topics that the users can select from, depending on what type of feedback they'd like to give. I always recommend ending the list with an "Other" category. If you're soliciting feedback, users will be frustrated if they can't find a topic relating to what they are concerned about.

Caution

Keep in mind that a majority of the feedback you'll get through this method can be negative. People are more apt to complain about something than to praise it, particularly when it takes time out of their "busy day" to provide the feedback. Although it may not make the most cheerful reading, hearing about what problems users encounter is pretty darn helpful when it comes to improving the site.

Web Forms

An alternative to open feedback prompts is to ask users to complete a more guided Web usability form. There's a double edge to this approach, however. While forms can supply you with the kind of data that you are looking for to determine how effective your Web site is, users tend to be much less willing to complete them. So there's an automatic filtering process that goes on from your user base. Chances are that the more hard-core Web enthusiasts will disproportionately respond to your request.

Be sure to include questions about such things as the user's familiarity and comfort with the Web early in your Web forms so that you can ascertain just which portion of your user base is giving you feedback.

When the Audubon Society decided to revise their Web site at http://www.audubon.org, they added a pop-up request to complete a ten-minute user survey. The survey provided them with very timely user feedback about a number of issues that helped them make the site "more user-friendly, informative, and effective." Note in the following screens how they roughly divided the questions between Web site usage (questions #1–11) and demographics (questions #12–16). They also provided two avenues for users to express their thoughts in their own words, the first as question #5 and then again at the very end of the survey. This takes into account that some of the best user feedback may not be anticipated by a specific question.

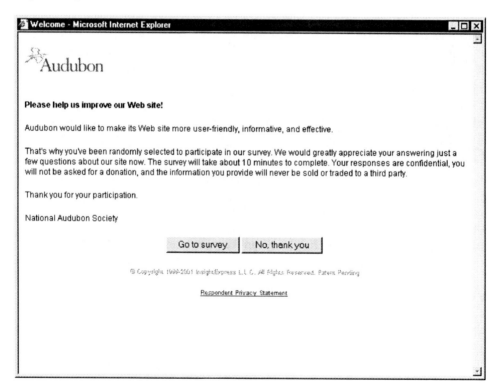

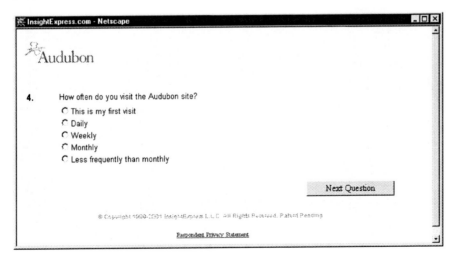

InsightExpress.com - Netscape

1. How did you first find out about the Audubon Web site?
    ○ Word of mouth from friends or family
    ○ Audubon materials (magazine, newsletter, direct mail)
    ○ An online advertisement
    ○ An advertisement not online (TV, radio, magazine, newspaper)
    ○ A news item online
    ○ A news item not online (TV, radio, magazine, newspaper)
    ○ A search engine
    ○ A link from another Web site
    ○ A link to the Web site in an e-mail
    ○ Other
    ○ Don□t know/remember

2. Why are you visiting the Audubon site today? (Check all that apply.)
    ☐ For information about birds
    ☐ For information about Audubon
    ☐ For information about upcoming events
    ☐ For state, local or chapter Audubon resources
    ☐ For information about conservation and environmental issues
    ☐ To read Audubon magazine online
    ☐ For membership or donor information
    ☐ To subscribe to an email distribution list
    ☐ For information about Audubon jobs
    ☐ Other

3. Are you an employee of Audubon?
    ○ Yes
    ○ No

Next Question

InsightExpress.com - Netscape

Audubon

4. How often do you visit the Audubon site?
    ○ This is my first visit
    ○ Daily
    ○ Weekly
    ○ Monthly
    ○ Less frequently than monthly

Next Question

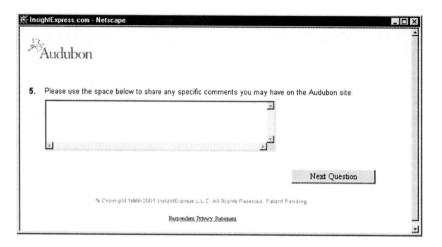

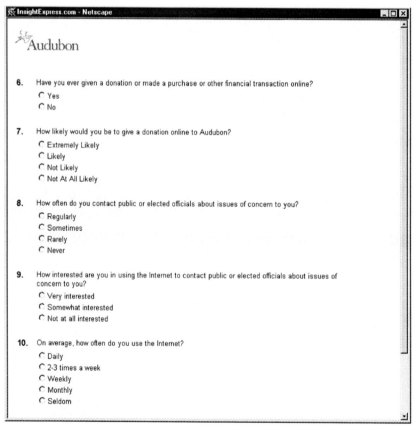

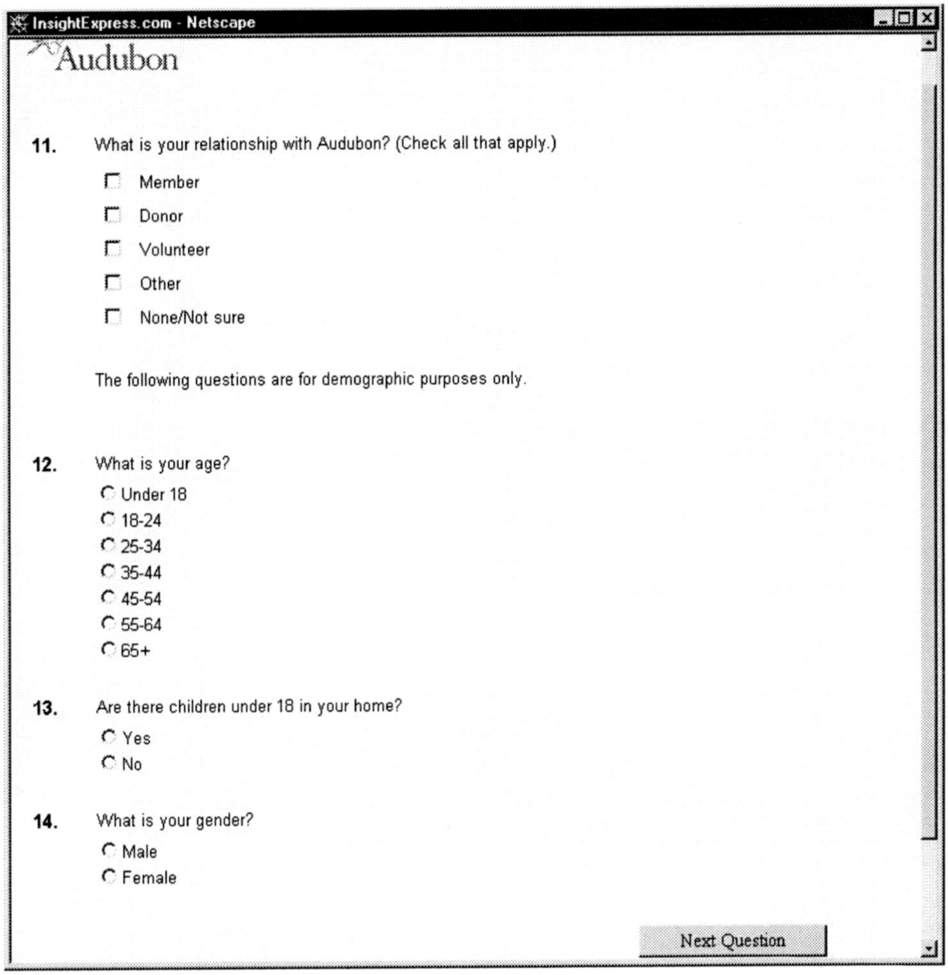

InsightExpress.com - Netscape

Audubon

11.   What is your relationship with Audubon? (Check all that apply.)

☐   Member

☐   Donor

☐   Volunteer

☐   Other

☐   None/Not sure

The following questions are for demographic purposes only.

12.   What is your age?
  ○ Under 18
  ○ 18-24
  ○ 25-34
  ○ 35-44
  ○ 45-54
  ○ 55-64
  ○ 65+

13.   Are there children under 18 in your home?
  ○ Yes
  ○ No

14.   What is your gender?
  ○ Male
  ○ Female

Next Question

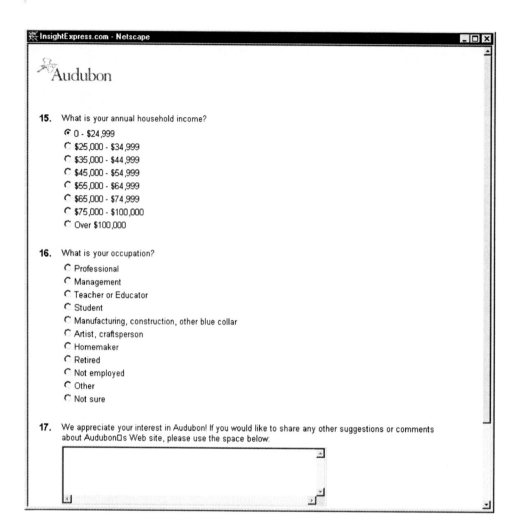

Tip

Consider using incentives to encourage users to complete Web forms. Free merchandise is always a good lure. Sweepstakes, discounts, gift certificates, or even cash can also be effective.

Web Usage Analysis

Data, raw data, more than you could ever know what to do with is being gathered by the gigabytes from the Web. There's a fine science out there somewhere, being developed as we speak, that can help you utilize that data for the purpose of understanding and improving usability issues. When the data pertains to usability, it is often called *usage metrics*.

The basic process of Web usage analysis goes something like this:

1. Establish criteria.

2. Gather data.

3. Analyze the data.

4. Use the data to decide how to best improve your Web site.

5. Implement the changes.

6. Start all over again.

Server Logs

You can establish a number of server logs for collecting data. Some of the most common logs include:

● **Access logs**   Collect information on date and time of connection, user identification, and what pages the user requested.

● **Error logs**   Collect information on error messages given to users.

● **Referral logs**   Collect information on the browser used to access the site and which URL the user visited immediately prior to visiting your site. (They are called "referral logs" because they were established to trace cross-referrals between partner sites, or sites that exchanged links. They are also used extensively now to capture how many hits a Web banner or advertisement brings in.)

Note

These logs are not automatically generated with every new Web site. It is necessary to coordinate what kind of information you would like to collect with the system administrator (often abbreviated sys admin) who is running the server.

The format of the logs also varies from server to server, but generally the kind of information gathered is the same. Also, you can arrange to have reports generated as either text or charts that show such things as the number of users who accessed your site or a specific page, per hour, per day, per month, etc. Figures 3-7 to 3-15 show a number of different kinds of reports generated by Funnel Web Analyzer and Webalizer, two out of a number of different Web reporting software companies.

Tip

You can download free trial versions of Funnel Web Analyzer and Webalizer from http://www.quest.com/funnel_web/analyzer and http://www.mrunix.net/webalizer, respectively. WebTrends, at http://webtrends.com, offers another such common tool, as does WebAlyser (not to be confused with Webalizer) at http://www.webalyser.com.

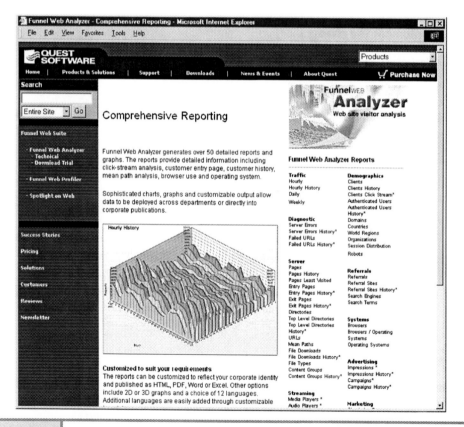

Figure 3-7   Funnel Web Analyzer can generate up to 50 detailed reports and graphs (http //quest.com/funnel_web/analyzer)

	Region	Requests	%	Bytes	%	Sessions	Visitors	Pages	Total Time	Errors
1	Oceania	5,651	40.29%	23.5MB	20.87%	1,128	561	3,108	50:05:42	92
2	Unknown	4,339	30.93%	40.4MB	35.86%	764	579	1,967	37:06:00	113
3	North America	2,532	18.05%	29.2MB	25.89%	512	392	984	16:20:59	52
4	Europe	963	6.87%	11.4MB	10.11%	164	138	315	07:16:18	10
5	Asia	470	3.35%	7.4MB	6.59%	116	51	166	05:59:18	16

Figure 3-8   This Funnel Web Analyzer report shows a breakdown of site visitors by geographic region, using a beautiful visual map as well as a table of text data

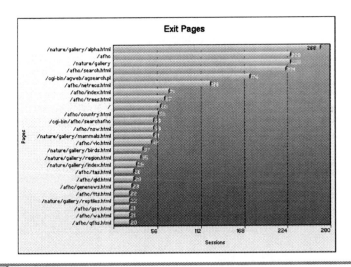

Figure 3-9   This Funnel Web Analyzer report shows the last page visited by users before exiting the site; a table of data also accompanies the graph

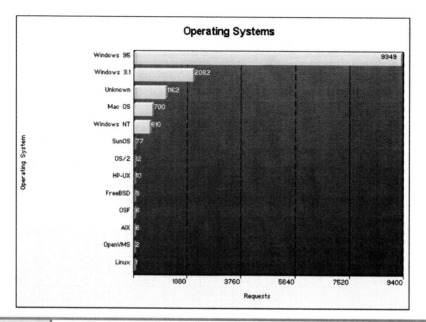

Figure 3-10 Knowing which operating systems site visitors are using, as can be seen in this Funnel Web Analyzer report, can be critical; other reports also give the details on which browsers were used

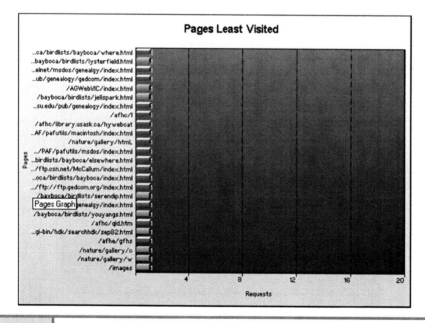

Figure 3-11 This Funnel Web Analyzer report shows which pages are least visited

If you want to find out what pages are *not* attracting visitors, reports on which pages are least visited can be very helpful (see Figure 3-11). Reports are also available on which search terms are most commonly requested, which can help you identify what content your users are looking for, and whether they are calling it by the same names as you are.

3

Monthly Statistics for August 2001		
Total Hits		3556
Total Files		2843
Total Pages		530
Total Visits		252
Total KBytes		15681
Total Unique Sites		322
Total Unique URLs		62
Total Unique Referrers		50
Total Unique User Agents		19
	Avg	**Max**
Hits per Hour	9	145
Hits per Day	222	532
Files per Day	177	416
Pages per Day	33	71
Visits per Day	15	32
KBytes per Day	980	2640
Hits by Response Code		
Code 200 - OK		2843
Code 206 - Partial Content		1
Code 304 - Not Modified		641
Code 404 - Not Found		71

Figure 3-12 The usage statistics for the Sanchez Art Center are generated by Webalizer; here, we see an overview of the monthly usage stats

#	Hits		KBytes		URL
colspan=6	**Top 10 of 62 Total URLs By KBytes**				
1	129	3.63%	4084	26.04%	/GeneratedItems/CSScriptLib.js
2	79	2.22%	1381	8.81%	/images/congratulations.jpg
3	181	5.09%	1160	7.40%	/
4	22	0.62%	958	6.11%	/2001-08/tibet.jpg
5	26	0.73%	825	5.26%	/mural.gif
6	36	1.01%	768	4.90%	/2001-00/joesan.jpg
7	50	1.41%	571	3.64%	/2001-08/awest.jpg
8	48	1.35%	325	2.07%	/eastwing.html
9	60	1.69%	317	2.02%	/westwing.html
10	149	4.19%	317	2.02%	/images/sacaddr.gif

Figure 3-13 This Webalizer report shows what the top ten URLs requested were, organized by their file size in kilobytes

#	Hits		Referrer
colspan=4	**Top 30 of 50 Total Referrers**		
1	1383	38.89%	http://www.sanchezartcenter.org/
2	426	11.98%	http://www.sanchezartcenter.org/westwing.html
3	353	9.93%	- (Direct Request)
4	245	6.89%	http://www.sanchezartcenter.org/about.html
5	198	5.57%	http://www.sanchezartcenter.org/main.html
6	187	5.26%	http://www.sanchezartcenter.org/eastwing.html
7	154	4.33%	http://sanchezartcenter.org/
8	124	3.49%	http://www.sanchezartcenter.org/artists.html
9	121	3.40%	http://www.sanchezartcenter.org/directions.html
10	94	2.64%	http://www.sanchezartcenter.org
11	74	2.08%	http://www.sanchezartcenter.org/2001-08/tibet.html
12	39	1.10%	http://www.sanchezartcenter.org/agp/agp.html
13	20	0.56%	http://www.google.com/search
14	17	0.48%	http://www.sanchezartcenter.org/agp/ewald.html
15	16	0.45%	http://www.sanchezartcenter.org/index.html
16	13	0.37%	http://sanchezartcenter.org/westwing.html
17	12	0.34%	http://sanchezartcenter.org/eastwing.html
18	7	0.20%	http://sanchezartcenter.org/about.html
19	6	0.17%	http://www.sanchezartcenter.org/agp/agpmember.html
20	5	0.14%	bookmarks

Figure 3-14 Referral tables, such as this one from Webalizer, itemize which Web site your users came from, immediately prior to visiting your site

Daily and hourly usage charts are also available and can help in planning future events and assessing the success of past events The kind of information on the hourly usage can be especially useful in determining server load and to help in timing live Web events. As you can see from Figure 3-15, 11 A.M. and 2 P.M. were the peak times during the month of August when users visited the Sanchez Art Center Web site.

User-Driven Navigation Patterns

In terms of ascertaining usability, some of the most useful information revolves around how users have navigated your site. From analyzing data gathered in a *click stream analysis*, an analysis of what your users clicked, you can actually trace their paths through the Web site. Of course, you can't know what their motivation was, or what they were looking for as you could if you were looking over their shoulder real-time and asking them questions as they proceeded. But you can detect patterns.

Take, for example, a set of usage data that indicates 80 percent of the users in the month of February started on the home page, clicked the special Hawaii travel promotion, completed the sweepstakes form, and then went on to a hula dance greeting card. These kinds of figures would indicate that your Hawaii promotion was probably simple to understand, was appealing, and could be deemed a success.

More typically, the data is not so conclusive, so it requires a lot more hemming and hawing over. Say your site offered a trip to Australia's Great

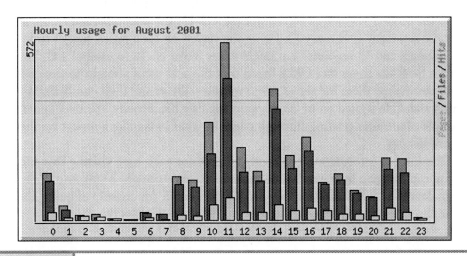

Figure 3-15   This hourly usage report for the Sanchez Art Center was generated by Webalizer

Barrier Reef in May, but only ten percent of the site's visitors that month completed the form. Off the bat, you need to consider a couple of significantly different causes. Maybe it's not a Web site issue at all; maybe your users are just not interested in visiting the Great Barrier Reef. Or maybe it was a usability issue, and there was some flaw within the Web site that discouraged them from completing the form.

If you are able to narrow the problem down to the latter flaw (using some other source than the server data, which cannot collect that kind of information), you then need to analyze a whole other series of possible causes. These could range from the graphic image used on the home page—maybe it showed a bloody knee scraped up from banging into coral instead of an appealing snorkeling shot?—to a broken link, to unclear directions, to an improperly set up form that consistently returned error messages to the users. Only some of these causes can be traced through your Web server usage data. There will be no data, for example, on whether or not the users found the graphic appealing or repulsive. A pile of error messages, however, could give you big clues about possible broken links or malfunctioning forms.

Figures 3-16 and 3-17 show an example of an individual's click stream analysis from Funnel Web Analyzer. This particular user visited the site twice, and his or her pathway is documented in each of the two sessions. During the first session, the user stayed on the site for seven minutes and 25 seconds and made a total of 432 clicks. I have captured only the top section of the session here for Figure 3-16 to save space. See http://www.quest.com/funnel_web/analyzer/sample/ClientStream-0.html for the full session history.

In the second session, depicted in Figure 3-17, the user returned to the site later the same day (February 7). He or she stayed on for a much longer time (15 minutes and 43 seconds) but made many fewer clicks (a total of 13). You can see from the times and URLs listed that the user went straight to the chat room and stayed there for about seven minutes. He or she then conducted a search and then signed on to the support mailing list. Finally, the user spent a couple of minutes reading through pages in what looks like a report on the client's history.

This kind of information has been gathered for each user visiting this site, so you can imagine how much data there is to sort through. Analyzing Web usage data is a bit like archaeology—with the benefit (or curse?) of being able to employ computers and programmers to help you process the data.

3

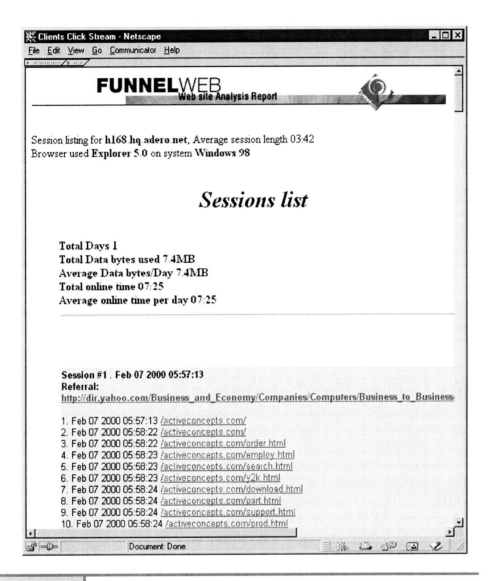

Figure 3-16   This report shows the beginning of a user's first visit to a Web site in a click stream analysis from Funnel Web Analyzer

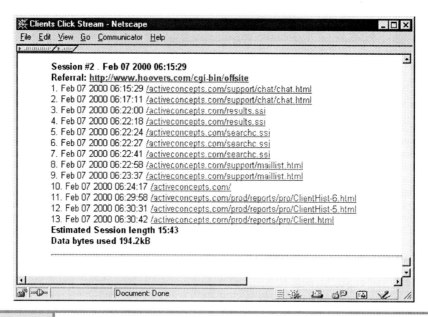

Figure 3-17 The same user's second visit to the site resulted in many fewer clicks but much more time being spent on the site

Back to Plain Old Observation

Have I mentioned to you that plain old observation can be a great way to gain insight into how effective your Web site is? Yeah, yeah, yeah, this is starting to become old hat to you, isn't it?

I don't believe I've mentioned field studies, though, have I? Visiting users in their natural environments ("in the field," so to speak, and thus the name "field studies") is probably the most effective way to observe users. They tend to be more relaxed in familiar environments, and their behavior, and more importantly their Web site usage, is more natural.

Just imagine if, two weeks into the Great Barrier Reef promotion, someone alerted you to the fact that nobody seemed to be participating in it. What would you rather do:

1. Dig out the logs and usage data and start to work analyzing them?

2. Go pick a user, point them to the home page, and observe them as they try to enter in the sweepstakes?

I know what I'd rather do.

Project 3-1: Develop a User Questionnaire

I'd really like to have you practice observing and interacting with potential users of a Web site, but I realize that can be a little logistically difficult for a self-study book. Instead, let's do the next best thing. Let's develop a set of questions as if you were going to distribute a questionnaire or conduct an interview with a group of users.

Step-by-Step

1. It can be helpful to have a specific Web site and its broad array of users in mind. Feel free to concentrate on the community art center Web site we discussed in Module 2 or another Web site scenario of your choice.

2. Write as many questions for the users as you can that would help you get to know a Web site's user base and be able to develop a set of user profiles. Aim for composing at least 15 distinct questions to get a good feel for the process, although I think you'll find that there's really no limit to the number of useful questions you could ask.

3. Feel free to start with the questions we developed in the "Level of Familiarity and Comfort with the Web" section earlier in this module if you like.

4. Just when you think you've exhausted the number of questions you could ask, give it one more try and jot down a few other categories of questions that would be pertinent for assessing usability issues.

Project Summary

If you have a friend or fellow student of the Web who is studying this book at the same time, compare and contrast the lists of questions you came up with. Or better yet, complete each other's questionnaire and give each other feedback on it from a usability perspective. I think you'll discover that there's plenty of room for variety in these questionnaires.

Module Conclusion

All these questions and techniques will help you get to know your users, and that's only half of it. In the next module, we will look more closely at what tools the users rely on, such as browsers, operating systems, computers, and just how those tools impact the usability of your Web sites.

☑ Mastery Check

1. Which of the following format(s) can a Web user profile take? (You may select more than one.)

A) Photographs

B) Text

C) Tables

D) Diagrams

E) Videos

2. List at least six prelaunch user analysis methods that are available to you.

_____

_____

_____

_____

_____

_____

3. Which of the following user analysis methods are available to you only after you launch a Web site? (You may select more than one.)

A) Observation

B) Web usage analyses

C) Web forms

D) Interviews

E) Questionnaires

☑ *Mastery Check*

4. What are two reasons why you can't always rely on what users tell you, instead of what they show you?

   _____

   _____

5. What is one of the most inexpensive, powerful tools available to you in assessing a Web site's usability?

   _____

6. Why is it a good idea to mentally separate the process of getting to know your users from that of getting to know their hardware and software constraints?

   _____

   _____

7. Which of the following are likely to suffer if you make assumptions without asking questions and find out months into a project that you were wrong? (You may select more than one.)

   A) Schedule

   B) Budget

   C) Morale

   D) Planning documents

   E) All of the above

8. Which of the following statements are true in regards to conducting field studies for usability purposes?

   A) You visit users in their natural environments.

   B) You should draw illustrations of the users and their behaviors in a notebook.

   C) They are one of the most effective ways to observe users.

☑ Mastery Check

9. What is a "click stream analysis"?

A) An analysis of what users clicked while visiting a site.

B) An analysis of how many clicks users can make within a given time period.

C) An analysis of whether a single-click or a double-click is more effective.

D) An analysis of the number of clicks it takes to get carpal-tunnel syndrome.

Module 4

Get to Know Your Users' Computer Constraints

The Goals of This Module

- Identify the primary hardware and software constraints affecting Web usability
- Understand the typical limits of our human attention spans
- Assess how user bandwidth affects Web page design
- Identify the key issues involved in cross-browser compatibility
- Identify the key issues involved in cross-platform compatibility
- Understand how best to work around differences in users' screen resolutions
- Consider the implications of designing Web sites for alternative devices

Now that you've gotten to know your users a bit better, it's time to get to know what tools they are using to access the Web. The Web-related hardware and software affect the user's experience with the Web immensely. In this module, we'll take a close look at a number of variations among the products that cause Web sites to be displayed and to behave differently for different users.

The four primary areas to investigate are

● Bandwidth

● Browsers

● Operating systems

● Monitor screen resolution

It's also important to keep an eye on all the developments going on right now with other, special devices that take the form of anything other than desktop computers. WebTV, cell phones, and PDAs (personal digital assistants like the Palm Pilot) are some of the most publicized nondesktop tools being used to access the Web. We will discuss those briefly as well at the end of the module.

Bandwidth

The terms *bandwidth* and *broadband* are misnomers, for they have nothing to do with the width or breadth of the cables or wires connecting users to the Internet and everything to do with the speed of connection. For example, in the case of digital subscriber lines (DSL), one of the more common residential "broadband" services, technologists found a way to add extra, speedier data streams to the existing copper telephone lines. In the case of satellite Internet services, there are no cables or wires required for receiving data; a satellite dish is used instead. Uploads, on the other hand, often need to be transmitted over the ground, but again that usually requires plain old telephone lines.

Bandwidth has everything to do with the speed of Web sites loading into a browser, or more typically, the lack thereof. Just how long do your users have to wait for a Web page to load? And how long are they willing to wait before clicking away to some other site? What is the quality of their experience in regard to download speed?

Human factors research gives us some insight into typical human attention spans. Back in 1968, Robert B. Miller delivered a paper at the Fall Joint Computer Conference that still has profound implications for Web design. In it, he gave three specifications for the amount of time people are able and willing to maintain a stream of thought.

- A response time of one-tenth of a second gives the user a feeling of instantaneous response. (This is a good rate of return. MTV and most television shows easily meet this criterion.)

4

- A one-second response time is about the maximum for the user's stream of thought to remain uninterrupted— although the user will probably notice the lag. (Wouldn't it be great if most Web sites could meet this criterion?)

- A ten-second response time is about the maximum tolerance level for staying focused. The user's stream of thought will almost certainly have been interrupted, and if one more fraction of a second elapses, that user is likely to start doing other tasks while waiting. Have you ever experienced the feeling, after a slow Web page loads, of wondering "Now what was it I was looking for?" This is why.

Tip

The goal for designing (minimally) usable Web pages for a broad audience is to keep each one's loading time under ten seconds. That's a tall order, and not easy to accomplish with typical modem connections. Did I ever say designing usable Web sites was easy? To achieve *ideally* usable Web sites, each page would have to load within one-tenth of a second.

Let's take a closer look at three key components regarding bandwidth and what impact they have on designing usable Web sites:

- What are the current bandwidth limitations?

- What about all the projections for increased bandwidth? When will we actually see it on a widespread basis?

- How do we design Web sites that will work well given the users' bandwidth capabilities?

Bandwidth Limitations

Many users make the assumption that the speed at which pages load onto their computers is entirely driven by what kind of modem or other connecting device they have. This is not the case. There are two limiting factors when it comes to bandwidth:

- The limitations of the modem or other connecting device on the user's computer

- The limitations of every other link along the network chain

Connection Device Limitations

In the early 1990s, as the Internet became accessible to the public, it was not uncommon to use a 2400 baud modem. That soon leapt up to 9600 baud, and then a 14.4 K (kilobit) modem hit the market, about the time the Web with its graphical user interface became available in the mid-1990s. Soon after, 28.8 K modems were all the rage, and 56 K modems are now the most typical setup for home users—which is not to say that all users with 56 K modems actually get 56 K per second transmission rates. These are all considered *low-bandwidth* connections.

?≥Ask the Expert

Question: What's the difference between all the size measurements such as kilobits, megabits, etc.?

Answer: Each increase in measurement reflects a 1000-fold magnification, as in the following:

> 1000 bits (b) = 1 kilobit (Kb or K)*
> 1000 kilobits (Kb or K) = 1 megabit (Mb)
> 1000 megabits (Mb) = 1 gigabit (Gb)
> 1000 gigabits (Gb) = 1 terabit (Tb)

And:

> 1000 bytes (B) = 1 kilobyte (KB)
> 1000 kilobytes (KB) = 1 megabyte (MB)
> 1000 megabytes (MB) = 1 gigabyte (GB)
> 1000 gigabytes (GB) = 1 terabyte (TB)

4

Question: What's the difference between bits and bytes?

Answer: Bits and bytes are much trickier to compute; they are related by a factor of 8, not 10, so there are eight bits to one byte. Also note, bits are designated by a lowercase *b*, while bytes get the upper case *B*. So, the relationships are as follows:

8 bits (b) = 1 byte (B)
8 kilobits (Kb or K)* = 1 kilobyte (KB)
8 megabits (Mb) = 1 megabyte (MB)
8 gigabits (Gb) = 1 gigabyte (GB)
8 terabits (Tb) = 1 terabyte (TB)

For some unknown reason, bandwidth connection speeds are usually given in kilobits per second, yet media files and Web page sizes are typically measured in kilobytes, so be prepared to do a lot of multiplication and division by a factor of 8.
*Note also that the abbreviation "K" by itself is often used to designate kilobit, as is the practice throughout this book.

Note

For comparison's sake, a 2400 baud modem transmits at a rate of 2400 bits per second, or 2.4 kilobits per second—*not* very fast!

Today there are a number of options for so-called *high-bandwidth* connections. Table 4-1 lists a few of them and some of their characteristics. The advertised

Kind of Connection	Source of Connection	Typical Maximum Connection Speeds (per second)	Notes
DSL	Through existing copper phone lines.	Actual performance varies considerably. Some vendors give a range of 144 K to 1.5 Mb. Others only up to 640 K.	Generally for residential and small business use. Costs run around $50/month, comparable to cable-modem and fixed wireless services.

Table 4-1 Typical "High-Bandwidth" Connections to the Internet

Kind of Connection	Source of Connection	Typical Maximum Connection Speeds (per second)	Notes
Cable modem	Through existing cable lines for cable TV. These lines are shared within neighborhoods, causing some performance problems during high-usage periods.	Downloads up to 5 Mb; uploads up to around 220 K. The cable companies limit the upload speed to prevent users from hosting servers on them. Technically, they should be capable of equal upload and download speeds.	Generally for residential use only because of the available cable lines. Costs are comparable to DSL.
Fixed wireless	Transceiver from your roof pointed toward a radio transmission tower.	Download speeds up to 5 Mb, but more typically 512 K to 1.5 Mb, similar to DSL. Maximum upload is 256 K.	Need to be within line of sight of a local transmission tower. Costs are comparable to DSL. Offered under other names such as "Sprint Broadband" or "Ricochet."
Satellite	Satellite dish plus indoor receiver and transmitter. For one-way satellite service, downloads are via the dish and uploads are via regular phone lines.	Download speeds up to 400 K. Uploads up to 128 K. For one-way service, uploads rely on a dial-up connection and modem.	To pick up the satellite transmissions, you need to have a clear view of the southern skies (if within the U.S.). Costs are around $100 per month.
Standard ISDN lines	Digital telephone lines / fiber optic lines	Up to 128 K	One of the oldest kinds of connections. Very few new installations are taking place now in light of the other options. Can still be found in homes and businesses, though.
T1/DS1 lines	ISDN fiber optic lines	1.5 Mb	Generally found only in businesses because costs runs as high as $1100 per month.

Table 4-1 Typical "High-Bandwidth" Connections to the Internet (*continued*)

Kind of Connection	Source of Connection	Typical Maximum Connection Speeds (per second)	Notes
T3/DS3 lines	ISDN fiber optic lines	Up to 45 Mb	Generally found only in businesses. Very expensive. The lowest price I've seen is $13,000 per month.
OC-3 lines	Synchronous Optical Network (SONET)	Up to 155 Mb	High-end business use only. Generally, prices aren't even quoted on Web sites for OC lines. You can be sure they're pricey.
OC-12 lines	Synchronous Optical Network (SONET)	Up to 644 Mb	High-end business use only.

4

Table 4-1 Typical "High-Bandwidth" Connections to the Internet (*continued*)

transfer speeds for high-bandwidth options vary widely from, say, standard ISDNs with *up to* 128 K per second to OC-12s with *up to* 644 Mb per second. There are even lab tests proving that optical fibers have the potential of transferring a *terabit* per second, although there are not any such commercial products out there at the time of this writing.

Note

Next time you see an ad for broadband access, note how the speeds are always advertised as "up to" a certain amount. In reality, those speeds are almost never reached due to all sorts of weak links along the chain. Even 56 K modems *never* reach transfer rates beyond 53 K, due to FCC regulations. Why aren't they called 53 K modems? Beats me. Let's attribute it to the evils of advertising.

Table 4-2 shows the *optimal* download capacity for different Internet connections in bytes. (As is customary, connection speed is in bits, while download speed is in bytes.) To stay in line with Miller's human factors research on attention spans, the last column, "Optimal Download per 10 Seconds," would also be the absolute *maximum* page size that you should create for a user with this type of connection. For any of the standard modem users, these are not very large pages, are they?

Kind of Connection	Maximum Speed (in Kb)	Optimal Download per 1/10 Second	Optimal Download per Second	Optimal Download per 10 Seconds
28.8 K modem	28.8 Kb	< 1 KB	3.6 KB	36 KB
33.6 K modem	33.6 Kb	< 1 KB	4.2 KB	42 KB
56 K modem	53 Kb	< 1 KB	6.6 KB	66 KB
Cable modem / fixed wireless	5 Mb	62.5 KB	625 KB	6 MB
Satellite	400 Kb	5 KB	50 KB	500 KB
DSL or T1/DS1	1.5 Mb	19 KB	188 KB	1.9 MB
T3/DS3	45 Mb	6 MB	5.6 MB	56 MB
OC-3	155 Mb	2 MB	19 MB	190 MB
OC-12	644 Mb	8 MB	80 MB	800 MB

Table 4-2   Optimal Download Sizes per Connection Type

Tip

To put this in perspective, consider a typical page that is 50 KB in total size, including the text and graphics. On a 56 K modem operating at maximum speed, that would take between nine and ten seconds to load, putting us within the tolerable download speed zone. On a 28.8 K modem, however, it would take nearly 14 seconds to load, well beyond our usability criteria, and that's the best case scenario, which rarely occurs in real life.

Limitations in the Other Links of the Chain

Unfortunately, in addition to the limitations on whatever bandwidth access your users have from their computers, there are other limiting factors along every link of the Internet chain. Just think about how many points of failure (or weakness) there are between your computer and each point on the Internet that you wish to access during any given session on the Web. Each request that you make goes through a long chain of physical hardware, including phone lines, cables, routers, and servers, plus the corresponding software for many of them.

Internet service providers (ISPs) sometimes handle millions of requests per hour. *Server lag*, a delay in responding to Web user requests, results from too many requests being made of a server at one time. And, of course, equipment periodically needs to be taken offline for maintenance or repair, and sometimes it just plain gets old and dies—unfortunately at times while it's "on the job" trying to answer your request for a Web page. In the best of cases, there will be a line of backup servers ready to take over your request, but sometimes there's a domino effect, and a chain of servers can be overloaded and all go down.

Tip
You cannot receive data any faster than it is being sent, so your transfer rate will always be reduced to the weakest link in the chain.

Thus, the *typical* connection speeds for most connecting devices is substantially lower than the *optimal* figures used in the previous section. The normal connection speed for 56 K modem users, for example, is usually between 44 K and 48 K. And it is not altogether uncommon for users with 56 K modems to connect at rates lower than 28.8. I frequently experienced this from my home office when I lived in the San Francisco Bay Area, neatly tucked in between Silicon Valley and Multimedia Gulch. (Right there in the Bay Area, we couldn't get DSL, fixed wireless, satellite, or cable modem service. Go figure!) The good side to this (the *only* good side, I might add) is that I was constantly reminded of what the experience of typical home users was like.

The real-world speeds for the most common residential high-bandwidth services are also often significantly lower than the optimal advertised speeds. DSL speeds, for instance, are often as low as 144 K to 640 K. Of course, in the advertisements and sales pitches they are often promoted as having speeds "up to 1.5 MB." That kind of difference results in your maximum page size needing to be 180 KB instead of 1.9 MB if it is to load in less than ten seconds, or 18 KB instead of 188 KB if it is to load within one second. That effectively limits what multimedia elements you could use to deliver "broadband" content.

Note
See how these real-world connection rates are often a far cry from the optimal rates listed in Table 4-2?

Projections of Increasing Bandwidth
It's easy for Web developers working from corporate offices with state-of-the-art bandwidth connections to forget about all the users without high-bandwidth

connections. When the connection is fast, and all your Web pages load quickly with extra features like Flash animations and Java applets popping into place in the blink of an eye, that hassle of waiting—interminably—for each segment of a page to download just disappears from your consciousness. If it wouldn't slow down the rate of Web development across the nation and probably impact the economy, I'd recommend every Web designer and developer work from such a setup, just so they could better keep in touch with the user experience!

There's been a lot of talk about high-bandwidth access since the early days of the Web, but the current numbers for *home users* are very small. Exactly how many current users there are is somewhat debated. On the upper end, according to the Nielsen//NetRatings, in 2001 13 percent of home users, roughly 12 million homes within the U.S., had something above 56 K modem access, and they were primarily based around major urban and technological centers. A September 2001 *Consumer Reports* article, however, reported that only 9 million households had high-bandwidth access. In either case, for general-interest Web sites, the answer is: not many.

In the workplace, as you might expect, the numbers are quite a bit higher, but still not overwhelming. In the year 2000, there were an estimated 24 million workers with high-bandwidth access. These figures are likely increasing at a much higher rate than for home users, as we'll discuss in a minute.

Eventually, then, the majority of people will have broadband access. But what's the current state of affairs? The Neilsen/Net Ratings service reports a little less than 100 million Americans currently on the Web. If you subtract from that the figures for broadband usage, we can determine how many people are still using low-bandwidth connections. To take a conservative approach, let's subtract the highest figures for broadband home access (12 million) and the figures for broadband office access (24 million). That leaves at least *64 million people* who have access at less than 56 K—and that's only the current, American users, excluding any potential duplicates from the home and office broadband figures which would make this figure higher. The next time a client asks you to create a site that will work well only with high-bandwidth access, pause for a moment and think about the numbers of people who will not be able to effectively use the site.

These figures bear repeating:

> 100 million Americans using the Web
> – 12 million who are using residential broadband access
> – <u>24 million who are using broadband access from work</u>

Total: 64 million Americans who currently have low-bandwidth access

Since the very first days of the Web, there have been constant predictions for high-bandwidth access being "just around the corner," but it just hasn't happened—yet. Two seemingly contradictory things are going on at the same time.

- On the one hand, by all reports consumer demand is high. Loads of users today would be willing to pay to have higher-bandwidth access to the Internet—if the service were available in their neighborhood. In a study released in August 2001 by J.D. Power and Associates, 10 percent of current dial-up subscribers said they are "extremely" or "very likely" to switch to DSL and/or cable modem in the next six months. (See http://www.jdpa.com/studies/pressrelease.asp?StudyID=548 for the full report.) This demand is especially high for those who work in any field related to the Internet or who are interested in playing games over the Internet. The demand for high-bandwidth residential access is expected to reach 18.5 million within the U.S. by 2003.

- On the other hand, in those areas where high-bandwidth service is available, lots of consumers are slow to adopt it—other than the handfuls who have been clamoring for it. There's a great deal of speculation as to the cause of this latter trend.

The cost of high-bandwidth service has proved to be one inhibiting factor. Typical prices at the end of 2001 for DSL, cable-modem, and fixed wireless access were between $40 and $50 per month, and rising.

Those are hefty sums for casual users of the Internet to fork out every month. And, unlike upgrading hardware components, where you know exactly what processing speed you will get with that new chip or how much storage space with that new external drive, paying for high-bandwidth access gives no guarantee of how quickly each and every Web site will load.

Around 90 percent of current DSL connections throughout the U.S., for example, transmit at a rate of less than 1 Mb per second. Generally, the further you are from a transmitting station, the slower your rate of access. That rate will make text and graphics-only Web sites load very quickly; that's a fast enough connection to have that satisfying instant load of most static Web pages. High-quality Web video, however, which is considered the premier broadband commodity and has long been considered the benchmark, needs around three times that bandwidth, around 3 Mb per second. Where's the incentive, I ask, for consumers to pay the extra bucks for "broadband" access if they can't really get "broadband" content such as video?

Ironically, cable modem users find themselves competing with each other for bandwidth because they share the television cable lines. Already, there are many complaints and jokes from cable modem users about getting bogged down during peak time periods. By mid-2001, cable modem services accounted for three-quarters of consumer broadband connections. Granted, this data was collected after a number of DSL providers went out of business in 2000 and early 2001. I think it would be safe to say that in the near future it is likely that DSL will gain ground on cable modems for two reasons:

- The telephone companies will get a handle on this new business opportunity and learn how to better market and manage it.

- As cable modem users get increasingly frustrated with the poor performance during peak periods, they will consider changing to DSL, which offers dedicated lines instead of shared ones.

In the workplace, users are gaining access to high bandwidth at a much greater rate. A report issued by Jupiter Research, a New York City firm that studies Internet commerce, indicated that users with on-the-job broadband access will double from 24 million in 2000 to 55 million by 2005. They also foresee difficulties, however, with peak demand periods in which users will be competing with their colleagues for bandwidth across shared networks. Thus, Web sites with high-bandwidth content may need to take into account the time of day and day of the week users will be accessing their site.

Add to these discouraging realizations the fact that broadband users are part of the same interlinked chain of access as everybody else. The access capability of any given user's computer is only one link along a long chain. The same external things that slow down Web sites for regular modem users are at play with high-bandwidth users: server lag, sites being down, overloaded servers, poorly designed and executed Web sites, etc.

How to Design Usable Web Sites Taking Bandwidth into Account

It seems we have two driving tenets regarding bandwidth in designing usable Web sites:

- Access speeds for desktop computer users will continue to increase, albeit more slowly than we might like.

- In the meantime, we still need to develop sites with our predominant user group in mind, which in most cases has less than 56 K per second access.

As with all Web site design, it is necessary to examine your user base for each and every site that you develop and to determine exactly what each user group's bandwidth needs are. Although most general-interest sites will need to cater to the less-than-56 K user crowd, that may not always be the case. A couple of exceptions might be:

4

- A business-to-business technology site aimed at Fortune 500 companies, where surveys have indicated 98 percent of the users have high-bandwidth access from work. The caveat here might be the growing trend of employees wanting to work from home, which unfortunately results in much lower access speeds.

- A broadband site that has partnered with a broadband delivery service. In this case, the target audience is going to be exclusively high-bandwidth users. The only danger here is that the numbers are small, so it may be hard to earn enough income to keep the business afloat.

- A site with distinct user groups and user needs that diverge directly along the lines of both access and content. In such cases, it may be necessary to develop different sections of the site for different user groups. Alternatively, it may be necessary to provide high-bandwidth and low-bandwidth versions of the site.

Good examples of this last scenario are sites that show movie trailers. It has become customary, for example, to give the user a choice between sizes of videos, so that they can weigh the pros and cons of download time versus quality and make their own decision. Providing such choice is almost always a good option.

A classic example is when the Apple site offered three versions of the trailer for the movie *Star Wars*. In line with typical usage scenarios, they predicted the low-bandwidth users would choose the smallest, postage stamp–sized version, the midbandwidth users, the midsized one, and only truly high-bandwidth users, the largest version, as users had done in the past. They were amazed to discover that by far the majority of the users chose the largest version. There must have been thousands of people who set up their computers to download the file and then walked to Australia and back while they were waiting. They each decided, however, that the content was worth the wait, and that's what is important. The choice was theirs.

Tip

Don't make assumptions based only on usage statistics. Put on those usability spectacles instead, and think from the user's perspective.

Ask the Expert

Question: So how do you find out what bandwidth your site's users have?

Answer: I'd recommend two methods:

● Study the current usage statistics for each user population demographic, if available. Sometimes the client sponsoring the site has this information. Other times, broad-scale studies can produce a lot of valuable information. Just knowing, for instance, that at least 64 million Americans have low-bandwidth access can help you make a lot of decisions. There are frequent articles on this topic in most of the Web-related publications, but to go straight to the source, here are a couple of good starting points:

   ● Nielsen//NetRatings, http://www.nielsen-netratings.com/

   ● StatMarket, http://statmarket.com

● Ask the users. If you're conducting interviews or surveys, it's very easy to include questions like: "How fast is your connection to the Internet?" or "What kind of Internet access do you have?" and give them a list of choices with various modems and high-bandwidth options. If they don't know, direct them to one of a number of bandwidth speed test sites on the Web. One good one is at the Bandwidth Place at http://bandwidthplace.com/speedtest. You might even ask users more qualitative questions about how

4

satisfied they are with their access speeds. If they are already generally frustrated with their Web experiences, for instance, that's a big clue to you that you'd better make your site simple and fast-loading.

Question: And once you have collected that data, what do you do with it?

Answer: The first thing is to sort it by user groups so that the distinction between each target audience remains clear. If you start averaging the data among all your users, you're likely to get a rather muddy picture.

And the second thing is to interpret it. Keep in mind that many users do not know what speed they are actually able to connect to the Internet. They tend to assume that they connect at whatever maximum speed their hardware is capable of. Users with 56 K modems, for example, will assume that they connect at 56 K, which is, unfortunately, never the case.

In this case, it can be helpful to use average statistics on connection speeds. If one of your target groups uses predominantly 56 K modems, it's a good idea to design the site as though it were being delivered at 44–48 kilobits per second.

Here are some tips on designing for low-bandwidth users. We will get into more specifics in Part II "Designing Web Sites for Their Users." Some of these tips get into specialized programming areas; see the suggested books on each topic to learn how to implement them.

- Make every page as small as you can, even if you've determined that pages *can* be larger to load within our ten-second limit.

- Use text generated by code such as HTML or Cascading Style Sheets (CSS) whenever possible instead of graphics. (See McGraw-Hill/Osborne's *HTML: A Beginner's Guide* and *CSS: A Beginner's Guide*.)

- Employ preloading scripts to load elements into the browser when you can anticipate the user will want them. (See *JavaScript: A Beginner's Guide* or other books specific to the program or application you are using. For example, to preload Flash animations, see the manual that ships with the product or *How to Do Everything with Flash 5*, published by McGraw-Hill/Osborne, 2001.)

● Make each graphic or other media element on a page as small as possible. To do this, you may need to:

   ● Choose the most efficient file format for each graphic or other media element.

   ● Use as few colors as possible in your graphics and other media.

   ● Use as narrow a tonal range as possible with your audio elements. In other words, avoid selecting clips that have lots of high as well as low notes.

   ● Reduce the actual size (height and width) of the graphics and other media.

● Slice illustrations or use progressive JPEGs for photographs for more active loading. (Slicing is a common method of cutting a graphic into smaller pieces.) The whole graphic may not load any faster, but the user will see part of it earlier, which is much more engaging than staring at a blank screen.

Note

See how a lot of these tips have to do with reducing the size of graphics? That's a big challenge in Web development. It is currently such a heavily visual medium, but graphics can really slow down the loading of a Web page.

1-Minute Drill

● How many Americans currently have low-bandwidth Web access?

● What rate of throughput does high-quality video require on the Web?

● 64 million
● 3 Mb per second

Browsers

Have you ever heard of the "browser wars"? That was an apt description of the intense competition between the early Web browsers in the mid-to-late 1990s. Netscape Navigator and Microsoft Internet Explorer were the key contenders, with the W3C (World Wide Web Consortium) playing the role of a rather buffeted and sometimes angry referee.

Note

The W3C is composed of key industry leaders and innovators. Tim Berners-Lee, the founder of the Web is a driving force within it. If you haven't already, take a look at its Web site at http://w3.org and bookmark it for future reference. It's an invaluable resource.

Looking back, the browser wars had some rather humorous aspects. Essentially, the players were desperately trying to win a game that did not have any fixed rules. (Picture a game of mud football, for instance.) It was a time of great invention and entrepreneurial spirit and incredible energy. Every few months somebody released a new version of a browser, touting the greatest and latest features, durability, and ease of use.

And, every few months, Web designers and developers had to reassess their options, retool, and refocus in developing Web sites that could work on the new browsers, as well as the old browsers.

The "wars" have settled down quite a bit with the new century. The W3C has gained the upper hand on setting a body of standards that most people like and think they can live with (and better yet, design and develop Web sites with). For better or worse, Microsoft gained the upper hand on the commercial side with close to 75 percent market adoption by Web users of its Internet Explorer browser. This is not to say, however, that they have declared an outright victory. Netscape has been hanging in there with a grip on its dedicated user base, and there have been a number of new "rogue" browsers introduced lately from all corners of the world that will help keep the dominant browsers from becoming too sedate.

Although we designers and developers may not be in a state of "war" today, we are, however, still dealing with the fallout. Many of those old browsers with their quirky and inconsistent feature support are still out there. If we count their users as potential users of our Web sites, then we have quite a challenge in creating sites that work on the old and new browsers.

The data on browser usage changes every month, with wide swings whenever a new version is released, so I highly recommend looking up the latest figures before beginning any new Web site project. The year 2001 saw the release of both Netscape 6.0 and Internet Explorer 6.0, spurring increases in user adoption of browers that more closely comply with the W3C standards. According to StatMarket.com, as of November 15, 2001, the use of Internet Explorer 6.0 had risen to 13.79 percent of the global population of Web users with expectation to continue rising. Data was not available specifically on Netscape 6.0, but as of October 15, 2001, 13.17 percent of overall Web users preferred some version of Netscape over the other browers. The share of Netscape users has been holding steady between 12 and 14 percent since a fairly precipitous drop from 33 percent in 1999.

The good news is that by the time this book is published and gets into your hands, the adoption rate of the newer, more standards-conforming browsers will have likely increased even more. Today, on the other hand, around ten percent of Web users are using some browser other than versions 4.0 and above of Netscape Navigator and Internet Explorer; by the time you read this, that figure may be closer to nine percent. Better yet, the next time you refer back to this book, that figure may be eight percent, and at the same time, the number of users moving up from the 4.x versions to the 5.x versions and the 6.x versions will be increasing. So although the use of the antique browsers will eventually drop off, there will probably always be a range of more sophisticated browsers.

Tip

StatMarket.com is an excellent source of usage data for the Web, including browser stats. They make some of the data available for free on their Web site, but they do charge a hefty subscription fee upward of $600 for full access to their reports and archives. News services like WebReview.com, though, often quote StatMarket data in their news reports, so with a little more effort, it is still possible to unearth the data that you need.

4

So how do you design usable Web sites taking into account the various browsers in use? Essentially, you need to do three things:

1. Determine what browsers your users have so that you can design your Web site accordingly. Conduct surveys or interviews, observe your users at their computers, and/or review current usage statistics for your specific user base, if available. If you have an existing site, check the data collected in the server logs. That will give you hard and fast information about the current users' browsers. Don't necessarily limit your user base to that in the future, though. It may be that the original site didn't work properly on other browsers and, thus, drove those users away.

2. Become intimately familiar with the browsers your users have. It's not necessary to memorize every single feature and tag that they support, but it sure is a good idea to review their support data—before you start designing or developing.

Tip
You may download the different versions of browsers at http://www.upsdell.com/ BrowserNews/find_old.htm.

3. Test, test, test—in every browser you think your users will possibly use. This includes testing in the prototype stage, during development, and before release. And, although development tools such as Macromedia Dreamweaver and Adobe GoLive can be helpful in identifying and resolving browser conflicts, they are no replacement for the real thing: load your site within the actual browsers for testing purposes.

You have a fourth thing to do, actually, but we'll get to that in a minute.

4. Write code that will work in future browsers.

Tip

It is easy to install multiple versions of both Explorer and Netscape on a Mac, but on Windows PCs it's only easy to have multiple versions of Netscape—unless you perform some sophisticated computer wizardry or have split partitions for your Windows PC hard drive. The Microsoft Explorer installer is set to remove prior versions of the browser. This makes it necessary to have multiple PCs in order to test multiple versions of the browser.

Ask the Expert

Question: How can I become familiar with what each browser supports and doesn't support?

Answer: Sometimes this requires quite a bit of digging. The product specifications include some of this information, but the browser companies tend to be rather too discrete about mentioning what their browsers don't support, or what their bugs are. Newsgroups, however, can be invaluable for straight-up answers from developers' own experiences and research. The other good place to look is objective publications and Web sites.

HitBox and WebReview, for example, have good "Browser Compatibility Charts" (see Figure 4-1 for an example). These charts indicate support for Java, frames, tables, plug-ins, JavaScript, CSS, GIF89a, DHTML, I-frames, and XML, which they periodically update.

- For HitBox's version, see http://www.hitbox.com/ cgi-bin/page.cgi?reference/browser.

- For WebReview's, see http://www.webreview.com/ browsers/browsers.shtml.

Be sure to read all the footnotes, too; these kinds of charts, by necessity, have to be riddled with exceptions and further explanations. Even then, they're usually not complete. Even if they say a particular browser supports a feature such as CSS1, most browsers typically have not supported every one of the specification's features. There's no way to get around testing.

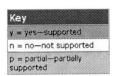

Key
y = yes—supported
n = no—not supported
p = partial—partially supported

Platform	Browser	java	frames	tables	plug-ins	jscript	CSS	gif89	dhtml	I-frames	XML
Win	MS IE 5.5	JDK 1.1[1]	y	y[2]	y	1.5 ECMA[3]	CSS2[4]	y	y[5]	y	p[6]
Win	MS IE 5.0	y	y	y	y	1.3 ECMA	CSS2	y	y	y	p
Win	MS IE 4.0	y	y	y	y	1.2 ECMA	CSS1	y	y	y	n
Win	MS IE 3.0	y	y	y	y	1.0 (k)	p	y	n	y	n
Win	MS IE 2.0	n	n	y	n	n	n	n	n	n	n
Mac	MS IE 5.0	JDK 1.1[21]	y	y	y	1.3 ECMA	CSS2[20]	y	y,18	y	p[19]
Mac	MS IE 4.0	y	y	y	y	1.2 ECMA	CSS1	y	y	y	n
Mac	MS IE 3.0	y	y	y	y	1.0 (k)	p	y	n	y	n
Mac	MS IE 2.0	n	y	y	y	n	n	n	n	n	n
UNIX	MS IE 4.01		y	y	y	1.2 ECMA	CSS1	y	y	y	n
Platform	Browser	java	frames	tables	plug-ins	jscript	CSS	gif89	dhtml	I-frames	XML
Win	NN 6	JDK 1.3[7]	y	y[2]	y	1.5 ECMA[8]	CSS2[9]	y	y[10]	y[11]	p[12]
Win	NN 4.7/4.5	JDK 1.1	y	y	y	1.3 ECMA	CSS1	y	y	n	n
Win	NN 4	y	y	y	y	1.2	CSS1	y	y	n	n
Win	NN 3.0	y	y	y	y	1.1	n	y	n	n	n
Win	NN 2.0	y	y	y	y	1.0	n	y	n	n	n
Mac	NN 4.7/4.5	JDK 1.1	y	y	y	1.3 ECMA	CSS1	y	y	n	n
Mac	NN 4.06	y	y	y	y	1.2	CSS1	y	y	n	n
Mac	NN 3.0	y	y	y	y	1.1	p	y	n	n	n
Mac	NN 2.0	n	y	y	y	1.0 (k)	n	y	n	n	n
Mac	NN 3.0	y	y	y	y	1.1	p	y	n	n	n
Mac	NN 2.0	n	y	y	y	1.0 (k)	n	y	n	n	n
UNIX	NN 4.06	y	y	y	y	1.1?	n	y	y	n	n
UNIX	NN 3.0	y	y	y	y	1.1	n	y	n	n	n
UNIX	NN 2.0	y	y	y	y	1.0	n	y	n	n	n
OS/2	NN 2.02	n	n	y	n	n	n	n	n	n	n
Platform	Browser	java	frames	tables	plug-ins	jscript	CSS	gif89	dhtml	I-frames	XML
Win	Opera 4.02	JDK 1.3[13]	y[14]	y[2]	y	1.3 ECMA	CSS2	y	p[15]	y[16]	p[17]
Platform	Browser	java	frames	tables	plug-ins	jscript	CSS	gif89	dhtml	I-frames	XML
Mac	Mosaic 3.07	n	y	y	n	n	n	n	n	n	n
Win	Mosaic 3.0	n	y	y	n	n	n	n	n	n	n
Platform	Browser	java	frames	tables	plug-ins	jscript	CSS	gif89	dhtml	I-frames	XML
Win	AOL 3.0	n	y	y	n	n	n	n	n	n	n
Mac	AOL 2.7	n	n	n	n	n	n	n	n	n	n
Win	AOL 1.0	n	n	n	n	n	n	n	n	n	n
Mac	AOL 1.0	n	n	n	n	n	n	n	n	n	n
Platform	Browser	java	frames	tables	plug-ins	jscript	CSS	gif89	dhtml	I-frames	XML
Win	Lynx	n	y	y	n	n	n	n	n	n	n
UNIX	Lynx	n	y	y	n	n	n	n	n	n	n
OS/2	Lynx	n	y	y	n	n	n	n	n	n	n
Platform	Browser	java	frames	tables	plug-ins	jscript	CSS	gif89	dhtml	I-frames	XML
NextStep	OmniWeb 2.1	n	y	y	n	y	n	n	y	n	n
NextStep	OmniWeb 1.0	n	n	n	n	n	n	n	n	n	n
Platform	Browser	java	frames	tables	plug-ins	jscript	CSS	gif89	dhtml	I-frames	XML
WebTV	MS WebTV	n	y	y	n	1.1	n	y	n	n	n

Figure 4-1   Browser Comparison Chart from WeReview.com and CMP Media LLC (Data compiled by Steve Franklin; http://www.webreview.com/browsers/browsers.shtml)

4

Notes on Figure 4-1:

1) Java & IE 5.5: By default, Java Runtime Environment 1.1.4 (JRE 1.1.4) is installed with IE 5.5. You can quickly upgrade to Java Development Kit 1.3 (JDK 1.3) with Sun's plug-in.

2) Table support for header and footer: Most browsers do not understand THEAD, TBODY, and TFOOT, which is unfortunate given the power these tags can have for printing and viewing long tables.

3) JavaScript in IE 5.5: IE 5.5 uses JScript, which is basically ECMA-compliant in recent versions. JScript maps relatively cleanly to the JavaScript versions used by Netscape and Opera. IE 5.5 uses JScript 5.5, which is compatible with ECMA-262 and (for the most part) supports JavaScript 1.5 features.

4) CSS and IE 5.5: There are a few problems with CSS1, although CSS1 is pretty well supported. CSS2 is weak, even for XML support and positioning. Watch for IE 6.0 to fix up much of the CSS2 and CSS Positioning (CSS-P) support.

5) DHTML in IE 5.5: DOM2 is not well supported in IE 5.5, and proprietary extensions are still frequently used when manipulating the IE document (e.g., innerHTML) even though these features are not yet approved by W3C.

6) XML in IE 5.5: XML 1.0 is partly supported, and XHTML 1.0 is pretty well supported. IE 5.5 has included an XSLT engine via MSXML (unlike Netscape's CSS/XML solution). A new MSXML release (3.0) includes an upgraded XSL engine that is much improved—look for it in IE 6.0. CSS/XML integration in IE 5.5 is minimal.

7) JDK & NN 6: Netscape 6 comes with JRE 1.3, but only a specific Sun version of the JRE (J2SE 1.30_01) is supported at present.

8) JavaScript in NN 6: Netscape has provided good JavaScript 1.5/ECMA-262 support in their new browser. However, they have made a very significant (and unfortunate) decision to rule out some of their noncompliant JavaScript additions that were introduced with NN 4.x contrary to specifications. Consequently, some of your JavaScript may have to test for NN 4.x, IE 4/5 and NN 6.x now, as document.layers, document embeds, and so on are now missing. Even more surprising, Netscape now supports some of IE 5.x's proprietary features, like innerHTML.

9) CSS2 in NN 6: CSS1 is well supported in NN 6, thanks to the new Gecko rendering engine. CSS2 is partially implemented, and excellent integration for XML/DOM support is provided.

10) DHTML in NN 6: DOM1 is well supported, and DOM2 partial support (e.g., events) are also integrated into the browser. The DOM Model now complies with the W3C standard, but as mentioned in note 9, Netscape has chosen to forego its noncompliant additions introduced in NN 4.x, meaning that some of your code may still detect NN 6 as non-IE, yet break due to the lack of support for legacy DOM interface elements.

11) I-Frames in NN 6: I-Frames are now supported in NN 6, but don't look for layers anymore! As already discussed above (note 9), Netscape has tossed many of its noncompliant features.

12) XML in NN 6: XML is well supported, as is XHTML 1.0. Netscape has also provided support for RDF metadata definition. Unlike IE 5.x, Netscape has not integrated XSLT capability into the rendering engine, forcing you to rely on simpler CSS/XML capabilities instead.

13) Java & Opera 4.02: JRE 1.3 is provided, but as an optional download configuration and installation option.

14) Frames in Opera 4.02: Realize that frames can be turned off, so frames behavior is not guaranteed.

15) JavaScript & Opera 4.02: JavaScript 1.3/ECMA are partially supported in Opera. Not only are some features missing, but many have been broken since the latest 3.x release. They are working hard to fix this up. Also, realize that Opera can spoof NN or IE, meaning that your browser detection script may not detect Opera properly. Check out Netscape's "Ultimate Sniffer Script" for pretty reliable detection.

16) CSS & Opera 4.02: CSS1 and CSS2 are both partially supported in Opera. Unfortunately, there are bugs and missing features that make CSS rendering in Opera a bit uncertain for some code that validates and displays properly in IE 5.x and NN 6.

17) I-Frames in Opera 4.02: By default, these were disabled in my installation. You can turn this feature on from the preferences.

4

18) DOM 1 in Mac IE 5: A good portion of DOM1 is supported in IE 5 for the Mac (chunks of DOM1 core are missing). However, the DOM support in Mac and Windows IE 5 is not consistent. This code is not cross-platform, and the Macintosh engine, while perhaps better at implementing DOM 1.0, is not consistent with IE 5 for Windows in all areas.

19) XML in Mac IE 5: Mac IE 5 has partial XML 1.0 support.

20) CSS and Mac IE 5: Our tests indicate that CSS1 is exceptionally well supported in Macintosh IE 5, but that CSS2 is quite partial.

21) Java and Mac IE 5: IE 5 lets you upgrade your JRE independent of your browser, as it leverages the MRJ provided from Apple. Tests and reports indicate that MRJ 2.2.3 (compatible with JDK 1.1.8) is relatively stable with IE 5 on the Mac, but earlier versions of MRJ may not be nearly as stable or predictable.

Project 4-1: Determining Appropriate Browser-Related Questions for Your User

With this new information about browsers and all their variability, you may be able to imagine how difficult it can be to ascertain from general users exactly what kinds of systems they are using. They often don't know themselves! Use this project to identify pertinent questions you can ask them to help pull this information or clues about it from them.

Step-by-Step

Write a list of questions for general user surveys or interviews that can help you identify exactly what browsers they are using and what they are set up to support. (See the Project Summary if you need some sample questions to get you started.)

_____

_____

_____

_____

_____

_____

Project Summary

Some questions might include the following:

- What browser or browsers do you use?

- What version of the browser do you use?

- Have you changed default browser settings such as making the text size larger or changing the appearance of the toolbar?

- How long have you been using this (these) browser(s)?

- Have you downloaded and installed any plug-ins or add-ons to your browser?

- If you use multiple browsers, which one do you prefer for visiting Web sites?

- Does your browser support the following plug-ins? (List the ones you are particularly interested in using on the site, such as QuickTime or Flash.)

- Does your browser support Java?

- Does your browser support JavaScript?

It's also helpful to include instructions on how to check to see what plug-ins or programming languages their browser supports.

Chances are many users will not know all the answers to the above questions. That's okay. There are certain assumptions you can make if you know only which browser and which version (or, by extrapolation, how long they have been using it). For example, if they don't know the answer to "What version of browser do you use?" but they do know they've been using it since 1999, then there's a good chance that it's still a 3.x version.

Note that many companies intentionally keep older versions of a browser installed on all their employees' computers for the following reasons:

- **Bugs**   They like to wait until all the bugs have been fixed before upgrading.

- **Hassle**   The more employees they have, the more time and resources it will take to upgrade everybody and answer everyone's questions.

- **Compatibility**   Companies often stay with the browser version that their intranet site was developed for, so they can be sure the site continues to work flawlessly.

With users who have not changed any of the preference settings or upgraded any components, there's also a good chance that the browser still has its default settings. In cases like these, browser compatibility charts can be immensely helpful and give you a fairly accurate representation of what their browser supports.

For example, if you are interested in determining whether you could use Java or JavaScript on a site, the 3.x and 4.x versions of Netscape and Explorer both included support for these in the default installation. It has typically only been for security reasons that users have disabled them. Many U.S. government employees, in particular, have been required to disable them, so you may be able to deduce that some users would not be able to see any sections of the site developed with Java or JavaScript from learning in an interview that they work for the government.

With some of the more recent versions of the browsers, however, such as Netscape 6.1, Java is not always included in the default installation. At the time of installation, users have to select the "Custom Install" and hand-pick that feature to install it. Automatically, this eliminates Java from the vast majority of Netscape 6.1 users.

There are also rumors at this time that Microsoft may be planning to discontinue support of Java as well as QuickTime and RealMedia in future versions of Internet Explorer. There are always rumors about what Microsoft is planning to do, aren't there? In any case, keep your ears tuned for any final decisions such as those that would have a marked influence on what you could or could not include.

Tip

The plug-ins for Macromedia's Flash and Apple's QuickTime started being included with the 4.0 browsers, so they have become *fairly* widespread. I emphasize "fairly" though, because Macromedia and Apple have continued to make improvements to the plug-ins, so full support can become a question of what version of plug-in the users have installed. Their functionality is not such a neat and tidy assumption as the vendors would have you believe. Also, plug-ins, or other browser features, sometimes get deleted or broken.

Prepare for Future Browers

My final recommendation for creating Web sites that will work on your users' browsers is to write HTML that will work in future browsers. That may sound like a bit of a stretch, but we can actually see a bit into the future in this regard. (Isn't that a nice change?!)

Extensible Markup Language (XML) is where HTML is headed. Because there is such a vast difference between HTML and XML in terms of how the page is coded, the W3C has developed an intermediate set of standards that one might consider a baby step between HTML and XML. That standard is called XHTML.

When the XHTML 1.0 standard was released by the W3C in January 2000, it cleared a pathway in the direction the Web is headed and established some very clear guidelines. Some of the major points are

4

- All code should be written in lowercase.

- All HTML tags must be closed. For example, the open paragraph tag <p> must now be concluded with a corresponding closing tag </p>.

- All HTML attribute values must be enclosed within quotation marks.

- All HTML tags must be properly nested; they can no longer overlap.

- The "id" attribute is to replace the "name" attribute.

- XHMTL has also *deprecated* (recommended the retirement of) a number of HTML tags such as the <font> tag in favor of the corresponding, and generally better, Cascading Style Sheets.

Tip

For a full discussion of how to properly implement these items and write HTML that will concur with the XHTML 1.0 standards see Wendy Willard's *HTML: A Beginners' Guide* (McGraw-Hill/Osborne, 2000).

Note

The World Wide Consortium is the organization responsible for setting standards for the Web. See their Web site at http://www.w3.org for more details on HTML, XHTML, and CSS standards and the Web Standards Project.

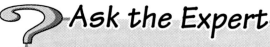

Ask the Expert

Question: What happens if my HTML code doesn't comply with the XHTML standard?

Answer: A variety of things can happen. At the moment, there will be no noticeable difference on a number of browsers. This is because many of the browsers being used today were developed prior to the release of the XHTML standard, so they still support the 4.0 version of HTML and in some cases even older versions of HTML.

Future versions of the browsers, however, are increasingly likely to conform with the XHTML standards and will start discarding support for old features. Netscape 6.0, for example, has thrown out support for a bunch of its own previous inventions because they had not been incorporated into the XHTML standards. This has particularly impacted its support of existing sites using JavaScript or Netscape layers. These sites now appear broken in the new browser because they do not fully comply with XHTML 1.0.

So to avoid your site's breaking in the future, it's best to write HTML that complies with the XHTML standard.

1-Minute Drill

● What three things do you need to do in order to effectively design Web sites for cross-browser use?

● Why should you write all your HTML code in lowercase?

Operating Systems

You may think that designing usable Web sites for a variety of computer operating systems is much simpler than designing for all the Web browsers, and for the most part it is. But that does not mean that it is a piece of cake either.

● Determine what browsers your users have; become intimately familiar with those browsers; and test your Web site on those browsers—thoroughly.
● To conform with the XHTML 1.0 standard and, thus, the likely development of future browsers

Note

The terms "operating system" and "platform" are often used interchangeably. Technically, the operating system is the software (such as Windows 98, Windows 2000, or Mac OS X) that runs a computer system, whereas the platform is the hardware, such as a Dell PC box or a Macintosh computer. It is possible to run multiple operating systems on different partitions of a computer, however, so I will use the term "operating systems" throughout this book to refer specifically to the software component.

4

Too many Web developers make the mistake of designing sites to work exclusively in the Windows environment since, by far and away, it is the dominant operating system among Web and other computer users across the world. There are, however, three other important operating systems to consider, and at least three good reasons why you might want to include each one's users in your user base:

● **Mac OS**   Apple's Macintosh computers are generally thought to have lost the "Operating System War" with Microsoft Windows, about the time Netscape lost its market advantage to Microsoft Internet Explorer. Like Netscape, Apple has maintained a devoted user base, but if anything it has shown better signs of regaining ground as it continues to improve its product line. When considering whether or not to go to the effort of making your Web site usable on a Mac, keep in mind the following market segments that hold it close to their hearts: schools, desktop publishers, graphics professionals, and many government organizations. Would you want any of them among your user base? Schools, in particular, have a disproportionately high number of Macintosh computers.

● **Unix**   Predating both the Windows PC and the Mac, Unix is still a mainstay operating system for many technical professions, including a high number of system administrators and Web developers. It's best not to overlook Unix users if you want to reach these audiences.

● **Linux**   A rogue operating system, Linux was created by Linus Torvalds, a student at the University of Helsinki in Finland, in the early 1990s. It is essentially a version of Unix, designed to run on most IBM-compatible PCs. Unlike Unix, however, it has an unbeatable price tag; it was designed from the beginning to be distributed free of charge or for nominal distribution fees. Linux has open source code, inviting anyone to review it and improve upon it. As such, Linux instantly became a popular operating system among programmers and technophiles, and it is slowly gaining acceptance worldwide. There are currently rumors, for example, that China is planning to adopt it as its formal operating system, no doubt causing Microsoft unending grief. Do you have any plans for sharing your Web sites with the millions of Chinese users coming online? If so, I'd recommend keeping a very close eye on Linux and making sure your Web sites work on that operating system.

The fat and sassy penguin in Figure 4-2 has become the visual symbol for the free-spirited Linux. In response to some criticism, Linus Torvalds defended it by saying, "Some people have told me they don't think a fat penguin really embodies the grace of Linux, which just tells me they have never seen an angry penguin charging at them in excess of 100 mph. They'd be a lot more careful about what they say if they had."

Tip

To stay up with new developments with Linux, see http://www.linux.org or http://www.linuxplanet.com.

Figure 4-2   The Linux penguin has been the cause of much brouhaha

When designing Web sites for cross-platform usability, you have six primary areas to consider:

- **Font availability**   Each operating system has a different set of fonts that ship with it, so if you want to specify certain font faces for your text, be sure to include fonts from each operating system that you intend it to be delivered across. It's also a good idea to test how your site also looks using the default font settings in each browser on each respective platform.

- **Font sizes**   In some cases, fonts will appear larger or smaller on different operating systems even when assigned an identical point size. Typically, letters in a Windows environment, for example, will appear about two points larger than the same letters on a Macintosh. This can be especially troublesome during the development stage when a graphic designer may be creating comprehensive designs or mock-ups on a Mac and then a client representative reviews them under Windows. Some of the more recent browsers have started automatically accommodating for these differences, but again it's best to test—especially if you are using a small type size that may become unreadable for your users if it loses another two points in size.

- **Filenames**   Each operating system has its own set of rules for naming files, including length of filenames and extensions, characters that are recognized within filenames, and case sensitivity. In general, you should:

  - Use filenames that are no longer than 31 characters long (shorter is okay).
  - Use no more than a three-letter extension (.jpg instead of .jpeg for example).
  - Use only lowercase letters. NO CAPITALS.
  - Only use the characters *a* through *z*, the numbers "1" through "9," plus the hyphen (-) and underscore (_). (Nothing fancier!)
  - Also avoid spaces; instead consider running words in together (page1.htm) or separating words by hyphens or underscores (page-1.htm or page_1.htm)

- **Color palettes**   Each operating system has its own system palette. What has commonly been referred to as the "Web-safe palette" consists of the 216 colors that overlapped between the Mac and the Windows operating

4

system palettes. This palette is not actually "Web-safe"; all but a handful of colors may display differently on different users' computers depending on the color resolution settings of their monitors. It is, however, a good starting point for finding *relatively* safe colors. Nonetheless, it is imperative to test for color changes across all platforms from which you intend users to view your Web site.

● **Gamma** The factory default settings for gamma, the color midtones, also vary from platform to platform. In general, images running under Windows, Unix, or Linux appear darker than under the Mac OS. Apple has long specified an exact setting of 1.8 for all of its monitors, but the generic PC world, which supplies monitors for most of the other operating systems, has been much looser. Its monitors can range anywhere from 2.2 to 2.5. And then, of course, the monitor's gamma and other color settings can deteriorate over time or be changed by the users. The important thing is to be aware of the possible differences, and to tightly control your development environment so that you can at least emulate the factory default settings to make sure that your site will work well on those monitors.

● **Feature support** Windows and Mac OS typically support the same Web file formats, programming languages, and other Web features. (Thank goodness for some compatibility!) Unix and Linux are a different matter, though, and may support some or none of the same features as the other two popular operating systems. If you want to do anything other than straight HTML, check very carefully to see what your target systems actually support.

Note

A few Unix users, and some Windows users, still employ the Lynx Web browser, which is essentially a text-only browser. It does not support the GIF89a file format, Java, JavaScript, CSS, DHTML, frames, or XML, among others.

The last word on designing for multiple operating systems is, of course, *testing*. After taking each of the preceding points into consideration, it's still imperative that you test your Web site on each of the intended delivery platforms. Some things just don't show up until you test.

1-Minute Drill

●   What are the four primary operating systems you may want to design
   Web sites for?

●   What are the six key, cross-platform Web design issues?

Monitor Screen Resolution

4

A sometimes hotly debated topic among Web developers is what *screen
resolution* to design their sites for. The screen resolution, also called the *screen
area* within the Windows Display Settings, is the viewable area on the monitor
measured in pixels. A common resolution for small monitors, for example, is
640×480, meaning 640 pixels wide by 480 pixels high. But knowing what size
monitors your users have does not necessarily indicate what resolution they
are set at. In most cases, users may change the resolutions on their monitors
through the operating system's preference settings.

Table 4-4 lists a number of common resolution options available to desktop
computer users.

Monitor Size	Typical Screen Resolutions Available
14–15"	640×480
	800×600
17"	640×480
	800×600
	1024×768
21"	800×600
	1024×768
	1152×870
	1280×960
	1280×1024

Table 4-3   Typical Screen Resolutions Available to Different Monitor Sizes

●   Windows, Mac OS, Unix, and Linux
●   Font availability, font sizes, filenames, color palettes, gamma, and feature support

The screen resolutions for laptop monitors vary widely, as do their monitor sizes, but typically they have the same proportional ratios with default resolution settings of either 800×600 or 1024×768. Note, however, that with liquid crystal display (LCD) technology, used on laptops and, increasingly, as flat panel displays for desktops, it is much more difficult for users to change the resolution and retain a high-quality image. Unix workstations also tend to have extra-large resolution settings, commonly 1400×1050 or 1600×1200.

Note

The screen resolutions of alternative devices such as WebTV and PDAs differ enormously from traditional computers, but we'll get to that in a minute.

Throughout most of the 1990s, designing Web sites for 640×480 viewing was considered the de facto standard. As larger monitors have become more common, however, that's not a safe assumption anymore. It has become even more important to query your particular user base to find out what resolutions they prefer to view Web sites on.

Tip

Just because users may have their monitors set to a particular resolution, say 800×600, that does not mean that the size of your Web pages can be 800 pixels wide by 600 pixels high. Even if the browser is maximized, which is not always the case, the operating system menu and the Web browser take up space, too. All those layers of gray-blue navigation options may slip out of your mind when you're designing Web pages, but they're very much present on the screen when your users are on the Web. Subtract the space these other elements take up from your 800×600 pixel count before you start designing pages. For more details, see WebMonkey's article on "Sizing up the Browsers" at http://hotwired.lycos.com/webmonkey/99/41/index3a.html.

You will periodically find surveys that indicate usage statistics for screen resolution, but review them with caution. I recall a survey done by StatMarket in 1999, for example, that indicated only 13 percent of Web users had their monitors set to 640×480, while 54 percent were using 800×600, 26 percent were using 1,024×768, and the remaining 7 percent were using a higher resolution or some other resolution. This report had Web development teams hopping; designers and developers long frustrated with the limited screen area afforded by a 640×480 monitor settings were keen to start designing Web pages for 800×600 viewing areas.

4

But there was a twist. When you examined the fine print, it was apparent that StatMarket had based its survey on voluntary participants who had come to their site and completed a questionnaire about their resolution settings. Well, I don't know many casual Web users who happen to frequent StatMarket. This is a site driven largely by and for Web developers. The results of their surveys indicated that Web developers, not typical Web users, were largely using 800×600 or higher resolutions. Their usage statistics still remained uncollected.

This is in no way meant to malign StatMarket. They provided the information on where they got their data, but lots of people just skipped over those details. Since then, StatMarket has expanded its research methods and, rather coincidentally, started charging for its data. Table 4-4 reproduces their latest statistics on screen resolution, as reported by newmedia.com. Ironically, the 800×600 numbers are rather similar to the less useful 1999 figures.

You might think that since these figures were gathered worldwide, they could be applied worldwide, but that's not necessarily the case. Once again, it depends upon where your user base is located. In Germany, apparently, Web users with a 1024×768 resolution accounted for more than 50 percent of the surfing population, while in China, they accounted for a little more than 18 percent.

There are actually two lessons to be learned here:

1. It's best to collect data specific to your user base and/or examine general usage statistics very carefully to determine whether their criteria match your user base.

2. As WebReview author James Kalbach put it so well, "Developing fixed-size Web pages is a fundamentally flawed practice." Scalable, or relative-width, Web sites take much better advantage of this amazingly flexible medium.

Screen Resolution Setting	Percent of Users
640×480	5.71%
800×600	52.47%
1024×768	32.72%
1152×864	2.32%
1280×1024	2.88%
Other	3.9%

Table 4-4   Screen Resolution Usage (Source: July 23, 2001, report from StatMarket.com; their information is gathered from more than 50 million Internet users a day to more than 150,000 sites worldwide.)

Instead of setting a table to be exactly 590 pixels wide, for instance, make it 90 percent wide. That way your Web site might work better for all your users.

Tip

See James Kalbach's full article on scalable versus absolute-width Web pages, "The Myth of 800×600" at http://www.WebReview.com/2001/03_16/webauthors/ index01.shtml.

Tip

When it comes to designing scalable Web sites, I recommend optimizing them for the monitor resolutions of your largest user group and then testing it on all the others to make sure the design is still workable. Also, it's a good idea to place your most important content in the upper-left portion of the screen. That way, even if a user has reduced the size of their browser window, they'll still see it.

Alternative Devices

PDAs, cell phones with Web access, WebTV, Internet appliances…there is an increasing number of what are currently called *alternative devices* for the Web. It won't be long until these "alternatives" are considered mainstream, and a number of visionaries predict what we know as the standard desktop computer and Web browser will just go away. The question they seem to debate is when, not if.

Each of the key hardware and software constraints we have discussed so far in this module—bandwidth, browsers, operating systems, and monitor screen resolution—will likely have an entirely different spin with these devices. It would take another book to fully address the usability issues of all these new Web-ready applications, but Table 4-5 lists a few tips for the three most common kinds of devices.

Tip

A 350-page book entirely dedicated to usability for wireless devices is expected to be published in early 2002. Keep an eye out for Mark Pearrow's *The Wireless Web Usability Handbook,* published by Charles River Media, 2001.

Device	Bandwidth	Browsers	Operating Systems	Screen Characteristics	Additional Notes
PDAs (personal digital assistants)	Low/ Wireless	New / product-specific, generally "clip" Web sites to text only	New / product-specific	Tiny resolution, very limited color, if any.	Limited ability to display graphics or other media.
Cell phones	Low / wireless	New / product-specific, generally "clip" Web sites to text only	New / product-specific	Tiny resolution, very limited color, if any.	Limited ability to display graphics or other media. Strong audio potential.
WebTV	High / cable modem	New / product-specific	New / product-specific	Typically 544×372; High definition TV is 1600×1900. Both have different ratios than the traditional 4:3 ratio of desktop computer monitors. More heavily saturated colors. Different gamma settings.	Users typically view WebTV from much farther away than desktop computers. The lower screen resolution of typical TV also means less detail will be visible.

Table 4-5   Hardware and Software Constraints for Alternative Web Devices

Tip

For WebTV development guidelines, see http://developer.webtv.net.

Project 4-2: Expand Your Usage Scenarios to Account for the Users' Hardware and Software Constraints

Now that you know so much more about how a user's hardware and software can affect their experiences with a Web site, apply that knowledge to expanding your usage scenarios developed in Module 2. For the purpose of this fictional project, it is necessary to imagine the user data. If you have another Web site that you are currently working on, feel free to gather data from that real-world project and develop usage scenarios for that user base.

Step-by-Step

1. Pick two different user groups for the community art center Web site, either from your earlier user profiles or starting afresh. Some of your choices might include the following user groups, each of which could be further broken down if necessary:

- Artists who are currently members of the center
- Children who may be interested in taking art classes
- Administrative staff of the center
- Members of the public who are interested in attending art events or classes
- Patrons of the arts

2. Outline what hardware and software each user group is likely to use and where they would be accessing the Web from (home, work, school, etc.). Consider bandwidth, browser, operating system, and monitor resolution, and research what the limitations of each one might be in the context of the Web site you envision creating. For example, if one of the groups predominantly uses a 3.x version of Internet Explorer, you will likely discover that Cascading Style Sheets are very poorly supported, so that may influence your decision whether or not to use style sheets in designing the Web site.

3. Pick a couple of imaginary individuals from each group. (Feel free to use characters developed for your previous usage scenarios if you like.) Finally, develop usage scenarios for how these individuals might use the community art center, taking into account their hardware and software, as well as all the earlier information you have collected on them.

Project Summary

There's nothing like reviewing current hardware and software constraints to bring your Web site designs into real-world scenarios. Knowing that the maximum size of each Web page should be no more than, say, 50 K for a particular project makes you examine each and every one of the lovely graphics that you might like to include. Economy of scale definitely becomes a priority.

Module Conclusion

With all the technological developments going on, the hardware and software used to access the Web are changing constantly. If you memorized today's usage statistics for all these tools, it would serve you well for only a few months. In some ways, today's statistics are already outdated. By the time the studies are completed, published, distributed, and read by Web designers and developers like us, they can be months old. So be prepared to update your insights into your user's hardware and software as often as you find yourself updating any similar items.

Keep asking your audience what tools they use, how they like them, if they plan to upgrade, and, if so, when. Keep track of your own server logs to see who is actually visiting the site and what tools they are using to do so. And always keep an eye out for what users are *not* coming to your site (yet!) and consider whether or not the cause could be a usability issue.

In the next module, we will stop seeing through your current users' eyes—not permanently, just long enough to look around and see what's out there on the Web that your users might not be aware of. As a Web designer and developer, you may find it immensely helpful to periodically assess the state of the Web and to pause and consider what possibilities might open up in the future. Hang on to your own usability spectacles, though. You might want to alternate assessing the Web from a designer's viewpoint and as your most familiar user.

4

☑ Mastery Check

1. What are the four primary hardware and software constraints that are most likely to affect the user's experience?

_____

_____

2. Which of the following lag times in a Web site will allow the user's stream of thought to remain uninterrupted?

   A) 1 second

   B) 5 seconds

   C) 10 seconds

   D) 15 seconds

3. For typical users with 56 K modem Web access, which of the following page sizes will download quickly enough that you will not have lost the user's focus? You may select more than one:

   A) 25 K

   B) 50 K

   C) 75 K

   D) 100 K

4. True or False: Broadband connectivity is gaining acceptance quickly enough that we can soon stop designing Web sites for regular modem users.

5. Which of the following browsers is the de facto design standard for most general-interest Web sites?

   A) Internet Explorer 3.x

   B) Internet Explorer 4.x

   C) Internet Explorer 5.x

   D) Internet Explorer 6.x

   E) Netscape Navigator 3.x

☑ Mastery Check

F) Netscape Navigator 4.x

G) Netscape Navigator 6.x

H) None of the above

6. True or False: A number of Web authoring tools have the capability to thoroughly test for cross-browser compatibility, thereby eliminating the need to test browsers individually.

7. Which of the following guidelines will help ensure that your Web sites will work in future browsers? You may select more than one:

   A) Write all your code in uppercase.

   B) Write all your code in lowercase.

   C) Use only the tags deprecated in the XHTML 1.0 standard.

   D) Use only the tags specified in the HTML 4.0 standard.

8. What audiences are you likely to lose users from if you choose not to design your site to work on the Macintosh operating system?

   _____

   _____

9. Which of the following guidelines should you follow in naming files for optimal cross-platform compatibility? You may select more than one answer:

   A) Use filenames that are no longer than ten characters long.

   B) Use no more than a three-letter extension.

   C) Use only lowercase letters.

   D) Use only uppercase letters.

   E) Use only the regular letters of the alphabet.

10. True or False: Designing Web sites for 640×480 screen resolutions is the de facto design standard.

4

Module 5

Know the Web Even Better Than Your Users Do

The Goals of This Module

- Understand what is involved in knowing the Web better than your users do
- Identify the limitations of the Web
- Identify the potential of the Web
- Explore ways to stay current regarding the state of the Web
- Expand your Web Site Library

Know the Web. Repeat ten times after me: "Know the Web. Know the Web. Know the Web...." It's just common sense to know all the ins and outs of the medium that you are designing for.

Have you ever heard of the saying, "A little knowledge is a dangerous thing?" Well, welcome to the "Web of the Wild West," an alternative interpretation of the acronym "WWW." You could say that the Web has been made by gangs of gun-slinging, program-thumping entrepreneurs on wild horses armed with "a little knowledge." To be honest with you, traditionally, *nobody* has had very much knowledge about the Web. Most of us have spent the last eight years trying to figure out what the heck this thing really is. Problem is, "most of us" haven't admitted it.

You are not being asked to put down all your Web tools with the intent to create Web sites until you can gain a full, comprehensive knowledge about the most intricate details of the Web. It's not an easy feat to gain a full understanding of any new medium, much less the Web. A great deal of what the Web is and what it is capable of as a medium has been invisible and/or unarticulated. Our understanding of it has been marred, in part, by the limitations of its technology *and* by the limitations of our own preconceptions.

What you can do is to arm yourself, so to speak, with current knowledge and ideas about the Web as a medium. There are an awful lot of smart, creative people out there thinking about and fooling around with the Web. It only makes sense to pay attention to them. In order to help create Web sites that will truly be able to provide a service that cannot be offered by other mediums, you've got to know two things:

- What are the Web's limitations?

- What is the Web's potential?

Tip

While you may not be able to know every facet of the Web's limitations and potential, you can understand the issues surrounding them significantly *better* than your users do. So our mantra becomes "Know the Web better than your users do." Repeat that ten times.

Ask the Expert

Question: So if you know the Web, or any medium, better than your users do, how can you rely on them to tell you what to design to meet their needs?

Answer: You can't exclusively rely on the users, or at least not their ability to express themselves. While they can often give you a good indication of what they want or need, they cannot always tell you what they want or even what would be useful to them. Oftentimes, they may not even realize that their needs could be met in a better way.

But that does not mean that you can ever ignore the users. This is the part of "seeing through the users' eyes" where you need to train yourself to see what they *will* be able to see but may not even be able to imagine yet.

Keep in mind, too, that while you may know the Web better than your users, they know what they're looking for on any given Web site or on the Web as a whole better than you do. It's a team effort.

Question: Can you give an example of how to design for users who don't know what they want?

Answer: Sure. Throughout the history of product development, there are cases where users have reported that a product was perfectly fine. Only after a new, better one was developed that they "couldn't live without" have they realized that the original product was flawed or inferior in some way.

One such example, well before the Web was even invented, was the improvement of the telephone by Henry Dreyfuss in 1930 for Bell Telephone Laboratories. As Mark Pearrow recounts in his *Web Site Usability Handbook* (Charles River Media, 2000):

> Dreyfuss believed that machines that were adapted to people's physical requirements would be the most functional and the easiest to use. Toward this end, he measured 2,000 sample faces from mouth to ear. He ensured that the hand grip wouldn't slip in the user's hand, and that the instrument could be easily handled by a variety of sizes of hands under different environmental circumstances. Through his collection of data on the human body's proportions and capabilities, Dreyfuss helped establish the science of ergonomics.

5

> During some of the research performed by his team, Dreyfuss found that telephone users reported that they were completely satisfied with the weight and feel of the old-style handset; it was heavy, and weight imparted an image of quality. However, when prototypes of a newer, lightweight handset were given to users to try, they changed their tune quickly....
>
> I'd say in terms of the development of the Web that we are still in the days of that heavy, old-style handset. Recent developments have moved us past the point of having the mouthpiece attached to a wall, at least, but it will only be with continued probing into the nature of the medium that we will be able to really help it reach its potential. To effectively design Web sites requires a fine balance between studying the medium and studying the users it is intended to serve. In this module, we will be studying that medium, primarily in terms of its limitations and potential.

Limitations of the Medium

We've already discussed a number of the technological limitations of the Web in earlier modules. In Module 4, for example, we discussed the constraints of bandwidth, browsers, operating systems, and screen resolutions in terms of developing Web sites that could be displayed across all the users' computer systems. There are a slew of other technological limitations, however, that all users experience just in the process of using computers to access the Web. We'll discuss those first.

Then, in addition to the technological limitations of the delivery platform, I'd also like to point out three other important limitations that may be a bit more intrinsic to the medium, depending on where you draw the boundaries:

- Multimedia, or the lack thereof
- Language difficulties
- The vast amounts of information available on the Web

Computer Limitations

A number of limitations that are inherent to current computer systems in general affect our perceptions about the Web as well. It can be very easy to overlook these when discussing the Web simply because they are so commonplace. But don't let that fool you; just because they are part of our daily experience does not mean that you should ignore their consequences for your Web designs.

Computer Ambiance

Face it, curling up with your computer in bed or relaxing with it out on the lounge chair are not as sensually appealing as, say, a good old book with its lovely book smell. Nor can it compete in this regard with being ensconced in your favorite recliner watching a big-screen TV set across the living room. Hard, putty gray plastic cases, the tippety tapping sound of the keyboard, the whir of fans and drives in the background, and the incandescent glow from the monitor make computers a rather cold medium.

Okay, you can put that warm and fuzzy cover over your mouse to make it feel like a teddy bear, or buy an iMac with translucent blueberry coloring, but that's hardly going to soften up the whole experience. No matter where you take your computer, it brings along something of its own ambiance, and if as a Web designer you are trying to convey some kind of warmth, you've got a built-in challenge inherent to the medium.

Monitor Quality

Yuck. Who has *not* gotten bleary-eyed from trying to read material on a computer screen for any length of time? How about headaches? You're not alone. Compared to the print medium in this regard, the Web comes out a big loser. It takes other, strong motivating factors to get people on the Web reading text. And many of them, if given a choice, would rather print out long documents on their home printers than have to read them on-screen.

HCI Constraints

Human-computer interactions, or HCI as it's commonly referred to, is a whole field that has been developed to help address the inherent physical strains of using computers. The eyestrain caused by monitors is only one such example. There are also all of the repetitive motion injuries that come hand-in-hand (or rather mouse-in-hand) with using these darn things, as well as the impact on posture, breathing, and the limited range of motion we experience while using computers—and, thus, the Web in its current manifestation.

Hint

Keep in mind that these technological limitations of the computers are not necessarily permanent and that they are not essential to the medium of the Web. Try to imagine the Web accessed through technologies other than our current computer systems. In understanding the medium of the Web, it can be helpful to differentiate it from its delivery platform.

Multimedia, or the Lack Thereof

"Multimedia" was the biggest buzzword of the industry throughout much of the 1990s. By this, people generally thought of the combination of text, graphics, audio, video, and animation. CD-ROMs made big headway into combining these elements in an interactive venue. When it came to the Web, though, our common perception then and now is that well, yes, all of these things *could* be on the Web if only it weren't for the bandwidth constraints.

But think again. Even if there were no bandwidth constraints, the Web was primarily created to display text. Even graphics were something of an afterthought. Consequently, much of the structure of the Web is geared toward text.

HTML, for example, is the acronym for Hyper*text* Markup Language, not Hyper*media*. Search engines find information based on strings of text. The biggest debates within the Web design field have mostly revolved around how to control the display of text and whether or not designers should even try to control its appearance.

Cascading Style Sheets have, to a large degree, been developed in response to this debate. They were conceived of as a way to amend the original functionality of HTML to give designers the control that they have been clamoring for. Their less obvious purpose is to prevent designers from "abusing" the text-based system by introducing such things as graphical text (text that is created in an image-editing program as opposed to generated by the code) or subverting the table tags into page layout tools.

Consider also the debates revolving around Macromedia's Flash animation. Unlike QuickTime video or RealAudio or even Shockwave Director, Flash is one of very few multimedia venues that were created specifically for the Web, so you might think that it would smoothly fit into the underlying structure. The strongest early criticisms against using Flash animation on the Web, however, were essentially that it did not have the same functionality as Web text. People complained that it wasn't searchable; nothing other than the beginning was bookmarkable; it couldn't be stopped and started at the user's pace, or accessed from any point. In other words, it wasn't like the medium of the Web as we understood it; it wasn't like text.

Many of these criticisms can be applied to the other multimedia formats for the Web today, and engineers across the field are trying to resolve them by adapting their products to this text-based medium, or creating temporary workarounds. For example, in order to make multimedia elements searchable, developers find themselves typing into the HTML a string of key search words that pertain to the content of the multimedia. This is not unlike the practice of assigning Alternative Text tags (<alt>) to all the graphics that appear on a Web page, so that browsers without graphics capability can at least convey to the user what image was intended to appear.

Wouldn't you agree, though, that there's a whole lot more information and subtle cues available in graphics and multimedia than can be conveyed in a short string of words? Whatever happened to the maxim that "a picture conveys a thousand words"? As Web designers and developers, keep in mind that the allure of integrating multimedia on the Web is at least partly illusory. There are, at present, structural limitations to how it can be fully integrated into the existing medium. Keep an eye out for the adoption of Scaleable Vector Graphics, commonly referred to as SVG. This new file format may resolve some of these dilemmas as well, although it may be a couple years before browsers that support them are in common usage.

You may be wondering by this point what concrete things you can do in designing Web sites to "solve" some of these inherent limitations. Unfortunately, there aren't any ready answers to most of them. Think of them, instead, as ongoing challenges in the design of the Web itself, in which you can play an active role. Much of the evolution of the Web has been prompted by designers and developers working on individual Web sites and coming up with brilliant ideas. Sometimes the designers themselves don't even realize the implications until others start copying and further improving their ideas.

My best advice to you is to stay aware of what these overall limitations are and keep an eye out for ways to eventually solve them—either by coming up with solutions yourself or by recognizing them when somebody else does. This process may come easiest to you if you have natural tendencies toward the *global learning* style we discussed in Module 2. (Do you remember what that was? Learning by seeing the big picture first, then diving into the details.) Also use your *intuitive learning* capabilities to explore the relationships between new technologies as they emerge and the existing technologies and applications of them.

Language Difficulties

Consider, too, the implications of this text-based medium regarding language and culture. The minute you have a medium that relies on text, predominantly text written in any one language such as English, you run into language difficulties.

At this moment, bands of programmers are intensely working on developing increasingly sophisticated translation programs. But even if they are able to someday create a program that flawlessly translates all the subtleties of every language into every other language (which is not going to happen anytime very soon), what about the page layout, the graphics, the other media, the use of color, etc.? How will those be translated appropriately depending on the user?

Translating from one Latin-based language to another, say from English to Spanish, requires a different amount of space, in some cases as much as 30 percent more. As you can imagine, this can play havoc with page design. Translating between English and Japanese, however, or English to Hebrew, also requires a change in orientation. A page designed to read from left to right does not easily adapt to languages that read from top to bottom or right to left.

One way around this straight translation process is to create a unique Web site for each intended audience in a different geographic locale. This process, often called *localization*, is time- and resource-intensive, but gives you the maximum control over otherwise iffy translation programs. Macromedia has employed this technique on a broad scale for several years. For example, compare and contrast Macromedia's home pages for the United States, United Kingdom, Korea, and Japan in Figures 5-1 through 5-4 or the current versions on the Web.

Figure 5-1 The home page for Macromedia's main U.S. site
(http://www.macromedia.com)

Hint

Macromedia constantly updates the content and design of its Web sites, so I'd encourage you to visit the current versions of its various localized sites to compare and contrast them with the screen shots taken at the time of this writing.

As you can see, Macromedia has not only provided a translation of the text from one site to another but has also selectively chosen content, graphics, colors, and page layout for each audience. (To see the color differences, you will need to visit the live sites on the Web.) You might at first think it unnecessary to have separate Web sites for the United States and the United Kingdom since the

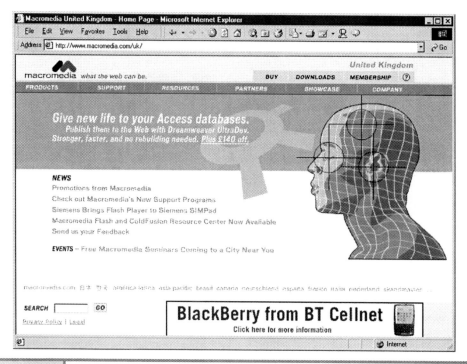

Figure 5-2 The home page for Macromedia's United Kingdom site
(http://www.macromedia.com/uk)

majority language in both countries in English. There are, however, some subtle but important differences between the two markets and the respective approaches of the two sales offices, such as the choice between "Store" and "Buy" in the primary navigation. Just as important, there are also much more obvious differences in content selected for each audience, from the featured promotion (Flash JumpStart Kit for the U.S. and Dreamweaver UltraDev for the U.K., site) to the news items and the events.

Tip

When localizing a site, it pays to hire a translator who is fluent in the language and intimately familiar with the culture. Always check out their background or get referrals from professional organizations such as the Silicon Valley Localization Forum at http://www.tgpconsulting.com/translators.htm.

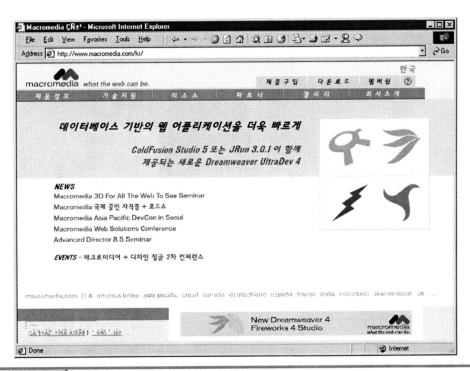

Figure 5-3   The home page for Macromedia's Korean site
(http://www.macromedia.com/kr)

The Web has long been touted as a "global" medium, and it does, indeed, have an underlying delivery mechanism that could provide world-wide access, providing, of course, that everyone in the world had access to a computer linked to this enormous network. But the Web does not have the intrinsic ability to transcend global differences in language or culture. It does not even have the capacity to accurately translate anything other than the text between cultures, and even that is severely limited at present. If you're looking for a good challenge to apply years of research and development to, this would be a really valuable one to take on.

Project 5-1: Experiment with Site Translations

See for yourself how translations can affect the page site design and test the effectiveness of on-the-fly translation programs.

Figure 5-4   The home page for Macromedia's Japanese site
(http://www.macromedia.com/jp)

Step-by-Step

1. First off, pick a site that has a fairly complex page design, including graphics, text, and perhaps columns such as the PBS site at http://www.pbs.org, the BBC site at http://www.bbc.co.uk, WebReview at http://www.webreview. com, or another site of your choice.

2. Pick one fairly complex page, open it at a standard monitor resolution, say 800×600, and study its design. Also, if you know any foreign languages that you'll be able to compare a translation to, read all of the text on the page to become familiar with the choice of words, nuance, tone, grammar, etc. Keep a copy of that page handy as well for reference by printing it out, taking a screen grab of it, or opening a new browser window beside it on your monitor.

3. Now go to one of the following Web site translation services, and enter the URL of that page:

- http://babel.altavista.com/tr?
- http://www.itools.com/lang/ (The Web page translator is currently near the bottom of the page. You may have to scroll to find it.)

4. Select a language to translate the site to from their menu. If you speak more than one language, I'd suggest choosing one of the languages that you are most familiar with so that you can gauge the accuracy of the translation.

5. Compare the page layout and the text (if you are able) to the original version. In particular, note differences in the following:

- Overall look and feel of the page
- Alignment of elements, such as captions fitting beneath images, or text fitting into columns
- Total page length
- Changes in material that is visible within a 640×480 or 800×600 screen size. For example, has any of the primary navigation dropped out of site?
- Changes in the need to scroll horizontally or vertically
- Accuracy of translation (if you know the language)

6. Select a couple of different languages for the same page and compare those results as well. (Note: You may find you are limited in the languages you can translate to by what character sets your computer supports.)

7. Back at the translation service site, enter a couple of sentences into the text translator, and translate your text several times. For instance, translate it first into Spanish, and then from Spanish into French, and then from French into Japanese. (Note: You may need to cut and paste the translation each time into the text entry box. Also, you may be limited here by what ability each translation service has to translate between languages other than English. This is just one more indicator of how heavily English-centric the Web is.)

8. Finally, translate your text back into English and compare those results with what you originally entered.

Project Summary

As good as they are, the current on-the-fly translation services leave a bit to be desired. You may be able to see now why companies like Macromedia go to the effort of localizing their site. In Macromedia's case, it has chosen to develop and maintain *12* versions of its site for different geographic audiences: U.S., United Kingdom, Korea, Japan, Asia Pacific, France, Spain, Latin America, Germany, Brazil, Canada, Italy, and Scandinavia. Note how a number of these sites overlap languages (such as the use of English for the U.S., U.K., Canadian, and Asian Pacific versions and Spanish for Latin America and Spain). Each of the sites has somewhat different content, targeted at those users in those distinct regions.

As for the chain of text translation, one time I did this and started with what I thought was a fairly simple sentence, "What do you think about eating purple lemons as a snack mid-morning?" I translated it in a three-step process to French, then to German, then back to English. It came back as "What do you, the pure-pure lemons, think as center mornings casse croÃ. te to eat?" What a riot. I would just hate to be depending on such a chain for communication purposes!

Vast Amounts of Information

One aspect of the Web that we know and love—and sometimes love to hate—is the vast amount of information accessible through the Web. Generally, there's more information readily available to us through the Web today than anybody accurately predicted. The terms "information glut" and "information overload" predated the Web, but the Web seems to have been created to test their limits.

Now, for the most part, I would say this abundance of information is *not* a limitation. After all, the more access to information the better, right? There are two aspects of the situation, however, which have proved to be a constant challenge for Web designers and developers, and which, frankly, we still have not mastered. The limitations, therefore, are due in part to our inability to answer the following two sets of questions or to integrate their solutions into the structure of the Web. You could also say that the Web's limitation in terms of the quantity of information is that it does not provide a structure that would eliminate the need for these questions. It was not built for the vast amount of information that is available through it today, nor the ever-increasing uploads.

Tip

Many users, especially serious researchers, will discount information found on a Web site if it does not include the source and date it was last updated.

- **How do we as users assess the quality of the information that is so freely available to us on the Web?** What criteria do we use? Who can

5

we trust to conduct reviews, etc.? These are all issues of authority and reliability. With all this information on the Web, how do we determine what is *good* information? Conversely, as Web designers we have the constant challenge to assure the user of the quality of the information we are providing to them. Merely including the source and date of information can do worlds of good in this regard. You might be surprised, however, at the number of Web sites that neglect even to include that information—or at least not on the page where you may be reading any given piece of information. And, as you well know, pages can get easily separated from the context of the rest of the Web site. We can print out isolated pages, bookmark them, or link to them and never glance again at the other sections of a Web site. It's a bit like tearing a page out of a book, but there's a lot less inhibition about doing it on the Web! And the second key issue is:

● **How do we get to the information that we need?**   Or to put in more industry-standard terminology, how do we navigate the Web? The core navigational feature of the Web as a medium is the hypertext link. This, by itself, does not make a coherent, organized system that everybody can use. Nope, it's up to us as designers and developers of the Web to create navigational systems that can handle this vast amount of information. This applies across the breadth of the Web and organizational bodies like the W3C to the browser engineers and, finally, down to individual Web site designers. Navigation is a huge issue, and one that needs constant attention and improvement. We will discuss this in much more depth in Modules 8 and 9.

1-Minute Drill

● What are three key limitations of the Web as a medium?

● What are the drawbacks to the abundance of information available on the Web?

● Multimedia, or the lack thereof, language difficulties, and the difficulty in assessing the vast amounts of information available on the Web and assessing its validity

● The difficulty in assessing the quality of the information and easily finding (or navigating to) the information on the Web

Potential of the Medium

Has the discussion of the limitations of the medium depressed you? Don't let it. Now we can make an about-face and look at the great potential of the medium, which in some ways has been barely tapped into. There are all sorts of possibilities for Web sites to take advantage of the medium in ways that cannot be so effectively accomplished through other mediums.

Let's look closely at four key elements that the Web has the ability to harness:

- Interactivity

- Currency of information

- Media

- Databases

We will then look at a few examples of ways in which the Web is or can be used.

Tip

While you may not find appropriate opportunities to integrate every one of the following possibilities into a new Web site design, it can be worth your while to make a habit of considering each one during the design process. That can prevent you from falling into the rut of creating the same kind of Web site each time and missing the perfect opportunity to really add value to a Web site.

Interactivity

The Web offers ways in which people can interact with the content of Web sites and with each other that are not possible in any other medium. The concept behind its core element, hypertext, is brilliant: if you want more information on any particular topic, click it and it will take you to that information. It's one of those things that is so simple and obvious that you wonder how we ever got along without it.

Suddenly, with a concept like hypertext you can implode the separation between different books or other sources of information. It's no longer necessary, in principal, to have a dictionary or set of encyclopedias or an archive of any sort. Anything that can be represented on a computer screen can, theoretically, be accessed through the Web. Thus, you could not currently replace access to a petting zoo through the Web, but you could replace the need to access books, photographs, videos, or audio equipment in order to learn about baby giraffes. One computer, one network, a bunch of hypertext links, and the world is our oyster.

The network that forms the backbone of the Internet also gives us the technology to interact with each other in a way that was not previously available. Just look at e-mail for a moment. On the one hand, it appears to be very similar to existing ways of communicating, such as writing letters or talking on the phone. Like our network of phone lines, e-mail has enabled friends, family members, business colleagues, and even strangers to communicate with each other and share whatever information they like. Unlike phone lines, however, e-mail has also given us the ability to do the following things:

- To communicate the same information with as many people as we like (and for whom we have e-mail addresses) at the same time.

- To share or access that information whenever we like (and not be dependent on the other people being on the phone or online at the same time).

- To share a broader range of information than is typical of phone conversations, from seemingly insignificant jokes to full-sized research documents. (Tell me, when was the last time you called someone on the phone just to share a joke with them? For whatever reason, this isn't typically done, but on the Web it is commonplace. It's more readily understandable why we typically do not share lengthy documents over the phone because of the time involved.)

Interacting with other people via the Web also gives us more options than we previously had, although there is some criticism that the Web has taken away from some real-world interactions. Web interactions allow for the following things:

- Being able to discuss shared interests through online chat rooms or discussion groups. Yes, this is also done outside the Web, but it can be more difficult to find a sizeable group of people with the same interests. Does your hometown, for instance, have a reptile lovers forum? Or a mystery writers workshop? The more particular your interest is, the greater chance you have of forming a sizeable body of participants via the Web than in real-world interactions.

● Forming more direct business relationships than a company's previous structure may have allowed. Business sites all over the Web have started to take advantage of one-to-one marketing, customized orders, increased customer service, increased feedback from their user base, and increased communication between business partners, to name a few advantages. There's much more potential within this area as well to increase efficiency and personalization.

● Meeting a larger pool of people than we might otherwise encounter in our "real" or "non-Web" based lives. True to its global nature, geographic distances are minimized on the Web, whereas time differences and language barriers still impact real-time conversation.

● Forming friendships or romantic relationships that are not influenced by physical characteristics. I'd like to tread very lightly here because there certainly are some weird and generally unhealthy relationships that are formed via the Web. But overall, you have to admit that there are opportunities via the Web for the development of honest human-to-human contact that is primarily conversation-based. On the Web, the basic relationships can form long before we are influenced by each other's physical traits that play such a big role in forming our first impressions when we meet somebody in person.

Currency of Information

The Web has a huge advantage over most other media; it can be updated with current up-to-the-minute information. Unlike television news, though, which also can have up-to-the-minute information, the Web also hosts an archive of past information that can be readily available. Other media can handle the archive, but none other than the Web have both archival and current information so readily available.

Take the same example of learning about baby giraffes. It may be that you could fit all of the information currently available about giraffes on one CD-ROM, including photographs, text, audio, and video. That's great; it could be a wonderful CD, imploding the need for all those same books, videos, and such we've already discussed, and you could access it from any computer (that reads that particular kind of CD-ROM) without needing an Internet connection. It would necessarily be limited to the information that was available at the time the CD-ROM was created, however, and that limitation is not intrinsic to the Web.

The Web has the wonderful capability to be updated on a moment-to-moment basis. Find a new bit of information about the chemicals transferred from mother to baby giraffe in its first feeding, and with a line of code—poof—the information can be made available to Web users who are just dying for that bit of information all across the world. This kind of currency combined with its vast body of existing information is a marvelous feature.

Media

Didn't I just include "multimedia" in the section on limitations? Yes, well, it is *more* limited than we might assume, but the capability for integrating all kinds of media is a wonderful possibility for the Web as well. It just has a long way to go before it can be as fully integrated into the structure of the Web as text is, and in the meantime be sure to assign alternative text using the <alt> attribute and descriptive search strings for the content of any media you employ.

Graphics, audio, video, even scent files and technology that can convey the sensation of touch or heat and cold all have tremendous potential in terms of increasing your ability to communicate whatever message you need to get across on a Web site. There may be definite limitations within the technology that you can't avoid at present, but you can avoid the mental limitations of just failing to envision how media may add value to a Web site.

Tip

When dealing with any kind of media on the Web, it's always a good idea to think about ways of giving the user options. Consider options to turn media on or off (especially audio for work or other environments where sounds may be obtrusive). See the Carbon 42 site (Figure 5-5) or the Barbie site at http://www.barbie.com for some examples of audio on/off options. Options for downloading different-sized files depending on a user's bandwidth are also always a good idea, as are options for being able to read what the content of the media is for those users who cannot access the media because of either technological or human factors constraints. Visit Apple's QuickTime movie trailers site at http://www.apple.com/trailers or the upcoming MovieFly site at http://www.moviefly.com for some examples of good user options. See Figure 5-6 for an extensive set of options for viewing a movie trailer.

5

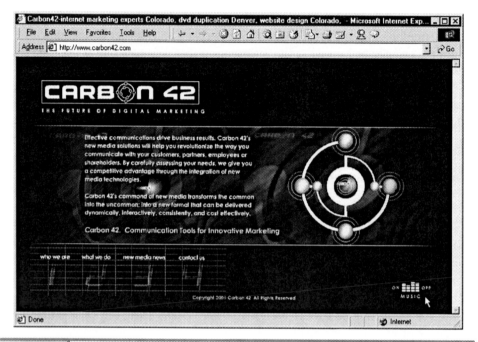

Figure 5-5 The Carbon42 site automatically loads a background soundtrack, but it gives users the option to turn it off in the lower right-hand corner (http://www.carbon42.com)

Databases

Databases are playing a huge role in helping alleviate the limitations we're encountering from the extraordinary amount of information available on the Web. In fact, the very purpose of databases is to store and retrieve data in an organized, automated fashion—just the ticket for helping us sort through the information glut.

Just having bigger and better databases won't solve all our information difficulties, though. They inherently follow a centralized management model wherein a database is designed for a particular set of purposes and then all of its users or developers need to supply or retrieve information according to that model. The Web as a whole is an intrinsically decentralized structure, with millions of small Web sites being created for as many different purposes.

For individual Web site designs, however, consider how employing a database may help automate the maintenance of that site's information. This

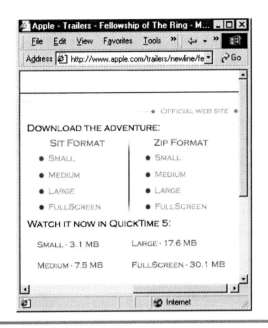

Figure 5-6 The Apple QuickTime site gave the user this slew of options for downloading or viewing the *Lord of the Rings* trailer (http://www.apple.com/trailers)

is particularly true for business or large-scale sites where there's a pattern to the kinds of information that periodically change. A typical retail business, for example, has a database that includes prices for its merchandise and shipping. When the business wants to have a 20 percent sale on a particular line of products, it is generally much easier to automate the updating of the prices reflected on the Web site by employing the database than to try to manually go in and update the figures for each item. The same would go for universally changing shipping rates or taxes, etc.

For example, think about the scale of a retail site like Amazon.com. At one point, they offered a sales promotion that included free UPS shipping on orders of two or more books. With such a promotion, they set up a fairly complex set of changes that had to go into effect for only a couple of weeks and then revert to the original process. It was not a simple process of just eliminating the UPS element from the database altogether. For each order, they still had to arrange for UPS to pick up and deliver the books and arrange to pay UPS for each delivery. It was only on the customer invoice that they needed to give a credit for the shipping costs—and only when the customers ordered two or more books. This is a complex process. Without a database to automatically compute the figures and coordinate the delivery, they would have spent thousands of extra man-hours processing each invoice.

Tip

Database design is an art unto itself. Unless you have a particular interest and strength in database programming, I'd highly recommend working with professional database personnel instead of trying to master it by yourself. Your knowledge of the Web and their knowledge about databases can make for very productive teamwork.

1-Minute Drill

● What are four key areas of potential of the Web?

● True or False: Having bigger and better databases will solve the problems with information glut on the Web.

Uses of the Web

Enough of all that theory. Let's take a look at some actual uses of the Web. Before reading this section, I'd suggest taking a sheet of paper and jotting down all the ways in which the Web is currently being used or that you can envision it being used. Chances are your list will overlap quite a bit with the following material. There probably aren't any big surprises here, but it can be useful to periodically review what the Web is being used for and how your particular Web sites fit into that schema.

Tip

In designing a Web site, it's a good idea to determine what its primary and secondary purposes are. They may often be a combination of the following typical uses of the Web, but having articulated the importance of each facet will help you keep your focus on those purposes and, thus, deliver the right site.

● Interactivity, currency of information, media, and databases
● False

Information Resource

This is the biggie. Many, many users of the Web are looking for information, and there are millions of sites whose primary focus is to provide information. There are also thousands of sites whose purpose is to provide links to other sites sorted by topic, providing layers of information resources. Visit The Library Spot for a typical example that combines the resources from encyclopedias, maps, online libraries, quotations, and dictionaries (see Figure 5-7).

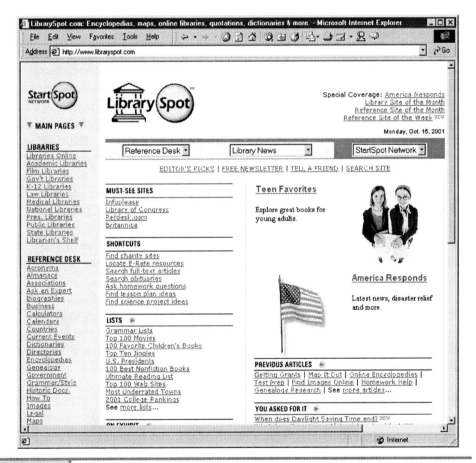

Figure 5-7   The Library Spot is a library of libraries, perhaps the ultimate in information resouces on the Web (http://www.libraryspot.com)

Business as Usual / E-Commerce

E-commerce is only one component of business sites. These concentrate on the selling of goods and services via the Web. Amazon.com (http://www.amazon.com) is one of the biggest e-commerce sites, and it's still growing. You are probably familiar with others such as E-toys, Barnes and Noble, PCMall, Nordstrom's…. This list can go on and on; essentially most of the major retail stores in the U.S. now have a presence on the Web, and there's a host of Web-only e-commerce sites as well.

Business-to-business and Extranets

Business-to-business sites and *extranets* are making enormous strides in terms of streamlining business practices. (Extranets fall somewhere between public *Inter*net sites and private *intra*net sites; they generally are password-protected sites hosted by a business to streamline transactions with its partners or special clients.) The increased communications made possible by these sites is increasing the efficiency of operations. Such tasks as ordering and providing the right amount of supplies at the right time, for example, minimize the need for (and costs of) warehousing.

Compaq computers at http://www.compaq.com is a good example of a successful business-to-business site. They set up a small extranet for each of their clients, facilitating the ordering of new computers at any time. The extranets have seamless integration with the publicly available Web site. At the time of this writing, Compaq is discussing a merger with Hewlett-Packard, so it's yet to be seen how their Web sites will change.

See also the GE Small Business site at http://www.gesmallbusiness.com/customer_service/bsns_net.jsp. Both of these sites, interestingly enough, are clients of Bowstreet, a business-focused solutions company. You can find other, similar business sites at the Solutions in Action part of their Web site at http://www.bowstreet.com/solutionsinaction/customers/index.html.

Intranets

Intranets are private Web sites created primarily for a company and its employees. Typical components include information on health and human resources, a description of the departments and personnel, phone and e-mail lists, calendars of events, conference room scheduling, and, increasingly, new employee training.

Unfortunately, due to their concern over privacy and security, it can be difficult to see many intranets unless you have a personal connection with the company. Visit http://www.intranets.com to set up your own Intranet or just get an idea of how one might work.

Shared Work Flow

Shared work flow was part of Tim Berners-Lee's early vision for how the Web could be used in the workplace. He imagined research scientists and academicians being able to collaborate on projects over the Web either at the same time (synchronously) or at different times throughout the day (ansynchronously). Developments in this area have occurred at a slower pace than have some of the other, more common Web uses, but an increasing amount of attention is being dedicated to it.

See Yahoo Groups at http://groups.yahoo.com for a simple consumer-level approach. It allows a group of people to share one e-mail address and a Web site from which they can plan events, send a newsletter, share photos, or discuss whatever topic has brought them together.

Visit eProject at http://www.eproject.com for more complex, business-oriented applications that are more in line with Berners-Lee's original vision (see Figure 5-8). It calls itself project management and collaboration software

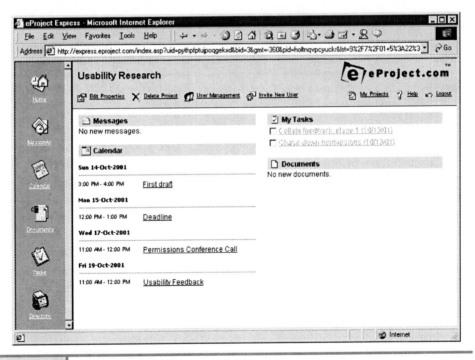

Figure 5-8   eProject offers a basic "Express" collaboration service for free (pictured here) as well as a more advanced "Enterprise" package (http://www.eproject.com)

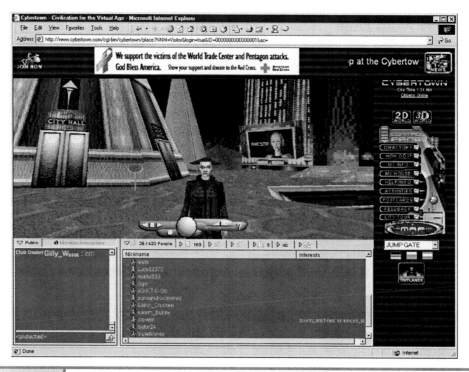

Figure 5-9 As a community site, Cybertown ofers sophisticated 2-D and 3-D chat environments (http://www.cybertown.com)

and provides an interactive Web site and document repository that allows project teams around the world to develop a project plan, improve communication between team members, and provide progress updates to managers and stakeholders. Its document management features allow members to check documents in and out while they work on them with a lock file option while it keeps track of version management and activity history.

Some examples of more strictly synchronous tools (where everyone meets and works at the same time) range from such free tools as MS NetMeeting, Sun Microsystems' Sun Forum, JXTA, Rat/Vat, and other chat tools to more costly tools such as Groove and Lotus Notes.

Community Sites

There's nothing quite like the human-to-human contact you can find in community sites. They provide a venue for people to connect with each other and communicate about shared interests or just to explore this new medium together. Community sites tend to employ chat rooms or discussion groups more than other types of sites, but an increasing number of sites are trying to incorporate some aspects of community into their overall design. Community aspects of the Web have gone a long way to soften the rather technology-heavy, intimidating aspects of the Web's computer-based delivery system.

Visit Cybertown for a good chat room environment, complete with avatars, that revolves around a science-fiction theme (see Figure 5-9). Visit Craig's List (Figure 5-10) for a very practical site that started as a community service site

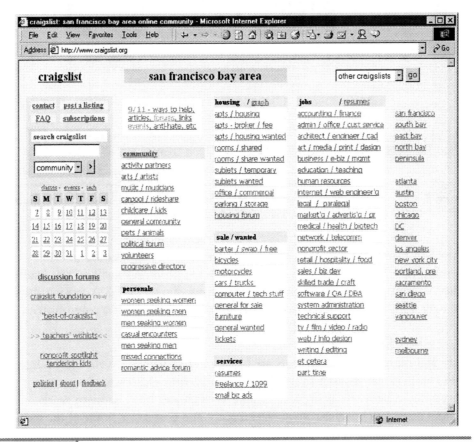

5

Figure 5-10 | Craig's List uses a simple text-based approach to provide a wide variety of services for a growing number of communities (http://www.craigslist.org)

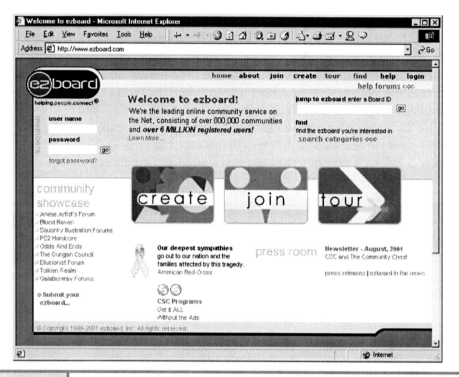

Figure 5-11   Part of ezboard's success as a community site can be attributed to its user focus (http:www.ezboard.com)

in the San Francisco Bay Area and is now successfully expanding to other communities. And the ezboard site (Figure 5-11) promotes itself as "the leading online community service on the Net, consisting of over 800,000 communities and over 6 million registered users!" Six million—that's quite a community.

Education Sites

More and more classes of all sorts are being offered over the Web. They range from complete self-studies to instructor-led real-time classes, and of course everything in between. Being able to take Web classes from home or work without having to travel is a great convenience and cost-saver. Some of the most effective classes also combine elements of community or entertainment sites. See some of the sample courses at http://www.digitalthink.com, http://www. macromedia.com/university, or http://www.ehandson.com (see Figures 5-12 and 5-13). DigitalThink currently offers more than 250 courses online across a broad range of categories; eHandsOn offers about 20.

Games / Entertainment

Don't forget this last, more lighthearted category. The Web can be a wonderful vehicle for games and entertainment. And by games, I do not mean exclusively Dungeons and Dragons role-playing games or shoot-em-up types of games. At last count, simple card and board games that had been ported to the Web were gaining in numbers far in excess of the hard-core games. Women and men, girls and boys, are enjoying playing games over the Web, either with existing friends or as a means to make new friends.

Games and entertainment sites often overlap a number of different uses for the Web from developing community to education. There's no reason why fun couldn't be part of all the other categories as well. See http://games.yahoo.com for a typical low-key gaming site.

5

Ask the Expert

Question: How can I stay up on what good Web sites are being developed? Should I just randomly surf the Web?

Answer: Randomly surfing is a good way to get a bird's-eye view of the current state of the Web, but chances are you will find a pretty high number of mediocre sites. To focus on some of the good designs and developments occurring on the Web, try keeping tabs on some of the major Web review sites or established competitions. It's a good idea to always remind yourself of what their bias might be. There's a good chance the staff of Print Magazine, for example, is going to be interested in high-quality graphic design and page layout and perhaps less interested in taking advantage of some of the less print-like qualities of the Web, like interactivity.

Question: Can you recommend a few sites to get me started?

Answer: Sure. A good general site that continues to develop an archive of thought-provoking sites is http://www.coolhomepages.com. Conversely, check out http://www.websitesthatsuck.com as well. Their premise is that you can learn a lot about design by looking at designs

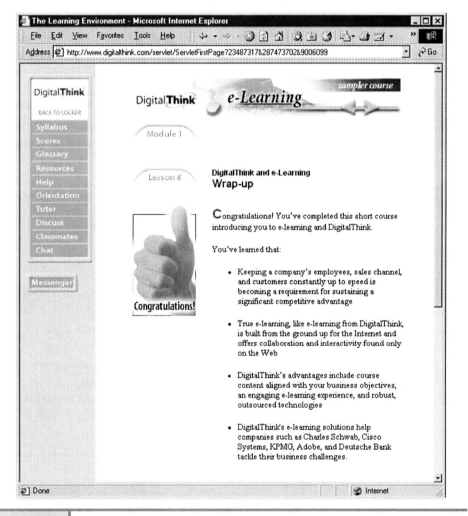

Figure 5-12   DigitalThink offers this introductory course on e-learning (http://www.digitalthink.com) (© 2001 DigitalThink, Inc.)

that *don't* work. For competitions, the Webby Awards is one of the biggest now. They have an annual competition with open judging for the first round, so it can be fun and educational to review and cast your vote for the contenders and then to review the final award winners. See their Web site at http://www.webbyawards.com.

If you're interested in developing sites with any of the Macromedia products, especially Flash or Shockwave Director, check out Macromedia's Shocked Site of the Day and their biannual People's Choice Awards at http://www.macromedia.com. See also http://www. shockwave.com for

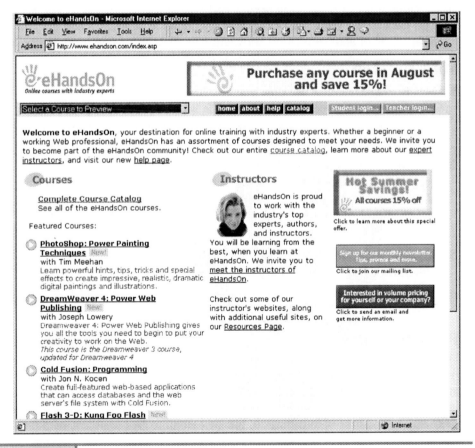

Figure 5-13   eHandsOn focuses on Web development topics for its courses
(http://www.ehandson.com)

an array of animations and interactive games or other uses of their products.

In fact, most of the companies that develop tools for creating Web sites such as Adobe, Apple's QuickTime department, or RealMedia also generally feature successful sites that were developed with their tools, so visit their Web sites or sign up for their newsletters. If you haven't already bookmarked them, WebReview and WebMonkey are great resources as well.

Project 5-2: Expand Your Web Site Library

To conclude this first part of the book, "Part I: Seeing Through the Users' Eyes," we'll go back to the Web Site Library that we began in Module 1 and expand it. Try to apply all of your newfound knowledge in analyzing a few more Web sites

Step-by-Step

1. First off, review each of the sites that you have already included in your library and add any more information that may be pertinent, such as its primary and secondary uses (informational, business, community, educational, games/entertainment, etc.).

2. Then, visit a few more sites in each of the previously described categories. Feel free to start with the sites I included in the brief description of each category or start by going to one of the Web review or competition sites such as http://www.coolhomepages.com and evaluating some of the sites they recommend.

3. Complete the columns that you have already identified, and add any extraneous notes to the "Other Notes" column.

4. Add screen grabs showing the pertinent features that you have commented on to the file.

Project Summary

This Web Site Library gives you a consistent framework for reviewing sites. You may well find that, as your interests grow and change, you start writing more and more notes in particular columns or keep commenting on consistent issues in the "Other" column. Feel free to adapt your template at any time by adding or changing columns of information, but be careful to be consistent with the entries you have already made.

The goal of this kind of library is twofold: one, to keep you consistently analyzing the same types of things; and two, to provide a useful document that you can easily skim or search to find useful examples of any particular issue you'd like to explore.

Module Conclusion

Knowing the Web even better than your users do isn't such a tough thing to do, is it? The trick is to be able to continue learning more and more about the Web without impairing your ability to see through the users' eyes. This is where so many Web designers and developers get off track. It's easy to get caught up in the fine details of creating Web sites and lose that overall perspective.

In Part II, we will explore some of the practical aspects of how to design Web sites for their users. Obviously, this is an impossible task if you don't know who your users are or how they perceive Web sites, so keep those usability spectacles handy. You'll be needing them a lot throughout the rest of your career in Web design and development.

5

☑ *Mastery Check*

1. True or False: You don't need to know more than your users do in order to design effective Web sites.

2. True or False: You should not participate in creating Web sites until you can gain a full, comprehensive knowledge of how the Web works and what its potential and limitations are.

3. If you know the Web better than your users do, how can you rely on them to tell you what to design to meet their needs?

   _____

   _____

   _____

4. Which of the following are limitations imposed by the computer environment? (You may select more than one.)

   A) Navigational confusion

   B) Monitor quality

   C) Information architecture

   D) Repetitive motion injuries

   E) Computer ambiance

5. Which of the following are true statements about the limitations and potential of the Web as a medium?

   A) Interactivity is one of the limitations of the Web as a medium.

   B) Multimedia is one of the limitations of the Web as a medium.

   C) Multimedia is one of the potentials of the Web as a medium.

   D) The global nature of the Web is one of its limitations.

☑ *Mastery Check*

6. What are five common uses of the Web?

_____

_____

_____

7. What are the two key benefits of creating your own Web Site Library?

_____

_____

5

Part II

Designing Web Sites for Your Users

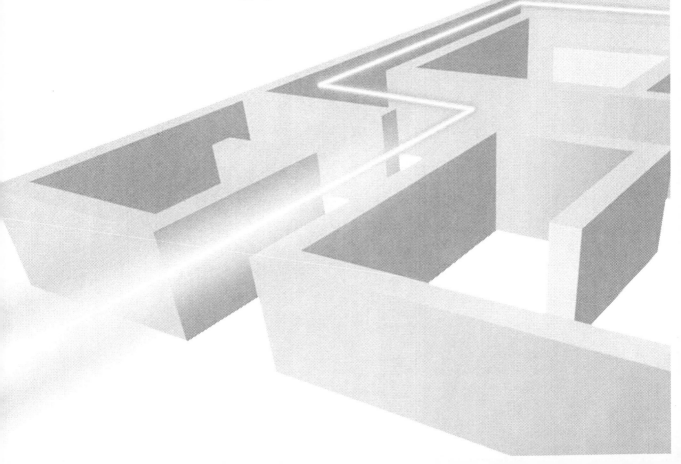

Module 6

Stick to a User-Centric Design Process

The Goals of This Module

- Identify the key roles in a Web design team
- Identify the phases of Web site design
- Identify ways to include the user in the Web design process
- Recognize common mistakes in a user-centric design process and learn how to avoid them
- Practice a planning session

Now that we've identified how to get to know your Web site's users and learn how to look at Web sites *through their eyes*, we can move on to how to effectively design Web sites that they can use—in short, how to design usable Web sites. All of Part II addresses this challenge.

In this module, we will discuss the underlying *modus operandi* of designing usable Web sites—sticking to a user-centric design process. It's not enough to do the groundwork and learn what would best serve the users and then to disappear into a production den for several months to create the final, splendiferous Web site. Unfortunately, it generally just doesn't work that way. It is more effective to constantly check in with the users, to get their opinions and observe their reactions to each step of the planning and implementation of your design ideas. This enables you to fine-tune the Web site, so that by the time you launch it, it is in perfect harmony with the users' needs.

Designing and developing Web sites is an iterative process. If you mapped the process out, it would look more like a spiral than a straight line. It's rather like a multistepped translation process. Remember the funny results we obtained in Module 5 by using a translation program to translate a sentence or two from English to French to German and back to English? That was the result of following a wholly linear process without a backward glance. If we had, instead, stopped at each stage and checked the language against the original wording and intent, we would likely have ended with phrasing much closer to the original.

The same applies to Web site design. By following an iterative process and constantly going back to confirm that you are indeed accomplishing what you set out to do, you can more effectively *translate* the design ideas to an effective Web site design.

Tip

The process of seeing through the users' eyes is also iterative. It doesn't really end with Part I or with the initial preparation for designing a Web site. You'll find that you will need to use those skills throughout the design process to develop a better, cumulative understanding of the users and how their needs can best be met through your Web site.

In this module, we will look at the following three necessary elements of a user-centric design process:

- Think of the user as a member of the design team.

- Involve the user throughout the design process.

● Avoid the most common mistakes made in following a user-centric design process.

As we conclude this module, you will

● Practice a planning session, one of the most important phases that you can involve users in.

1-Minute Drill

● Is the Web design process a sequential process or an iterative one?

● True or False: A user-centric design process involves finding out everything you can about the users and then creating the site.

● Iterative
● False. It is more effective to constantly check in with the users, to get their opinions and observe their reactions to each step of the planning and implementation of your design ideas.

The Design Team Composite

The Web started out with a lot of "Web teams" consisting of one person wearing a lot of different hats. One individual would take on the responsibility for designing, producing the graphics, writing the copy, programming, and maintaining the Web site. Even with the increasing complexity of the Web and its technologies, this is still possible today, but it's not likely to produce the very best Web site.

There are a number of reasons why teams can create higher-quality Web sites than lone individuals, not the least of which is the benefit of specialization. But more important than that for our purposes in creating *usable* Web sites is the breadth of perspective that comes from working with a team. At a minimum, I would say that to effectively design a usable Web site, you need three perspectives:

- **Technical viewpoint** To inform what can and cannot be done and how to most efficiently implement the site design

- **Creative viewpoint** To inform how the content can be most effectively communicated through the use of design elements

- **Usability viewpoint** To inform what the content should be

In many cases, you also need a fourth perspective:

- **Investment viewpoint (often called the business perspective)** To inform whether or not the return on investment (ROI) will likely be worth the investment in the first place and whether or not the project is even feasible in terms of budget, schedule, and available resources.

Note

A Web site's return on investment need not always be measured in dollar figures. In the case of nonprofit organizations, for example, a Web site's success could be measured in the number of people it is able to serve. If a site takes two-thirds of an organization's budget and reaches only one-quarter of its clientele, it may not be deemed worth the investment; their resources could be more effectively spent elsewhere. Alternatively, a number of businesses measure the success of their sites in terms of marketing and public relations gains, areas that are hard to assign a dollar figure to.

Whenever you are building a Web team, think about creating a composite of these perspectives. This does not necessarily mean that every Web team should have four individuals on it, each representing one of these perspectives. Oftentimes, a knowledgeable individual can bring overlapping perspectives to the table. But even more frequently, you may need more than one person to fully present the perspective of any one of these areas.

Just think about the technical complexity of a large e-commerce site for a moment. To fully understand what can and cannot be done on a particular site, you may need a number of different technical specialists, say a database programmer, a Java programmer, a JavaScript programmer, HTML and XML specialists, and a system administrator. The usability perspective also often requires more than one person. As you now know, a site often has several key user groups, each of which will likely need to be represented to give an accurate representation of the usability viewpoint.

The team does not need to be composed of people within a single company, either. Many teams include clients, users, and freelance Web professionals from outside the Web development company. In some cases, all but the coordinator are from outside the company.

A key member of most large Web teams is a project manager. Their job is not to represent any one viewpoint but to help meld the various viewpoints into a single vision and to coordinate the logistics of the project.

6

?⟩Ask the Expert

Question: What is the client's role in the Web design process?

Answer: A number of Web team models include the client, or whoever is footing the bill, as a separate role on the Web team. While I think the client is an invaluable source of information and ideas, I believe their role can and should be subsumed within the four primary perspectives. Very often, for example, the client needs to contribute a great deal to the usability perspective in helping to determine who will be using the site. Too many Web sites exist in which the client insisted upon its idea of what the Web site should be to the detriment of its users and, thus, ultimately, itself.

In general, to best serve the interests of the client, you need to create a site that gives preeminence to the client's target audience—i.e., the Web site users, *not* the client itself. This is not exactly business as usual; it is, however, one more way in which the medium of the Web is impacting the world around it.

Question: Are there any exceptions where the client should play a distinct role?

Answer: Yes, there are exceptions to almost every rule. One such exception may be when a client has a message that they want to get out to the world. In other words, when they want to use the Web as a broadcast medium. There's nothing user-centric about the intent, design, or execution of such sites, though.

Most often, the exceptions occur when the client thinks they know exactly what they want. In cases like these, they are essentially designing their own Web site and hiring you just to produce it and make it look pretty. I consider this a straight fee-for-services arrangement. You can make a living this way, but it's not really *designing* Web sites.

1-Minute Drill

● What three perspectives do you need to consider to effectively design a usable Web site?

● What role does a project manager play on a Web team?

The Web Site Design Process: Including the User

The typical phases in the Web site design process are quite similar to those of many other design and engineering fields. Although the terms may vary from

---

● Technical, creative, and usability
● The project manager's job is not to represent any one viewpoint but to help meld the various viewpoints into a single vision and to coordinate the logistics of the project.

field to field or even team to team, typically the process includes the following phases, which occur roughly in the following order:

- Planning

- Design

- Development

- Deployment

- Rediscovery and beginning the whole process over again for the next version

For the Web, add to that list "Maintenance and Updating" as the second-to-last phase. Unlike so many of its counterparts, no Web site is a final product that can be shipped out the door and forgotten more or less until the next version goes into design. Part of the magic of the Web is its currency and capacity to change practically moment to moment.

In shifting to a user-centric design process, it's not necessary to change the basic production process. The phases remain the same; we need only look for appropriate opportunities for including the user.

Planning Phase

The planning phase offers some of the greatest opportunities (and needs) for user involvement. This is the core conceptual phase in which the major decisions—like what purpose the Web site will serve and who it will serve—need to be made. It may sound obvious that you would want to include users in this process, but don't take that for granted. You might be surprised at the number of Web sites that have been created in the past without even considering what the users would want.

Employing a user-centric design process, however, necessitates that you find out during this phase all you can about the users and what they'd want or need in the Web site. You can employ many of the techniques we discussed in Part I to obtain much of this information, including market research, questionnaires, interviews, observation, usage scenarios, etc. I would also encourage you to involve some of the users in your planning sessions with the other team members.

Brainstorming sessions can be immensely helpful in identifying and articulating the Web site goals and detailing issues surrounding content and structure—if they are conducted effectively. Here are two valuable tips that can help you do that:

- Choose your planning environment carefully.

- Use proven brainstorming techniques.

Choose Your Planning Environment Carefully

It's not necessary to go on an expensive retreat to a tropical island to have an effective planning session. It is necessary, however, to have a room that everyone is comfortable in, that has plenty of tools available for recording ideas (whiteboards, flip charts, scratch paper, index cards, sticky notes, different colored pens, etc.), and that allows freedom of movement. It can be very helpful if team members can get up and walk around to write things on the board, point to a previous idea or drawing, draw arrows connecting ideas, or just pace back and forth if that is how they think best.

It's also necessary to ensure that the group will not be interrupted for at least an hour, maybe an hour and a half. In this day and age, this applies as much to devices the participants might bring in with them as it does to external events or intruders. Instruct all the participants to turn their cell phones and pagers off, and instruct other staff not to interrupt. It's also a good idea to avoid scheduling planning sessions when you know there's going to be a fire drill.

It never hurts to bring in treats as well, preferably something fresh and stimulating, not the same old pastries that the company provides for every other meeting. You can do to a lot to set the tone for the work session by infusing the environment with a little something out of the norm.

Use Proven Brainstorming Techniques

The product design firm IDEO takes brainstorming more seriously than just about any other firm I've encountered, and, perhaps not coincidentally, they are also one of the most innovative design firms today. They have itemized "Seven Secrets for Better Brainstorming," roughly paraphrased as the following:

1. **Sharpen the focus**   Start with a clearly defined problem. An example for Web design might be "How can we help safety-conscious parents research and buy the best toys for their children over the Web?"

2. **Playful rules**   Establish a set of rules that encourages the sharing of wild, random ideas. A number of IDEO's conference rooms have stenciled in six-inch-high letters such rules as "Be visual" or "Go for quantity." The idea is to avoid critiquing or allowing anybody to critique anybody else's ideas. One thoughtless criticism can be the death-knell of the entire group's efforts.

3. **Number your ideas**   IDEO advocates numbering each idea as it is written down. First, this encourages the quantity of ideas recorded (a "Hey gang, let's see if we can come up with 100 ideas" sort of mentality). Second, it provides an easy mechanism for referring to the earlier ideas without losing your place.

4. **Build and jump**   As one idea starts to peak, use some part of it to launch a second train of thought. In our toy example, for instance, as the ideas start to slow down in discussing how to secure the credit card transactions, jump to another related subject by saying something like, "Secure socket layers are a great idea; what are some other ways to *reassure* the parents about the safety of buying the toys over the Web?" Or: "That's all good and well for securing the safety of the purchasing process; how do we reassure the parents about the safety of the kids' interactions online or even the safety of the toys themselves?"

6

Tip

Be prepared to jump back to earlier ideas as well. Brainstorming is not just forward motion. Very often people will continue thinking about possible solutions to a problem even after the group has moved on to other topics. Or sometimes the new topic will spark ideas for other solutions.

5. **The space remembers**   Write the ideas down so that they are all visible to everyone in the group at all times. As tempting as it may be to stop and tidy up the quickly scrawled suggestions, don't do it. When returning to an idea, perhaps to jump to a new topic, the spatial memory of that notation amid all the other scrawls will help people recapture the mind-set of the discussion that prompted the idea in the first place. The idea is that everyone should be able to see the whole progression at a glance and be able to jump to and fro between various ideas with ease. This may require covering the entire room with butcher paper. If that's what's needed, then you've got a great brainstorming session going.

6. **Stretch your mental muscles** By this, IDEO means to do a gentle warm-up such as playing an on-the-spot word game or to assign homework that will get the participants into the mind-set of the users. Surfing a few Web sites might be all it takes to get the creative juices flowing for our example. This tactic can be especially useful if the group has not worked together before, or if they are new to brainstorming.

7. **Get physical** We've already mentioned how important it can be to have ample room for movement. To get the greatest number of ideas in the shortest period of time, it helps to enlist the help of everyone in the room to record the ideas. Just letting one person write down all the ideas while everybody else sits and watches doesn't always keep the momentum up. Better to have people take turns or write or draw sketches of their ideas on butcher paper or scratch paper while the rest of the group goes on. Brainstorms can be extremely visual, and drawing, mapping, diagramming, and the like should be encouraged. IDEO's teams also often start building things with whatever supplies they have on hand, but this is in part because they are a product design firm. Web sites brainstorming sessions tend to stay in the visual realm.

Tip

See *The Art of Innovation* by Tom Kelley, the general manager of IDEO, for more insight into how IDEO manages to produce some of the most innovative product designs in America (Doubleday, 2001).

Ask the Expert

Question: What do you do when a brainstorm grinds to a halt or just fizzles?

Answer: There are a number of techniques that you can try— hopefully *before* the session has completely ground to a halt or fizzled. The quicker you can catch the sagging momentum, the better your chances are at reviving the energy.

One good technique is to use the "build and jump" approach discussed in the "Seven Secrets to Better Brainstorming." The minute the ideas start to slow down, look for an aspect that has more potential that could be explored and direct the conversation that way.

Alternatively, if that avenue seems to have been fully explored, backtrack to an earlier point in the brainstorming session that may not have been fully explored. Choosing one from a period of high-intensity contributions may also serve as a little reminder of that energy and enthusiasm and get everyone back on track.

It also helps to have a series of questions prepared ahead of time that can help guide the discussion. In the example of designing a Web site to help safety-conscious parents research and buy the best toys for their children, you could identify ahead of time that those parents are likely to be concerned about the safety of the toys as well as the safety of conducting purchase transactions over the Web. If any part of the site encourages participation by the kids, the parents could also be concerned about the safety implications of that interaction.

Finally, having a defined period of time and a set goal in terms of numbers of ideas can go a long way toward keeping everyone focused on the task at hand. IDEO suggests one hour and one hundred ideas.

Design Phase

For the most part, users get to take a back seat during the design phase, or perhaps playing the role of a consultant would be a better way of putting it. The baton is handed to the designers for this leg of the journey, and they get to do their job. It would be a mistake to expect too much from the users during this phase. After all, they are not designers, and although they may enjoy playing around with image editing tools, they are unlikely to produce the best set of comprehensive designs (also commonly called comps or mock-ups). Just as I would have difficulty producing anything close to the Mona Lisa if handed a set of oil paints.

Where the user can play a valuable role, though, is as a checkpoint for the designers. Once the designers come up with some graphical representations of the ideas everyone agreed on within the planning phase, users can give them feedback as to whether or not they will work for their needs.

It's typical for a design team to present two or three sets of comprehensive designs. This reflects the inherent difficulty in translating design concepts to an actual design. Sometimes talking about it is not enough; you need to dive in and come up with visual interpretations, then discuss why they work or don't work and refine them accordingly.

Paper prototyping is one of the oldest and most proven methods for communicating site design ideas quickly. Instead of spending any time at a computer at all, pull out a stack of paper and start sketching. Draw buttons, navigation bars, and text blocks in place and then ask the users to give it a test run. If they tap on a button, for example, to emulate a mouse click, you can whip out the page that would link to. If they tap on something that you hadn't considered to be a button, you can change your plans right there, draw a box around it and turn it into a button. User Interface Engineering is one of the masters of paper prototyping for Web sites as well as software design. They also conduct a number of short courses in it. See their Web site at http://world.std .com/~uieweb/prototyp.htm for a more detailed discussion on this method. Also see "Five Paper Prototyping Tips" at http://world.std.com/~uieweb/ paperproto.htm.

Tip

At every stage of the development process, find ways to communicate your ideas in the least resource-intensive way possible. Instead of spending ten hours carefully drawing a set of graphics, for instance, sketch them out in pencil or cut and paste existing images and present them as ideas to the rest of the team. Only when you get approval should you spend the time to fully develop them.

Development Phase

Users have it pretty easy during the development phase as well, until it comes to testing. Although development often takes up to 80 percent of the time and resources allocated to any particular project, in some ways it is more straightforward than the other phases. Ideally, it should not begin until the design plans are finalized and everyone has agreed upon the blueprint, so it is just a question of executing the plans (and making the darned thing work!). Of course, in the real world, it's often not this simple, and the short schedules necessitate that some parts of the site start being developed while the site design continues to evolve. This is a tricky maneuver at best and almost always requires more revision.

Even when the design plans are considered to be final, it's still necessary to periodically review the site as it is being developed to ensure that it is in alignment with the site goals and meets the established usability criteria. (This is one more point at which you can see how Web site development is an iterative process.) The latter may involve hosting mini-usability tests, perhaps asking half a dozen users to perform a handful of tasks on a particularly problematic section of a site. It may be that part way through the development, the technical team decides to change tactics—either because they realize something may not work as proposed or because they discover what appears to be a more efficient way of accomplishing the same task.

Or, in some cases, the team suspects that the original design plan was flawed and may not prove to be as usable as everyone thought. Rather than completing the entire site before testing, in these cases it makes much more sense to test just that bit of the site earlier, since changing its design may affect other portions of the site.

The final step before launching or deploying the site is full-scale testing, both for functionality and usability. A dedicated team of testers equipped with an array of tools usually takes on the functionality testing. At this time, they check to make sure everything is working as it should on all the specified user platforms, operating systems, and browsers. They check for broken links and missing pages, graphics or media that load too slowly or not at all, and anything else that may affect how well the site performs from a technical standpoint.

Usability, however, is far too subjective to rely on other members of the Web team to test. To properly test usability, it is necessary to bring in representative users to observe how easily they can accomplish tasks such as finding information or placing orders on the site.

Tip

Even testing with just three to five members of the target audience is a worthwhile step to take at each one of these points along the development lifecycle.

I lied when I said this was the final step. The very final step is actually making the necessary revisions prompted by the results of the tests and then retesting those sections to ensure that they work properly.

Deployment Phase

Launching the Web site—that's a time for the whole Web team to celebrate and then slip off for some rest and recreation before moving on to the next project. Except, of course, for the users, who now have the biggest opportunity for user involvement of all: actually using the live Web site to accomplish whatever tasks they want. In many ways, this is an extended and far more informative usability test.

Maintenance and Updating Phase

The maintenance and updating of a Web site involves several members of the Web team, including the users, and is often quite a bit more complex than people give it credit for. Or at least it is if it is done properly!

Updating a site is not nearly as straightforward as implementing the design plan and involves quite a bit of decision making, including determining what to update and how to integrate additions within the existing design.

Of primary importance is inviting user feedback—and listening to it. Ideally, some mechanism for inviting the feedback should be built into the site design from the beginning, such as online feedback links and forms. Also, technical support teams should be given instructions and a process for recording usability issues reported to them by users. Non–Web-based information gathering is also important, since it may be the only means to solicit information from users that the Web site is *not* serving well.

Many of the requests for adding or changing information on the site will come from company employees as a business changes, whether change takes the form of new product lines, special promotions, or news releases. Some of this can be anticipated and a place for such changes incorporated into the overall design. For example, if a retail store always offers a seasonal special, you can build in a place on the home page for the rotating special. Similarly, a lot of sites have a News or Press Release section in anticipation of semiregular updates.

Of course, certain big events such as mergers almost always come as surprises and are nearly impossible to plan for in advance. They are often on such a scale, though, that they may require short-term modifications to a site to provide enough time for an entirely new Web site design to be conceived and implemented.

Caution

Be wary of what I call *sludge creep*, where a client keeps adding more and more material to a site without integrating it into the design or considering whether or not this will be valuable material for the users. These sites tend to become less and less usable as they get bogged down with stuff.

Rediscovery Phase

There's a very fine line between launching a Web site and beginning the design process for its next revision. In many cases, these stages completely overlap, and you may find yourself taking notes on what you might be able to do with version two while you are still designing version one. It is not uncommon, in fact, for a budget, a schedule, or the existing technology to impose limits on the first version of a Web site design. You can use your ideas for an even better Web site, however, to lobby for the necessary budget or schedule to implement your ideas in the next version. Also, we can see the technological changes coming to some degree, so it's always a good idea to be thinking about what you could do with a site once that technology becomes available and adopted by the site's user base.

If you know, for example, that the majority of your users will be using an upcoming version of Internet Explorer or Netscape by the end of your deployment period, then you can plan a site that takes better advantage of the Cascading Style Sheets features supported by those browsers to be launched at that time. All of this is premised upon the assumption, of course, that those features will better serve your users than the existing site features. User needs first, applicable technologies second.

Think of this rediscovery phase, then, as overlapping all of the other phases of Web site design. It is a natural outcome of keeping those usability spectacles handy and seeing the Web afresh from other perspectives. Don't let yourself get too bogged down with the details of getting a site produced and launched. There's another version due around the corner, and now is always the best time to start envisioning it.

6

1-Minute Drill

● What are the six phases of the Web design process?

● What occurs during the deployment phase, and how can the user be involved?

Common Mistakes in a User-Centric Design Process

By opening up the design process to more user involvement, you also risk making a few additional mistakes. (As if there aren't enough possible mistakes to make anyway!) Here are a few of them and some suggestions on how to avoid them.

Relying on Too Narrow a Group of Users

Relying on too narrow a group of users is a cardinal mistake that can badly skew your usability results. You may invite 100 users to review a prototype of a kidsware site, but if they are all parents then you won't have an accurate assessment of how well the site works for a kid. Think proportional representation here. If 40 percent of your target audience are parents, 40 percent kids under age 12, and 20 percent potential investors, then hold to those percentages in selecting users to help with the various phases of design and development.

In a focus group or a brainstorming session, for example, invite two parents, two kids, and one potential investor; or four, four, and two; or eight, eight, and four; etc.

Relying on Too Few Users

Individuals do tend to have personalities and quirks, don't they? If allowed too large a presence during the design process, these traits can skew your results as well. In order to nullify any such quirks and get a more even representation of

---

● Planning, design, development, deployment, maintenance and updating, and rediscovery
● The Web site is launched during the deployment phase, and the users now have the biggest opportunity for user involvement of all: actually using the live Web site to accomplish whatever tasks they want.

your defined users groups, it's necessary to keep drawing from a pool of users for different phases of the design process. Don't use the same four parents, for example, in the focus group, the first brainstorming session, and the review of the comps phases.

It can be okay for individuals to participate in more than one phase, but typically only if the total number of users involved is quite high. It is not uncommon for users involved in the early stages to be asked back for the final usability testing, which involves many more total users. This way their unique influence is diluted.

Not Doing Enough Usability Spot-Testing

Quite a few Web teams do usability testing only at the end of the development phase along with all the technical testing. By this point in the project, they've generally spent all the time and money allotted for development, however, so if they discover a critical usability issue, they may not have the resources to correct it.

6

As I've said before, it always takes more resources to correct something after it's been developed than to get it right the first time.

Allowing Too Much User Influence in Specialized Areas

This comes up most frequently within the design phase. Lots of people like to be involved in creating the look and feel of a Web site, and unfortunately lots of them think they know more than they do. This problem extends beyond user involvement to other members of the Web team as well as client involvement.

You need to maintain a fine balance between listening to their feedback and inviting too much participation. It can be helpful, for example, for a user to point out that he or she doesn't understand what an icon represents. It's not always as helpful though if the user recommends a different illustration style or color scheme. There are always exceptions, of course, based on any given user's talents, but in general trust your designers to do their job.

Alienating or Intimidating Users

Most users are not as intimately familiar with the medium of the Web or the process of creating Web sites as the other members of the Web team. It can be remarkably easy to alienate or intimidate them by offhand comments, the use of jargon that they don't understand, or any criticism either spoken or implied.

Even though they may be surrounded by people whom they consider experts, it can be necessary to reassure them that they are an invaluable asset to the team and that they bring a fresh perspective that you are interested in hearing.

Project 6-1: Practice a Web Planning Session

I can't overemphasize the importance of learning brainstorming techniques, or improving upon whatever brainstorming skills you already have. Even IDEO admits that there's room for improvement within their ranks, and they're pretty diehard brainstormers. They've even launched a research project recently to look for new approaches and variations. (Just think, they're probably hosting a brainstorming session on new ways to brainstorm at this moment.)

So use this activity to practice brainstorming within the context of Web design. If you have any friends or colleagues who would like to participate with you, all the better. If not, solo work will be fine, too.

Step-by-Step

1. Pick one of the following Web challenges to focus on during your planning session:

- Helping users find names for their adopted pets from the human society
- Helping overwhelmed users decide among an array of high-bandwidth Internet access options
- Helping exhausted, stressed-out caregivers for Alzheimer patients connect and share information among themselves

2. Analyze your choice in terms of components and write a few questions about it that may help redirect the focus and energy during the session. If you need assistance here, review the Ask the Expert sidebar earlier in this module.

3. Choose a good environment for your brainstorming session and reserve it for a designated time—anywhere from 15 to 60 minutes for this activity will be fine. And set for yourself the goal of coming up with as many ideas as you've allowed minutes: 15 minutes would correspond to 15 ideas, etc. Be careful to ensure that you will not have any interruptions. Turn off the ringer on your phone, make sure the laundry buzzer won't go off if you're at home, and otherwise clear the decks.

4. Prepare the environment by making any tools available that you might feel like using during the session. A good supply of paper and pens are a must. Post-it notes or index cards and scotch tape can also be very helpful. Also, bring something wacky to the environment if possible that might help stimulate ideas. If designing a Web site that sells toys, for example, it wouldn't hurt to have a few of them around!

5. Write out a few playful rules for yourself and set them up in your environment. Some examples might be "Let the ideas flow," "Quantity not quality," or "Going for 100" (or 60 or 15, depending on how many minutes you have chosen).

6. Are you ready? On your mark—get set—go! See how many ideas you can come up with for solving this challenge.

Project Summary

One of the hardest things to control within a brainstorming session is self-criticism. Did you find yourself at any point thinking "Oh that is a dumb idea" and then pausing while trying to think of a "more intelligent" idea? That's the bane of brainstorming; it breaks the pace and starts to eliminate the more wild ideas that may lead to something really innovative. If you didn't experience this, then good for you!

Brainstorming is definitely a skill that improves with practice, so try to incorporate it into your life in any way that you can. Topics do not have to be limited to your professional field, such as Web design. Try brainstorming with a spouse or a parent for instance over what to have for dinner next Saturday. But watch out, you might be surprised at what ends up on your plate!

6

Module Conclusion

Involving the users in the design process can lead to a really dynamic, fulfilling experience—and much better Web sites in the end. Most Web teams find it empowering to actually interact with some of the users; it brings the focus of the site much closer to home when you know exactly who you are developing it for and how it will be useful to them.

In the upcoming modules, we will delve further into the logistics of how to design usable Web sites.

☑ Mastery Check

1. What is the underlying *modus operandi* of designing usable Web sites?

_____

_____

2. What can enable you to fine-tune a Web site during production so that by the time you launch it, it is in perfect harmony with the users' needs?

_____

_____

3. In a user-centric design process, what role do the users play in relation to the Web team?

_____

_____

4. Which of the following is the correct definition for a "Web team composite" in terms of a user-centric design process?

   A. An individual who manages all aspects of Web design and production

   B. A team composed of a designer, a developer, and a project manager

   C. A team that includes members who represent the creative, technical, and usability perspectives

   D. A team hired by a client to implement its design

5. What is the client's role in a user-centric Web design process?

_____

_____

6. In general, to serve the best interests of the client, do you need to create a site that gives preeminence to the client's ideas for a Web site or those of the client's target audience?

_____

_____

☑ *Mastery Check*

7. Which phase of the Web development process is fairly unique to the Web industry and why?

_____

_____

8. Which of the following decisions need to be made during the planning phase?

   A. What will the look and feel of the site be?

   B. What purpose will the Web site serve?

   C. What technologies will be employed on the Web site?

   D. Who will execute which portions of the design?

9. What two things can you do to best ensure the success of a brainstorming planning session?

_____

_____

10. Which of the following is an appropriate level of user involvement during the design phase?

   A. To sketch out ideas for the designers to implement.

   B. To select the color scheme.

   C. To provide feedback as to whether or not the comps will work for them.

6

Module 7

Site Design, First Steps: Getting Users to Your Site

The Goals of This Module

- Understand how to facilitate getting users to your site
- Recognize the importance of domain names and URLs
- Identify ways to make your Web site findable
- Distinguish between core and supplemental content
- Practice determining appropriate core and supplemental content for a Web site

What's the first thing you do when you want to go to a particular Web site? Typically, people will launch a browser and type in the URL if they know it. If they don't, they begin a search, either based on what they think the company name or URL is or based on the content they are looking for.

This module will look at what you need to do to facilitate that process of getting users to your site. There really are only two aspects that you need to deal with in such a task: the logistics of it, such as having an appropriate domain name and listing it with search engines; and the meatier challenge of providing the right content in the first place to attract them. No matter how neatly you pave the way for visitors, if you don't have content they are interested in, you're not going to be able to lure them to, or keep them at, your site.

The Logistics of Getting Users to Your Site

The logistics side of getting users to your site is relatively simple. There are three things that you need to do:

- Choose appropriate domain names and URLs.

- Make your Web site findable.

- Implement a promotional plan beyond your Web site.

Choose Appropriate Domain Names and URLs

Do you remember the URLs mentioned in Module 2 for the learning style assessments? Let's see—if I recall correctly, they were

- Richard M. Felder's Index of Learning Styles at http://www2.ncsu.edu/unity/lockers/users/f/felder/public/ILSdir/ilsweb.html

- Canfield's Learning Style Inventory at http://www.tecweb.org/styles/stylesframe.html

- Howard Gardner's Multiple Intelligence Inventory at http://surfaquarium.com/MIinvent.htm

I have to admit I cheated there. There's no way I can remember those URLs. Every time I want to refer to them, I have to look them up. I didn't even retype them here; I copied and pasted them. The chances of introducing errors by retyping cumbersome URLs such as these seemed too great. These URLs do very little to facilitate users getting to the learning style assessments. Only the last one, in fact, conveys any clues within the URL about the content, although it abbreviates it in a rather unorthodox fashion: "Multiple Intelligence Inventory" becomes "MIinvent." It makes sense after you see it, but it would be next to impossible to guess that's how it would be abbreviated while trying to look for it.

On the other hand, can you list the URLs for three search engines from memory? How about http://www.yahoo.com, http://www.google.com, and http://www.excite.com for starters? Easy to remember, easy to type, and hundreds of thousands of visitors find them with relative ease. My only criticism is that the names don't give any clues at all to the fact that they have anything to do with search engines. These sites rely entirely on name recognition. Fortunately, they chose very easy domain names to remember.

Ask the Expert

Question: What's the difference between a "URL" and a "domain name"?

Answer: Domain names are the part of the URL (Uniform Resource Locator or Web address) that people most often refer to when they talk about a site: yahoo.com, google.com, and excite.com are all domain names. Their full URLs include the "http://" prefix and often include "www." So http://www.google.com is an example of a URL.

Additionally, subsections of the site *typically* follow the domain name portion of a URL, so to direct someone to the jobs sections of google.com, you would give them the URL http://www.google.com/jobs.

Question: Why is it that I sometimes, but not always, see "www" included in URLs ?

Answer: The "www" was originally used to designate the World Wide Web portion of the Internet, but it's not essential to include the actual letters nowadays. In fact, a number of the larger sites use that space to designate what are in effect subsections of a site, so they have in a sense inverted the hierarchy. This is why I mentioned that subsections only *typically* follow the domain name. For example, to go to the movies section of yahoo.com, you need to go to http://movies.yahoo.com, not http://www.yahoo.com/movies as you would expect.

7

> To see any additional pages within that section, however, the old pattern resumes, and the URL places the remaining path information after the domain name. To find out more about the movie *Lord of the Rings*, for instance, you would go to http://movies.yahoo.com/shop?d=hv&cf=info&id=1800362180.
>
> That last section of the URL is by no means easy to memorize or type in, which is a typical problem of URLs that are dynamically generated. Yahoo.com relies on users clicking the link labeled by the movie name, in this case "Lord of the Rings," instead of needing to memorize it or type it in. Later in this section, we will discuss some of the other problems this kind of autogenerated URL can pose.

One more set of mind puzzles for you: What do you suppose are the correct domain names for the following businesses? Can you identify what the challenges are that make choosing the domain names difficult?

● AT&T, the telecommunications company

● Barnes & Noble, the booksellers

● The Better Business Bureau

● Macy's, the department store

● Consumer Reports, product review guide

Table 7-1 lists these businesses, what their challenges were in selecting a domain name, what their solutions or current domain names are at the time of this writing, and some domain names that you might have guessed would be the correct ones, but that aren't.

There are a few simple and easy-to-follow guidelines for choosing appropriate domain names and URLs.

Creating Good Domain Names

If you are starting with an existing business name that you need to find an appropriate domain name for, you may find some of your options are limited and you'll need to pick and choose from the following tips. If starting completely

Business Name	Challenge in Selecting a Domain Name	Current Domain Names	Nonfunctional Domain Names
AT&T	•Use of a nonstandard character, in this case an ampersand	att.com	at&t.com—You can't use ampersands in a domain name. atandt.com—This domain exists, but it directs users to the AT&T Shop or eBay, not to the main AT&T site, oddly enough.
Barnes & Noble	•Multiple words •Use of a nonstandard character, in this case an ampersand •The last word is easily misspelled as Nobles, Nobel, or Nobels	bn.com barnesandnoble.com barnesandnobel.com barnesnoble.com	barnes&noble.com—You can't use ampersands in a domain name. barnesandnobles.com—A common misspelling. This domain directs users to information on the Barnes & Nobles Foundation, not the bookstore site. barnesandnobels.com—Another common misspelling. Currently not owned by anybody. barnes_and_noble.com barnes-and-noble.com Nothing is wrong with these two choices or the use of underscores or hyphens in domain names. Barnes & Noble just didn't choose to use them. Oddly, Barnes & Noble is aware of the common misspellings because they include them in the site's Meta tags for search engines. By not purchasing all of these alternative domain names, however, they risk someone else buying them and getting their misdirected traffic.
Better Business Bureau	•Multiple words •Length of name	bbb.org bbb.com betterbusinessbureau.com	betterbusinessbureau.org—This domain has an "Under Construction" notice on it, perhaps signifying that they plan to use it as an alias to their primary site. Additionally, they could have used hyphens or underscores but chose not to.
Macy's	•Use of punctuation, in this case an apostrophe	macys.com	macy's.com—You can't use apostrophes or other punctuation in domain names. macy.com—A common misspelling that no one currently owns.
Consumer Reports	•Multiple words •Duplicate letters at the end of one word and beginning of next. This sometimes confuses users and can lead to misspellings. •Lengthy name, which can also lead to typos	consumerreports.org consumerreports.com consumereports.com (spelled with a single "r") All of these domain names direct the user to consumerreports.org	consumereports.org (The .org variation of the most common misspelling)—Because this is a common misspelling, it would be a good idea for them to register this domain before someone else does. At least consumereports.com (single r) is owned by Consumer Reports and indeed is an alias for consumerreports.org. cr.org—This would be a simple abbreviation for Consumer Reports, but they weren't quick enough off the mark. The domain belongs to another site, the Applied Computational Research Society, which may get some of Consumer Reports' misdirected traffic. cr.com—Still available.

7

Table 7-1   Business Names with Inherent Difficulties in Selecting a Domain Name and Their Current Solutions

from scratch, though, I would use the following as a checklist. Don't settle on a name until it meets all of the following criteria.

Tip

The extensions used in domain names (.com, .gov, etc.) signify the type of Web site. Commercial ventures, for example, use .com; government sites, .gov; nonprofit organizations, .org; educational institutions, .edu; and network providers, .net. Due to the boom in the Web and the corresponding search for good domain names, new extensions are being introduced periodically. Some of the latest ones are .biz for businesses and .info for information sites. Additionally, most non-U.S. countries also have a two-letter extension: .uk for the United Kingdom, .fr for France, etc. These are generally preceded with .co to indicate country. For example, Macromedia's United Kingdom site can be found at http://www.macromedia.co.uk.

To ensure the most easily accessible sites, keep your domain names:

● **Short and simple** The fewer letters and words, the better. Yahoo.com, amazon.com, pbs.org—these are hallmarks of good domain names. Everybody can remember them.

● **Easy to say** Think about what your domain name will sound like, and avoid anything that could be easily mistaken or work as a pun. CtoC could be heard in any number of ways, including "Sea to Sea," "See 2 See," or "C2C." An unfortunate result of my company name, Hot Tea Productions, and its corresponding domain name, hottea.com, arises from the American tendency to pronounce "t"s and "d"s the same. So although it's crystal clear in print, we almost always need to spell it when we are speaking. Otherwise, people can think they hear "hoddee" or even worse "haughty"!

● **Easy to memorize** This comes much more naturally if a domain name is short and simple and easy to say, but, even so, make sure your domain name is distinct enough that it won't be easily confused with other names. Sites that begin with "e-" can be especially prone to this problem: e-biz, e-business, e-buzz... After a while, they start to all sound the same, and your users may find themselves groping: "What is the name of that site? E- something or other?"

- **Easy to type and easy to spell** You want those fingers to just magically transport the user to your site without any hitches, so practice typing our your domain name three dozen times before committing to it. If you find you are frequently inverting any of the letters, consider changing the name. Common misspellings will also commonly result in your users going off to some other site or getting an error message, something it would be best to avoid. Whenever possible, register any common misspellings and use them as aliases to direct users to your primary domain name.

- **Only use lowercase letters if possible.** Spaces and special characters such as ! @ # $ % ^ & * ( ) ? are invalid and will not be recognized, and numbers can be problematic. (See the next item.) Mixing upper- and lowercase letters can also be problematic for servers that are case sensitive, so it is best to use only lowercase.

- **Avoid numbers.** One good reason to avoid numbers is that people never know whether to spell numbers out or to use numerals. My favorite Web mail service is onebox.com; they offer all the right features and have excellent service. My only scruple with them is how frequently I have to spell out their domain name because I can't just say it. If I don't do this, someone could easily send my mail to "1box.com," and I would miss it. Also, numbers can easily be mistaken for letters and vice versa. The numeral one (1) and the letter "l" are often mistaken, as are the numeral zero (0) and the capital letter "O" Two is even worse. It can be interpreted as "two," "2," "too," or "to."

- **Avoid duplicate letters between words, if possible.** By this, I mean when one word ends with the same letter that the next word begins with, such as the duplicate of the letter "r" in Consumer Reports. You can't easily avoid this if you have an existing name, because you wouldn't want people to start misspelling the name of your company; Consume Reports would not be nearly so effective! Additionally, companies that have intentionally overlapped letters also can cause confusion. For example, if you pronounce my friend Wendy's design business you would say "Willard Designs," for example, but it's spelled willarDESIGNS. Wendy has purchased the domain names willardesigns.com and willarddesigns.com for just that reason.

- **Run in words** Generally run multiple words together and avoid using hyphens or underscores to separate the words. For example,

7

consumerreports.org instead of consumer_reports.org. I don't have any emphatically strong reasons for this recommendation; it is as much a convention of the Web as anything. Keep in mind, though, that this convention probably evolved because it is easier to type run-in names, and users can get confused in their memory over whether the words should be separated by underscores, hyphens, or dashes.

Caution

Avoid the temptation to "clarify" awkward domain names by using capital letters when you refer to them in print, such as ConsumerReports.org and BetterBusinessBureau.org. While many servers and browsers ignore the case, not all of them do and you can inadvertently cause users to form bad habits. For example, if you type in http://www.esig.ucar.edu/Whatsnew.html (with a capital "W") you will get a server error message reporting that the page can not be found. If you just use lowercase, however, it will deliver the page straight away.

- **Make names logical and guessable.** Above all, make sure your domain name is logical and guessable. Ideally, you want users to be able to reconstruct your domain name if they can't remember it.

- **Use multiple, similar domain names if you need to.** This is what some of the businesses in Table 7-1 with problematic domain name choices chose to do. The Better Business Bureau is an excellent example, with bbb.org, bbb.com, and betterbusinessbureau.com. Although it costs a bit more money to secure and retain multiple domain names, it tremendously simplifies the process of accessing the Web site for users who may be encountering the same difficulties with the business name every day. If you have to think twice about what the most appropriate domain name would be for your business, then you can be sure the users will as well.

Tip

You can now secure domain names through a number of vendors. For a complete list, see InterNIC's Accredited Registrar Directory at http://www.internic.com. For more information on the domain name registration process, also see the Network Solutions site at http://www.networksolutions.com.

Creating Good URLs for Subsections

There are two problems with subsection URLs that are dynamically generated, such as the link to information on *Lord of the Rings* at yahoo.com at http://movies.yahoo.com/shop?d=hv&cf=info&id=1800362180. One problem is that they are just plain ugly and non–user friendly. It would be very difficult to speak or type out that URL, and your chances of making a mistake are much higher than with a more word-based URL. Wouldn't http://movies.yahoo.com/lordoftherings, for instance, be much easier to handle?

The second problem is that dynamically generated URLs can use symbols that trip up search engines, particularly question marks (?) and ampersands (&). As a consequence, the contents of these pages are omitted from most search inquiries. It is possible to fix these kinds of URLs, but it takes some server-side programming expertise.

Tip

For more information on fixing the URLs for most popular e-commerce servers, see J.K. Bowman's article entitled "Dynamic Web Page Optimization" at http://spider-food.net/dynamic-page-optimization-b.html. We'll examine additional ways to facilitate users searching your site in the next section.

7

Make Your Web Site Findable

There are lots and lots of services out there that promote themselves as being able to increase the search penetration of your Web site. Between you and me, though, they can employ a lot of tricks to get people to initially come to your site, but they are not necessarily going to increase your dedicated user base. Besides, if they managed to promote everybody to the top 10 search results, the top 10 would become the top 10,000. What good will that do anybody? With a little extra time and know-how, however, you can increase how well search engines can identify the content of your site to users who are looking for that content—without having to pay an extra cent.

There are two primary activities that you need to do to make your Web site findable:

- Prepare your HTML pages for searching
- Submit your site to the search engines

Prepare Your HTML Pages for Searching

If you know HTML, you are probably already familiar with the <head> tag. This is a required tag near the beginning of each page that includes mostly hidden information that does not appear on the Web page when it is viewed by the browser. You are not required to have anything at all within this tag, but if you want to make your site easily searchable by search engines, then you need to take advantage of two opportunities that are available to you within that space:

- **Give every page a good title using the <title> tag.** This is the text that appears at the very top of the browser along with the name of the browser when users view your Web site. It is also, however, one of the first things that the search engines review and index. Be sure to include words that reflect the content of that page. For example, "Page One" does not convey nearly so much helpful information as "Consumer Reports Auto Preview 2002."

- **Include a description and list of keywords used in your site by using the <meta> tag.** Use clear language, preferably in sentence form, for the description, since this is the text that users will see in the search reports. Typically, they should see a sentence or two, running from around 20 words to as many as 50. Also, create a list of the keywords people may use to search for the content of your site. Prioritize them and include the most important ones first, since some engines will index only the first few.

Tip

A good starting point for learning HTML, including coding the tags we are discussing in this section, is *HTML: A Beginner's Guide* by Wendy Willard (McGraw-Hill/Osborne, 2001).

An example of good header information from the Conscience Records site (http://www.conscience.com) is

```
<head>
<title>[conscience records]</title>

<meta name="description" content="Conscience Records - Conscience was
founded in 1995 to help new and established artists create high-quality
records, and to provide a dedicated staff and the business infrastructure
```

```
necessary to produce, market, promote and distribute those records. To date,
Conscience has released albums from five artists: Powerman 5000, Grind, and
El Dopa, Acumen Nation, and Mocean Worker, and is currently in negotiation
with other talented artists to join the roster in the near future." />

<meta name="keywords" content="Conscience records music independent label
industrial metal electronica drum and bass jungle hardcore animation edge
sound artists art evil real audio live audio brain spinning el dopa powerman
5000 grind acumen nation mocean worker enno vandermeer jen kriesel eric
bohnenstiel auriea harvey" />

</head>
```

In addition to preparing the information within the header of each HTML document, the actual content of your Web pages can increase its ranking in the eye of a search engine. So don't be bashful about repeating your keywords in section heads or other prominent places. On the other hand, don't go overboard. Search engines also look for excessive repetition and consider it spamming. Generally speaking, if you're honest about the use of keywords on your pages, you'll be fine. Just don't try to trick a search engine into thinking you're something you're not, as it may backfire on you.

Submit Your Site to the Search Engines

You could spend the better part of a lifetime tracking down and submitting your site to every single Web search engine and directory that exists. Or you could strategize and submit it to a handful of sites that have the lion's share of user requests. Paul Boutin narrows it down even further in an article on webmonkey.com. He says, "The Yahoo directory accounts for half the traffic referred to most sites. So get your site listed on Yahoo, and your traffic can literally double overnight. Beyond that, most search engine traffic comes from two places: Google and Inktomi."

Keep a close eye on google.com. It has been increasing its base very quickly. For example, according to Jakob Nielsen on useit.com, Google went from being the number six search engine in 1999 to a clear winner in 2001. As of April 2001, Google accounted for 46 percent of all search referrals to the useit.com site.

This does not mean that you should completely ignore all the other search engines, but focus first on the ones that will get you the most traffic. For the others, you may want to implement a "blanket strategy," as Boutin calls it. For example, you might choose to pay a small fee to have a service submit your site

7

to the others. For a fee of $59/year, for example, submitit.com will submit your site to your choice of up to 400 search engines and directories. Alternatively, you can submit your site yourself to the sites you feel it's worth the time and effort for.

This is just the tip of the iceberg. Here are a few resources for further investigation:

- For more information in general on how to make your Web site more search-engine friendly, see Paul Boutin's seven-page article "Search Engine Optimization FREE!" at http://hotwired.lycos.com/webmonkey/01/23/index1a.html.

- For information on improving your site's ranking or other details about how search engines work, see http://www.searchenginewatch.com.

- See Jakob Nielsen's site at http://www.useit.com/about/searchreferrals.html for a list of some of the smaller search engines if you'd like to submit your site to them directly.

Implement a Promotional Plan Beyond Your Web Site

Launching your Web site and getting it listed in the major directories and indexed in the search engines can be very effective at getting Web users to visit your site. But don't forget all those other potential users. It can be very helpful to implement a promotional plan for media other than the Web. The first step, for example, is to include the URL on all other print publications and marketing collateral that the company or organization is already producing.

Sometimes it takes a more concerted effort, though, to inform your potential users that your Web site exists and in what way(s) it could be useful to them. You've probably noticed an increasing amount of print and television advertising promoting Web sites over the past couple of years. It takes a big budget to fund this kind of marketing plan, but it is definitely an effective route to take. Flyers and brochures are another option.

Consider, too, all of the Web users who may not think to look for your site, especially if you are providing a service that has not typically been offered on the Web yet. Although placing banner ads on other sites is of questionable value, in some cases they have been effective. Certainly coordinating reciprocal links with related Web sites or industry organizations can help alert users that your site exists.

Tip

It's a good idea to ask a site's owner before adding a link to it from your Web site. For one, it's common courtesy. For another, it's a good opportunity to ask them to place a reciprocal link to your Web site on theirs. In some cases, sites will ask you to pay a fee to become a member of their organization before including a link to your site.

In a few cases, sites will pay you to link to them. Amazon.com, for example, got a head start in the Internet business by launching an affiliate's program in which referring sites got a percentage of the cost of books bought by the individuals that clicked through to amazon.com from their site.

Chances are you'd like to secure repeat traffic as well. Just having visitors come once and then never return usually doesn't support site goals such as building a dedicated user base. You should plan ways of encouraging return visits as well in your promotional plan. These can cover a wide range of options, from predictably offering new content, such as news sites do on a daily or even hourly basis, to one-time events or special promotions.

This takes us directly to the crux of the matter. To get users to come to your site repeatedly, you need to offer them the content that they need.

7

1-Minute Drill

● What are the three logistical tactics that you need to take to get users to your Web site?

● What are the two things you can do with Meta tags?

● Choose appropriate domain names and URLs, make your Web site findable, and implement a promotional plan beyond your Web site
● Give a description of your Web site and include a list of keywords

The Crux of Getting Users to Your Site: Provide the Content the User Needs

It may sound obvious that if you want to attract users to your site to buy books, then you need to have a selection of books available online for them to buy. But the task of providing the content that the user needs is typically a little more complicated than that. What information about the books, for example, do users need in order to decide which book to buy? Do they need to see images of the cover? What about sample pages or tables of contents? Author biographies? What kind of mechanism for actually purchasing the books do users need? Will they want to pay by cash, check, credit card, or even barter?

In deciding exactly what content your Web site needs to provide, it can be helpful to break it down into the two primary kinds of content and to examine each in light of the site goals:

- Core content

- Supplemental content

Tip

For our purposes, I am using the terms *core* and *supplemental* content to distinguish between the roles that the content plays within the Web site. The core content is the information or material that the users may seek, and the supplemental content is all the Web paraphernalia that is needed to support those efforts, such as navigation bars.

Core Content

The core content provided by a site should tie in directly to the site goals and should be established during the planning stages of the site design process. The primary goals of e-commerce sites can be the easiest to determine the core content for, since they are generally encouraging the purchase of goods or services. An adequate description of those goods or services then tops the list of the core content that needs to be provided for the user. A site whose purpose is to sell books, for example, must provide a description of the books.

On the other hand, consider a typical marketing site. A site goal may read something like "Establish XYZ Corporation as a responsible company that is vested in the community." What content should be provided is not as clear at first glance. A goal like this would require you to dig deeper to find out exactly how XYZ is (1) responsible and (2) vested in the community. You may discover, for example, that XYZ responded immediately to a devastating hurricane in the area by donating the use of inflatable rafts to the rescue efforts and then followed up by helping the residents relocate to temporary housing. This may then become some of the core content that needs to be included in the site.

But there's a problem with emphasizing information like that as the primary content of a Web site. No matter how generous or beneficial such services may be, over-promoting anything that has been done in the past can seem to be self-aggrandizing and thus work against the site goal. It's also not user-centered. That may be the information the company thinks it wants to get out to the public, but what might provide more convincing primary content would be something that would be of immediate use to the community. Perhaps this company could offer an ongoing relocation or job service through the Web. That immediate service could form the initial impression, which could then be supported by additional information on other contributions to the community that XYZ had made.

Of course, most sites have multiple site goals that require several layers of content. It can be helpful to rank the core content in terms of importance, using such terms as primary, secondary, tertiary, and so on, that may later help you establish the structure of the site. In the XYZ example, the relocation and job service would be considered the primary content, and the background information on their involvement in the aftermath of the hurricane would be secondary.

Don't limit your thoughts just to text content either. It's necessary to determine what's appropriate in terms of other media as well, including graphics, audio, video, animation, etc. This step also requires that you consider the user's hardware and software limitations and to decide whether it might be necessary to provide different versions of the media for different bandwidths.

7

Project 7-1: Determine Some of the Core Content for a Web Site

Try your hand at determining some of the core content for a site whose primary goal is to sell books and books-on-tape. Remember, for our purposes here, the core content is the material that users may be looking for, not the supplemental Web content such as navigation bars that will facilitate that process for them.

Step-by-Step

1. Consider the following primary Web site goal: "To increase sales through the Web of our books and books-on-tape from our two major product lines: Science Fiction and Science & Technology."

2. Write down all of the core content that you think will be necessary to provide on the Web site. Approach this from a user perspective. If you were interested in buying such books or tapes, what would you want to have available to you? Include what media other than text you would like to have included on the site as well.

3. Rank your list of contents in terms of priority: primary, secondary, tertiary, etc.

4. Compare your notes with some existing Web sites, such as the following:

   ● Amazon.com (http://www.amazon.com)

   ● Barnes & Noble (http://bn.com)

   ● Books on Tape (http://www.booksontape.com)

   ● InformIt.com (http://www.informit.com)

Project Summary

Amazon.com takes the cake for being one of the first sites to really probe the depths of what kind of content could be provided to users via the Web to help them make decisions about buying books. They started with the retail model of including book covers, text from the book jackets, sample text from the books in some cases, and then added a whole slew of options for getting other people's opinions.

They recognized the very important role that "word of mouth" plays in such decisions in the real world, even though that was not catered to within traditional retail establishments. Even more importantly, they recognized that they could facilitate the gaining of that information through the Web in a way that could not be easily done in the traditional bookstore. In addition to providing full editorial reviews from their own staff as well as the publishing houses, they also provide a venue for readers to share their opinions about books and to rank each other's opinions. Oh, and they provide their own sales ranking, based on purchases made through their site and numerous kinds of cross-referrals and services such as wish lists and lots of personalization features.

When they expanded beyond selling books, however, they did not always think as far afield. In the case of selling books-on-tape or even music CDs, for example, they only rarely take the obvious step of providing audio clips for the users. Generally, the only form of media they provide in addition to text is the jacket, in a thumbnail and enlarged versions. As a user, I would find lots more audio clips much more beneficial.

There are, of course, some good reasons that may be influencing the decision not to provide audio clips, but for the most part they have to do with production costs, not usability or user preferences.

Most of the other book Web sites have emulated amazon.com's model and offer many of the same features and content. The Books on Tape site does offer audio samples, but only for a few of their tapes. At the time of this writing, they offered 50 audio samples out of approximately 2000 books-on-tape.

Supplemental Content

The supplemental content supports the core content and site goals. Navigation bars and menus are a common example. Users are often not even conscious of this material or would not include it if you asked them to describe the contents of a site. When it comes to creating the Web site, however, it is rather essential to include this kind of material on your content list. If someone on your Web team doesn't produce it, you will be in quite a pickle when it comes to creating a usable Web site!

Tip

We will be covering the information architecture and navigation design each in their own module, since they are so important. These will be in Modules 8 and 9.

Additionally, there is a fair bit of supplemental content that is necessary to provide the underpinnings of a usable Web site. For example, an inherent subset of the goal to sell books, or to sell *anything* via the Web, is to secure the trust of the user. The lack of trust was one of the biggest obstacles to e-commerce taking off on the Web, and there are still many people who profess they will not buy anything over the Web.

In part, this is a result of their distrust of computers and Web technology, but to an equal degree it can be a distrust of the company just because they are interfacing with it through a Web site. Web sites can come and go very quickly, can be hosted anywhere in the world, and could potentially dodge their legal responsibilities more easily than businesses with a fixed address on Main Street, where the customers can go knock on its door if there's a problem. Ironically, however, many of the same individuals appear to feel comfortable in giving out their credit card information over the phone, which can be just as susceptible to credit card fraud.

In addition to the site navigation, which will have its own module, there are three areas that frequently require the development of supplemental content. They are

- Securing user trust

- Securing your own or your client's protection

- Producing advertising revenue

Secure User Trust

To help secure the user's trust, provide the following supplemental content:

- **Context of the material provided on the site** To validate the information available on your site, provide such information as the date it was last updated, authorship, and sources—right on the page that holds the information. You might be surprised by how many sites neglect to do this. To validate the Web site as a whole, provide information about the company or organization that's behind it. Answering the questions who, what, where, when, and how can be a great way to start. Just communicating with the users that this is a real business, with real people and real history, can do wonders for establishing trust.

- **Contact info beyond the Web** This is actually a subset of providing context, but it's so important that it deserves a bullet point unto itself.

There's no better way to ensure a business is legitimate than revealing its physical address and phone number. If people know where they could go to knock on its door if there's a problem, they are much more likely to enter into a business arrangement with it.

- **Privacy statements**   This is a huge (and legitimate) concern about the Web. The databases behind many Web sites are practically inhaling our personal information—including names, addresses, phone numbers, social security numbers, credit card numbers, number and kinds of pets, favorite restaurants…. You name it and there's a database out there with an empty field waiting for that bit of information so that somebody can sell it to someone else. Web users want to know what you plan to do with the information that you may be asking them to give you, so by all means let them know. Preferably also instigate a reasonable privacy policy!

- **Security notices**   Along the same lines as privacy, inform the users of what technical security measures your site employs to ensure the safety of the information, such as credit card numbers, that you are asking them to share with you.

7

Tip

A highly usable and well-designed Web site also automatically engenders trust. That's an added benefit to all your hard work!

Secure Your Own or Your Client's Protection

The flip side of the coin for securing user trust is to secure your own or your client's protection from abuse by your users.

- **Copyright and terms of use notices**   If you do not wish any of the contents of your Web site to be copied and used in other commercial applications it's in your best interest to include a copyright notice. This can apply to individual graphic images or other media files as well as just text. Most Web sites these days include a blanket copyright notice for their entire Web site. Terms of use notices can also specify under what conditions portions of the Web site can or cannot be used.

● **Disclaimers**   Additionally, provide disclaimers for anything that you don't want to be held liable for. If your site provides advice on dealing with psychological trauma, for instance, it is probably best to make it clear that you are offering advice on a general basis, but that individuals should consult with their doctor to ensure the best treatment for their individual cases.

Produce Advertising Revenue for the Site

You're probably more familiar with ad banners than you care to be. Many people find them annoying or irritating (especially the ones with repeating animations) and will scroll up and down pages trying to get them off the screen. If that's not possible, many users will cover the ad on-screen with the palm of their hand while they examine the rest of the Web site.

Not all ad banners are evil, though, and in many cases they are the only source of revenue for great sites that provide a free service to their users. The trick is to try to make the ads useful to your users as well. I'd recommend, for example, keeping editorial and aesthetic control over the ads that you agree to publish on your Web site. You can establish guidelines, for example, that specify animations should run no more than two times within any five-minute period, just as you provide the dimensions to fit in a consistent space on your Web page. And you can solicit advertising from companies or organizations that can offer something related to the content of your Web site.

Caution

Be sure to keep the distinction between your core content and any advertising absolutely clear. If the purpose of your site is to provide unbiased information but the users form the mistaken impression that "you" are trying to sell them something, it will undermine the credibility of your whole site.

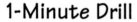

1-Minute Drill

● What is the difference between core content and supplemental content?

● What measures can you take to protect you or your client on a Web site?

● The core content is the information or material that the users may seek, and the supplemental content is all the Web paraphernalia that is needed to support those efforts, such as navigation bars.
● Provide copyright and terms of use notices and disclaimers.

Project 7-2: Determine Some Supplemental Content for a Web Site

Following through with the books and books-on-tape Web site from Project 7-1, determine some of the supplemental content needed for the Web site.

Step-by-Step

1. Review Project 7-1, if necessary, to recall the details of the books and books-on-tape Web site.

2. List all of the supplemental content that you can think of that will need to be developed to support the site's primary goal of selling books and books-on-tape. Focus on the ways of securing user trust and securing your client's protection. Even though we have not discussed the navigational elements in detail yet, jot down some notes on what kinds of navigation would be most useful to the user.

3. Compare your notes with the same Web sites as before, and look closely at the actual content they provide for these purposes. Which ones do you think are most reassuring to you as a user? Also note whether or not you had to hunt to find this information:

- Amazon.com (http://www.amazon.com)
- Barnes & Noble (http://bn.com)
- Books on Tape (http://www.booksontape.com)
- InformIt.com (http://www.informit.com)

4. Add some notes regarding these examples of supplemental content to your Web Site Library.

Project Summary

As you've probably discovered, most of the supplemental content that we discussed earlier in this module is fairly standard practice for a lot of Web sites. There can be some significant differences in the fine print, however. Even the length of the legal-type documents can vary considerably.

Note, too, how the links to most of these documents are in very small print at the bottom of the pages. Most users do not actually read these documents, but I think a lot of them derive comfort or a sense of security from just knowing they are there.

In terms of navigation, you may have noticed that the sites use a number of different tools to facilitate the users' movement through the Web sites. These

7

range from navigation bars and menus by one kind of category (such as best sellers or new releases), to a drop-down selection by more specific topic categories (such as architecture or business), and a heavy reliance on search engines. Interestingly enough, none of these sites really take advantage of site maps.

Tip

See Appendix D for a checklist regarding Web site content.

Module Conclusion

At least half the task of getting users to your site and keeping them there, or encouraging return visits, is dependent on offering them the content that they are looking for, so take care in determining that content. The second half of the equation, of course, is designing a site that can facilitate access to that content.

With the preview on navigational elements in the last project, you ought to be primed for our next two modules. They focus on helping users find the content that they're looking for. Module 8 explores how to organize the content of your Web site and create its information architecture, and Module 9 shows how to design the navigation for your Web site around that architecture.

☑ *Mastery Check*

1. Which of the following are techniques for creating good domain names? (You may select more than one.)

   A) Make them easy to say

   B) Make them easy to type

   C) Avoid using numbers in them

   D) Run the words in together

   E) All of the above

2. Which of the following are domain names and which are URLs?

   A) hottea.com

   B) http://bn.com

   C) http://go.yahoo.com

   D) excite.com

3. Why should you generally avoid using the number 2 in your domain name?

   _____

   _____

4. Above all, what is the most important thing to do in selecting a domain name?

   _____

   _____

5. What two tags can you use within the <head> tag to make your Web pages findable?

   A) <title>

   B) <description>

   C) <meta>

   D) <list>

   E) <search>

7

☑ Mastery Check

6. What can you do with each of the two correct tags to question #5?

_____

_____

7. What roles do the core and supplemental content fulfill on a Web site?

_____

_____

8. True or False: The core content provided by a site should tie in directly to the site goals and should be established during the planning stages of the site design process.

9. True or False: The media other than text to be included on a Web site are considered part of the supplemental content.

10. Which of the following can be accomplished through the use of supplemental content? (You may choose more than one.)

A) Provide a means of navigating the site

B) Provide information that the user is looking for

C) Provide a sense of security for the user

D) Produce advertising revenue

E) Produce a community of users

Module 8

Information Architecture: Organizing Your Web Site

The Goals of This Module

- Understand how to organize Web site information from the users' point of view

- Identify the classification systems available to you for organizing information for a Web site

- Determine how to present the information architecture on the Web site

- Determine how to choose appropriate labels and metaphors

- Implement guidelines for establishing the depth and breadth of Web sites

- Practice organizing content for a Web site

Once you've figured out what content to include on a Web site, all you need to do is create an attractive interface and start programming, right? Wrong. Although many Web sites have been built that way, it is certainly not the most reliable way to create a successful site. In fact, if you were to use that approach in cooking, it would be like gathering the ingredients needed for all the dishes from appetizers to dessert, dumping them into a big pot, and then serving it on beautiful plates. The results might provide the necessary nutrients for sustenance, but you're certainly not going to have many satisfied customers, or get many return visitors!

Deciding on what content your users would like is only one of a number of important steps toward creating a solid, usable Web site. The next step is to decide how to organize it, or, to follow through with our cooking metaphor, what dishes each ingredient will go into to create the tastiest meal possible. Unlike most cooking situations, however, where you begin with a menu and then select the ingredients, most Web sites begin with identifying the contents or ingredients first, rather like assessing what is in your refrigerator. Then it's your job as the master chef to create a delectable meal out of those contents. The key is to create a harmonious array of dishes that complement each other.

Keeping the goal of following a user-centric design process in mind, there are two stages within this process as well. It is necessary to

- Organize the information from the users' point of view.

- Determine how to best present those clusters of information on the Web site for your particular users, such as choosing the best labels to go in a navigation bar.

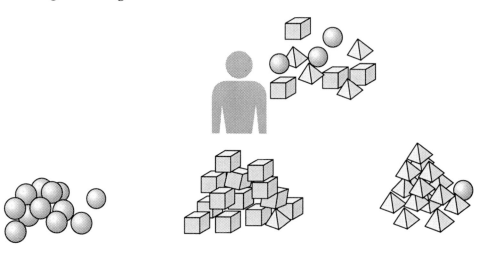

Organize Information from the Users' Point of View

Some of the earliest tasks we tend to give young children are sorting tasks. Providing a box full of cubes, pyramids, spheres, and donut-shaped toys, we encourage them to sort the objects into piles based on shape. With a stack of brightly colored cards, we encourage them to sort by color: put all the blues together, all the reds together, etc.

For the most part with these tasks, we operate under the assumption that there is one right answer to each challenge. Unfortunately, that simplicity goes away very early on. The minute you introduce color to the different-shaped toys, for instance, you introduce two competing organizational systems: Is it better to group together all the cubes, regardless of color? Or to group all the blue toys together, regardless of shape? And that term "better" is, of course, subjective. Both classification systems can be perfectly correct, but determining which one is "better" depends entirely upon what function the groups are supposed to serve.

In Web site design, that translates to basing your decisions on how the Web site will be used. Once again, the user reigns supreme. It does no good to group all the toys on a Web site by color if your audience is going to be looking for them by brand. And vice versa.

8

?Ask the Expert

Question: How do you decide on an organizational structure for groups of users that may want different structures?

Answer: In Web site design, you often need to provide multiple solutions for multiple users. It may be, for instance, that little six-year-old Sue Jolie is determined to fill her traditional doll's house with bright yellow creatures and toys, so she would want to see all the yellow toys on a site. Old Uncle Derek, however, may want to buy a new Lego set every year for his niece's birthday, so he would want to be able to search for the Lego brand.

To accommodate both users, you would need to provide both color-based and brand-based organizational systems.

Question: Do I need to accommodate every user's favorite organizational style?

Answer: No. In fact, it is impossible to cater to every single user's organizational preferences without cluttering up your user interface with so many options that it becomes confusing to everybody. It is generally best to identify the two or three systems that users most want or need. Oftentimes, this takes the form of a clear navigation bar, a search function, and a site map.

In the case of the toy site, for example, it may be unlikely that a significant proportion of toy shoppers would want to search for toys by color, so you may decide not to accommodate little Sue Jolie after all for this site. In the case of a site that sells embroidery thread, however, a large body of your users may indeed want to search by color as well as brand, so you may decide it is necessary to provide both options, perhaps as alternate navigation bars. One could be a list of colors: Yellow, Red, Blue, Green, and so on. The other could be a list of embroidery thread brands.

The most typical conflict in determining the best organizational system for a Web site is between a company's method of organizing information for its own purposes and how its customers would naturally look for that information. Take the toy site, for example. If you asked the head of the warehouse what is the best organizational system, he or she might well say by size, because it may work best for the warehouse staff to stack the little toys on top of the big toys. If you asked the head of the accounting department, he or she might say by cost. The production manager might say by materials or quantities, etc. Every department has its own structure based on its particular needs. The public Web site, however, is not being built to meet those needs; it is being built to meet the needs of its users, the customers who may be interested in buying a specific toy for a specific person.

Rather than espousing any of the staff's organization systems, customers would probably be more interested in having the toys organized by appropriate age range, brand, type of toy, or price. They may be interested in seeing all the toys that are safe for children under five, for example, or all the toys made by Mattel, or all stuffed animals.

Very often, business managers have the most influence on the Web site's organizational scheme, and the differences between their perceptions and those of the users can be more subtle than the previous examples. Still, the differences can be substantial and should be checked against the user needs. The development of business intranet sites, for example, commonly begins with an assumption that the company's organizational chart will determine the Web site's organization. Thus, each department would have its own section, such as manufacturing, distribution, marketing, human resources, and so on. This may lead to Web sites that are easy to maintain and update because each department could be responsible for changing its own material, but it rarely provides the most useful interface for the employees. Academic sites tend to be poorly organized in this sense as well.

If you would like to schedule a meeting in a conference room, for example, would you think first "Let's see, that would be under the Operations Department's description" or "I need to schedule a meeting, where is the link to Conference Rooms or Scheduling?" The same goes for employee directories—now would that be under Operations or Human Resources? Who cares who is responsible for maintaining the information? The key really is to be able to find what you need—quickly. This is not to say that you need to eliminate all information about the departments. There may well be a need for a description and background information on what each department does and who its personnel are. That would, however, likely be of secondary importance to the tasks the employees need to carry out through the intranet site, much as the "About This Site" section of many public Web sites is of secondary importance to the users who are undertaking a task.

8

In organizing a Web site's content from the users' point of view, it can be immensely helpful to break it into two stages and then to test the results of each against each other:

● Task analysis, using such things as task-flow diagrams

● Information architecture analysis, using such things as site diagrams or flowcharts

Tip

The term "information architecture" is a fancy way of saying how information is organized. Like the traditional field of architecture, it encompasses the planning stage and focuses on establishing a sound structure. The end result is some kind of model on paper, often called a "blueprint," although it looks more like a flowchart, which can then be followed during the construction or development phase.

 ## 1-Minute Drill

● True or False: After deciding on the content, you can dive into the navigation design.

● What kinds of organization schemes could there be for a box of colored crayons that has been partly used?

● What is the most typical conflict in determining the best organizational system for a Web site?

Task Analysis

In organizing the content for a Web site, it's always a good idea to start with a user task analysis. If you are working on an e-commerce site, for example, you will want to trace the steps necessary toward buying an item. You can do this with simple flowcharting tools, like the following one created in MS Word, or you can write the steps out on Post-it notes or index cards so that you can easily shuffle them around to show various options.

● False. After deciding on the content, you must first develop the information architecture before diving into the navigation design.
● Three organizational schemes could include arranging the crayons by name, by hue following the pattern of the shades of the rainbow, or even by height, since some of the crayons have been used and are presumably of different heights.
● The most typical conflict is usually between a company's method of organizing information for its own purposes and how its customers would naturally look for that information.

Tip

In many cases, a task analysis can draw quite easily from your earlier usage scenarios if they are still consistent with the content and plan for the Web site. Remember, Web site design is an iterative process; you may feel as though you are returning to an earlier point when in fact you are progressing in a spiral-like manner.

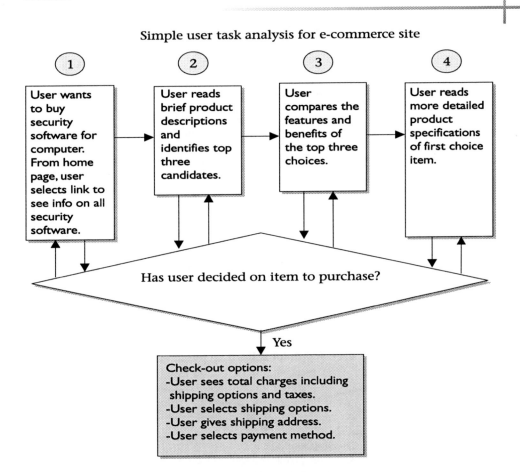

Simple user task analysis for e-commerce site

1 — User wants to buy security software for computer. From home page, user selects link to see info on all security software.

2 — User reads brief product descriptions and identifies top three candidates.

3 — User compares the features and benefits of the top three choices.

4 — User reads more detailed product specifications of first choice item.

Has user decided on item to purchase?

Yes

Check-out options:
- User sees total charges including shipping options and taxes.
- User selects shipping options.
- User gives shipping address.
- User selects payment method.

8

Finalize the task analysis by mapping each step to a definable chunk of the content that you have decided needs to be on the Web site, as in the next illustration. This stage can include a fair bit of tweaking—both of the content and of the task analysis. Using the example of the software retail site, it may be that you had included the full product specifications on your content list. When you get to the task analysis, however, you may realize that it may be better for the user if you present this information in two formats: one, a condensed version for comparative review, and the second, the full details for a more probing part of a decision-making process. Thus, your content list would need to expand to include both versions.

Simple user task analysis with content blocks for e-commerce site

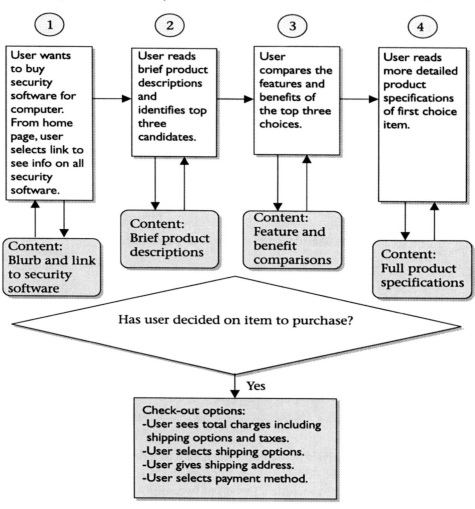

In contrast, sometimes you can determine from the user task analysis that a piece of content you previously identified as needing to be on the site now has no purpose. In such cases, it is worth revisiting the criteria for including that content on the site, and if they are not valid, then dropping it from the content list.

Information Architecture Analysis

Grocery shopping trips are the perfect opportunity for analyzing a common form of information architecture. Most grocery shoppers (a.k.a. users) usually approach such an expedition with a list in hand of items they would like to buy or with the general feeling that they should stock up on everything that they need at home. Both approaches are similar to how many users approach Web sites, ranging from precisely directed visits to a more free-ranging exploration. And there are innumerable ways that grocery stores decide to arrange their products with differing results in how easily most of their customers can find their desired items.

Off the top of your head, for instance, can you recall where the peanut butter is located at your favorite grocery store? Can you remember which section of the store, which aisle, or which shelf it is located on? How about the precise placement of the style that you most like? Is the Laura Scudders crunchy peanut butter to the right or the left of the creamy style and above or below the Skippy brand? What about the styles of peanut butter that are mixed with jelly? Are they in the peanut butter section, in the jelly section, or placed exactly between them? Are they even grouped together, or does each one stay with its respective brand of peanut butter?

Very few people would be able to answer *all* of those questions from memory—other than perhaps the people responsible for stocking those shelves. It's not even that it would be such an impossible task to remember these kinds of details; most people could remember them if they put their minds to it. But why should we memorize every detail of a scheme that could change at the manager's whim? It is better to rely on the information architecture of grocery stores, so that every time we go grocery shopping we learn or discover part of the process. It is a more efficient process than memorizing where every single item is in every store that we shop at.

8

Hint

Good information architecture is self-explanatory. It enables users to easily learn how to use that system to find what information they need.

When thinking about organizing any form of content, whether for a grocery store, a book such as this one, or a Web site, it can be helpful to consider all of the structural information models available to you. These can be classified within two kinds of systems—a nice and tidy organizational structure in itself:

- Exact systems

- Inexact systems

And then, of course, there's the less tidy option of a

- Combination of exact and inexact systems

Tip

From the user's point of view, a "searchable system" may also be an option. We will discuss that as a form of supplemental navigation options in Module 9. Web site search functions are generally a mechanism for searching a database, which in turn organizes information according to some combination of exact and inexact systems.

Exact Systems

An exact organizational system follows a set of well-defined rules that can assign every single piece of content a precise position within its scheme. Alphabetical order is one of the most common examples. Once the principles are explained, everybody can use the system to find words or names in alphabetical order, such as a dictionary or the white pages of a telephone book—assuming, of course, that they spell them correctly. The WhatIs? Web site emulates the dictionary model and offers an alphabetical organizational model (see Figure 8-1).

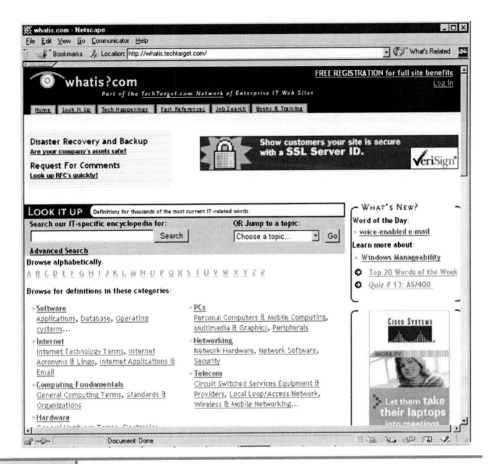

Figure 8-1 WhatIs? offers a straight alphabetical organizational system as its first method of looking up words (http://whatis.techtarget.com)

In addition to the alphabetical model, other exact systems include:

● **Numeric** The Dewey Decimal System is an example. See Dr. Weil's 8 Weeks to a Healthy America site at http://www.askdrweil.com/eightweeks/proj/ 0,1997,1,00.html? Web sites that direct you along a step-by-step process such as http://www.igeneration.com (see Figure 8-2) also employ this kind of organizational system, as do some other sites that require a registration process.

Figure 8-2   iGeneration employs a numeric organizational system to direct students through a step-by-step process toward getting certification

- **Chronological**   This variation of the numeric system organizes events by date. Calendars of events such as the one at the VW car site at http://www.vw.com/owners/calendar.htm are a common example on the Web. Timelines and discographies are other good examples (see Figure 8-3).

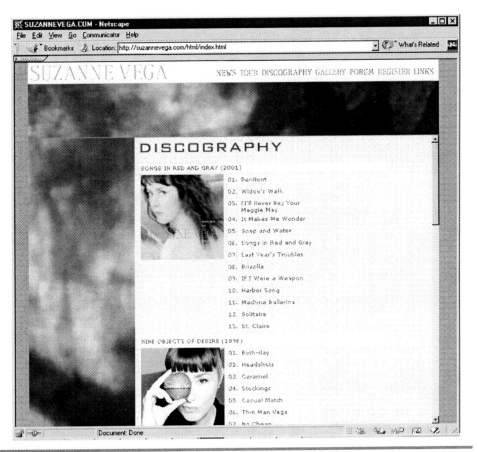

Figure 8-3   Discographies such as this one of singer/songwriter Suzanne Vega almost always follow a chronological organization system (http://suzannevega.com/html/index.html)

● **Geographic**   Organizing information by region. For example, you can look for summer jobs based on location at http://www.summerjobs.com/ do/where. The One Day Hikes and Grass-Roots Web sites use actual maps as an organizational and navigational feature to good effect. (See Figures 8-4 and 8-5).

Figure 8-4   One Day Hikes uses a map of the world to organize information about hikes by location (http://www.onedayhikes.com)

Tip

You may be interested to know that OneDayHikes.com is a database-driven site. Its geographical-based information architecture follows a strict hierarchical structure and was designed from the database out—i.e., the site design came only after the database structure had been finalized.

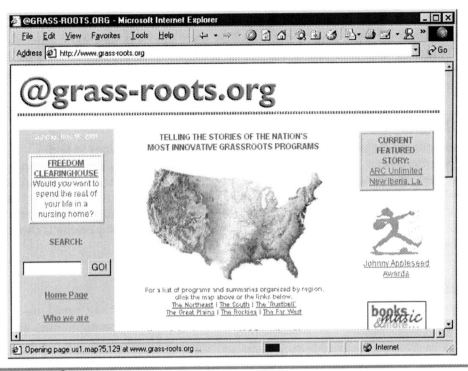

Figure 8-5   The Grass-Roots site uses a map of the United States to organize information on grass-roots efforts by region (http://www.grass-roots.org)

8

While exact systems may appear to be the surest means of organizing information, they are not necessarily the most efficient. Could you imagine, for example, if your grocery store organized its contents in alphabetical order? Indeed, peanut butter would be very easy to find; you could simply locate the aisle that had a big "P" on it and proceed past the peanut brittle to find the peanut butter. This would, however, eliminate the possibility of the peanut butter and jelly combinations being placed neatly between the peanut butter and the jelly, for the jelly would be several aisles away under "J."

Also, if you were looking for some kind of raspberry fruit preserves to put on your toast in the morning, you would probably need to go down the "F" aisle for fruit preserves and "J" for jam and jelly. These latter items would also have to be separated by such things as Jamaican rum and Jello (or would that be under "G" for gelatin?). Or perhaps you'd have to look under "R" for raspberry. The grocery store could even decide to organize all its contents alphabetically by brand, making it very easy to stock shelves, since products tend to be ordered by brand. But this kind of structure could send you quite literally all over the store seeking to compare different kinds of raspberry preserves. Or, more likely, right out the door and down the street to their competitor's.

Tip

Even with exact systems, users can be confused about which word to find information under. Thesauruses are full of words that have very similar meanings, and there are strong regional differences between word preferences. The American "parking lot" and the British "car park" offer one such example. Additionally, some exact systems such as the geographical system can change. Geographical regions and names change over time as national borders shift. Even voting precincts change on a more local level.

Inexact Systems

In order to be effective, inexact organizational systems have to be based on some form of logic that is identifiable to the user. The most common ones are

- Topic
- Task
- Audience
- Metaphor

While it may make perfect sense for you to use a structure that emulates a baseball game, for example, with first, second, third, and home base, it can succeed only if your users are familiar with that structure outside of your Web site. Otherwise, they would likely be confused with the sequence of going from third base to home base or with the three strikes, you're out rule.

This ties right back into the need for good information architecture to be self-explanatory. Most exact systems are based on common knowledge of patterns like alphabetization; this is not the case with many inexact systems. Ironically, the most common organizational structure used on the Web, clustering groups of content together by topic, is also the one that is most open to interpretation and debate by Web users. Primarily this is because topics often tend to overlap.

Topic Even what appears to be a simple, clear structure in the division of book subjects on the McGraw-Hill/Osborne Web site seen in Figure 8-6, reveals the complexity of this approach. The categories are defined as "Database and ERP," "Programming & Web Development," "Networking & Communication," "Certification & Career," "Applications, Internet & Hardware." The topics work well to show general distinctions between categories, but there are always overlapping exceptions. If you were interested in finding a book about programming databases for the Web, for example, would you look under "Database and ERP" or "Programming & Web Development"? And again, if you wanted a book to help you study for a certification exam on Web development, would you look under "Programming & Web Development" or "Certification & Career"? The answer in both of these cases is that you might need to look under more than one topic in order to find all the books related to your particular interest—or use the search function, an alternative to the organizational system McGraw-Hill/Osborne has chosen.

In any case, this system works better for this content than any exact system. Listing the books only alphabetically by title or author or chronologically by date of publication could give each one a precise placement on the Web site, but that would prove very cumbersome to most users who were interested in finding books about any given subject.

8

Task Organizing content by user task can create very engaging, interactive Web sites. As with tips for résumé building, active verbs generally carry a lot more punch than nouns. Consider the difference between seeing navigation buttons such as "Shop," "Compare," and "Buy" as opposed to "Products," "Specifications," and "Shopping Cart."

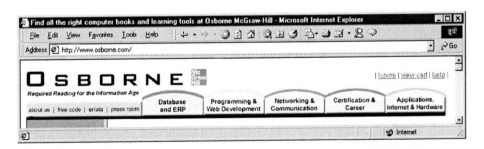

Figure 8-6 McGraw-Hill/Osborne's Web site divides books by topic into five categories (http://www.osborne.com)

Ask the Expert

Question: How can you decide what set of topics will make the most sense to your users?

Answer: One of the best ways is to enlist the help from a number of your users in organizing the content through what is commonly referred to as a *card sort*. This can be useful in determining user preferences for any number of organizational systems, but perhaps particularly so for deciding on clusters by topic.

On a stack of blank index cards, write a blurb about each kind of content that you want to include on the Web site on each card (one blurb per card). Make this as simple as you can. In the case of the McGraw-Hill/Osborne Web site, for instance, the title of each book would be sufficient plus additional cards for the non–book related information such as press releases and update patches.

You may also find it helpful to number the back of each card for ease of reference.

Shuffle the cards and hand them to one individual at a time and ask him or her to organize the cards in the way that would make the most sense. It can sometimes be helpful to give your helpers some guidelines regarding the number of groups to aim for: 5 to 10 generally works well.

Observe and record the groupings each user selects and then compare them all. Usually some strong patterns will emerge that can point you in the right direction.

Question: What if the results indicate two or more organizational patterns?

Answer: It's not unusual for two or more organizational patterns to surface. There are, after all, many "correct" ways to organize most information. Many of the final user decisions come down to preferences. When you have multiple patterns, identify the one that was favored by the most users. Chances are, these numbers will be true in the real world as well.

In some cases, two or more patterns will be prevalent. It may be necessary to conduct further usability testing to determine which of these is the best system, or you may find that you can offer both systems within the same Web site.

For example, Ofoto, a photo-processing site located at http://www.ofoto.com, separates the parts of its Web site into "view and edit photos," "share albums," "buy prints," "add photos," and (a non-task item) "ofoto store." This last section could easily have followed through with the theme with a label like "buy accessories," since it sells things like frames, albums, and photo cards. Contrast that scheme to the more static Kodak site at http://www.kodak.com, with more typical, non-active category heads like "Products," "Service and Support," "About Kodak," and "Kodak Worldwide." Which site structure do you find more engaging?

Audience Organizing content by audience can be a great solution if you have clearly distinct audiences that will be looking for very different content. The iGeneration site, for example, divides its content on the home page between prospective employers who are looking for IT-certified employees and potential employees looking for certification and an employer (see Figure 8-7).

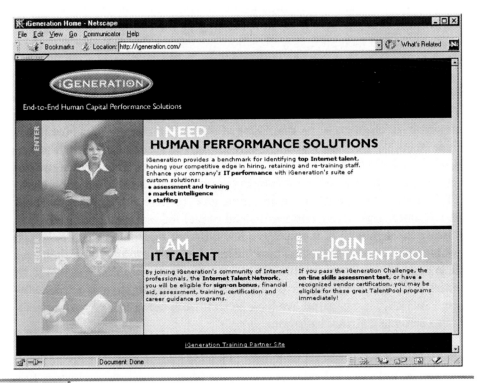

8

Figure 8-7 iGeneration divides the content of its Web site between employers, employees, and students (http://www.igeneration.com)

Bryant Heating and Cooling Systems at http://bryant.com has changed over time from an entirely audience-driven organizational scheme where it had only two parts, a "Homeowner's Section" and a "Dealer's Section." Today it has a more mixed format with "consumer resources" and "dealer resources" but also a separate "products" section. Banking Web sites such as http://www.fleet.com also frequently separate sections by audience such as personal and business customers or potential and existing customers.

Caution

Dividing a site by audience does not work well if much of the content overlaps between them or if the audiences are not distinct. A book site, for example, might have a hard time if it tried to distinguish between "businessmen" and "fathers," since one man can easily be both, and indeed, a father may well be interested in buying a business book for his son or daughter.

Metaphor   Metaphor-driven organizational systems can be terrific or terrible. Their success depends heavily on how thoroughly the content can be aligned within the chosen metaphor as well as how responsive the audience is to the metaphor. If a metaphor is perceived as "dorky," there's no saving the site.

Perhaps in part because of the difficulty in using metaphors successfully, there seem to be fewer sites that attempt them. The Paper Veins Museum of Art in Figure 8-8 is one. It uses the construct of the interior of a museum building to organize the contents of its site. Some of the special content areas (or floors) include labels like the Film Theater, Poetry Room, and Artist's Café, but the others just rely on labels like First Floor, Second Floor, and so on. This kind of division works pretty well because that is how museum buildings are often organized.

Take a look also at NetGrocer, an online grocery store at http://netgrocer.com. This is a more text-based example. Instead of picking one metaphor and following through with it, it employs a few different metaphors that don't quite work together. Food is organized into "aisles" (logically enough), and then each aisle is organized by category, but not necessarily categories that you would find in aisles in the real world. In the drugs "aisle," for example, there is a "medicine chest." Suddenly in our mind, we have to shift from being in a virtual grocery store to being in a virtual bathroom.

Other common metaphors often include office settings, where desk accessories and office furniture are labeled with links to related information. The desk calendar, for example, links to a calendar of events; the filing cabinet, to the history files;

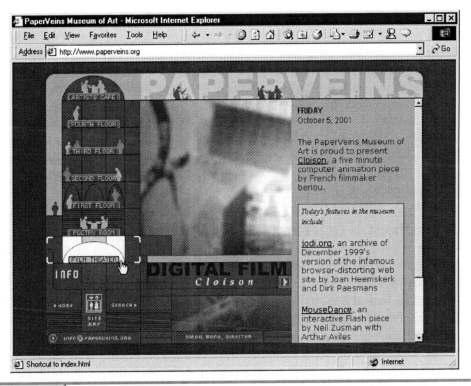

Figure 8-8   The PaperVeins Museum of Internet Art uses the metaphor of the floors of a building (http://www.paperveins.org)

the phone, to the contact information or e-mail link; and so on. Kitchen metaphors are another relatively common device. An old version of the Kraft site at http://www.kraftfoods.com, for example, used to have an illustration of a kitchen on the home page with links to different sections from the toaster, the pots and pans, etc. They have since revised the site and eliminated the image map, but they have retained a title of "The Interactive Kitchen" with some residual links to things like "Your Recipe Box."

Cityscapes have also often been used as metaphors with links from buildings or monuments, for instance. Clicking "City Hall," for example, may take you to the government issues; the town library, to background information; a post box or telephone box, to contact information; and so on. These metaphors can be particularly tricky to work with because the real-world counterparts change.

When using any metaphors, think especially hard about any content that will not naturally fit in—whether it's current content that you want to include or future content that you'll need to allow space for and an appropriate venue to link from within the metaphor. Some of the most troubling material is often the kind of information that fits under "About This Site" or "About This Company" labels on Web sites. Just where in a kitchen metaphor, for example, can this naturally fit in?

The Paper Veins site cleverly incorporates some of this kind of extraneous material in what appears to be an information booth on the ground floor. When you go to the site, roll your cursor over each letter of the "Info" sign to see how they link to four different kinds of generic information.

Combinations of Exact and Inexact Systems

So which organizational system generally works best? Often, the best solutions lie in a combination of systems. Look at the telephone book, for example. It's divided between an alphabetical listing of names (generally the white pages) and another alphabetical listing by subject with further subdivisions in alphabetical order (generally the yellow pages).

The Whatis? site we previously looked at (Figure 8-1) also uses multiple systems. The primary system is alphabetical, and the secondary is by topic. The McGraw-Hill/Osborne site uses subsets within each topic category to indicate series of books like this "Beginner's Guide" series.

Tip

Although it is sometimes necessary to use more than one kind of organizational system, I'd encourage you to try to be consistent within each type of navigation. Thus, ideally, your main navigation bar will follow one kind of system, such as by task or audience, and secondary navigation may provide an alternative system. This is especially true of metaphor-driven sites.

Even our earlier examination of the grocery store reflects a number of different systems; all the produce, for example, goes in one section but then is further broken down by vegetable or fruit, species, and whether it is organically grown or commercially produced. Compare that as well to how you organize your groceries once you bring them home. (I bet it's not alphabetical!)

The key is to organize the information from the user's point of view and develop a logical system that the users will be able to readily learn.

Site Diagrams

A key tool in developing the information architecture for a Web site and communicating it to the rest of the development team is the *site diagram*. These diagrams, usually in flowchart form, give a visual representation of the placement of and relationship between all the information on the site. For example, the following illustration shows a rough overview of an art site's structure. Note how it displays the organization of the content without much care given to the precise language.

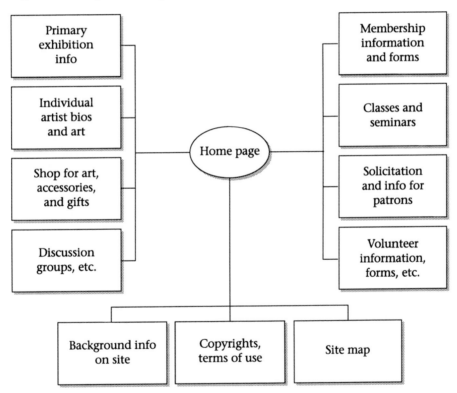

Typically, there are many drafts of these documents. The next illustration shows the final version of this document including the wording that will actually be used on the Web site. (We will be discussing how to determine navigation labels in just a moment.) The full site diagram is a multipage document that includes the details on every subsection of the site as well.

Note the different organizational schemes employed on the Web site. A rooms metaphor is employed for the bulk of the site, from Main Gallery to Volunteer Office. The supplemental information About this Site, Legal Information, and Site Map are in a separate menu. In the final site, they appeared in small print at the bottom of the page.

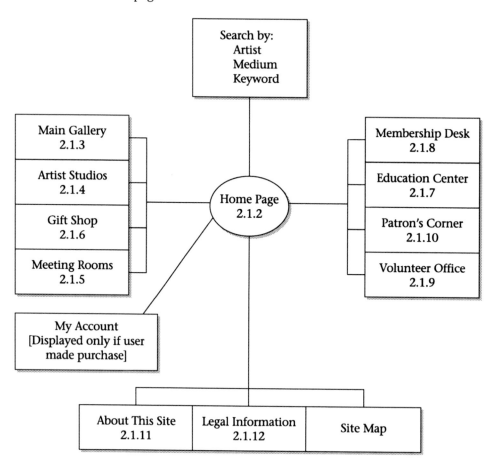

The next illustration shows one such subset, the Patron's Corner. (These last two illustrations are reprinted with permission from iGeneration, Inc., copyright 2000.)

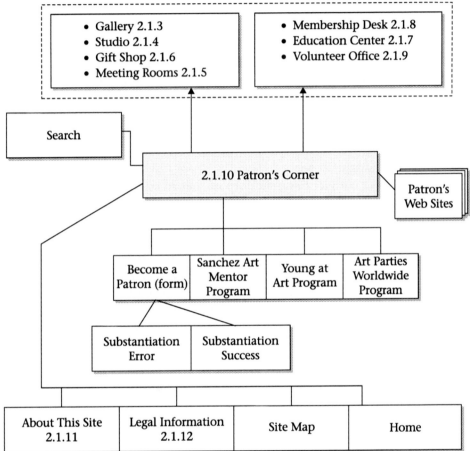

8

1-Minute Drill

● What role can usage scenarios play in the development of a Web site's information architecture?

● What two key information models are available to you when organizing any groups of information?

● Usage scenarios can be very helpful in doing a task analysis to examine how a user might use the content of the site.
● Exact systems and inexact systems.

Determine How to Present the Information Architecture on the Site

Organizing the content of a Web site into coherent groupings provides the foundation and structure for the whole site, but you can't stop there. Just as you need to "finish" a building by installing door knobs, light switches, and so on, you need to "finish" the information architecture of a Web site to make it user friendly. You do this by determining how to best present those clusters of information on the Web site for your particular users, such as choosing the best labels to go in a navigation bar.

This step serves both a utilitarian purpose and an aesthetic one, just as does the selection of plates, bowls, and silverware in serving a meal. You wouldn't typically choose to serve ice cream in a wine glass with a fork as the utensil, would you? Just so, on a Web site you might not choose to label a group of items with an ugly, cumbersome title like "Fat-Producing Chemical Properties" even if that is an accurate description from a scientific and organizational viewpoint.

There's a fine line between this stage and the navigation design phase, and frankly, on some teams the duties overlap. For our purposes here, though, we'll include in the information architecture phase three factors that are more conceptual in nature and that do not require the input of a graphic designer. They are

- Content labels

- The three-clicks guideline

- The seven, plus or minus two, guideline

In Module 9, we'll address all the remaining aspects of integrating and building upon the information architecture to design a usable Web site.

Content Labels

Short and sweet is generally the rule when assigning content labels that will appear on the Web site. You need to translate that "Fat-Producing Chemical Properties" description into "Ice Cream," so to speak.

Here are some guidelines for creating effective labels:

- **Clarity of meaning is of the utmost importance.** I can't stress enough how often this is overlooked. Watch out for labels that sound cool but don't convey what content they will link to. For an example, take a look at the award-winning 7-Up site at http://www.7up.com. This site was showcased on Macromedia.com, but its most prominent button (in this case in the center of the screen) is labeled "Nice Package." Can you guess what is behind it? Only after you roll your mouse over the button do you get a clue as to what's behind it—in small print in brackets: "[The Store]."

  Another site (that, perhaps coincidentally, is no longer in business) had the following set of labels: Money, Work, Life, Stuff, and Dream. They certainly may sound catchy, but if you're like me, you'll be hard pressed to guess what content was included in the Life, Stuff, and Dream categories. Industry jargon, on the other hand, can be equally as alienating to users who are not subsumed in that industry. Confirm if something is clear to you that it is also clear to your users.

- **Single words are better than multiple words** because users sometimes mistake multiple-word labels for multiple labels. "Career Fashions," for example, could theoretically be interpreted as two labels: "Career" and "Fashions." If you need to have multiple words, pay particular attention during the navigation design phase to make sure that the words do not appear to be separate buttons. See the Macy's navigation bar at http://www.macys.com for a simple and effective example of how to separate multiple-word labels with a thin vertical lines. Sometimes this can be as simple as running the words in together, such as CareerFashions. By the same token, don't try to force a link label into a single word if it makes more sense to use it as a phrase.

- **Avoid words that have double meanings.** Puns don't always work in your favor, especially if you don't think about them ahead of time. Look at the Macy's site again. The button on the far left, "At Home," links to the section of the site that sells household items like linens and kitchen gadgets. Do you think there's any chance users might confuse that with the customary "Home" button, which takes them to the home page of the site? I do.

8

●   **Think about each label on a navigation bar** as being part of a set and strive for consistency in tone and language. The labels should also be consistent with the tone and language you want the whole site to convey. For example, it doesn't work well to mix business-like labels such as Company, News, and Products with more hip labels like Rockin' or CoolDude.

Three-Clicks Guideline

User studies have indicated that frustration quickly accelerates with the number of clicks users have to make to get to the information they are looking for. As a rule of thumb, you should strive to make all the material on your Web site available within three clicks of the home page. This is called the "three-clicks guideline."

The intent of this guideline is to control the *depth* of Web sites and to make the content easily discoverable. On large sites, it's not always possible to conform to this rule, but it's in your best interest to come as close to it as possible.

Seven, Plus or Minus Two, Guideline

This guideline aims to control the *breadth* of Web sites and thus complements the three-clicks guideline's focus on depth. When creating navigational elements, strive to have around between five and nine content groups (seven, plus or minus two). Any more than that and you risk overwhelming the user. Any less than that and you may run into problems with the three-clicks limit.

Oddly enough, this guideline originated in an entirely different context—in memory studies that indicated people generally had difficulty memorizing strings of information that had more than seven, plus or minus two, elements. (Thus, we memorize seven-digit phone numbers with relative ease.) When applied to the Web, the original premise isn't particularly relevant because we don't require the users to memorize the navigation menu; it is there as a constant reminder of what is available on the site. All the same and without any scientific evidence, users just seem to prefer dealing with this range of information.

There are, of course, exceptions to this rule as to any rule. Some of the portal sites, for instance, such as yahoo.com have a home page chock full of links. But even Yahoo has six primary icons at the top of its home page (Calendar, Messenger, Check E-mail, What's New, Personalize, and Help). It then presents other sets of information links in clusters that roughly fall within the seven, plus or minus two, guideline, although the design runs them in together to save space on the page. As of this writing, with the exception of "Connect," all of the subsections have fewer than nine elements:

Shop Auctions · Autos · Classifieds · Shopping · Travel · Yellow Pgs · Maps

Media Finance/Quotes · News · Sports · Weather

Connect Careers · Chat · Clubs · GeoCities · Greetings · Mail · Members · Messenger · Mobile · Personals · People Search · Photos

Personal Addr Book · Briefcase · Calendar · My Yahoo! · PayDirect

Fun Games · Kids · Movies · Music · Radio · TV

Project 8-1: Organize Content for a Web Site

Now it's your turn to practice developing the information architecture for a Web site. If you have a Web site that you are currently working on or would like to develop, feel free to adapt this activity for that site. Otherwise, let's return to the example of the community art site that you developed usage scenarios for earlier.

Use the following as a preliminary content list, and develop a workable structure for that content:

- Mission statement

- Three-year plan for art center

- History of art center

- List of key personnel in art center

- Current exhibition photos and text for main gallery and student gallery

- Past exhibition photos and text for main gallery and student gallery

- Artist biographies of members

8

- Photos of member artists' individual works
- Artist statements about their work
- Artist contact information
- Art center contact information
- Legal disclaimer
- Copyright notice
- Solicitation for new members with list of benefits and costs
- New membership application form

Step-by-Step

1. Practice the card sort by writing a synopsis of each item from the content list on an index card and then seeing how many different logical groupings you can come up with that include every item.

2. Select your favorite set of groupings.

3. Assign appropriate labels to the information groups. Be sure to make them internally consistent in terms of tone and language.

4. Create a flowchart showing where each item will be placed and how it will relate to the other items on the Web site. (If you do not have access to a flowcharting application, feel free to do this by taping your index cards in place on a huge sheet of paper and drawing brackets and arrows between them.)

5. Confirm that your information architecture plan concurs with the three-clicks and the seven, plus or minus two, guidelines.

Project Summary

As you have probably discovered, there are numerous ways that you could effectively arrange this information—and, unfortunately, there are many more that just won't quite work. It's sometimes necessary to explore several dead-ends before finding a good solution in this process. The flowcharts we discussed earlier in this module for the structure of an art site demonstrate one way a similar group of information could be organized.

Tip

See Appendix D for a checklist regarding Web site design.

Module Conclusion

Creating a solid, user-friendly information architecture plan is essential to the success of a Web site. It must be logical, self-explanatory, and clearly understandable to the users.

With that as the foundation of your Web site, you can now move on to the graphical design stages and the task of communicating the content and structure of the Web site to the users in as effective a way as possible. We will turn next to designing the navigational components.

☑ *Mastery Check*

1. What are the two stages in establishing a Web site's information architecture?

_____

_____

2. What is information architecture?

_____

_____

3. What trait is essential to good information architecture?

_____

_____

4. List the four common kinds of exact organizational systems:

_____

_____

5. List the four common kinds of inexact organizational systems:

_____

_____

8

☑ Mastery Check

6. What is the greatest benefit from following an exact organizational system?

_____

_____

7. True or False: Exact systems are the most efficient and surest means of organizing information.

8. What is the chief challenge in organizing a site's content by topic?

_____

_____

9. Under what circumstances is organizing a site's content by audience most effective?

_____

_____

10. What two things can determine how successful a metaphor-driven site will be?

_____

_____

11. What purpose does a site diagram serve?

A) To help supply the users with information necessary to make purchase decisions

B) To show the client what the navigation design will look like

C) To give an accurate depiction of a user task analysis

D) To give a visual representation of the placement of and relationship of the site's contents

Module 9

Navigation Design

The Goals of This Module

- Identify the components of navigation design
- Identify the relative importance of aesthetics and functionality within navigation design
- Determine how to provide effective navigation from multiple entryways
- Identify the differences between navigation controls and navigation aids
- Recognize the importance of sitewide consistency in navigational elements
- Practice creating part of a site's navigation design

There's one key principle behind creating good navigation design, and that is to give users the navigational tools they need to find whatever they may be looking for. Navigation design and usability are inseparable. If the navigation is unusable by the people it is intended for, you might as well just pull the site off the Web.

Following this principle may, of course, sound simpler than it is. The good news is that by paying attention to a handful of important tasks, you can learn to create effective navigation designs with *relative* ease.

The five primary tasks are

- Stay true to the information architecture blueprint.

- Make every page feel like home.

- Design user-friendly navigation controls and navigation aids.

- Integrate the look and feel of supplemental navigation.

- Establish sitewide consistency in navigation.

Stay True to the Information Architecture Blueprint

At its most fundamental level, navigation design is a manifestation of information architecture. The task of the navigation designer is to transform the ideas articulated in the paper-based information architecture blueprint, complete with site diagrams or flowcharts, into the various media employed by the Web.

Graphic design is a key skill employed during this phase, but it is not the only skill needed. Just as the Web differs from print, navigation design for the Web requires skills in developing motion graphics, audio production, and interactivity design in addition to graphic design.

This is also the phase where aesthetics comes into play with their wonderful, intangible issues like the "look and feel" of a Web site. It is important to note that aesthetics need to play a *supporting* role to functionality in this phase, not the other way around. Designers need to stay right in line with the old adage, "form follows function."

Tip

Whereas the first failure in creating usable Web sites lies in ignoring the users' needs in the planning stages, the second surely lies in losing sight of those needs during the graphic design phase. It's all too easy to let the lure of bright colors and cool graphics supplant or eclipse the necessary functionality.

This is not to go to the other extreme, however, and say that there is *no* need for aesthetics in navigation design for the Web. There is, indeed, a great deal of need for aesthetics in a process *whose goal is to maximize communication.* Having brightly colored buttons can do a tremendous amount to facilitate navigation, as can good icons that immediately suggest to the user what the content of a section entails as well as implying its subtext—such as tone and atmosphere—far more successfully than the text label alone could do. Pictures can convey a thousand words, as can the choice of fonts, color, placement, or layout, and conveying meaning is what this phase is all about.

Ask the Expert

Question: What do I need to do or know in order to undertake the whole design process—aesthetic and functional?

Answer: Have you ever heard that vague phrase about needing "a good eye?" It is really true. "A good eye" will carry you a long way in any design field. It's hard to say exactly how one can develop a good eye, though. There aren't any certification programs I know of in "Good Eye Training," but there are many paths to it.

A good starting point is to learn about design in general. This can be through traditional graphic design courses or books, but you can also transfer a tremendous amount of knowledge from practicing any fine art such as painting, illustration, or photography.

Don't forget about the media design component. Many Web teams overlook this aspect—in Web design and in team building, too. Many forms of media conjoin in the Web, and they each benefit from the touch of a skilled craftsman or craftswoman. All the graphic design courses in the world are not going to fully prepare you for video editing, for example. Television experience is not going to fully prepare you for interactivity design, etc.

9

So the first half of the task is to learn as much as you can about aesthetics in any field. The second half of it is to learn how to communicate with the user. Oftentimes (although not always), fine arts are about self-expression, and issues like communication and usability are secondary. Design is fundamentally about forming a bridge between an idea and the end user. You're in the right place to learn about that side of things!

A couple books that might be helpful to start out with are

- *The Non-Designer's Design Book* by Robin Williams (Peachpit Press, 1994)

- *Visual Literacy: A Conceptual Approach to Graphic Problem Solving* by Judith and Richard Wilde (Watson-Guptill Publishing, 2000)

Keep in mind, too, the different learning styles we discussed in Module 2 as well as the broad array of non-English speakers on the Web. In general, the more techniques and media you can employ to convey a message, the more effective you will be in reaching a broad audience.

Just don't get caught up in all these lovely techniques and media and stray from your original purpose. Stay true to the information architecture. Think of it as your blueprint as much as if you were building a high-rise office complex. It will provide a solid structure and foundation for your Web site. If you stray from its specifications, you may leave out a vital screw or support beam, and you will leave your users at the door, so to speak, scratching their heads in confusion.

It's also vital to test your interpretation of the ideas against actual users. Once you have some comps or even a working prototype, be sure and give them a test run with some real users to confirm you are on the right track.

1-Minute Drill

- What are the two biggest failure points in creating usable Web sites?
- True or False: In navigation design for the Web, function should follow form.

- Ignoring the users' needs in the planning stages and losing sight of those needs during the graphic design phase
- False. Form should follow function.

Make Every Page Feel Like Home

I have a secret to tell you. I really dislike the preeminence given to "home" pages, and even the convention of calling them "home." They may be the most commonly accessed page on any given site because their URL corresponds to the domain name (typing "osborne.com" into a browser links to http://www.osborne.com/ index.htm, which is commonly referred to as the "home" page). But such pages are by no means the *only* entry point, nor should they be. The Internet is structured like a "web" after all, not like a hierarchy where you have to enter through a common doorway every time. If we needed to have such a familiar metaphor to make the Web seem comfortable to us, "hallway" would at least have been a more appropriate term for the function this so-called "home page" serves.

There are so few conventions on the Web that I suppose I have to live with this one. My advice to you, though, is to not think of these pages as "home" pages but as one of multiple entry points. The important function they serve—of greeting the guests and offering them a range of navigation options (rather like doorways in a hall)—should permeate the entire Web site. Every page, in this case, should feel like home. Users should not need to hit the "Home" button in order to reorient themselves to the Web site.

There are two key ways to do this:

- Provide sitewide context at all times.
- Provide descriptive text every place it may be needed.

Provide Sitewide Context at All Times

"Where am I?" "Where have I been?" "Where can I go?" Providing answers to these questions is the lifeblood of a good navigation system. If a user gets up, walks away from the computer, and comes back two hours later—perhaps after lunch and a rousing game of foosball?!—he or she ought to be able to assess his or her current position on the site and continue merrily along the way.

Unfortunately, very few sites manage to answer all of those questions at a glance, but in Project 9-1, we'll examine a couple that do make pretty good headway. The example sites both use a method called "bread crumbs," among other things. The "bread crumbs" terminology comes from the Hansel and Gretel fairytale in which the children leave a trail of bread crumbs behind them as they enter a forest, hoping it will help them find their way out. This is an apt metaphor for how lost users often feel on the Web, and the development of the use of such "bread crumb trails" on the Web was a direct response to the users' needs.

Tip

Most bread crumbs actually show where the page is within the site's overall structure. Few actually show the path you've taken to reach that page because that would require cookies to do so.

Project 9-1: Examine Navigation Clues for Context

The Macromedia and Adobe sites give their users clues about where in the site they are at any given time, although using slightly different approaches. Note, both of these companies revise their sites fairly frequently, so don't be surprised if you see something different from visit to visit. As a rule, both companies have been employing some kind of bread crumb trail to help orient the users for several years now, so keep an eye on the sites to see what kinds of changes they introduce pertaining to this concept.

Step-by-Step

1. On the Web, go to http://www.macromedia.com and navigate to information on the Flash feature tour.

2. In a new window, go to http://www.adobe.com and navigate to the complete feature list of LiveMotion.

3. If possible, position the windows side by side on your monitor so that you can compare them easily, or place them slightly off kilter with each other so that you can easily toggle between them. Figures 9-1 and 9-2 show the sites at the time of this writing for your reference. You will need to go to the sites, however, to see such components as color and interactivity.

4. First off, compare the URLs and consider how well they indicate the path the user has followed to get to that point.

5. Locate this book, *Web Usability and Navigation: A Beginner' Guide* on amazon.com (http://www.amazon.com) and compare that URL to the Macromedia and Adobe URLs. Would you be able to retrace your path any more or less easily on amazon.com by just looking at the URL? Which one is more user-friendly?

6. Next, compare the primary navigation bars of the Macromedia and Adobe sites. Is it clear at a glance which section of the site you are in? Why or why not?

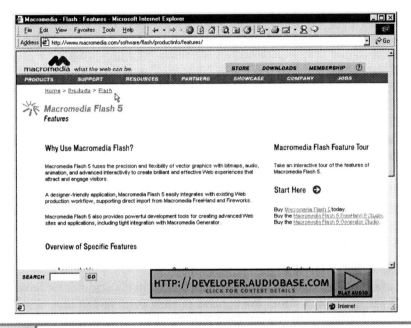

Figure 9-1 Macromedia FlashFeature Information at http://www.macromedia.com/software/flash/productinfo/features

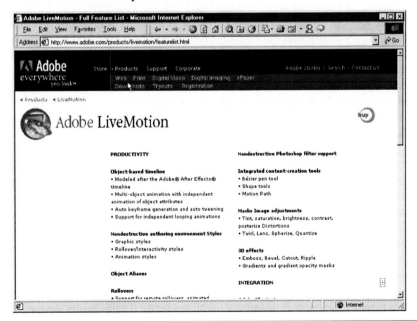

Figure 9-2 Adobe LiveMotion Feature List at http://www.adobe.com/products/livemotion/featurelist.html (© 2001 Adobe Systems Incorporated. Adobe and LiveMotion are registered trademarks of Adobe Systems Incorporated in the United States and/or other countries)

7. Then compare the bread crumb trails of both sites, the navigational text that appears against the white background just below the navigation bars. At the time of this writing, Macromedia's site reads "<u>Home</u> > <u>Products</u> > <u>Flash</u>" and the Adobe site uses the words "Products" and "LiveMotion" with a little arrow pointing to the left in front of each word. Does one communicate more effectively than the other where you are, where you have been, and where you can go on the sites? Why or why not?

8. Finally, evaluate how the "features" subsection that each of these pages is in is communicated to the users. For example, is it incorporated into the bread crumbs? Indicated by text headers? Highlighted in menu options? Conveyed by some other means, or not well conveyed at all?

9. Make a list of the media devices other than text labels that each site uses to communicate the navigation options and history to the user. Consider such things as color, font choices, placement, cursor behavior, size, and link colors.

Project Summary

There are pros and cons to the ways both Macromedia and Adobe have chosen to give the users clues about the context of each page within their respective Web sites. Starting from the top (and looking at the sites in their current incarnation at the time of this writing), the URLs of both sites also indicate the pathway in clear English, which makes it easy for users to see where they have come from. This is a welcome change from database-driven sites like Amazon .com that spit out lengthy, complex URLs that are very difficult to interpret.

The primary navigation bar of each site is also very simple and straightforward, although Macromedia's current site does not give any indication at all within that bar as to which section you are currently in. This is unlike Adobe's, which employs three clues: a dotted line, a little orange arrowhead, and the appearance of the submenu of navigation options. In past versions of its site, Macromedia has employed a number of techniques like these, as well as color changes to highlight which section the user is in, but not in this iteration. Go figure.

As far as the bread crumbs are concerned, however, Macromedia's approach is markedly more functional than Adobe's. It's very clear from looking at Macromedia's links that they are indeed links and form a progressive chain. Adobe's are not so revealing at a glance. I would hazard to guess that a number of users do not even realize they are active links and may be a bit confused about the relationship between them. They may be interpreted as yet another submenu of options. For example, the middle step of the progression (selecting "Web" after "Products") is omitted. There is no visual indication anywhere in the navigation that Adobe LiveMotion is one of the products designed for the Web.

The bread crumbs feature on Adobe's site looks a little more elegant, but this appears to be a case where the graphic design eclipsed the information architecture, and form was allowed to lead instead of follow function.

Provide Descriptive Text

One disadvantage of relying on everyone visiting a "home" page, rather like you'd expect people to read a book's table of contents before diving into the book, is that sites too often use the home page to explain the navigational system. Some sites, for example, give a sentence-length description of what appears in each section of the site. Occasionally, sites have even introduced text labels underneath icons on the home page but then not carried the labels through to the subsections, apparently thinking that users have started at the beginning and memorized what each icon represents.

All I can say is that if any information introduced on the home page is necessary to understanding how the navigation works or what to expect in each section, that information needs to be available on every other page. Books can get away with displaying partial information on a page. Note in this book, for example, that the headers alternate between left (verso) and right (recto) pages. The title of the book appears on one, and <u>the</u> module number and title on the other. No information about the other modules in the book appears anywhere in the headers or on any page except the table of contents. Books can rely on the reader to look elsewhere in the book for the full context.

Unlike a book page, every Web page needs to be able to stand on its own as a host welcoming visitors to the site. Users can link to any page of a site from a bookmark or a referral from another site. If that page does not convey the context of the site or, even worse, does not provide any navigation at all to the rest of the site, it is merely a dead end. Users will visit that page and then leave the Web site without even knowing what they have missed.

It is best to leave room for all the necessary information in the page design. If your icons need text labels, for example, then allow enough space in the navigation bar for both icons and text. If they need full-sentence descriptions, then leave that space.

Assigning a good URL and using the HTML <title> tag appropriately are easy ways to give the user a summary of each page. The information you assign to the "title" for each page appears at the very top of the browser window and is the text that appears with any bookmarks that users make for that page. Figures 9-3 and 9-4 offer two examples with slightly different levels of effectiveness. In Figure 9-3, the title and the URL of the Web page for McGraw-Hill/Osborne's Beginner's Guide series tell the users exactly what they are seeing: "BEGINNER'S GUIDE Title List." In Figure 9-4, on the other hand, the title of the Web page for the HTML beginner's guide gives the exact title of the book, but note how the URL indicates the ISBN number instead, which may be useful for the publishers or Web developers but not so much for the user.

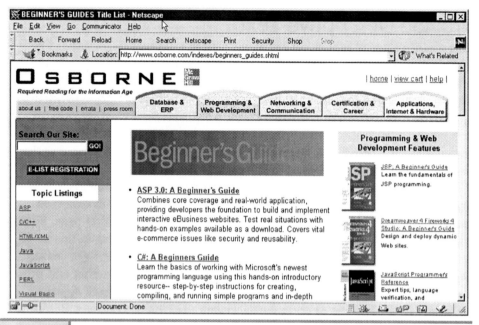

Figure 9-3   The Web page for McGraw-Hill/Osborne's Beginner's Guide series
(http://www.osborne.com/indexes/beginners_guides.shtml)

Tip

Avoid using generic titles like "Introduction" or "Page One," which could appear on any Web site. Give the user as much context as possible within the title, such as "An Introduction to Fine-Toothed Combs." Also, keep in mind that overly long titles will be truncated in the browser window, so keep them short and sweet.

There are two other approaches you can use, but I'd caution you that they may not work on every browser, so it's best not to *rely* on them:

- Alternative text designated by the Alt and Title attributes
- Other rollover link descriptions

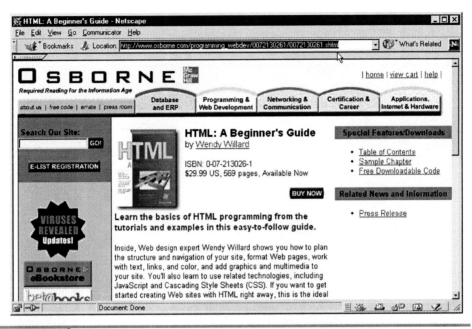

Figure 9-4   The Web page for the HTML Beginner's Guide (http://www.osborne.com/
programming_webdev/0072130261/ 0072130261.shtml)

Alternative Text

As we've previously discussed, it's always a good idea to assign alternative text to
all graphics using the Alt attribute in case of problems with the graphics loading
or for visually impaired users who may be using voice readers. In many cases, this
text will also appear if the cursor hangs over an item (otherwise known as upon
rollover), thus providing an easy labeling system, but it is best not to rely on that
text for basic navigation. If the PaperVeins sites in Figure 9-5, for example, tried
to rely on the alternative text and removed its label "Artist's Café" from the top
floor icon, users would have no clue what the icon represented at a glance. If by
chance they rolled their cursor over the icon and the alternative text failed to
appear, they would continue to be stymied. The presence of the label contributes
a great deal toward the ease of navigation. Applications like Adobe Photoshop
and Macromedia Dreamweaver rely on this kind of ToolTips instructional cue
for their toolbars, but they expect their users to learn to recognize the icons at
a glance through repeated use.

9

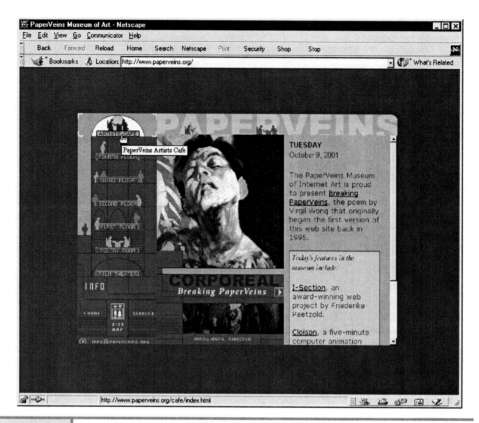

Figure 9-5 The PaperVeins.org Web site does not rely on the alternative text for labels, and for good reason

Additionally, you can use the Title attribute to assign descriptive text to many other elements, in addition to graphics. I'd encourage you to use this attribute with all of your hypertext links and every other page element that seems important to identify, particularly for uses that are using audio browsers to "read out loud" each Web page. This attribute, however, is newer than the Alt attribute, so older browsers do not support it.

Caution

It is easy to confuse the <title> tag with the Title attribute. The former controls the title of the Web page, which displays at the very top of the browser, while the latter can control the title, or text description, of a number of elements within the page design.

Keep in mind, however, that not every browser on every computer always reveals the alternative text, regardless of whether it is controlled by the Alt attribute or the Title attribute. Nor does every user know how to position his or her cursor just so and to let it sit there for a moment until the Alt text appears, so it is not a good idea to exclusively rely on this technique. It should just be thought of as one more navigational aid.

Other Rollover Link Descriptions and Expanded Menu Options

Scripting languages such as JavaScript and Web development programs such as Flash and LiveMotion can be used to create rollovers (also called mouseovers) on navigation icons or text to give a more complete description of the link or to show expanded menu options. You may have noticed this feature on the Adobe site, for example, as in the LiveMotion menu options featured in Figure 9-6. The screen on the left loads automatically, but you see the submenus only when you roll your cursor over one of the topics, as on the right.

This approach can work beautifully to give additional information without cluttering up the page, but—there always has to be a but, doesn't there?—they may not work in every browser. Any time you use anything other than standard HTML, you run the risk of complications on the end user's machine. Users can disable browser features such as these, sometimes consciously or sometimes unconsciously.

In the case of JavaScript, a number of users who are very concerned about security issues will intentionally disable JavaScript. This includes many government employees who are required to disable it. Similarly, Flash and LiveMotion are both dependent on the browser having the correct plug-in installed and operable.

The Flash plug-in (which LiveMotion also uses) has become much more widespread and is currently included as an option with new versions of Netscape and Internet Explorer, but not every user chooses to install it. Nor does every user upgrade it whenever a new version is available, so a dependence on plug-ins can still be problematic. (We will address this issue more fully in Module 10.) So once again, it is best not to rely exclusively on this approach.

When you do use such rollovers, take care to make sure that they are, indeed, clear to the user and fully functional. For example, I've seen sites that have links that are actually hidden *until* the user rolls over something. This is not a very useful navigation aid although it may be "cool." Even that may be questionable. It places the burden entirely upon the user to discover what portions of the site are navigable. The same goes for sites that turn off the underline indicating a hypertext link and then program a rollover, so that if

9

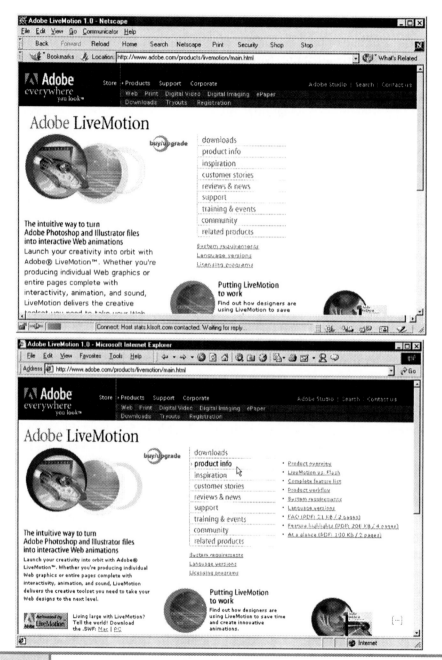

Figure 9-6   The LiveMotion main product page use rollorvers to give an expanded navagation bar at http://www.adobe.com/products/livemotion/main.html (© 2001 Adobe Systems Incorporated. Adobe and LiveMotion are registered trademarks of Adobe Systems Incorporated in the United States and/or other countries)

the user happens to mouse over that text, the underline magically appears and indicates that it's a live link. I'm sure there must be cases where this is appropriate, such as Easter egg hunts, but by and large for typical Web sites, it's in your best interest to make the navigation visible to the user.

It is also possible to use many different type treatments and special effects for the different rollover states, which can add a great deal of interest and liveliness to a site. Be wary of overdoing it, though. One rule to follow is to always ensure links are readable at every stage.

Also, if you're going to use rollovers, make sure that you take full advantage of their capabilities. Occasionally, I've come across rollovers that show the contents of a section but do not include active links to any portions of it. This is just silly. It forces the users to click to the main section then search again and click whatever topic they are interested in.

 ## 1-Minute Drill

- What three navigation questions provide a sitewide context?
- Why can't you rely on ToolTips to display alternative text designated by the Alt attribute?

Design Navigation Controls and Navigation Aids

In navigation design, you need to create two kinds of elements: navigation controls and navigation aids. *Navigation controls* are the actual devices that transport the user from one page or section to another. The hypertext link is the most fundamental example on the Web. Other examples are buttons; navigation bars; or hot spots in image maps, videos, or QuickTime VR. Navigation controls almost always map directly to the information architecture blueprint.

Navigation aids, on the other hand, help guide the users around the Web sites, like the color-coded labels in parking garages. They give the users clues about what elements function as navigation controls—for example, they indicate the presence of hyperlinks by the use of underscores and the color blue. They also help convey the sitewide information architecture and convey

---

- "Where am I?" "Where have I been?" "Where can I go?"
- Not every browser on every computer always reveals the alternative text. Nor does every user know how to position his or her cursor just so and to let it sit there for a moment until the Alt text appears.

the context we discussed in the last section. Assigning different colors to different sections of the site, for example, helps the users to realize at a glance what section of the site they are in. A number of the large retail sites such as Amazon.com and Drugstore.com employ this device. The latter makes particularly effective use of it. Visit http://www.drugstore.com to see the color at work.

Other common examples of navigational aids are icons, the images used in image maps, the various states of buttons and links (for example, the state while the cursor is over the link, while it is being clicked, and once it has been clicked), sound cues, and metaphors used in navigation.

Hint

In navigation design, judiciously employ navigational aids to make sure that the users know that every navigational control is, indeed, functional. For example, you can use a graphics editing program to make a text label look like an interactive button and then create a rollover effect that will highlight the button when users place their cursor over it, further suggesting that something will happen if they click it.

Navigation Controls: Design Tips

Here are a number of design tips, particular to navigation controls.

Hypertext Links

- Use plain old hypertext links whenever speedy download time is critical and you need to keep your page size to a minimum. There's nothing faster.

- In general, use hypertext links sparingly within paragraphs. Too many of them in one paragraph can really interrupt the flow of reading. One or two is generally not too obtrusive.

- Hypertext links automatically include navigation aids that indicate with underlines and color that they are, indeed, a functional link. They also automatically change color after having been linked on, indicating to the users that they have visited that portion of the site.

- Avoid stating "click here." Make the navigation obvious by context and the default hypertext link indicators. Instead of "<u>Click here</u> for information on travel to Maui," for instance, "<u>Travel to Maui</u>" or even just "<u>Maui</u>" is much more efficient and informative. That way, if a user is scanning a page, he or she sees the topic, not the instructions.

- Avoid changing the default colors of the links and overriding preference settings disabled users may have set in their browser.

Buttons

- Convention has made buttons easily recognizable as navigation controls. If something looks like a button, most users will place their cursor over it to see if it is indeed an active link.

- Buttons can come in all shapes and sizes, but they are typically thumbnail-sized and often have a 3-D look and feel to easily reflect different button states. If they have an illustration on them, they are generally considered to be icons. See the following section on "navigation aids" for some tips on designing icons.

- Employ navigation aids to create variations on each button to indicate their various state (on mouse over, mouse down, and mouse up). These can take the form of different colors, expanding or contracting sizes, or other graphical variations.

Navigation Bars

- Include the primary navigation bar on all pages of the Web site.

- Keep the navigation bar consistent in appearance, functionality, and placement on every page.

- Establishing visual relationships within the navigation is essential. For example, determine the levels of navigation (primary, secondary, and so on) and design them accordingly to convey that relationship to the users. Look again at the McGraw-Hill/Osborne or the PaperVeins sites (Figures 9-3 through 9-5) again for some examples. The Osborne site has four navigation clusters. The primary one, as you might expect, is about their books. It has the largest buttons, the most prominent use of color, and a graphic design accent in the shape of the arc over the text, all of which contribute to drawing the user's eye. The secondary content is contained within the small buttons to the left, including "about us," "free code," etc. The third

9

level has supplemental navigation options: the small HTML text in the upper-right corner with "home," "view cart," and "help." And the fourth level (not visible in the figures) is at the bottom of the Web page and provides links to "Terms of Use," "Privacy Policy," and "Contact Information Page." Take a look at the live version of the PaperVeins site (http://www.paperveins.org) to practice identifying the levels of navigation there; basically, it moves in clusters from top to bottom.

- Convention and typical usage calls for the placement of the primary navigation bar along the top of each page or in the upper-left corner.

- Also, employ navigation aids to create different button states for each component of a graphical navigation bar.

- In general, include seven-plus-or-minus-two categories in each navigation bar.

- If you include subcategories in a navigation bar, it's also generally a good idea to limit them to around seven in number.

- If you use a graphical navigation bar, be sure to assign alternative text for every navigational element.

Hot Spots

- Hot spots can be used in image maps, video, or QuickTime VR to indicate a clickable area. By assigning a hypertext link to that area, you arrange that the cursor will automatically change from an arrow to a hand, indicating it is active.

- Whenever possible, add additional navigation aids to indicate that hot spots are active links. Highlighting the areas when the cursor passes over them or having them wiggle just a little, for example, can draw attention to their clickability.

- Make the hot spot large enough and hold still long enough that users can easily click it. There's nothing more frustrating than not being able to click a navigation link quickly and easily.

- If the hot spots in an image map can be organized in distinct rectangular areas, it is better to splice the image and make each piece an individual button than to load the entire image as an image map. The page will load much more quickly.

Ask the Expert

Question: Is convention the only reason to place the primary navigation bar at the top or in the upper-left?

Answer: No, that's not the only reason, although so few conventions have been established for the Web that when one does arise it's worth considering before discarding it. More importantly, however, it's important to evaluate why that convention may have been established and how it may help your Web site design. This particular convention of placing the navigation bar at the top or upper-left took hold because of its high usability. For one, it is useful for the navigation bar to be near the browser's navigation, particularly the "Back" and "Stop" buttons, as well as the location/URL slot. That way, if the users are confused about the navigation, they need only look in one general area. The convention has probably also contributed to the development of user habits—that subtle movement of the eye up and to the left.

Perhaps even more importantly, the upper-left corner is the only spot that people are guaranteed to see. If you put something over on the right-hand side and people minimize their browser window, you've lost them.

Question: Are there any instances when Web conventions aren't supportive of good usability?

Answer: The example of the use of the term "Home Page" we discussed earlier in this module is one. Jakob Nielsen also discusses this issue in an article, appropriately named "When Bad Design Elements Become the Standard." In it, he broaches the color of hypertext links, navigation tabs, navigation rails, and bread crumb trails. He also gives a good methodology for evaluating conventions:

> Web design is easy: If you are thinking about how to design a certain page element, all you have to do is to look at the twenty most-visited sites on the Internet and see how they do it.
>
> - If 90% or more of the big sites do things in a single way, then this is the de-facto standard and you have to comply. Only deviate from a design standard if your alternative design has at least 100% higher measured usability.

9

- If 60–90% of the big sites do things in a single way, then this is a strong convention and you should comply unless your alternative design has at least 50% higher measured usability.

- If less than 60% of the big sites do things in a single way, then there are no dominant conventions yet and you are free to design in an alternative way. Even so, if there are a few options, each of which [is] used by at least 20% of big sites, you should limit yourself to choosing one of these reasonably well-known designs unless your alternative design has at least 25% higher measured usability than the best of the choices used by the big sites.

Admittedly, the percentages in this list are my own best estimates. There is currently too little research on consistency theory to know exactly how many sites it takes for a certain design element to reach the level of a convention or a standard. Similarly, we don't know exactly how much it harms users to deviate from the two levels of expectations, though it is absolutely certain that it does hurt.

Therefore, I recommend following the conventions even in those cases where a different design would be better if seen in isolation. The fact is, no website is seen in isolation: users come to your site expecting things to work the same way they are already used to.

For the full article, see http://www.useit.com/alertbox/991114.html.

Navigation Aids: Design Tips

Here are a number of design tips particular to navigation aids.

Color-Coding

- Consistency is of the utmost importance. Once you designate a color for a section, carry through with applying that color to each page within that section.

- There is some debate over whether it is better to include all the colors for each assigned section in the navigation bar at all times. In general, it can work well to include all the colors if you have a small number of sections, but the navigation bar quickly gets too busy if you have a lot of different sections. A number of large sites, such as Amazon.com, have changed recently to omit all but the current section color. They lose a bit on the ease of navigating to other sections, but they gain in the simplicity of page design and the comfort of using the Web site.

- There is a natural limitation to the number of colors that can be effectively used to color-code sections. Once you start using similar shades of orange, for example, users will have a very difficult time differentiating the sections.

- It's difficult to work with a set of colors with widely different contrasts, especially when you need to integrate text labels into the colors. If you are using black text, for example, it will be difficult or impossible to read it when set against black or dark shades of blues or reds. Conversely, if you are using white text, yellows and light colors become problematic because the white drops out against them.

Icons

- Tie icons as closely as possible to the subject matter they are supposed to represent. Wholly abstract icons often do little to aid navigation.

- Aim for a high *visual fidelity:* In other words, make icons look like the thing they are supposed to represent.

- Icons are generally best used with text labels. Very rarely are they so self-explanatory or memorable that all users will understand what they represent by themselves.

- When creating sets of icons, design them as a set instead of individual pieces. They should share traits such as illustration style, complementary colors, fonts, size, and shape.

- Make sure the look and feel of the icons integrate well with the look and feel of the site and suggest an appropriate tone for the content of the site.

Button States

- As mentioned, buttons should convey what state of interactivity they are in. Generally, slightly different variations of buttons are needed for the

9

normal position (mouse off), mouse over, and selected (mouse down). In some cases, it can also be helpful to have a change to indicate that part of the site has been visited, just as hyperlinks change color after having been visited. Unfortunately, however, this is not possible with regular HTML for anything other than text links. You have to use cookies and some scripting language to track where users have been on a site.

● The various button states can employ a number of different methods. The default, as with hypertext links, is a change in the state of the cursor from an arrow to a hand. Some others include:

  ● Changes in color

  ● Changes in visual effects such as drop shadows and glows or highlights

  ● Movement, oftentimes a little wiggle to indicate it's active

  ● An auditory cue, most often a hissing sound to indicate a button or hot spot is active and a clicking sound when the button is selected. These are most often used in conjunction with changes in the visual state as well. A word of caution with this method, however: Avoid sounds that will annoy your users—or their colleagues if users are accessing your site from work.

Sound Cues

Although there is not currently much use of audio to aid in navigation on the Web other than in conjunction with button states, it can be done. Here are a couple possibilities:

● Different background music used with each section rather like using different color coding

● The use of sound to indicate proximity to an active link: sounds coming from the right or left or growing or diminishing in volume

Metaphors

● As we discussed in Module 8, a key component of the success of metaphor-driven Web sites is making sure that the metaphor is appropriate for the content. For the Barbie site at http://www.barbie.com, for example, a playfully illustrated girl's bedroom is a reasonable place for Barbie to be; whereas a seriously illustrated technical computer lab would not be.

● Align as much of the content as possible with the metaphor and avoid leaving bits and pieces off to the side as other kinds of links. It can work, however, to have a clearly separate navigation bar, just as you can have clearly divided primary and secondary navigation bars.

● Avoid mixing metaphors. Pick one and carry it through.

Project 9-2: Identify and Analyze Navigation Controls and Aids

The best way to familiarize yourself with the wide variety of navigation controls and aids in use on the Web is to visit a number of Web sites and analyze them in terms of their controls and aids.

Step-by-Step

1. Visit several of the following sites and assess their use of navigational controls and aids:

● http://www.drugstore.com
● http://www.amazon.com
● http://www.crayola.com
● http://www.barbie.com
● http://www.boowakwala.com
● http://www.sleepinheaven.com
● http://www.bbdo.dk
● http://www.120seconds.com
● http://www.egomedia.com
● http://www.vw.com
● http://www.cadillac.com
● http://www.creaturelabs.com
● http://www.gmunk.com
● http://www.shockwave.com

Hint
Use this activity to build up the Web Site Library you started in Module 1.

9

2. On each site, itemize what elements act as actual navigation controls (result in some action) and which are merely navigation aids (inform you about your navigational choices).

3. Make notes in your Web Site Library regarding particularly effective or ineffective controls or devices.

4. Compare your notes with other colleagues or students, if possible.

Project Summary

This navigation design is a complex process, isn't it? There are many options available to you in terms of designing navigation controls and aids. The developers of Drugstore.com, for example, used a color-coding approach effectively throughout the site. Did you notice, though, how they show all of the colors on the home page, but then in every subsection proceed to gray out all colors except the section the user is in? Also, instead of drop-down menus showing all that is available within each section, they opted to give a brief description without additional links.

Amazon.com, in contrast, has removed all the section colors from the home page and employs a color only within each respective subsection. They've also run into problems, however, with the repetition of the color blue. At the time of this writing, they use a similar shade of blue for the home page, "Merlyn's store" (my personalized portion of the site), electronics, music, and computers. Overall, I'd say that the use of color as a navigational aid has been diminished on this site to a minimal level.

This is another site to keep an eye on over time, however, and observe how they continue to revise it. Not long ago, for instance, Amazon.com included all their stores in the navigation bar on the home page, which ended up looking like a towering pile of file folders. There were at least three rows of them. At present, they have narrowed the navigation bar to the primary seven stores (does this remind you of that seven-plus-or-minus-two guideline?) plus the welcome, or home, page and added a separate button to "see more stores."

While you'll undoubtedly find some navigational aids and controls you like, you'll also find some you don't like. Use this experience to remind yourself what it's like to be a first-time visitor to a Web site, to be better equipped to build usable navigation systems of your own.

Integrate the Look and Feel of Supplemental Navigation

Most sites also contain supplementation navigation such as search engines, site maps, help functions, and FAQs (frequently asked questions). The design of these should not be overlooked. Search engines require a form field and Submit buttons, which almost always look like dull little gray boxes, as in the following illustration. Some designers or developers seem to forget that it is possible to modify the appearance of the Submit button. You can easily control elements such as the length and height, the wording, the look and feel of the instructions (in this case, just the word "Search"), and of course, the background and placement on the Web page.

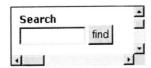

Site maps, on the other hand, have no technical restrictions on them beyond the usual HTML, yet there is sometimes a surprising lack of imagination or aesthetics in designing them. Yes, their functionality is of supreme importance—although you might be surprised by the occasional site that does not have any active links from within its site map and that employs it purely as a navigational reference. (How that happens is beyond me.) As with the rest of the site, though, there is plenty of room for aesthetics and certainly a need to tie the site map into a consistent look and feel with the rest of the site.

Generally, the same design style should be applied to the site map as to the rest of the site. This includes such things as the selection of fonts, colors, and backgrounds and general page layout. On large sites, it may be necessary to include much more information on a single page for the site map than anywhere else in the site. It is generally considered more important to make a complete site map available to the users than to stick to a nonscrolling rule.

The Quest Software site map in Figure 9-7 is a typical site map that keeps in style with the rest of the site. Note how this is one case where it works to turn the underlines off all the hypertext links because the whole page is composed of such links. Quest has kept the words in blue, however, to suggest they are all links, and the underlines appear when users move their mouse over them.

Of the Web sites we examined in Project 9-2, only a handful even have site maps, so compare and contrast the following site maps. To also test the navigation design, I'd recommend trying to find the site map from the home

9

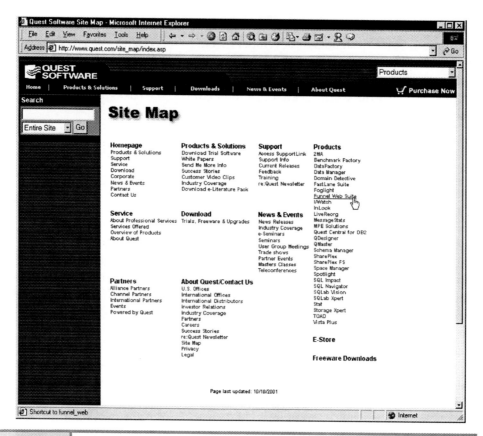

Figure 9-7 Quest has a "typical" site map (http://www.quest.com/site_map)

page first and consulting the information in the right column of the following table only if you can't find it:

http://www.amazon.com	Directory of all stores
http://www.boowakwala.com	Actually is at bottom of home page
http://www.vw.com	Under 3 out of 4 of the drop-down menus
http://www.cadillac.com	Middle of top navigation bar
http://www.apple.com	Bottom of home page
http://www.sharp-usa.com	Lower-left corner
http://www.warnerbros.com	Gray navigation bar near the top
http://www.digitalthink.com	Gray navigation—far right edge

Consistency, Consistency, Consistency

Have you ever heard that saying by Ralph Waldo Emerson that "Foolish consistency is the hobgobblin of little minds"? Well, if you have, please erase that from your memory (along with the dozen pink elephants dancing by the river).

When it comes to navigation design, you cannot get too much consistency. Slip on your usability spectacles if you don't have them on and think about all those users who feel lost or disoriented on the Web. It would be hard enough if every single site used the same style of navigation, but that would be impossible to dictate. As it is, users have to contend with thousands of different styles and approaches. Making your Web site easy to navigate and easy to remember requires having a consistent navigation design.

Additionally, the company identity is also often integrated into the navigation design. For example, it has now become common practice to use a company logo in the upper-left corner as a link to the home page. Establishing a consistent navigation design can thus further promote the company identity as well. Take a look at the IBM site, for example at http://www.ibm.com. Just as you would expect, the company logo, the colors, even the pin-striped pattern are clearly evident throughout the site.

9

Project 9-3: Create Part of the Navigation Design for a Web Site

Carry the community art center example from Module 8 one step further into the navigation design.

Step-by-Step

1. Review the information architecture blueprint that you developed in Project 8-1 or go back to the similar example in Figures 8-5 and 8-6 in Module 8.

2. Go as far as you can to create the navigation design for this site, taking into consideration the following factors:

- Stay true to the information architecture blueprint.

- Make every page feel like home.

- Design user-friendly navigation controls and navigation aids.
- Integrate the look and feel of supplemental navigation.
- Establish sitewide consistency in navigation.

3. Adjust the scope of your efforts to the time and resources you have available. If all you have on hand, for example, are paper and pencil, then draw out two or three possible variations. In fact, this would be a good starting place in any case. Whatever you do, don't let the tools get in the way of the design ideas. Conceptualize the design first and then render it through the use of software applications and programming.

4. Present your design ideas to some potential users of such a site if at all possible. Also compare them with other colleagues or students if available. Record all the observations and feedback, and revise your design accordingly.

Project Summary

Entering the navigation design phase requires a mental leap. It is altogether a different experience than the logical, even intellectual process we've followed to date. There are no single right answers, but there are clearly better and worse interpretations. The final check, of course, must be with the users themselves. Only they can truly determine which site provides the navigation tools that they need.

Tip
See Appendix D for a checklist regarding Web site design.

Module Conclusion

Establishing the information architecture and navigation design are two of the most complex and important steps in creating usable Web sites. We will now turn to more general Web site design usability issues. Module 10, for example, takes a look at a number of key site design dilemmas.

☑ Mastery Check

1. At its most fundamental level, what is navigation design?

_____

_____

2. What is the role of graphic design within navigation design?

_____

_____

3. What is meant by "making every page feel like home"?

   A) Make every page low-key and comfortable.

   B) Make every page present the site's navigation options.

   C) Post a welcome message on every page.

   D) Direct users to the home page from every other page.

4. What are "bread crumbs" in the context of navigation design?

_____

_____

5. True or False: It is not necessary to provide descriptive text throughout the site explaining the navigation functions if this has been carefully explained on the home page.

6. What is the difference between navigation controls and navigation aids? And what are some examples of both?

_____

_____

7. True or False: The button states that indicate when a button is active, depressed, or released are navigation aids.

9

☑ Mastery Check

8. Where does convention indicate the navigation bar should be placed on a Web site? You may select more than one answer.

A) The top of each page

B) The center of each page

C) The upper-right corner

D) The upper-left corner

9. What are the limitations when using color-coding of different sections of a Web site?

_____

_____

10. What two things benefit from having a consistent navigation design?

A) Site identity

B) Usability

C) Entertainment

D) Ad revenue

Module 10

Site Design
Usability Dilemmas

The Goals of This Module

- Understand some common design dilemmas and how they can be addressed

- Evaluate the advantages and disadvantages of some of the solutions to these dilemmas

- Practice resolving Web site design dilemmas

As with any field, there is a handful of recurring design dilemmas in creating Web sites, particularly if you are aiming to create good, usable Web sites. These are the kinds of dilemmas where there are no easy answers; there are pros and cons that need to be considered in light of the specific Web site project and its audience. In this module, we will discuss the issues and some general guidelines for the following dilemmas from a usability perspective:

- The plug-ins conundrum

- Browser version dilemmas

- Splash page dilemmas

- Frames dilemmas

- The challenge of designing really large sites

The Plug-ins Conundrum

Wonderful tools are available to create elaborate animations, soundscapes, video with hot spots, QuickTimeVR, 3-D environments, CD-quality audio, and other fancy media for the Web. So why aren't we all hip-deep in developing things like that right now? There are, of course, the bandwidth limitations that we discussed in Module 4. And then there is what I call "the plug-ins conundrum."

Bandwidth aside, anything beyond plain old HTML requires browser plug-ins to properly display these wonderful creations, and the minute you start complicating the browser requirements, you are likely to bypass a number of your users' systems. So designers and developers have been tearing their hair out weighing the pros and cons between being able to use these cool development tools and the costs of losing some of their users. (Now you know why there are prevalent signs of early hair loss among Web developers!)

The good news is that some of the most common plug-ins have been included with the browser installation programs for the past two years. Most notable of these are Apple QuickTime and Macromedia Flash (which also supports Adobe's LiveMotion animation files). In October 2001, Macromedia announced that over 386 million Web users now have the Macromedia Flash Player. This sounds especially promising in that Flash files *can* be relatively low-bandwidth if care is taken to make them so. But hang on a second before rushing out to start developing all-Flash sites: There has to be a downside, doesn't there?

The bad news comes in two forms:

1. Not everybody chooses to install the plug-ins when they install the browser, so knowing that 20 percent of your users have the latest version of Netscape, for instance, does not guarantee that those users have the QuickTime or Flash plug-ins installed.

2. New, improved versions of each of the plug-ins keep being developed. You probably know what that means: users tend to upgrade very slowly or not at all. Additionally, the new plug-ins are not always fully backward compatible, so in order to view all of the current Web sites, you would need to have multiple versions of all the plug-ins installed, which you can't do.

It's a bit of a conundrum, isn't it?

The easy answer, of course, is to avoid using any of these fancy tools. That's a good rule to follow for general-interest Web sites that are primarily composed of text content and that need to have broad accessibility to all sorts of users.

And then there are the more complicated answers. *If* the content of your site would truly benefit from taking advantage of one or more of these presentation modes that rely on browser plug-ins, then consider each of the following possible solutions:

- **Links to download plug-ins** Provide a way to install the necessary plug-ins.

- **Multiple versions** Create one version of the site that uses only HTML and fancier ones that require plug-ins.

- **Mixed use** Prioritize the content on your site and develop the most important portions in HTML only and the nonessential content with plug-in-dependent applications.

- **Version control** Check and advise on the version of the plug-ins.

10

Note

Whenever you are considering making any part of your site dependent on browser plug-ins, first ask yourself if there is any other way to effectively present the content. If you can do it in straight HTML, then by all means do so.

Provide a Way to Install the Necessary Plug-ins

Some Web developers have chosen the "do or die" approach to using plug-ins. If users do not have the necessary plug-ins, they must download and install them before being able to view the site. Figure 10-1 shows a worst-case scenario of what such sites sometimes present to users who do not have the plug-in. We'll talk about version control, where users just have the wrong version of a plug-in, in a minute.

As you can see, pages that rely entirely on plug-ins do not provide many options for the users, who may feel as though they have hit a dead-end.

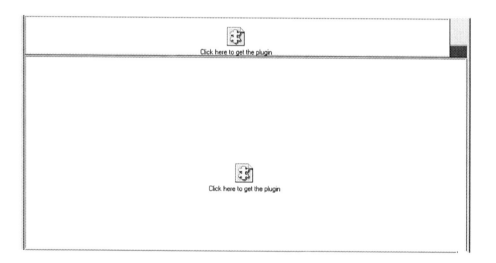

Figure 10-1 An anonymous site as it appears through a browser without the Flash plug-in; you probably wouldn't want your users to be welcomed with this sort of page

Ask the Expert

Question: If your browser has the plug-ins, how can you see what sites that require plug-ins look like to browsers that lack them?

Answer: You need to disable the plug-ins from your browser. The easiest way to do this is to temporarily move them from the browser's "Plug-ins" folder and then relaunch the browser. Don't forget to move them back into the folder once you have finished.

Question: The names of the plug-ins don't make sense to me. How do you tell which plug-in is which?

Answer: This can be a bit tricky. There are some clues in the names; for instance, "swf" stands for Shockwave Flash, Macromedia's original name for Flash, so I recognized the "npswf32.dll" file in my Netscape "Plug-ins" folder. Shockwave Director, on the other hand (what is now commonly called Shockwave), is abbreviated "dsw." Apple's QuickTime files always have a "qt" in them; RealMedia, RealAudio, and RealVideo files can have "rm," "ra," or "rv"; and so on.

If you have a PC, you can also right-click each plug-in to determine who has produced it. Thus, you can identify all of the Macromedia files, the Apple files, etc.

A German dance instruction site, Die-Tanzschule, addresses the plug-in problem head on. (See Figures 10-2 and 10-3. How's your German, by the way? You'll need it to discover what the users' options are. Or you could use one of the translation sites from http://www.babelfish.com if you like.) If possible, visit the site so that you can actually see the Flash animation and differentiate between it and the static HTML.

Users without the Flash plug-in have two options: to download and install the plug-in, as suggested by the large white box, or to click the small text in the lower left-hand corner: "Sehen Sie nichts??? Hier klicken." Translated, that means "Don't you see anything??? Click here." That link takes the users to an

10

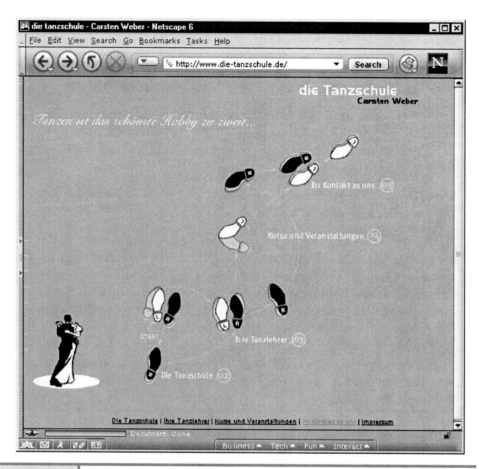

Figure 10-2 If users have the Flash plug-in, they see a lovely Flash-animated intro that results in this home page at the Die-Tanzschule site (http://www.die-tanzschule.de)

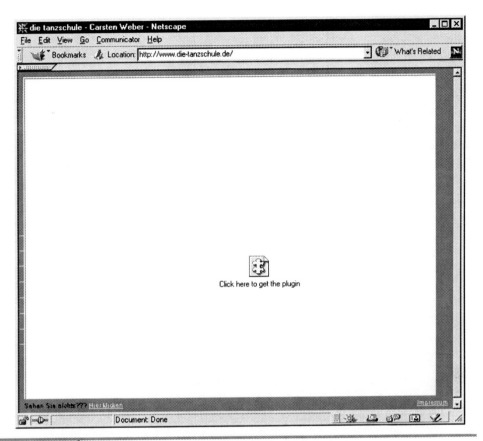

Figure 10-3 If users do not have the Flash plug-in, this is all they see of the Die-Tanzschule site

10

HTML-only page that looks exactly like the Flash page, although its behavior is slightly different.

Take a look also at the Conscience Records site pictured in Figure 10-4. This jazzy-looking site integrates the feeling of being on the cutting edge of Web technology with its look and feel. The home page presents users with the following message: "If you are using Netscape or IE 3.0+ and have your plug-ins you are ready for the hardcore version of the site. We've removed some of the browser-crashing treats, so go ahead…Live Dangerously."

Caution

Phrases like "Get plug-in" by themselves may well baffle many users, especially beginners. Foremost in their thoughts are questions like "Which plug-ins? What are they used for? How can I get them? Why do I need them? Do they cost anything?" Most Web sites, unfortunately, fail to give this information.

Figure 10-4   Conscience Records describes its technology needs in a language that ties in with the overall look and feel of the site (http://www.conscience.com)

Ironically, the developers of the Conscience Records site have simplified the technology used in the site so that it's not particularly "hardcore" by today's standards. It relies solely on HTML programming and the RealMedia plug-in to listen to music samples in the "Sounds" section; its graphic design contributes most of the "hardcore" feeling. Also, given the way that introductory blurb is written, I would expect they would also have a "softcore" version of the site somewhere. If we were not ready for the "hardcore version," for instance, where would we go? All the same, it can be a good idea to use language to describe the technological needs of your site that fit in with the content and overall tone.

Another site that is worth a visit for this same reason is the Homewrecker site at http://www.homewrecker.com. A message on its home page reads:

Recommended:

● 4.0 Browsers, IE or Mac – 5.0+ Works

● Flash 4 Plug-In

● Focused Noggin

● Cozy Lounger

This approach encourages the users to adopt a whole attitude—toward both the technology and the site. In fact, a previous version of the site went even further. It provided a checklist:

- got the Shockwave plug-in!
- volume is cranked up!
- brain is undeniably focused!
- chillin' in comfortable chair!
I, the clicker, solemnly swear that all the above is accounted for and I am of sound mind—or at least I was before I got here. (Users then needed to click a button that said "let me in!")

Unlike all of the previous sites, however, this one does not give the users any options but to have the Flash plug-in installed. If you click the "enter" sign without having the Flash plug-in, all you get is the large white box with the "Click here to get the plug-in" message. Perhaps stating "Required" instead of "Recommended" would have been more apt in this case. Ironically, if you view the current site with the Flash 5 plug-in instead of the Flash 4 version specified, it appears to work just fine.

10

Fancy and Plain: Multiple Sites for Multiple Users

A tried and true way of resolving the plug-in conundrum is to provide multiple versions of the site and give the users a choice between them. Take a look at Suzanne Vega's Web site, for example (see Figure 10-5). The home page presents users with a choice between a "HIFI (Flash)" or "LOFI (HTML)" version of the site.

Madonna's Web site, at http://www.madonnamusic.com, uses a similar technique but without associating the language with the content of the site. Users have what appears to be a straightforward choice between "Enter Flash Site" or "Enter Non-Flash Site." The choice is not quite that easy, however. The small print by the "Enter Flash Site" states that it requires not only Flash 4 but also the QuickTime plug-in. Even the small print by the non-Flash states that it requires QuickTime. This may be a case where a more abstract labeling system like "HiFi" and "LoFi" would more effectively communicate the

Figure 10-5   Suzanne Vega's Web site gives users the choice between entering the HIFI (Flash) or LOFI (HTML) version of the site (http://www.suzannevega.com)

technological needs to the user. They would prompt the user to read the fine print instead of assuming the titles have given all the necessary information.

Note

Did you notice on Madonna's site how the links to download the plug-ins are not underlined? There's no easy way to tell that they are, indeed, links unless you roll your mouse over the words. Only then do the underlines appear to suggest that the words are hypertext links. This could easily confuse users who read the text but do not know where to download the plug-ins from.

The Carbon 42 site couches the choice between versions of its site in terms of bandwidth. As you can see in Figure 10-6, the home page presents users with the options: Click for Flash Version | High Bandwidth or Click for HTML Version | Low Bandwidth. If users click the Flash Version, however, but do not have the Flash plug-in, they are taken to a page with just the large white box and the "Click here to get the plug-in."

10

Figure 10-6   Carbon 42 gives users a choice between high- and low-bandwidth sites (http://www.carbon42.com)

Tip

Rather than relying on any technology terms, try to describe to users what their choices actually mean in their own language. Choices like "Version of site for regular, old modem connection " and "Version of site for fast cable modem, satellite dish, or high-speed office network connection" will mean a lot more to many Web users than simply offering "low-bandwidth" and "high-bandwidth" choices.

There are a couple other options, however, for presenting multiple sites. They are

- Use one version as the default
- Auto-direct users to the most appropriate page

Use One Version as the Default

A number of sites that previously gave the user a choice between versions of a site on the home page have changed recently to provide only one default site. The Die-Tanzschule home page, for example, used to present a choice between entering the Flash or HTML versions of the site. As we discussed with Figures 10-2 and 10-3, however, they now present the Flash version as the default, and provide the HTML version only as a backup in case the Flash version does not work.

The Sharp site at http://www.sharp-usa.com used to present a choice between "plugged" and "unplugged" versions on its home pages, where "plugged" led to a Flash site and "unplugged" to a straightforward HTML site. Currently, they provide only a single, more sophisticated HTML plus JavaScript version of the site; they have dropped the Flash version altogether.

The strongest benefit for using this kind of approach is that it frees up the home page from all the technological clutter of explaining what options are available to the user, and it allows the user to get into the content of the site much more quickly. This trend goes hand in hand with a move away from the early self-consciousness of developing for the Web toward concentrating on the content that the user is most likely to be interested in.

Auto-Direct Users to the Most Appropriate Page

An alternative method to presenting the user with a choice on the home page is to run a browser-detection script to identify what system the users have and then direct them to the most appropriate page. The 120 Seconds site in Figures 10-7 and 10-8 uses this approach. When users type in the

URL http://www.120seconds.com, the browser checks to see whether or not they have the Flash plug-in installed. If they do, it directs them to the main site at http://www.120seconds.com/index.cfm (Figure 10-7). If not, it auto-directs the user to http://www.120seconds.com/noflash.html, which gives them instructions on downloading the Flash plug-in (Figure 10-8). The only thing this site omits that would be of great interest to inexperienced Web users is how easy and cheap (free) it is to download and install the plug-in.

Caution

Browser-detection scripts are often written in JavaScript, which some organizations require their employees to disable because of security concerns.

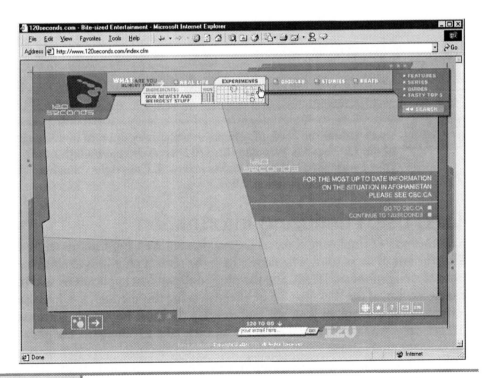

10

| **Figure 10-7** | Users *with* the Flash plug-in are automatically directed to this page of the 120 Seconds Web site (http://120seconds.com/index.cfm) (Used with permission, all rights reserved. Copyright Canadian Broadcasting Corporation, 2001.) |

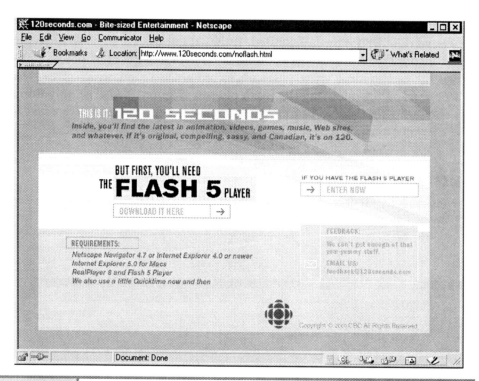

Figure 10-8   Users *without* the Flash plug-in are automatically directed to this page of the 120 Seconds Web site (http://120seconds.com/noflash.html) (Used with permission, all rights reserved. Copyright Canadian Broadcasting Corporation, 2001.)

Mixed Use: Prioritizing Information

Yet another way of employing some of the multimedia Web applications without risking the loss of those users who do not have the correct plug-in is to combine the use of straightforward HTML and the plug-in-dependent applications within the same version of the Web site. To be effective using this method, it is necessary to prioritize the content on your site and develop the most important portions in HTML only. Any nonessential content can then take advantage of the plug-in-dependent applications.

The Hillman Curtis Web site employs this method to good effect. (See Figures 10-9 and 10-10 or visit the site to see the full Flash animation.)

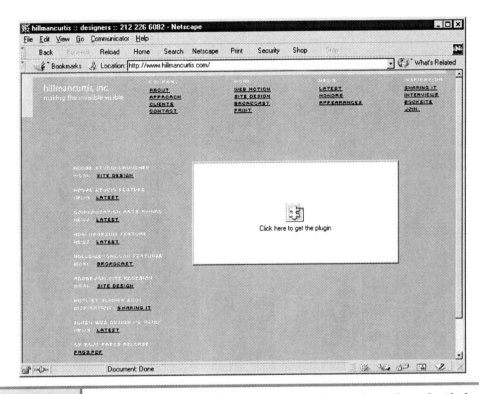

Figure 10-9 The Hillman Curtis Web site as it appears if users do not have the Flash plug-in (http://www.hillmancurtis.com); note how all the navigation is still visible to the user

One section of the home page has been designated as a Flash showcase of some of the work this studio has created (the box on the right-hand side). Because this is a motion graphics design studio, it would be very important to the clients to be able to see some of the motion graphics up-front on or very near the home page, yet the designer has wisely stayed away from making the entire site Flash-dependent. With this balance of technologies, all users are guaranteed to be able to see the most important content of the site. And most users, those with the Flash plug-in, will be able to view the entire site.

Another similar example is the Cybertown site. This site uses a very specific 3-D application produced by Blaxxun Interactive for its chat room environment. The front of the site, however, is built in HTML (with JavaScript rollovers that

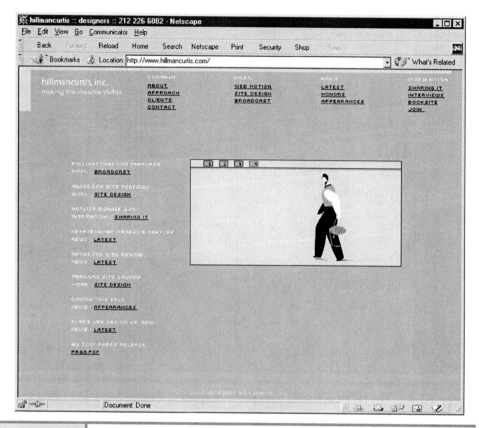

Figure 10-10   The Hillman Curtis Web site as it appears if users have the correct plug-in installed

make the description of the navigation buttons appear when you roll your cursor over them). It isn't until users reach the third level of the site, seen in Figure 10-11, that the choice between 2-D and 3-D worlds prompts the installation information for this application and plug-in.

Version Control: Check and Advise on the Version of the Plug-ins

Further complicating the design decisions revolving around plug-ins is the fact that different versions of the plug-ins do not all support prior applications; they are often not fully backward compatible. Thus, identifying which version of

Figure 10-11   Cybertown uses a specialized 3-D viewing application, but it's not employed until the third level of the site (http://www.cybertown.com)

the plug-in your users have installed can become critical to determining the performance of a site. In most cases, you can employ a browser-detection script to determine what version of the plug-in any given user has installed. If that version will not work with the current site, however, then you are faced with the design challenge of communicating that information to the user. There are, of course, a number of ways of doing this.

The Macromedia Web site, for example, adds a small blurb with a warning sign, the exclamation point within a triangle saying "To view this site, install Macromedia Flash Player 5."

It does not, however, force the user to upgrade in order to view the contents of the page. Instead, it integrates that blurb directly into the page, as in Figure 10-12, and replaces some of the Flash-dependent elements with non-Flash counterparts. In the case of this page, for example, both versions have the picture of the head, but the Flash version has rollovers (see Figure 10-13).

The EgoMedia site also runs a browser-detect script, but it does not provide an alternative set of non-Flash pages. Instead, it chooses to inform users

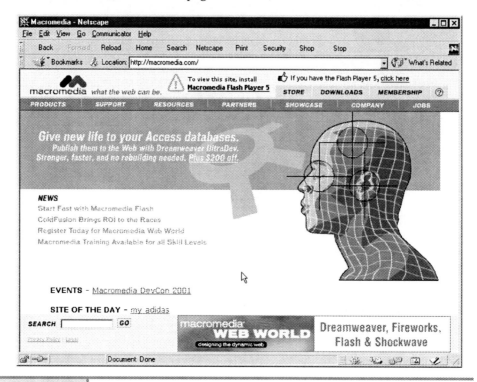

Figure 10-12   At the top of the page, the Macromedia site alerts the user to the need to upgrade to the newer version of Flash

Figure 10-13 The Flash-enabled version of the same page has added functionality, such as the rollovers from points in the illustration of the head

without the proper plug-in about the situation: "We couldn't detect a Flash 5 player plug in. You might have Flash 4, but to enter this site you'll need Flash 5. Please click on the icon below and follow instructions in order to download and install the correct software" (see Figure 10-14). As Figure 10-15 shows, users with the right Flash version installed go right to the site's home page.

10

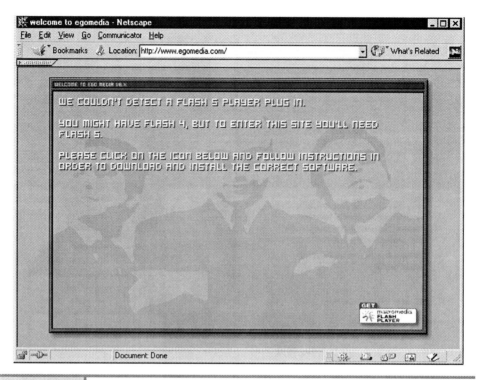

Figure 10-14 The EgoMedia site gives users this notice about having the wrong version of the Flash plug-in installed and what to do about it (http://www.egomedia.com)

Note

The EgoMedia site, at http://www.egomedia.com, is well worth checking out. It offers several interesting features such as a desktop metaphor and customizable user options.

Figure 10-15 When the right plug-in is installed, users can go straight to the home page of the EgoMedia site

The Suzanne Vega site, as we discussed earlier, does give users the choice of a HIFI (Flash) or LOFI (HTML) site, but if users without the correct plug-in try to enter the Flash portion of the site, they are given a Flash upgrade notice, as in Figure 10-16. They see the following message: "We suggest you upgrade your player to Flash 5. We found an older version of the Flash player on this browser. Please <u>upgrade</u> and try again. If you feel you've reached this page in error, click <u>here</u>. Or, if you'd like to visit the HTML version of the site, click <u>here</u>." (As a test of your skills, try rewriting that statement to avoid the "click here" syndrome.)

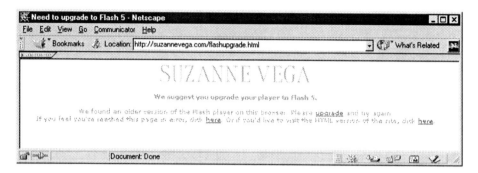

Figure 10-16　The Flash portion of the Suzanne Vega site requires version 5 of the plug-in; if users do not have that plug-in, they are directed to upgrade or try the HTML-only version of the site (http://www.suzannevega.com)

Tip

Before designing any site with Macromedia Flash, see Macromedia's "Top 10 Usability Tips" for designing Flash Web sites at http://www.macromedia.com/software/flash/productinfo/usability/tips.

Ask the Expert

Question:　Are there any other problems than the bandwidth and plug-in issues with using multimedia applications?

Answer:　Yes, in fact, one area of major concern is that it's very difficult for Web search engines, which are text-based, to read any text content within multimedia presentations such as Flash or QuickTime files. A lot of research and development is going into developing ways to do this, but in the meantime, it's left to the developers to essentially index the content themselves by including a list of keywords for this content within the HTML file. That adds yet another complication to the development process and often omits some important material.

Another cause of concern for some developers is the linear nature of many multimedia pieces. A number of Web sites force users to watch movies or animations from beginning to end when the users may, in fact, be most interested in a bit in the middle. This is less true of audio and video files that have a controller than of Flash or Shockwave files without a controller; however, it's still virtually impossible to bookmark a section that you would like to revisit with any of these types of files.

1-Minute Drill

- What two limitations do multimedia Web files, like Flash or QuickTime, have in Web sites?
- What issues complicate the industry numbers suggesting the total number of users who have any given plug-in?

Browser Version Dilemmas

In our discussion of plug-ins, we've already touched on a few Web site examples that include information about what browsers, or what versions of browsers, the site is best viewed with. Take a closer look at the Conscious Records site (Figure 10-4), the 120 Seconds site (Figure 10-8), and the Homewrecker site (http://www.homewrecker.com) in light of their browser specifications.

Most often this kind of information is included in a litany of other requirements—such as the required plug-ins. In the early days of Web development when the browsers were changing at a breathtaking pace and Netscape and Explorer were each introducing their own tags, building Web sites to work on specific browsers made some sort of sense from the developer's perspective. However, they have never made much sense from the user's perspective. How many users do you know who would actually upgrade their browser in order to be able to view a particular site? Unless you have an unusual group of acquaintances, the answer is typically "not many" or "none."

The Web standards are much more consolidated today, and there are very few legitimate reasons to launch a Web site that does not work on most users' browsers. In fact, I can think of only two possible reasons, and they are not very good ones from a user's perspective:

10

1. If your site employs Cascading Style Sheets, you will have to work very hard to make sure all the code works on all versions of Netscape and Explorer from version 4.x forward. The 3.x browsers did not support CSS. Support for CSS is inconsistent enough at this point even among versions

---

- Bandwidth and dependence on browser plug-ins
- Users do not necessarily install plug-ins that ship with their browsers; nor do they quickly upgrade them whenever a new version comes out.

of Netscape and Explorer, however, that I would advise you to optimize your site for one browser but thoroughly test it in all browsers to make sure the variations are acceptable. It is also a very good idea to develop non-CSS code for those browsers that do not support CSS at all. If you are merely using CSS to affect the display of type within a document structured in HTML, you can interweave the CSS and the non-CSS code into the same pages, so they aren't actually alternative versions. The older browsers, for example, will just ignore the CSS code and interpret the HTML code that they recognize. In the case of using CSS for layout and positioning, however, it is extremely difficult to use the same page for browsers that don't understand CSS because the CSS formatting does indeed change the meaning or purpose of the content.

2. The second possible excuse is when the new versions of the browsers drop support for some of the old features. Netscape 6 did this in its efforts to more fully comply with the W3C's XHTML 1.0 standards, which had deprecated a number of HTML tags. In such cases, I'd consider it acceptable for sites to put up *temporary* notices, like the following from the Sharp site at http://www.sharp-usa.com:

> Attention Netscape 6 Users:
>
> The Sharp-USA site uses DHTML and other advanced techniques supported by Netscape Version 4 and Internet Explorer Version 4 and above. We are in the process of upgrading so that Netscape Version 6 will be supported. We apologize for any inconvenience this may have caused you.

Splash Page Dilemmas

Splash pages are the screens that fill up your browser before the home page is loaded. They are often elaborate Flash-based animations, such as the introduction to the Harry Potter movie Web site at http://harrypotter.warnerbros.com, or the simpler example of the Die-Tanzschule Web site (http://www.die-tanzschule.de). They can also be very simple, functional screens such as the plug-in check from the EgoMedia site (see Figure 10-17) or the Harley-Davidson check for preferred language/country (http://www.harley-davidson.com).

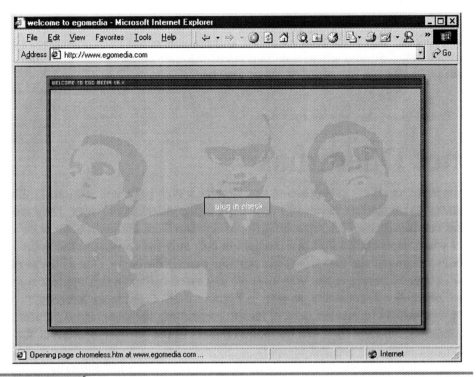

Figure 10-17 | EgoMedia employs a very simple splash screen while it is
confirming whether the user has the correct Flash plug-in
(http://www.egomedia.com)

10

Nobody seems to mind the little splash pages, but there can be quite heated
controversy about the merits of large, high-bandwidth splash pages. I am firmly
entrenched in the middle of the road on this argument. I have to admit that *if*
I'm not pushed for time and *if* I'm using a high-bandwidth connection, I rather
enjoy some of the more elaborate multimedia splash pages. (I just watched the
Harry Potter one a second time just for kicks!) But those two "ifs" are pretty big
ones, and there are also people who feel strongly that such splash pages are a
complete waste of their time.

The one clear solution for this dilemma is to always, always, always include
a way out for your users so that they can opt out of viewing your meticulously
crafted splash page. A "Skip Intro" link works very well and has become a de
facto standard for this task.

Tip

Make sure all "Skip Intro" links are HTML and not part of the Flash animation. I have actually seen sites where the "Skip Intro" link isn't available until after the Flash animation has downloaded. What a waste.

There. Now, that was an easy one.

Frames Dilemmas

Frames are an HTML construction that divides a Web page into sections (called "frames") that operate rather like miniature independent Web pages. They are most commonly used for separating the navigation from the main content so that when users click a link in a navigation bar, only the content in the main window changes; the navigation bar remains exactly the same. One of the most visible uses of frames in the Web sites we discussed earlier in this module is in the Conscience Records site, as seen in Figure 10-18. Conscience Records employs vertical frames on most of its site (separating the page into right and left halves), but then they add horizontal frames in the business section of the site (separating into top and bottom).

The white bar across the middle of the business section indicates the separation between the top and bottom frames. When users click one of the menu options in the top right-hand section, only the content in the bottom half changes. If they click the white brain animation in the top left-hand section, the whole screen is directed back to the home page.

Visit the site on the Web and note what happens to the URL in the Address field when you click each of the business links. Although the content in the bottom field changes with each click, the URL does not. This is one of the aspects of frames that causes confusion among users. Not only do frames make

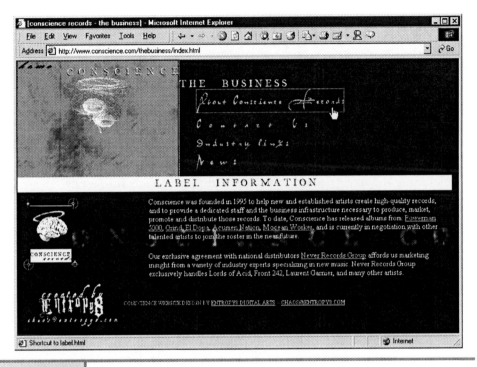

Figure 10-18   The top and bottom frames of Conscious Records'
business section are separated by a white bar, pictured here
(http://www.conscience.com/thebusiness/index.html)

it difficult to identify exactly where you are on a site, they also make it difficult
to bookmark any given content area to return to later or to communicate its
whereabouts to other users.

10

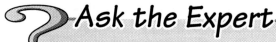

Ask the Expert

Question: How can you tell whether or not a site uses frames?

Answer: An easy way is to watch what changes on the screen when you click a link. If part of the screen remains visible while other parts change, chances are the site is using frames. The converse is not as straightforward as you might think, though, because of the various options available within the HTML for frames. If the whole page, including the navigation, disappears and then reloads into a new screen, the site may or may not be employing frames. In the case of the Conscience Records site, for example, if you click the white brain animation in the upper left-hand frame, it directs the whole page back to the home page.

To be absolutely sure, you can also check the source code to see if any of the HTML tags for frames are being used. These are pretty easy to recognize because they contain the word "frame" in them, such as <frameset> and <frame src=...>.

Since frames are a collection of mini–Web pages, they also require several pages of source code, one for each frame plus a primary one to determine the frame structure. The primary one is available through your browser options. In Explorer, for example, you can select View | Source. In Netscape, that would be View | Page Source. To see the individual coding for each frame, if you have a Windows PC, try right-clicking each section that looks as if it might be a frame and viewing the page source or the frame source. If you have a Mac, activate a frame by clicking somewhere within it, then use CTRL-click to open that page into its own window. You can then view the source code from the pop-up menu.

Debating whether or not it was okay to use frames used to keep Web designers up arguing late into the night. The controversy has quieted down somewhat, but that's more because people got tired of arguing about it than because there's an easy answer. From a usability perspective, however, guru Jakob Nielsen still considers frames one of the top ten mistakes in Web design, although he assigns it a "medium" score in terms of negatively impacting usability. As he says in his May 2, 1999, column:

"Frames are no longer the disaster they were in 1995 and early 1996 due to some advances in browser technology: Netscape fixed the Back button with version 3, and since virtually nobody uses version 1 and 2 any more, this means that users can now navigate through frames with fewer problems. Version 4 reduced the problems printing frames (though users still often get a different printout than they expected), and Internet Explorer 5 has finally regained the ability to bookmark pages despite the use of frames. Frames still prevent users from emailing a recommended URL to other users and they also make the page more clumsy to interact with." (For the full newsletter, see http://www.useit.com/alertbox/990502.html.)

Instead of banning the use of frames altogether, however, I would advise scrutinizing your user base. If they are a fairly Web-savvy group, they may be able to handle the difficulties with frames and thus appreciate some of the advantages frames afford, such as quicker loading time, since only the targeted frame needs to be reloaded. They are by no means a perfect solution, but frankly very little on the Web is!

In no case, however, would I recommend any efforts be made to prevent users from breaking out of your frames if you use them. If you try to view any of the band information in its own (bookmarkable) window on the current Herschel Freeman Agency site, for example, you may see this message: "This site is designed using frames. You have somehow followed a link which has brought you to this site without accessing the main index page. Click below to go to the Herschel Freeman Agency main page." Visit http://www .herschelfreemanagency.com/Kornog.html for this example.

A number of the Web sites we've been examining in this module, however, make good use of frames. In addition to the Conscience Records site we've discussed, the Macromedia site also uses frames for the navigation and search function and advertisement at the bottom of the page, and the Suzanne Vega site uses frames for the navigation.

10

Tip

Since frames did not become an official part of the W3C's HTML specifications until version 4, a number of the older browsers do not support them. Generally, you should provide an alternative non-frames-dependent version of the site for those users.

If your users are just learning how to navigate the Web, I would advise avoiding the use of frames, since they can be confusing.

1-Minute Drill

● True or False: Requiring users to have a particular browser to see a Web site is a common and accepted practice in Web development.

● Which version of the HTML specification formally adopted the use of frames?

The Challenge of Really Large Sites

If you didn't spend much time on the Harry Potter Web site when we were discussing splash pages, go back to it at http://harrypotter.warnerbros.com or pick another Warner Bros. movie that you are interested in from the Apple QuickTime site at http://www.apple.com/trailers. (Up until this moment, I have never seen a use for the way this site organizes movies by studio; I'd think most users would want to look up movies by title, wouldn't you?) For the moment, do *not* go to the main Warner Brothers Web site to choose one of their movies. Choose one instead from the Apple site. You'll see why in a minute.

Spend five to ten minutes exploring the site and finding out whatever you might like to know about the movie. When you've finished, click the Home button in the upper left-hand corner. Did you expect to go back to the home page of the Harry Potter site (or whichever site you chose)? I sure did. What a surprise to find that I was suddenly at what appeared to be a completely different site. Mind you, I wasn't really paying careful attention to the interface design when I first visited the site. I was, well, rather interested in the content— behaving rather like a user, I'm afraid. If I had scrutinized it, I would have noticed that, indeed, that top- level navigation bar was not for the Harry Potter site at all; it is for a Warner Bros. umbrella site. The Harry Potter site is a subsite of this much larger site.

Now reverse the process. From the Warner Bros. main site (http://www.warnerbros.com), navigate to the movie site you've just explored. Once there, the whole structure and process seem much more "intuitive." Many users coming from this direction might think, "Of course, that top navigation bar is for the Warner Brothers site, and the Harry Potter site uses the far left for its navigation menu. Duh!"

● False
● Version 4

That initial confusion, however, is a common experience on really large sites, and it is a usability problem. A judicious use of the bread crumbs that we discussed in Module 9 would go a long way toward eliminating some of this confusion. Just imagine an extra line near the top navigation of the Harry Potter Web site that looked like this: Warner Bros | Movies | Harry Potter.

With large Web sites, however, there is one huge dilemma: the seven, plus or minus two, guideline clashes with the three-clicks guideline we discussed in Module 8 whenever there are more than 729 distinct content areas on a Web site. If you allowed the maximum of nine category heads, each with nine subtopics, and each with nine sub-subtopics, users could reach only 729 content areas within three clicks: ($9\times9\times9$ = 729).

Some of the really large Web sites have thousands or even tens of thousands of pages. Creating a usable organizational system for this much information is a real challenge. Just about the only way to do it is to create subsites, like the Harry Potter site. If you look closely at the Warner Bros. main site, you can see that they have dozens of subsites, one for every television show, every movie, every DVD, etc.

Here are some guidelines for increasing the usability of large Web sites:

- Establish the context. Make it clear on every subsite, that it is, indeed, a subsite of a larger site.

- Treat every page as though it is some user's entry point. Users need to be able to determine very quickly exactly where they are in a site if they are to successfully navigate it. This means indicating where they are within a subsite and how that subsite relates to the larger umbrella site.

- Balance that fine line between establishing sitewide consistency and creating a distinct look and feel for each subsite. Yes, this is asking rather a lot, but it's not impossible. One avenue that I would highly recommend is to include the same global navigation for the umbrella site on all subsites. At the time of this writing, Warner Bros. does this for all of the recent movie sites, but if you delve deeper into the old movies, this breaks down. The link for *See Spot Run*, for example, takes you to an entirely separate site. Also, many of the nonmovie subsites have different global navigation systems, or again, none at all.

10

Project 10-1: Analyze a Large Site and Suggest Usability Improvements for Its Architecture and Navigation

The Disney Web site is a classic example of an enormous, unwieldy amount of information. Its business encompasses a wide range of components from producing cartoons and movies to hosting business conferences at its facilities like Disney World. As such, creating a single umbrella Web site with a number of coordinated subsites is a real challenge.

Disney continually evaluates and revises its clutch of sites, but I hazard to guess that, whatever stage the site is in while you are reading this book, there will be room for improvement.

Step-by-Step

1. Visit the main Disney site at http://www.disney.com and spend a good chunk of time exploring and evaluating it.

2. Assign yourself a set of tasks that would represent a good cross-section of users. These could include children, parents, business people, tourists or other travelers, international fans, etc. Repeatedly, starting at the home page, try to complete each task with as few clicks as possible. Put your usability spectacles on for this activity, and try to think like each one of the targeted user groups.

3. Take notes on any missteps that you make and your thoughts on what might have led you astray or confused you.

4. Finally, compose a list of suggestions for improving the usability of the site, particularly paying attention to the information architecture and navigation. Be on the lookout, among other things, for better ways to establish the context of the whole site from any point within the site and to balancing the line between sitewide consistency and subsite distinction.

5. E-mail the list, if you feel so inclined, to the Disney Webmaster.

Project Summary

As you can see, there are many possibilities for improving upon even the most established sites, such as Disney.com. As a rule of thumb, the larger and more diverse the content is, the more difficult it will be to create an easy-to-use Web site. The key is in finding a good way to break the site into coherent subsites *without* losing the integrity of the whole. Maintaining the context of the overall site is crucial.

Module Conclusion

Now that we've gotten the site design usability dilemmas out of the way, the rest of the process should be a breeze. All that's left for us now is to focus on specific aspects of the design process. We'll discuss screen design in the next module, and then content preparation in Module 12.

10

☑ *Mastery Check*

1. Which of the following are valid components of the "plug-in conundrum"?

   A. Version of plug-ins

   B. Screen resolution support

   C. Manufacturer of plug-ins

   D. User adoption of plug-ins

2. Which of the following is the common abbreviation for Flash files?

   A. swf

   B. dir

   C. fla

   D. fls

   E. swd

3. Which of the following is the common abbreviation for Shockwave files?

   A. swf

   B. dir

   C. fla

   D. fls

   E. swd

4. Which of the following concerns should be the first one addressed whenever you are considering making any part of your site dependent on browser plug-ins?

   A. Consider how to tell your users how to install the plug-ins.

   B. Consider which version of the plug-in to require.

   C. Consider how to perform a plug-in check on your users' systems.

   D. Consider alternative ways to present the content.

☑ *Mastery Check*

5. True or False: In the early days of the Web, building Web sites to work on specific browsers made some sort of sense from a usability perspective.

_____

_____

6. True or False: In designing a Web site with Cascading Style Sheets, it is best to optimize it for one version of one browser, but it is also important to test it on other browsers.

_____

_____

7. Which of the following is a surefire solution for the splash page dilemma?

    A. Avoid creating any splash pages for any site.

    B. Always include a link to bypass the splash page.

    C. Give your users a choice between small and large versions of the splash page.

    D. Include vital information in the splash page, so users have to watch it.

8. Which of the following statements are *not* true about frames?

    A. Frames always link from one to the other. They are never self-referential.

    B. If a navigation bar is included in a frame, it will stay visible when a user clicks one of the links.

    C. There is a limit of six frames per Web page.

    D. Horizontal and vertical frames can be mixed on the same page.

    E. You can always determine whether or not a site uses frames by observing its behavior.

10

Mastery Check

9. True or False: Bookmarking a section of a site contained within a frame is problematic.

   _____

   _____

10. Which of the following approaches will help ensure a large Web site is also usable?

    A. Divide the site up into a number of independent, smaller sites and forget the idea of one large one.

    B. Create a single information architecture map that will include all the components of the site.

    C. Treat every page as though it is some user's entry point.

    D. Establish a consistent, sitewide global navigation system.

Module 11

Screen Design for Usability

The Goals of This Module

- Identify the elements of screen design for the Web that affect usability
- Determine the appropriate screen size for your design
- Determine the appropriate amount of content to include on each screen
- Understand how to direct the user's eye with the screen design
- Understand the color limitations of screen design for the Web
- Identify how to ensure on-screen readability
- Understand the importance of establishing consistency in screen design

Screen design is a huge task unto itself and requires a great deal of creativity, talent, and aesthetics, among other things. In this module, we will address some of the key aspects that affect Web sites' usability, so we will focus primarily on the following functional aspects of the design:

- What screen size do you design for?

- How much content should be included on one screen?

- Telling a story/directing the user's eye

- Using color on the Web

- Ensuring readability

- Establishing consistency

What Screen Size?

So you're creating some comps (comprehensive designs) for a Web site whose target audience predominantly use an 800×600 screen resolution. What's the first thing you do? Start a new file in an image-editing program like Photoshop that is 800 pixels wide by 600 pixels high, as in the following illustration?

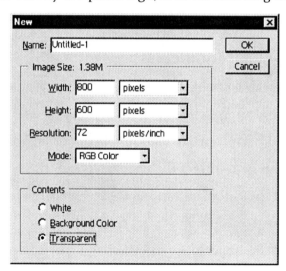

Not on your life. If you design a Web site for the full screen resolution, you will guarantee that some of the contents will be cut off because of all the space taken up on computer monitors by the browser and operating system paraphernalia. It is necessary, instead, to subtract all of these space-grabbing components to determine the maximum viewable screen size that you can design for. Use the following as a generic formula for determining the viewable screen size in pixels:

User screen resolution, 640×480, etc.
– Operating system space
– Browser space
Viewable screen size

Unfortunately, however, there's no magical single set of numbers for the amount of space taken up by the operating systems and browsers, because they vary just a little bit with each new version. Additionally, users can often set their own preferences, which may affect the size and placement of all this extra stuff. Take for instance the Windows PC taskbar (the menu bar that includes the "Start" menu). The default setting for the taskbar is at the bottom of the screen and takes up 28 pixels in height, but users may also choose to make it invisible or drag it to the side to convert it from horizontal to vertical, as in Figure 11-1.

Figure 11-1   When users change the position of such things as the Windows taskbar from, for instance, horizontal to vertical, it changes how much screen space is available for viewing Web sites

11

This otherwise harmless change alters the space available for viewing Web sites. In this case, it reduces the available width by 60 pixels while increasing the available height by 28 pixels.

Of course different operating systems have slightly different space needs as well. The Macintosh OS, for example, typically requires 20 pixels in height. The user can also move its menus around the screen as well, however.

As for browsers, each brand and each version of that brand requires a slightly different amount of space for its menus. Additionally, each browser requires an extra little bit of padding inside its own windows so that the contents of the Web site do not run up against the edge of the browser. This is commonly referred to as *browser offset*. There also are a myriad of settings the users can change that affect the size of the viewable area, such as which toolbars appear and whether or not text or icons (or both) appear, etc. And, of course, users can make the least predictable change of all: they can drag the corner of the browser window to make it whatever size with whatever proportions they want.

Hint

It is possible to override the browser offsets in HTML for versions 4.x and above of Netscape and Internet Explorer. To do this, you need to assign a value of 0 to the marginheight and marginwidth attributes (for Netscape) and the topmargin and leftmargin attributes (for Internet Explorer). It is necessary to use all four attributes if you want to override the offsets in both browsers. This will not, however, override the offsets of browsers prior to the 4.x version releases or browsers other than Netscape and Explorer.

Don't despair, however. Although you cannot determine exactly what screen size will be fully visible on every user's monitor, you can hedge your bets by using the largest dimensions required by the browser and operating system default settings. Table 11-1 lists these settings for Netscape versions 3.x–6.x and Internet Explorer 3.x–5.x. Fortunately for Web designers in this case, many users never change the default settings. This will give you the safest, or worst-case scenario, screen size for the default operating system and browser settings.

Tip

Whenever a new operating system or browser comes out, check its default space requirements against the maximum defaults listed in Table 11-1. If they require even more space, then substitute its numbers into your equations. Also, if you know your target audience is using a specific platform or browser, base your design screen size on those specific needs.

Maximum Sizes of Default Settings

	Operating System Menus	Browser Menus	Browser Offsets
Width	0 pixels	67 pixels	10 pixels
Height	28 pixels	162 pixels	15 pixels

Table 11-1	Maximum Current Space Taken Up by the Default Settings for Macintosh and Windows PC Operating Systems and Netscape and Internet Explorer Browsers

Hint

For a breakdown of the space available within each version of Netscape and Internet Explorer, visit the WebMonkey site at http://hotwired.lycos.com/webmonkey/99/41/index3a_page3.html or Module 3 of *Web Design: A Beginner's Guide* by Wendy Willard (McGraw-Hill/Osborne, 2001).

Thus, as a rule of thumb, you can plug the numbers from Table 11-1 into the generic formula. For example, if your user screen resolution is 640×480, you would get a viewable screen size of 563×275:

Width×Height		
User screen resolution	640	480
– Operating system space	0	28
– Browser menus	67	162
– Browser offset	10	15
Viewable screen size	563	275

There's one more factor to take into consideration if you are designing with frames. You need to allow extra space for the frame borders, or edges, and scroll bars. Each edge (top, bottom, and sides) generally takes up about 6 pixels, although you may customize this within the HTML.

The default sizes for scroll bars range from 13 to 16 pixels, again depending on which browser and operating system. It is possible to specify within your HTML that the scroll bars should be invisible. Use caution when doing this, however, since it will mean users who are looking at your site in a smaller viewable screen area than you have designed for may not be able to access all the information within the frame. This would also be the case for visually impaired users who increase the default type size for easier readability.

11

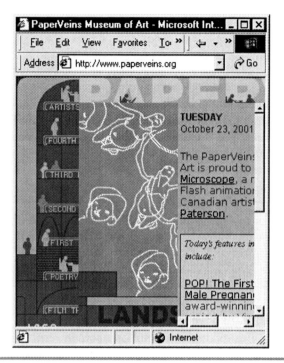

Figure 11-2   The scroll bars on the frame that contains the navigation in this example are invisible, so if the users reduce the size of the window, they lose access to some of that information (http://www.paperveins.org)

The PaperVeins site in Figure 11-2 is an example of a site for which the designer made a deliberate decision to enable scroll bars for the primary text areas and to disable them for the more visual areas. This solution works well by and large, except for the most extreme cases in which the user reduces the window to a tiny area, as I've done here. I would hazard to guess, however, that this extreme user behavior is pretty rare.

Project 11-1: Determine Viewable Screen Sizes

Now it's your turn: Using the material you have just learned, determine the viewable screen size for users with different systems.

Step-by-Step

1. Use the viewable screen size equation and the largest default settings from Table 11-1 to determine the viewable screen size for an 800×600 screen resolution: _____

2. Compute the viewable screen resolution for users with a 1024×768 screen resolution who are also using recent versions of Netscape and Explorer that will allow you to set the browser offset to 0: _____

Project Summary

Once you get the hang of it, this is a piece of cake. All you need to do is substitute the user screen resolution into the equation as follows to see that the viewable screen size for users with an 800×600 resolution is 723×395.

Width×Height		
User screen resolution	800	600
– Operating system space	0	28
– Browser menus	67	162
– Browser offset	10	15
Viewable screen size	723	395

In the second task, you need to substitute the 1024×768 resolution and delete the browser offset, since you will control the margins within the HTML file.

Width×Height		
User screen resolution	1024	768
– Operating system space	0	28
– Browser menus	67	162
– ~~Browser offset~~	~~10~~	~~15~~
Viewable screen size	957	578

1-Minute Drill

● What are the current maximum browser offsets?

● What are the current maximum default sizes for browser menus?

How Much Content Should Be Included on One Screen?

Now that you know how to determine the viewable screen size for a given set of users, you need to address the question of "What *all* do you include on each screen?" It may be possible to include an entire product catalog on a single, long, scrolling page, but this may not be your best choice in terms of usability!

● 10 pixels in width and 15 pixel in height
● 67 pixels in width and 162 pixels in height

Three factors can help determine how to distribute the content between pages:

● Content groups

● Download speed

● To scroll or not to scroll?

Content Groups

The first things to look for when determining what content to include on a single page are natural breaks by subject matter. If you are handed a booklet, for example, detailing the long history of a paper manufacturing company, chances are the information will already be broken into subtopics. There might be a biography of the founder, a list of former CEOs or other important employees, a timeline of improvements in machinery and the paper manufacturing process, and information on the company's involvement with the community.

Each of these topics may merit having its own page, or even its own set of pages. The information on the company's involvement with the community could be further broken down into, say, their support of the local high school's baseball team, a scholarship program for employee's children, and sponsorship of a series of business luncheons.

Length will often dictate how many topics can be most effectively grouped together. If you have only one sentence of material about each of three community programs, for example, it would be silly to put each sentence on its own page.

One crystal-clear guideline in determining how much content to include on each page is that it's a good idea to include as much related content as possible that can be displayed within the viewable screen area—without cluttering it up and without overwhelming your user's bandwidth limitations.

If a content group is larger in size than the viewable screen area or demands a larger download than is acceptable, then you need to consider the other factors as well.

Tip

Many of the decisions about how to distribute the content between pages should be done at the information architecture stage. In many cases, however, the information architects do not have all the content at hand in the early stages of planning a Web site. They may only know, for example, that there needs to be a section on a company's history, not whether or not there's one paragraph's worth of material or ten pages.

Download Speed

As we discussed in Module 4, no page should take longer than ten seconds to download on your users' systems. One second or one-tenth of a second would be even better!

You can fit a lot of HTML text into a ten-second download, but the minute you start introducing graphics or other media, you'd better start breaking your content into pages based on download speeds (preferably along content group division lines).

In the example of three community programs, for instance, if you also have an illustration or photograph to accompany each single sentence description, you might well be able to include all three on the same Web page. This is providing, of course, that you optimize each of the graphics and make them small enough that they don't surpass your download requirements.

If you have accompanying videos instead of graphics, it would be unwise to include all three on the same page—both for bandwidth reasons and to avoid overwhelming the user with multiple videos playing at the same time. It could work, though, to have a still shot taken from each video on the page, with a link from each to its corresponding video.

Likewise, if you have half a dozen photographs to accompany each description, it would make a lot of sense to break this section into three pages. Even then, to optimize the download speed, you might want to have small thumbnail images of the photographs grouped together with the option to link on each one to see a larger image. Keep in mind, however, that users with particularly large screen resolutions, such as 1600×1200 workstations, may have a hard time seeing very small thumbnails.

To Scroll or Not to Scroll?

Finally, there's a hotly debated question of whether or not to include so much content on a page that your users are forced to scroll to see it all. There is no easy black-and-white answer to this question; it has a wide gray area in the middle. Some users refuse to scroll, and some situations make it impossible not to design pages that have to scroll. There are, however, a few guidelines around the perimeter.

Users should *not* have to scroll to see primary navigation options; navigation should be considered vital information, and it should be clearly visible within the initial screen area when the page loads, often referred to as "above the fold." Nor should they have to scroll to see information that they have just clicked a link for. If a user has clicked a link, the information they have requested should take a high priority, and the beginning of it, at the very least, should be immediately visible. If users do not see what they have requested, they will often think a page is broken before thinking to scroll down to see if the material has appeared further down the page.

In general, only nonessential information should be presented outside this instantaneously viewable area above the fold. Keep in mind, however, that users rarely scroll down on a home page to read extra, nonessential information. If information is this nonessential, it is worth asking yourself if it should be included on the Web site at all.

When it comes right down to it, most users do not like to scroll. About the only time that users do willingly scroll is if they are interested in reading a longer block of text that has been introduced to them within the readily viewable screen area. Lengthy text-based articles or documents that users will either read in a linear fashion (from beginning to end without much skipping around) on-screen or print out for later reading are best presented as single, scrollable pages. This facilitates a continuous reading process and ease of printing the whole document. An exception is in the case of very lengthy documents, however, which should best be broken down into multiple, lengthy, scrollable pages to alleviate the cumbersome nature of such a long document; 1000 words per grouping is a good goal.

Lengthy documents that have clear divisions by sections and that users may want to read in a nonlinear fashion are best broken into appropriate content sections with a mini–table of contents available with each section. This provides the necessary flexibility for the readers.

Of course, it's always a good idea to give your users options. The online *New York Times* (http://www.nytimes.com) is an excellent example. Their default presentation breaks each article into scrollable chunks that are roughly five times as long as the viewable area within a browser at an 800×600 screen resolution (approximately 1000 words in length). At the bottom of the first such page, however, they give readers the option of viewing each of the subsequent groupings of similar length in sequence or the entire article on a single, long, scrollable page. They also include a "Printer-Friendly Format" button at the top of each page, which enables users to print out the entire article, instead of having to print each page by itself. Additionally, consider making such lengthy documents available in a downloadable form, such as Adobe Acrobat PDFs.

Caution

Horizontal scrolling is generally a no-no, and designing pages that require users to scroll horizontally will often elicit scathing remarks from other designers. This is largely due to usability problems. Users do not expect horizontal scrolling and are even less likely to observe that it is an option than in the case of vertical scrolling. To play devil's advocate, however, there are some cases where it can work well. Timelines are one that users are used to seeing in a horizontal format. Another example is the BrainCraft site. It employs an interesting interface for the portfolio section that uses horizontal scrolling. See the Flash version of http://www.braincraft.com. BrainCraft is not, however, the first, nor the only company to use this device contrary to all "design rules." Keep an eye out for others and add them to your Web Library.

1-Minute Drill

- What three factors help determine how to distribute the content between pages?
- What is the maximum time that should be allowed for a Web page to download?

Direct the User's Eye

Many graphic design courses emphasize that a designer's role is to tell a story through design. This applies to Web screen design as much as to page layout in print design. It is the screen designer's job not only to communicate each piece of information on a Web page to the user, complete with nuance and texture, but also to tell the story of the relationship of the content sharing a space. You can achieve this by building each page as though you are directing the user's eye.

Ask yourself the following questions: What should the user see first? Then second? Then third? What content is the most important, second most, etc., and how do all the other pieces relate to these? Are they subsets? Or perhaps tangents? If they appear to be unrelated, why do they appear on the same page?

11

- Content groups, download speed, and whether or not to scroll
- Ten seconds

Then design the screen to reveal the priority of content. There is a reason why company logos are often placed in the upper-left corner; they establish the identity of the Web site and preside over all the content rather like a king. Navigation is usually a handy bar either on the left side or across the top, again prominently placed in part of the screen that is most likely to be visible even in a worst-case scenario. The beginning of the key content for a page is often next in line, centered somewhere near the top. Depending on the site goals, this can appear to be either less or more prominent than the navigation and identifying logo. Or at least it *ought* to be determined by the site goals! Too often, the screen design is haphazard and is not tied into telling a coherent story.

But here, this all sounds rather vague. Why don't you try it out from the user's perspective?

Project 11-2: Observe How You "Read" a Web Page

If you have not paid attention in the past to the path your eye follows when you are viewing Web pages or even printed pieces, then this project is especially important. If you are already intimately familiar with this process, then consider using this project just as a reminder of a very important step.

Tip

Consider using this activity to add to your Web Library.

Step-by-Step

1. Open your browser window to a standard full-screen size with either 640×480 or 800×600 screen resolution.

2. Revisit some of your favorite Web sites, or pick a couple from the following list:

   - http://www.madxs.com
   - http://store.gofuse.com (after the Flash intro)
   - http://www.virtualflowers.com

● http://www.daycare.com

● http://www.att.com

3. If the page is slow to load, avert your eyes from the screen until it has fully loaded. In some cases, designers have carefully determined which items should load first, and at other times it is wholly random, so it is best to eliminate this influence on you for the purposes of analyzing screen designs as whole units.

4. As you view each Web page, pay close attention to what catches your eye first, second, third, and so on. Jot them down quickly before you judge them or change your own pattern. Include each time your eye returns to an item in this list as well.

5. Then from an objective distance, analyze the order to determine whether or not the design is intentionally directing your eye or if it seems random. Jot down what contributes to the success or the failures of such "story telling."

6. Finally, consider what role the *white space*, the space between elements, plays in each design as well.

Project Summary

The more you practice this, the more adept you will become at observing the pathway that your eye takes through a Web screen design and the manner in which it enables you to construct meaning. With the Virtual Flowers site, for example, it's very clear from first glance that it is an ornate—dare I say "flowery"?—site that has something to do with flowers. The actual content of the site and the navigation options are not apparent, however, until you read the text labels, which came sixth on my own documentation of the path my eye followed.

The GoFuse site, on the other hand (after the Flash intro), is such a welcome respite from busy home pages, isn't it? With only three items to view, it makes me stop and absorb each one. Thus, I enter the site much more fully comprehending what the options are than with most other sites.

As for the white space, this is another important tool in your design kit. I like to think of it as serving a purpose similar to punctuation in text or silence within musical pieces. For one thing, it gives the user's eye a rest, but it also helps arrange the space and establish priority among elements. It's not always necessary to use the largest typeface on the content with the highest priority, for instance. It's equally possible to emphasize it by using a small typeface surrounded by an ocean of white space. The eye goes straight to it and has the room to dwell on it.

11

Color and the Myth of the "Web-Safe Palette"

Most people think about color as something pretty that contributes to the aesthetic appeal of a design. The use of color in Web design, however, also has some pretty significant usability components. Generally, the easiest place to recognize this, of course, is when color is used badly.

The use of glaring, jarring colors in bad combinations, for instance, can elicit almost a physical revulsion. If you see users pull back from looking at a screen as though trying to put as much physical distance between themselves and the Web site as possible, then you have a pretty strong usability clue—unless, of course, that is the goal of the particular Web site.

Conversely, if you observe users leaning in more closely to the screen with a pursed brow, squinting as they try to make out the words, you also have a usability clue. In this case, you likely have a readability problem, which may be caused by a poor use of color (particularly low contrast between the text and background) or a number of other factors, which we'll be discussing in the later section "Ensure Readability."

Color Guidelines

In between these extremes, however, there are very fine gradations between the effective use of color. Here are some guidelines to follow when establishing color schemes for Web sites:

- Use appropriate colors for the audience and the site goals.

- Use colors within the navigation to support the information architecture (as we discussed in Module 9).

- Avoid unnecessary busyness through the overuse of color.

- Don't rely exclusively on color.

Tip

I highly recommend that you take this book with you to your computer and check out some of the Web sites while reading this section. We, umm, have a little usability problem here in discussing color within a black-and-white book!

Use Appropriate Colors for the Audience and the Site Goals

Take advantage of some common divisions in the use of color throughout our culture, such as the use of primary colors (bright reds, blues, greens, and yellows) for kids. These are bright and happy, playful colors. Take a look at the logo for Toys R Us at http://www.toysrus.com for one example. Or scan a number of other kids' sites such as the following:

- http://www.lego.com
- http://www.mattel.com
- http://www.boowakwala.com
- http://www.bbc.co.uk/littlekids/
- http://www.barneyonline.com

Business Colors   The IBM shade of blue is a cultural hallmark for business, particularly professional, somewhat conservative businesses that want to elicit a sense of security. Banks, management firms, and professional services firms fall right in this category. Try doing a search on any general business subject and glance at the home pages of the first ten entries. You might be surprised at just how many of them use predominantly blue in their design. Here are a few examples as well:

- http://www.ibm.com
- http://www.uofcfcu.com
- http://www.bankofamerica.com
- http://www.sba.gov
- http://www.prosavvy.com
- http://www.pmsinc.com

This is not to say you must use blue in all business Web sites. This audience can also be comfortable with other sedate, harmonizing colors. Review some of these women's business sites for their use of slightly more innovative color:

- http://www.womensbusinesscenter.org
- http://www.sbaonline.sba.gov/womeninbusiness

11

- http://www.cdnbizwomen.com

- http://www.wyomingwomen.org/

- http://www.graspnet.org/women.html

Energy Colors   High-contrasting colors may be targeted at youth or young adults and can convey a jazzy sense of energy. They may also certainly target other adults, even the same ones who use the more conservative business sites. Just as there are divisions within our own life between business and pleasure or daytime activities and nightlife, there can be divisions between color schemes that may appeal to users at different times in their day. Also, note how a number of "younger" companies or even whole industries, such as the dot-com industry, also sometimes take advantage of the energy conveyed by highly contrasting colors. Wired Magazine, for instance, set the tone in the early 1990s with bright, highly saturated colors. Its Web site today is considerably more subdued, but is still in the same vein. Check out some of these sites:

- http://www.wired.com

- http://www.girlshop.com

- http://forum-snowboards.com

- http://dreamworksrecords.com

- http://www.billabong-usa.com

- http://www.bonesmovie.com

Earth Tones   These are some of my personal favorite color schemes; they convey a much more down-to-earth attitude. They, perhaps not surprisingly, are used more on outdoors sites, gardening sites, environmentalist sites, or sites that convey a relaxed, weekend-like lifestyle. I'd encourage you to search topics or hobbies that you like to engage in on the middle of a Saturday afternoon to see if there are any correlations in color schemes. Additionally, here are some sites that make good use of earth tone color schemes:

- http://www.oneworldjourneys.com

- http://www.arizhwys.com

- http://www.audubon.org

- http://www.rei.com

● http://www.archcrafters.com

● http://www.onedayhikes.com

Use Colors Within the Navigation to Support the Information Architecture

As we discussed in Module 9, the colors used within the navigation design can be immensely helpful in supporting the information architecture. (See Module 9 for more details.)

Avoid Unnecessary Busyness Through the Overuse of Color

This ought to go without saying, but it's surprising how many Web sites are out there where the designer just went overboard with the color. Do not add color for color's sake. Just as with all the other elements of design, each introduction of a new element should have a justifiable rationale for how it will help the user better understand a message.

Don't Rely Exclusively on Color

This is an area where print design must by necessity vary a bit from Web design. In print design, you can rely exclusively on a color to impart information—so long as you avoid colors that a significant number of your audience are not color-blind to. The Web, however, has a much higher percentage of users who are visually impaired and, thus, are relying on things other than your color scheme or graphics.

Additionally, you cannot control the color that is displayed on a Web user's monitor with nearly the same precision that you can in print design. In print design, you can go stand by the printer and conduct press checks to confirm that the colors are exactly what you intended. Not so in Web design. Even with using colors from the so-called Web-safe palette, there are many factors that affect the display of colors on monitors, including such things as age, brand, and user adjustments to the settings.

With all that said, the next question is, "Which colors can you use with any chance of maintaining a consistent display?" Unfortunately, this does not have as simple an answer as I imagine you'd like to hear.

Which Colors Can You Use?

It wasn't so long ago that every Web designer "knew" there were exactly 216 colors that could be relied on to appear consistently across every browser and operating system. Well, it turns out that they've been wrong about that for some time now. As David Lehn and Hadley Stern have pointed out in a WebMonkey article, in reality, there are only 22 colors that are truly "Web-safe." The colors are listed in Table 11-2. (See their full article at http://www.hotwired.lycos.com/webmonkey/00/37/index2a.html.) The remaining 194 colors are consistent only in certain situations.

Tip

To see the truly Web-safe palette in color, visit Lehn's and Stern's article at http://www.hotwired.lycos.com/webmonkey/00/37/stuff2a/complete_websafe_216/reallysafe_palette.html. To see the original Web-safe palette, visit Lynda Weinman's Web site at http://www.lynda.com/hexh.html.

Having a palette limited to 22 rather randomly selected colors, with a decided leaning toward green, makes it a bit difficult to design unique, attractive, compelling screens, doesn't it? Well, right in line with so many other Web "solutions," there are a few options if you're willing to bend a little. Mind you, designers usually have no problem "bending" the rules, but realize that what's at stake here is the consistency of how your Web site will be presented on your users' systems. Thus, it is inherently a usability issue, so be cautious about bending too easily—or too far.

First off, it's necessary to understand that the key problem with the original Web-safe palette is that it does not display the colors properly on operating systems set to thousands of colors (16-bit). Ironically, the original Web-safe colors display correctly for the most part on both 256-color displays (8-bit) and millions of color displays (24-bit or 32-bit), catching the lowest and highest technology users. Unfortunately, however, at the time Lehn and Sterne wrote their article, the lion's share of users (56 percent) had systems set to display

FFFFFF	FF00FF	33FF33
FFFF33	FF0000	00FFCC
CCFF66	000033	00FF00
66FF33	FFFF66	FF0033
33FFFF	FFFF00	0000FF
33FF66	66FFFF	000000
00FFFF	66FF00	
00FF66	33FFCC	

Table 11-2   The Truly Web-Safe Palette, Discovered By David Lehn And Hadley Stern

thousands of colors. This spread makes it very difficult to ignore any one group. Increasingly, computers are sold with heavy-duty graphics cards, so eventually the vast majority of users will, hopefully, have their monitors set to millions of colors, but you can't rely on that for general-interest Web sites today.

Once again, the discussion comes around to needing to know exactly what technology any given Web site's user base has. If you can determine that the vast majority of all your users have 16-bit displays or a combination of 8-bit and 32-bit, for instance, then you can choose your palette accordingly. In most cases, however, the user base will encompass all three levels of technology. So what can you do? I can think of only three viable solutions:

- Stick to the really Web-safe palette of 22 colors.

- Add to the really Web-safe palette by creating hybrid colors by juxtaposing pixels of those 22 colors within an image editing program to give the illusion of a third color. (This only works within graphic images; you cannot specify a hybrid color within HTML.)

- Design to the majority of your user base and test like crazy on the other systems to ensure that the results are acceptable. Modify them as needed.

Ensure Readability

Ensuring readability is one of the preeminent usability issues for screen design. To begin with, the current monitor technologies don't make it very enjoyable to read on-screen; in fact, they contribute to a great deal of eyestrain. Thus, Web designers have to be even more diligent than print designers in doing everything they can to make all the text easily readable, right down to the small print commonly found at the bottom of Web pages with links to information about copyrights, licensing, security, etc.

The good news is that ensuring readability is fairly easy to accomplish. Here are four guidelines, some of which we have already touched on, so you're probably familiar with them.

11

Type Size

This may sound silly, it's so obvious—you know what I'm going to say, don't you?!—but I've got to say it anyway: Don't design Web sites using small type that is difficult to read. You might be surprised at just how many Web sites intentionally design screens using a tiny type size, just because it looks, well, cool. I'll be the first to admit that I *like* the look of really tiny type with generous leading (the space between the lines), but that does not make it usable or suitable or kosher or anything in the realm of acceptable. Don't do it—unless you are using type as a purely graphical accent and don't want the users to read it.

Keep in mind, too, as we discussed in Module 4, that different operating systems can display type in different sizes. The exact same font and type size on a Windows PC, for example, typically appears about two points smaller on Macintosh computers. The current browsers are beginning to compensate for this difference, but by all means, whenever you are using a type size bordering on small, test it on all the systems that your user base has to determine whether or not the type size is still *easily* readable. Oh, and make it larger if it is not. I've never heard anyone complain about a font being too large!

Font Choice

As you may recall from Module 4, there are a limited number of fonts that you can specify within HTML that are likely to be installed on *all* of your users' systems. This is largely due to the relatively small overlap between fonts automatically installed on both Windows PCs and Macintosh computers. The system default fonts are not necessarily the best fonts for designing Web pages either.

Your best bet is to specify a number of font faces, including one or more system fonts, and to make sure that your Web site design looks good with all of them. Also, it is a very good idea to specify as your last option the type of face that you envision. Typically, this is either *serif* or *sans serif*. These are fancy terms, but they're easy to remember once you understand what they are. Serif typefaces have extra little strokes, called serifs, along the edges, like this Times New Roman font face that you are reading. "Sans" means "without," so sans serif typefaces are without serifs. You can see the difference as follows:

T

T

Now, it's important to understand that in print design, serif typefaces have long been considered more readable than nonserif faces. Thus, the Times typeface has been used in newspapers like the *New York Times* for decades. The opposite *generally* holds true for screen design. I emphasize "generally" because this is a rather debated topic, and type designers are creating all sorts of wonderful fonts specifically for reading on-screen that may prove to be exceptions. In general, however, when designing on the Web, use sans serif typefaces for the major portion of the text, and restrict the use of serif typefaces for headlines or special uses.

Tip

In the long run, more of these new fonts designed specifically for the screen should be included in the default system font package as well as being included with browsers, so Web typography prospects are quite promising for the future.

In designing *graphics* that include text, you, of course, have many more choices for font faces. In fact, you can use any typeface that you want. When you optimize the file for the Web, it will automatically convert the whole graphic, including the letters, into bitmap form, which does not require the font to be installed on the user's system.

There are two downsides to using graphical text from a usability standpoint, however. One is that the files are larger and thus require more time to download. The second is that the words are no longer recognizable to any of the technologies as text, so text-readers or search engines, for example, perceive them only as a graphic. It is thus necessary to add a description of what the words say within the HTML file, using either the Alt or Title attributes.

This is not to say that you should never use graphical type. Take a look at how the Hillman Curtis Web site employs type in Figure 11-3. If possible, visit the site on the Web and analyze its source code as well. Although the navigation options look very simple, clean, and unpretentious, as though they were created in HTML, they are actually graphical type, and the links are created through the use of an image map.

Curtis uses quite a small type size, about the smallest you can get away with, but he has carefully selected a sans-serif font that is highly readable. This typeface is not available on most of his users' computers, so he maintains the consistency of its look, feel, and functionality by freezing it as graphical text. Additionally, he has optimized each of the graphics so that they are quite small in file size, 2KB and 3KB, respectively, so they do not hamper the download speed.

11

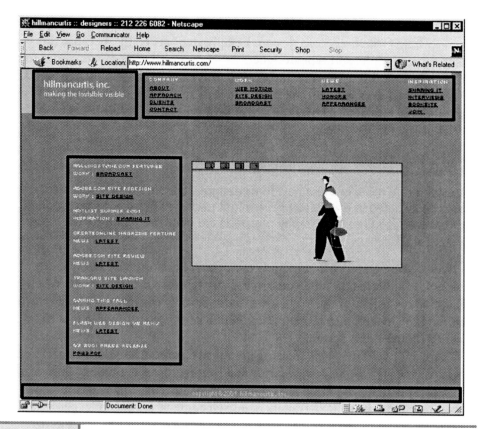

Figure 11-3 The HillmanCurtis home page uses four graphics (indicated by the black boxes) to control the display of type on the site (http://www.hillmancurtis.com)

Caution

Sites that rely predominantly on graphical text can also pose difficulties for search engines trying to index them, because these engines can't "read" the type. Providing alternative text thus becomes doubly important, as well as fleshing out the Meta tags. Search engines also give preference to sites that include multiple uses of a search term. Thus, a site with a search term included in a Meta tag and an HTML level-one head will get a higher ranking than a site that has the same term in a Meta tag and in a graphical type that fills the role of a level-one head.

Contrast

The higher the contrast between words and their background, the easier the text is to read. This applies to all forms of design. Here, let me show you what I'm talking about:

Having black type on black background is extremely low contrast (in fact, there is no contrast), making it impossible to distinguish the letters of the words from their backgrounds and, thus, rather impairing their readability.

If you have a light background, like the white pages of this book, then it's best to use a dark color for the type, like this black type. The same for Web sites. The converse is true as well. If you use a dark background, then by all means use a light color for the type.

There may be a certain intrigue to having murky type of a similar hue to the background, but if you actually want the users to be able to read the words, then you'll have to make some aesthetic sacrifices.

Tip

To check how well your pages hold up in compromised color situations, try switching your monitor to grayscale for a minute. If your content is unreadable because of a lack of contrast, consider changing some colors to increase that contrast.

11

Background Complications

It's wonderful to be able to create interesting backgrounds for Web sites. They can influence the whole mood and tone of the Web site in subtle, or not so subtle, ways. When it comes to being able to read text over them, however, backgrounds can certainly get in the way.

Here's a simple rule:

One of the challenges in Web site design is that different pages sometimes have different needs. It is not uncommon, for example, for a home page to have considerably more white space than pages deeper into the site. Thus, home pages can sometimes take advantage of more elaborate backgrounds than can more text-laden pages.

One good technique to keep in mind is that you can use the same background throughout the Web site but alter its opacity when text needs to appear over it. By reducing the opacity, you make it more transparent or "screen it back," as many Web designers refer to it. Thus, our wayward background in the previous illustration can become more text-friendly if the background is given only 30 percent opacity:

Admittedly, this is still not the most ideal background for a Web site. In order to increase the contrast between type and its background to increase readability, it is necessary to make the background have less internal contrast. In effect, if you have a background that has highly contrasting colors in it, such as black and white, it will be next to impossible to find a color that will contrast well with them both. In some cases, designers will change the color of individual letters to increase their contrast with whichever part of the background they are superimposed over. This is a labor-intensive approach, but it can be worth the effort.

Consistency, Consistency, Consistency (Again)

Do you have a strange déjà vu feeling that we already had a section called "Consistency, Consistency, Consistency?" If so, you're absolutely right. In Module 9, we discussed the importance of establishing consistent navigation throughout the site. This applies as well to the overall look, feel, and functionality of the screen design.

Once you've established the design, you need do only three things:

- **Create templates**   Electronic files that can be used as models for each page or section

- **Create style guides**   Documentation of all the design decisions needed to re-create any section of the Web site

- **Stick to them!**

Ask the Expert

Question: What exactly is a style guide?

Answer: A style guide is a document, often with supporting electronic files, that details all of the design parameters for a Web site including decisions made about format, structure, and layout. It is designed to be of use to anybody developing or updating the site and puts forth a set of rules (or design decisions) so that the site will maintain the integrity of its design, regardless of who is working on it.

Question: What all should be included in a style guide?

Answer: In the real world, the contents of style guides can vary quite a bit. They can be a bare-bones documentation of the graphical and media treatment of a site, or they can couch the design decisions in terms of the overall site purpose and philosophy to help enable good design decisions to be made in the future. Here are two sample table of contents:

1. **Introduction**

2. **Format and Structure**

   Directory Structure

   Overall Logic of Site Structure

   Guidelines for Adding Content

   Avoiding Dead Ends

   Provide Links to Home Throughout

11

3. **Graphics and Visual Style**

Page Elements

Logo Usage and Specifications

Colors

Fonts

---

1. **Site Purpose**

2. **Site Philosophy**

3. **Thematic Approaches**

4. **Color**

Color schemes

Color palettes

5. **Navigation**

Conventions for bars, buttons, and image maps

Required elements

6. **Graphics**

Graphics standards and formats

Conventions

Available sources

7. **Type**

Font faces

Font sizes

Conventions

8. **Media**

   Media standards and formats

   Conventions

   Available sources

9. **Screen Design**

   Templates

   Sample screens

10. **Programming**

    Operating system requirements

    Browser requirements

    HTML version requirements

    Page size maximums

    Conventions

    Templates

11. **Review and approval process**

    Quality and performance standards

    Chain of review

    Approval authorizations

11

Module Conclusion

If anyone ever tells you that screen design has little to do with usability, you
ought to have enough ammunition now to set them right. All aspects of designing
Web sites have some impact on usability. So much of the process uses aesthetic
judgment or intuition, though, and at first glance it may be difficult to realize

exactly why some design decisions seem right and some do not. I think you will find that learning how to look closely at a design, however, and to articulate just why it is or isn't effective, is invaluable to the process of becoming a better designer.

Next, we will turn to the production phase of Web site design and explore how to actually prepare the content for the site so that it is in the most user-friendly format.

☑ *Mastery Check*

1. If you know your users have a screen resolution of 640×480, why shouldn't you design your Web site to fill that space?

   _____

   _____

2. What is the generic formula for determining an appropriate screen size to design for?

   _____

   _____

3. What is the correct definition of the term "browser offset"?

   A) The amount of space taken up by the browser's menu

   B) The pad between the browser and the operating system menu

   C) The pad between the edge of the browser and the content of a Web page

   D) The space left over for the Web page after subtracting the space needed for the menus.

4. Which of the following permit you to adjust the browser offsets in versions 4 and above of Netscape and Explorer? (Select all that apply.)

   A) topmargin

   B) marginheight

   C) sidemargin

   D) offsetmargin

   E) marginwidth

   F) leftmargin

5. Why should you use caution in specifying that the scroll bars of frames be invisible?

   _____

   _____

11

☑ Mastery Check

6. What two limiting factors should influence the guideline that suggests in determining how much content to include on each page, you should include as much related content as possible that can be displayed within the viewable screen area?

   _____

   _____

7. Since it's the information architect's role to determine how the content of a site is organized, why are some decisions about how much content should go on any given page left to the screen design stage?

   _____

   _____

8. True or False: Most users generally prefer scrolling over linking.

9. What would be a key difference achieved in a Web site design by using a color palette of highly contrasting colors as opposed to a set of earth tones?

   _____

   _____

10. How many colors are in the truly Web-safe palette?

    _____

11. List four key factors that may impact readability.

    _____

    _____

Module 12

Preparing User-Friendly Content

The Goals of This Module

- Identify the two key components of content management
- Understand what's required to prepare user-friendly text for the Web
- Discern the differences between reading print and online materials
- Employ the key guidelines for writing for the Web
- Understand what's required to prepare user-friendly media for the Web
- Practice identifying appropriate media files for a Web site

One of the last steps in a user-centric design process is actually preparing the content and entering the production phase. Much of a design can be implemented by other members of a Web team without knowing all the ins and outs of why the design decisions were made. It can be tremendously helpful, however, for every member of a Web team to have at least a rudimentary understanding of the design process and particularly the importance of basing every decision upon the needs of the user. Even at the content production stage, issues of usability come into play.

For the purposes of this module, we will focus on the usability aspects of this stage, not *all* the production details. Separate books have been written on producing graphics, animation, audio, and video for the Web, so we couldn't possibly fit it all into this one module.

For ease of discussion, we'll break the content into two groups:

- Text
- Media

First let's take a brief look at how to manage all this content, a crucial step in the Web development process.

Content Management

Even a small Web site can contain hundreds of pieces of content. There may be dozens of small word processing files, one for each block of text to be included on the site. There may be dozens of photographs, dozens of illustrations, a couple handfuls of less typical media files, such as audio or video files, and, of course, at least as many HTML documents as there are pages in the Web site, more if the site uses frames. And, unfortunately, most of these pieces do not stand still but go through a development, revision, and integration process. Keeping track of all these components while they go through their various permutations can be a challenge.

Thus, before actually creating any user-friendly content, it is first necessary to set up a workable system in which you can develop, track, and manage the production of that content. For sanity's sake as well as efficiency's, this is more of an issue of creating a usable process for the team members than for the final Web site users.

With any such system, you need two components:

- A list or inventory of all the pieces of content that need to be included on the Web site

- A method for tracking the acquisition, development, revisions, and approval stages of each piece of content

Table 12-1 is an example of a simple form that combines both the inventory and tracking of content and that you could easily re-create yourself in any word processing or spreadsheet software. Large Web development teams will often have specialized project management software, such as Microsoft SourceSafe, that

Page Name	Comp Filename	Supporting Content Files: File Name / Type / Current Location	Status: Waiting / In Process / Ready	Current Ownership (by Team Member)
Home	final_comp_ home.psd	Intro.doc / MSWord / Editorial Review	In Process Due 2/15/02	Editor
		Disclaimer.doc / MSWord / text folder	Ready	Web Developer I
		Copyright.doc / MSWord / text folder	Ready	Web Developer I
		TermsOfUse.doc / MSWord / text folder	Ready	Web Developer I
		logo.gif / GIF / images folder	Ready	Web Developer I
		faces.jpg / JPEG / images folder	Ready	Web Developer I
		index.html / HTML / Programming	In Process Due 2/18/02	Web Developer I
About Us	final_comp_ about.psd	About.doc / MSWord / Editorial Review	In Process Due 2/19/02	Editor
		StaffList.doc / MSWord / text folder	Ready	Web Developer I
		office_illus.gif / GIF / Art Dept	In Process Due 2/29/02	Art Director
		staff.jpg / JPEG / Art Dept	In Process Due 2/19/02	Jr. Designer
		about.html / HTML / Programming	In Process Due 2/21/02	Web Developer I

Table 12-1   Sample Content Inventory

12

itemizes every piece of content along with every step it will need to go through before being fully integrated and launched as part of a Web site. Vignette (http://www.vignette.com) and Open Text Corporation (http://www.opentext.com) offer powerful applications specifically geared toward managing online content. A number of Web authoring products like Dreamweaver, GoLive, and FrontPage also have simpler file check-in and check-out management tools.

Tip

Regardless of the content inventory and tracking system that you employ, be sure to include clearly defined sign-off stages. Not getting the approval needed at the right time may be the number-one cause of inefficiency in Web site development. Say, for instance, that a piece of art is sketched, created, optimized, and placed on the Web site without the client ever seeing it or even approving the idea of it. If the client hates it, then not only will the time spent to create it have been wasted but so will the time of whoever designed the page, whoever optimized the graphic, and whoever integrated it into the HTML.

Preparing User-Friendly Text for the Web

As we discussed earlier in this book, a significant part of how usable text is perceived to be on a Web site revolves around its presentation and how readable it is. But don't stop there. Even more fundamental to the issue is the text itself. The choice of words, their arrangement, and their presentation all contribute to how appropriate and user-friendly the text is on a Web site.

Note

See Module 11 for a discussion of how the *display* of text on a Web site can affect readability, a key factor in how usable the text is.

Don't be fooled by some people's attitudes that "Oh well, this is the Web; the text can just be fast and dirty." That *may* be true for e-mail or online chat rooms—I largely disagree with that assumption as well, for there have been many senseless misunderstandings caused by sloppy writing—but it is clearly *not* true for the text included on Web sites. As you would with any other text-based medium, you need to carefully choose your words and craft them for the particular medium and the particular audience.

How People "Read" the Web

Many companies have made the mistake of thinking that they can simply use the text from their carefully thought out and developed print pieces on their Web site. After all, they likely invested considerable time, effort, and money in producing those materials, didn't they? They may have hired professional copywriters and editors, even an ad agency, to hone their corporate message into a carefully constructed presentation, which may have a proven track record of being effective with their customer base. So why shouldn't they just be able to port that message over to their Web site? Think about that for a moment, and take your best guess at answering it:

_____

_____

My answer is that the medium of the Web is significantly different than the print medium—different enough that the same company, the same message, and the same audience will produce a significantly different experience on the Web. For starters, the basic experience of reading online *is* different than that of reading printed material. It may be that you have the same little black letters forming the same sequence of words in sentences and paragraphs, but one medium you can hold in your hand as close to eyes as you like, sitting comfortably wherever you like with the capability of adjusting the lighting conditions to whatever seems most pleasant. For the other, however, you need to be sitting at a computer, probably at a desk, looking into a back-lit screen in a position that may or may not be ideal for both optimal ergonomic posture as well as optimal visual proximity to those little black letters. Today's computer monitors have significantly lower resolution than print or photographic resolution, adding the possibility of eye-strain to any Web site experience.

As Jakob Nielsen reported in his book *Designing Web Usability* (New Riders, 2000), reading from computer screens is about 25 percent slower than reading from paper. Add to that the eyestrain caused by today's computer monitors and the fact that people just don't like to read much online. Users also bring a different set of expectations to a Web site than to a printed piece. Often they are goal-oriented and very aware of the time passing. All these factors contribute to a

12

different reading experience and the need for a different approach to writing and presenting the text.

The most readily distinguishable difference in user behavior is they are much more likely to scan text on the Web than in print. While they may spend 20 seconds reading a blurb on a brochure word for word, the same users may spend only 5 seconds skimming the corresponding text on a Web site. Gone is the opportunity to wax eloquently in a luxurious preamble to your topic. With user expectations of finding the nugget of information they are seeking instantaneously, you'd better put that nugget right at the top and knock that preamble off the Web site.

Ironically, the more Web sites cater to this reading style, the more users come to expect it and even demand it. Once higher-quality monitors that facilitate the reading process become widespread, it is likely that users will continue to read in the same fashion for quite some time, just out of habit and expectation.

With all this scanning and skimming and the frequency of being able to change the content of Web sites, you may think that the text may not matter very much beyond making fleeting impressions. While this is true to a degree, the medium also provides more opportunities to the users to capture your text. They have the means right at hand to print out a Web page or copy and paste portions of the text into other documents, so your words can be quoted and distributed with much greater ease than with traditional print media. An awkward paragraph or a silly typo can be perpetuated well beyond its life on your Web site—yet another reason to take care in crafting your words.

Guidelines on Writing for the Web

Here are some guidelines on writing for the Web:

● **Stick to the user-centric design process.** Write what the users want to know, not what you or your client may think will help promote a product. Web users resent padding and useless marketing hyperbole.

● **Write toward the task-oriented nature of the Web.** E-commerce sites, for example, actually enable users to purchase products, unlike marketing brochures that may be limited to encouraging users to take the next step—such as going to a store—to purchase a product. As such, e-commerce sites are best served by providing all the options necessary to make a purchase transaction. Oftentimes, these include the ability to research, compare, and buy.

● **Get to the point.**   Use an inverted pyramid approach wherein you present the conclusion first and the supporting facts second. This applies to all the text elements on your site, including the structure of Web pages, Web paragraphs, or Web lists. This also helps to keep the most important points above the fold as well so that users are sure to see them.

● **Use an appropriate editorial style for your users and their purpose.** You can't go wrong with an objective, straightforward tone on the Web, but you should not feel limited to that as your only option. Many Web sites have successfully integrated a certain hip attitude into their text. Hip or cool is okay (1) if it's appropriate for the audience, (2) if you can convey it in a minimal amount of words, and (3) if you can use it to support all the other writing guidelines. Once again, avoid fluff.

● **Get your grammar right.**   You need good grammar and spelling in any text-based medium, and the Web is no exception. If necessary, hire a professional copywriter and/or copy editor. No typos, no spelling mistakes, no bad word usage, no run-on sentences, etc. (Did you notice that last sentence is a sentence fragment, by the way?)

Tip

Use spellcheckers and grammar checkers as your first line of defense. They're easy, they're cheap, and they will generally flag the worst offenders. Do not, however, rely on them exclusively, for they are not perfect.

● **Be succinct.**   In other words, use as few words as possible. Jakob Nielsen goes so far as to recommend that Web authors and editors pare down the text for a Web site to *25 percent less* than its print counterparts. This takes into account both the 25 percent reduction in the speed of online reading and the dislike (and discomfort) of reading on today's computer screens.

● **Chunk your text.**   It just so happens that the term "chunking" came into popularity with the advent of the Web and the need to break material down into bite-sized portions. It's always given me the impression of taking a sledge hammer and breaking a huge ice block into chunks, an image that is not entirely inappropriate for the process, but I'd recommend using an ice pick or other tool to finish refining each chunk. Keep in mind that each chunk needs to be able to stand on its own—within a Web page or within the whole site.

12

- **Create a visible structure for the text.** Having a random display of chunked text is not nearly so effective as having a neatly ordered, logical structure. This, of course, involves first assigning priorities and then following through on the presentation. Take advantage of heads to summarize each block of text.

- **Keep your titles short and sweet.** Titles, heads, labels, captions, and callouts are the first items users tend to read, because they stand out from any block of text and are usually displayed more prominently. Take advantage of that prominence to get each title's particular message across as clearly as possible. Don't bog the title down with too many details (or too many words), and avoid using cute titles that don't accurately convey the meaning or that require a lot of thought to understand. By all means, however, feel free to use clever titles that *do* convey the meaning quickly and effectively.

Ask the Expert

Question: I've heard a lot about copyright infringement on the Web. How can I avoid that?

Answer: There are two sides to that question: you need to avoid inadvertently infringing upon somebody else's copyright and you need to be able to protect your own material. For the former, the best rule of thumb is to always ask before using anything someone else has created on your Web site. In many cases, people will be happy to give you permission, especially if they feel your Web site will give their work positive exposure. As a photographer, for example, I *love* it when somebody asks to use one of my photographs on their Web site—so long as they include a credit and preferably a link either to my Web site or my e-mail address.

That brings us to the second rule of thumb: Always give credit where credit is due. Do not, however, make the mistake of assuming that because you are citing the source, you are avoiding copyright infringement. It is still necessary to secure permission.

Here are a few other guidelines:

- Photographs, film clips, illustrations, text, even code—anything created by somebody else—are subject to copyright protection.

- Many sources distribute copyright-free materials either for free or for a fee. (See http://www.comstock.com, http://www.photodisc.com, or http://www.javascript.com for examples.) Read all licenses very carefully, however, prior to including the item on your Web site. Some companies exclude permission for reproducing their work on the Web just because it is so easy for someone else to steal the work once it is on the Web.

- You may use any material that is considered to be in the "public domain" free of charge. Public domain material is work that has never been copyrighted or whose copyright has expired. Be aware, though, that there are different expiration dates for different kinds of material. Also, absence of a copyright symbol does not mean that it has not been copyrighted.

Question: How do you prevent somebody else from using your copyrighted material?

Answer: This is a little trickier. The best protection, of course, is *not* to publish the material on the Web in the first place, but that hardly addresses most people's needs. In lieu of that, here are a few tips for helping to prevent such thefts:

- Embed copyright information into graphics, animation, audio, or video files using a digital watermark. See the Digimarc site at http://digimarc.com for one of the leading providers of this service or the EWatermark site at http://www.ewatermark.com.

- Employ a tracking service to track the use of your watermarked files across the Web. Digimarc also offers this through its MarcSpider subscription.

- Include copyright information on each page of your Web site, preferably in straight HTML so that everybody's sure to be able to see it.

- Including copyright information as a comment near the top of your HTML file.

12

> Make it easy for people to ask you for permission. Include a permissions or use statement on your Web site, outlining what is acceptable usage and who to contact for more information.

Project 12-1: Writing for Your Audience

Try your hand at converting a print-based article into text that is appropriate for the Web.

Step-by-Step

1. Choose a print-based article or brochure that you would like to work with to practice preparing text for the Web. This could be any news story from your local newspaper, a product brochure, a piece of promotional mail, or the call for action following this project adapted from an Audubon piece. (Do not feel that you have to agree with or support any of the items in order to do this activity.)

2. Rewrite the printed piece for presentation on the Web, taking into account all of the guidelines on writing for the Web we have discussed.

3. If possible, convert your version of the document to HTML and compare and contrast the experience of reading it on your computer monitor with reading the original in printed form.

4. Solicit a few friends or colleagues to also compare the two versions and to give you feedback on how clear and easy to read the online version is.

5. Incorporate any good suggestions your friends or colleagues were able to provide.

Project Summary

To take the best advantage of the Web, the arctic drilling example needs to be extensively rewritten per the guidelines on writing for the Web. Here are some of the key aspects that could benefit from being changed.

● **Write toward the task-oriented nature of the Web.** Placing a call to action on the Web can marry the action with the call. With a click of a button, you can take users to sample letters addressed to their particular representatives and thus tremendously facilitate their process of voicing their concerns.

● **Get to the point.** An inverted pyramid approach could work very easily with this article. The prompt for action is the most important point of such articles and could be placed at the top of the page, above the fold, followed by the background information.

● **Chunk your text and create a visible structure for the text.** This big block of text could be broken into a number of smaller "chunks," each with its own short and sweet title such as Background, This Week's Progress, and What You Can Do. Much of the information could also be presented chronologically, perhaps along a time line to give a better overview at a glance.

● **Be succinct.** Reducing the overall number of words in this article and breaking it into smaller chunks would help tremendously in making it more easily scannable. Most of the major points could be pulled out into abbreviated bullet point form.

● **Use an appropriate editorial style for your users and their purpose.** An objective, straightforward tone could be very effective in presenting most of the information in this article, perhaps with an impassioned plea for action, indicating how important each individual's response will be.

Sample Call for Action from an Environmental Organization

Week of October 22, 2001: On October 2, the U.S. Senate passed the Defense Authorization bill—a bill that did not include the House-passed energy bill or any provisions to open the Arctic National Wildlife Refuge to oil drilling. The vote came about after the Senate voted unanimously to invoke "cloture"—a Senate procedure that limited debate and forced a vote on the Defense Authorization bill. Pro-drilling Senators, led by Senator James Inhofe (R-Oklahoma) did try to add a "sense of the Senate" amendment to the Defense bill, claiming that a national energy policy was vital for providing fuel to the armed forces. His effort failed—ruled "non-germane" (meaning unrelated to pending legislation) and therefore out of order.

While this effort saved the Arctic Refuge for the week, pro-drilling Senators are not giving up. In fact, they have vowed to try and attach the House-passed energy bill and its Arctic drilling provisions to every single bill that comes before the Senate floor for the remainder of the year! And they'll likely have until the end of the year to try. On October 3rd, Senate Majority Leader Tom Daschle (D-South Dakota) said he expects the Senate to be in session "in one form or

12

another" until the end of the year. He stated that the Senate would tackle a number of bills dealing with national security, military policies, economic policies and airport security, then take on other issues, i.e., the 13 appropriations bills, patients bill of rights, minimum wage issues, education and energy legislation.

It appeared the next Arctic fight would happen between October 8–15, when the Senate Energy & Natural Resources Committee was to begin its hearings and debate on energy legislation. Then, on October 9th, at the request of Senate Majority Leader Tom Daschle, Committee Chairman Senator Jeff Bingaman (D-New Mexico) announced he would suspend these hearings for the remainder of the year. Instead, Chairman Bingaman will submit a comprehensive and balanced energy package to Senator Daschle, and let the Majority Leader decide whether the Senate will have time to act on the package this year or next.

We and our partners in conservation are working tirelessly to encourage Senate Members to keep Arctic Refuge drilling provisions out of Senator Bingaman's comprehensive energy package. And you can help. Regardless of where your lawmaker stands, if he or she is on the Committee, please call and urge your Senator to keep arctic drilling provisions out of Senator Bingaman's comprehensive energy package. You can reach your Senators by calling (202) 224-3121 and asking for your Senator by name. Be sure to ask where your lawmaker stands on the issue. And if we can ask you to do one more thing: let us know what you heard!

Meanwhile, if your lawmakers are not on the Committee, you can still help. Please continue to contact your two U.S. Senators and urge them to stay focused on national security, and oppose efforts to open the Arctic National Wildlife Refuge to oil drilling. Remember, you can instantly identify where your lawmakers stand on the issue of drilling in the Arctic Refuge and communicate with them by hitting the lawmaker position key to your left. Once you identify your Senators' positions, select the take action key to instantly send your letter, fax, or e-mail.

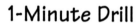

1-Minute Drill

- What two components do you need to manage the content of a Web site?
- What is the relative difference of reading onscreen from reading print materials?

- Inventory and tracking systems
- Reading onscreen is about 25 percent slower.

Preparing User-Friendly Media Files for the Web

As with preparing user-friendly text, many of the issues revolving around preparing user-friendly media files—including graphics, animation, audio, and video—also have to do with production and presentation on the Web. At the core level, however, it is important to identify which media files will be most appropriate for your users. Complex statistical charts, for example, may be the perfect means of communication for mathematicians but not for children wanting to buy toys or adults planning a vacation.

Conversely, having a nice looking photograph of a couple holding hands on the beach may convey loads of information about what the quality of a vacation would be at a particular locale but nothing about the comparative costs of flights to that destination. In addition, loading 12 such photographs onto a Web page or a half-screen video of the same shot may add little value but could well irritate the users because they may find themselves waiting for the images to load instead of being able to continue researching their holiday destination.

Tip

Before creating any visuals for your Web site, review the color guidelines in Module 11.

Once again, base the decisions about what to include on a Web site on what would be most helpful to the user. Only after that process should you figure out what is the best way to prepare and optimize those files for delivery via the Web. Following are some key questions you might ask yourself to help determine which media files to use on the Web site and how integral they are to your message:

- Will users find the media files appealing, informative, annoying, or irrelevant?

- Will the media files delay the users from finding the content they are looking for?

- Will the media files be a central, supporting component of the Web site, or just an optional frill?

12

- If users are not able to access the media files, will the Web site's content, message, and navigation be adversely affected?

- Does the presentation of the media files get in the way of the users' control over their own experience of the Web site?

- Could the content of the media files be effectively conveyed using plain text or with simpler media?

- Are the media dependent on Web technologies that your user base may not have installed?

Tip

In producing any media files for the Web, the primary challenge is to achieve the best quality in the smallest, fastest-loading format. Unfortunately, that formula often requires making compromises.

Once you have determined which media files can give your users the best value, you need to prepare and optimize those files for delivery via the Web. The key production considerations to take into account in optimizing media files for the Web are

- **File size** "Small" is the operative word here. The smaller the file, the faster it will load on your user's machines. Not coincidentally, smaller dimensions (height×width) also generally result in a smaller file size (in number of kilobytes).

- **Image (or audio) quality** You'll typically want the quality to be as high as possible, without compromising the file size and thus the download speed. The choice of file format and compression method can affect the quality a great deal. Some sites provide files at different quality levels, allowing the users to choose which ones they would like to experience (and wait for their download, if necessary).

- **File format** There are two considerations to file formats: One is to choose a file format that is broadly supported on the Web or by your targeted audience's systems. This is easy for still graphics; JPEGs and GIFs have long been supported by all the major browsers, and the PNG format will in all likelihood eventually gain the same level of support. It's trickier for most other media. With the exception of animated GIFs, which use the same GIF format as still images, most other media require plug-ins. The second consideration is choosing the format that will provide the best end result for any particular medium. The GIF file format typically is best for simple line art, while the JPEG format is best for photographs or very complex illustrations. There are a number of choices for audio and video files, each of which has its pros and cons to consider, chief of which are whether to provide streaming or downloadable content. In many cases, you may wish to make multiple file formats available and let the users decide which is best for them.

- **Compression method**   For still images and animations, the compression method is built into the file format, such as GIF, JPEG, or Flash files. For audio and video, however, they are distinct steps. You need to first decide on which compression method to use, each generally with its own pros and cons, and then what file format to save it in to deliver over the Web.

- **Alternative text**   You probably know the ropes on this by now, but I couldn't sleep well at night if I left it out here. Always provide a text description of your media files within your HTML code for users who cannot see or hear the files.

There is one additional point to take into consideration for multimedia files:

- **Give users on/off options**   Because of the downloading burden and possible intrusion of multimedia files such as animation, audio, and video, it is always a good idea to give users a way to turn them on or off.

1-Minute Drill

- List the five key issues to address in creating user-friendly media files for the Web.

- What is the primary challenge in creating media files for the Web?

12

- File size, image (or audio) quality, file type, compression method, and alternative text
- Achieving the best quality in the smallest, fastest-loading format

Project 12-2: Determine the Most Appropriate Use of Media Files for Your Users

With your usability spectacles firmly on your nose, consider which media would be most appropriate for users of any given Web site.

Step-by-Step

Consider from the user's perspective which media files might be most useful for the following scenario. Indicate your recommendations for which available media files would be most appropriate and any new ones that you would like to have created.

- **Scenario**
  - A dog and cat pet care Web site with sections on training, grooming, and veterinary care

- **Target user-base**
  - Children learning to care for pets and adults who are looking to increase their knowledge or solve particular problems. Both are accessing the site from home computers on a range of bandwidths.

- **Available media**
  - Photographs of different breeds of cats and dogs
  - Photographs of people (kids and adults) playing with their pets
  - Photographs of pets with various ailments
  - A series of illustrations of removing a burr from a dog's coat
  - A series of illustrations of brushing a cat's teeth
  - Audio of different barks and meows
  - Audio of a vet describing the symptoms and treatment of particular illnesses
  - Video of removing a burr from a dog's coat
  - Video of brushing a cat's teeth

- Videos of veterinary treatments, such as cauterizing a wound, applying a brace, giving shots, and feeding medicines
- Animations of the same veterinary treatments, such as cauterizing a wound, applying a brace, giving shots, and feeding medicines
- Humorous animation of giving a cat a bath
- **New media files to be created (budget permitting)**

Project Summary

There are, of course, many right choices for this project. Any number of good Web sites could stem from this content list. Part of the selection process, however, hopefully makes it clear that placing some of the available media on a Web site for home users would probably be a waste of bandwidth.

Video files, in particular, are so large that they are best sacrificed if *any* other media can effectively communicate the same information. A simple task like giving shots to a cat or dog, for instance, could surely be communicated with either line drawings or a simple animation. Making your pet swallow a pill, however, can be quite a bit trickier. As a user—and someone who has had difficulty with this particular operation!—I might appreciate having a video available demonstrating the various techniques. I would not, however, want this to automatically play, but would prefer to have the option to view it if and when I wanted to—like when my husband was right there with a promise that he'd learn to do it and take over the task for me! I also always appreciate seeing the size or expected download time of large media files, so that I know what to expect when I click on the file.

A few of the available media files are clearly gratuitous. There may be a place up front for one or two photographs of happy smiling people with their pets to set the tone for the Web site, or for a sample bark or meow audio file, but these would not be on my list of must-haves. The final selection of images would also largely depend on the actual file sizes of these images. For example, if the images were all 20K, perhaps you'd include only one at a time (rotating them out each time the page was loaded), but if they were all only 5K, you could include three or four at a time.

12

Module Conclusion

If you've done all the preparation and research up front, many of the decisions necessary to create user-friendly content will be a breeze. It's one of the last steps in a long process of user-centric design and is a natural extension of all of the previous decisions you may have made in designing a Web site. Knowing your users and knowing how they will use the site is essential to it.

In the next module, we will examine a couple of Web sites and apply all of the knowledge we have learned so far to determine just how usable they are and what improvements could be made to them to improve that usability.

Tip

See Appendix D for a checklist on providing usable content.

☑ *Mastery Check*

1. Why can it be helpful, during the content preparation stage, for every member of a Web team to have at least a rudimentary understanding of a user-centric design process?

   _____

   _____

2. Which of the following are benefits of a good content management system? (Select all that apply.)

   A. It facilitates an efficient development process.

   B. It facilitates version control.

   C. It promotes sanity among team members.

   D. It guarantees a more usable Web site.

3. True or False: Approval stages should be integrated into an effective content management system.

4. In the creation of user-friendly text for a Web site, what aspect is even more important than the presentation of text and its readability on a Web site?

   _____

   _____

5. True or False: On the Web, the text can just be fast and dirty.

6. Why doesn't it usually work to just lift copy developed for print publications and slot it into a Web site?

   _____

   _____

7. In what way could a document that has the following types of information be effectively reordered for presentation on the Web: preamble, supporting arguments, and conclusion?

   _____

   _____

12

☑ *Mastery Check*

8. Which of the following is/are *not* appropriate guidelines on writing for the Web?

   A. Write toward the task-oriented nature of the Web.

   B. Explain every point in full detail.

   C. Get to the point.

   D. Use an appropriate editorial style for your users and their purpose.

   E. Get your grammar right.

9. What is meant by the phrase "chunk your text"?

   _____

   _____

10. True or False: If you find a piece of art on the Web that does not have a stated copyright or digital watermark, it is okay to reproduce it on your Web site.

11. In preparing user-friendly media files for a Web site, what aspect is even more important than the presentation and delivery of the files across the Web?

   _____

   _____

Module 13

Case Studies:
Analyzing Web Sites

The Goals of This Module

- Practice analyzing Web sites for usability issues

In this module, we will look closely at some sites to analyze them for usability issues. This module varies a little in format from all of the other modules in this book. Think of it as a series of projects or opportunities to practice applying all that you have learned in the preceding modules.

At the time of this writing, each of the sites examined was in the planning stages of being redesigned. Each Web design team was aware that there were some flaws in the sites, or at least some areas that could be improved, but the best means of remedying them had not yet been determined. After discussing the sites in the next few pages, I will ask you to compare your findings and analysis to the revised sites on the Web. But don't look at the live sites ahead of time! Take advantage of this opportunity to evaluate the sites on your own; only after you have formed your own recommendations should you compare them to the final, revised sites. Even then, it may not be clear whether your ideas or those of the Web team actually working on the project are better.

The eProject Site

The Web team at eProject.com knew they had a usability problem when a single issue started to dominate the user feedback from the Web site and their customer service phone line. It became evident to them that users were being confused by the logon process on their home page much too frequently.

Home Page

Slip on your usability spectacles, take a look at the home page in Figure 13-1 from a user's perspective, and answer the following questions:

1. Does anything about the home page strike you as confusing? List all your possible concerns here (or on a separate piece of paper):

   _____

   _____

   _____

2. From just looking at the screen grab of the home page, what text or buttons would you expect to be active navigation links?

   _____

   _____

   _____

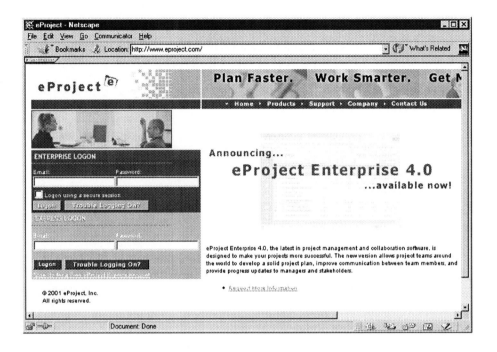

Figure 13-1   eProject home page

3. As a user, what would you do to resolve your confusion?

_____

_____

_____

Some questions you may have identified for the home page may include the following:

● Why are there two logon forms?

● What's the difference between the Enterprise Logon and the Express Logon?

● What is the rest of the text that has been cut off from the top line, starting with "Plan Faster," "Work Smarter," and "Get…."?

13

● I see the description of eProject Enterprise 4.0. Are they trying to sell something to me?

● Is the "Free eProject Express Account," mentioned at the bottom of the logon section, a trial version of eProject Enterprise 4.0 or something else?

● Does the check box to "Logon using a secure session" apply just to the top logon option or to both of them?

● What can I do with these accounts that I could theoretically log into?

● Is the "Support" button support for the software, or support for the Web site?

● Why are there two "Trouble Logging On?" buttons in the logon screen? And do they have the same information?

Text or buttons that you may expect to be active navigation links might include all of the text across the top of the page, from "Plan Faster" through "Contact Us," but in reality for this version of the site the very top row has no active links. Only the row with "Home," "Products," "Support," "Company," and "Contact Us" contains links.

The text that is cut off, "Get…" something, is an indication that there is more to the right-hand side of the page, which requires scrolling horizontally. We will discuss this feature in a moment. But for now, let's concentrate on the key areas of confusion: what the products and logon features are.

Products Page

Take a look at the product description page in Figure 13-2. This page was reached by clicking Products in the top navigation bar. There's a little problem straight off the bat in that the description of the Enterprise software is for version 3.6, when the version promoted on the home page is 4.0. eProject was updating their software and Web site at the time of this writing and had not updated that page yet, so ignore that discrepancy.

After reviewing the Products page, answer the following questions:

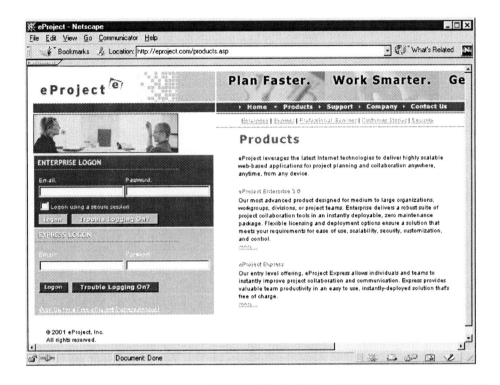

Figure 13-2   eProject product description page

1. Which points of the confusion caused by the home page are clarified by the Products page?

_____

_____

_____

2. Which ones are not clarified?

_____

_____

3. What new elements are introduced on this page? And how do you think they tie in to the existing options?

_____

_____

4. What do you think would be included under the "Professional Services" link?

_____

_____

5. What do you think would be included under the "Security" link?

_____

_____

At last, the Products page clearly explains the two product offerings and thus, by implication, the two logon options. Fortunately, the logon options are also included on this page, so it is not necessary to backtrack to the home page to log on. In many ways, the user would benefit from having this kind of material right on the home page so that he or she would not have to fumble around trying to figure out what the options meant. You can almost guess the line of reasoning that might have gone into omitting information about the Express product on the home page. It is a free product, and presumably the company is trying to promote the full-featured Enterprise product that is for sale. Unfortunately, the cost is in site usability.

In fact, it is evident only in the very last line of the description for the Express product that it is a free service. By implication, users may assume that the Enterprise product is _not_ free; however, this is not clearly spelled out anywhere on the existing site. The full product description, for instance, viewable by clicking either the "more" link at the end of the text blurb or the "Enterprise" option in the top navigation band, does not include anything about price or even give the user the option of purchasing the product online. It is necessary to use the "Request Information" link on the home page to submit a form to the company and then wait for them to contact you with more information. This is doubly ironic, since a substantial portion of eProject's services and products are offered online. Users just can't complete the purchase transaction through the Web site.

To make this page even more usable, it would be helpful to rewrite the text in a more scannable form. Converting the dense blocks of text in paragraph form into a series of bullet points would be an easy way to do this.

Note

You cannot tell this from any of the screen grabs, but the eProject logo in the upper left-hand corner is not an active link. It has become customary for logos in such a position to provide an easy link back to the home page. This is a missed opportunity on this site.

As for the main menu options, there is a new submenu for this section across the top of the page. Unfortunately, however, users can't tell at a glance which of the main sections they are in. You have to have really good eyesight and look to see that the little arrow beside "Products" is pointing downward to "Enterprise," "Express," etc. There are no other navigational aids—no color coding or visual aids connecting the main topic and the submenu.

In terms of content, you may be surprised to learn that the Professional Services link leads to services offered by eProject to its customers, including training, customized interfaces, application integration, and a partnership program. Thus, besides providing the Enterprise and Express software, they also offer additional services in support of their product and customers who adopt the product.

The Customer Stories link takes users to a page describing the kinds of customer success stories that are available. The actual examples are available, however, only by horizontal scrolling.

The term "Security" by itself may well be confusing. As it is, the link takes you to a page called "Product Security," yet it includes information about security measures taken for *both* the Web site and the use of the Enterprise and Express services online. It includes information on the secure server environment, the secure data transmission environment, the secure application environment, and data backup and protection. It specifies that eProject Express does not use SSL, which clarifies the absence of the "Logon using a secure session" check box underneath the Express section of the logon screen.

Security Issues

With this security information in mind, however, take a look at the warning message that popped up when I tried logging into the Enterprise software with the secure session box checked (see Figure 13-3). This did not reassure me of the security of the site. Apparently, my e-mail address and password are not secure. Despite the impressive back-end security systems, this little blip on the front end may do untold damage to consumer confidence and trust in the product.

13

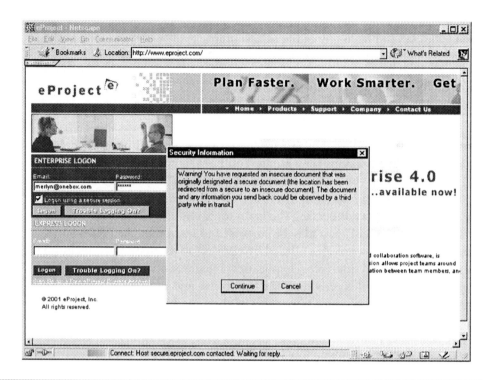

Figure 13-3   eProject login security warning

Trouble Logging On?

Look now at Figures 13-4 and 13-5, which show what users see after clicking the upper and lower "Trouble Logging On" buttons, respectively. As you can see, the information provided is completely different, depending on which button the user clicks. Most users would take the button labels literally. Since the button labels are identical, many users would click the first one they could get their mouse on if they were experiencing any trouble logging on. But with the page in its current form, they may not get what they are expecting.

Figure 13-4   Page reached when users click on the Trouble Logging On? button beneath the Enterprise Logon option

Note

The text fails to wrap on both of the "Trouble Logging On?" pages and gets cut off if users don't have their browser windows open wide enough. This is another area where using variable table widths instead of fixed widths would improve the usability.

13

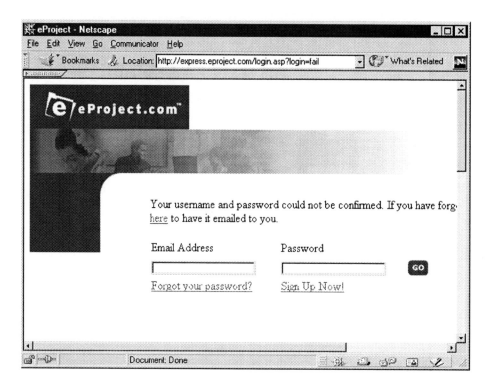

Figure 13-5
Page reached when users click on the Trouble Logging On? button beneath the Enterprise Logon option

Note

The use of contrasting colors further complicates the identification of the "Trouble Logging On?" buttons on the home page. The one for Enterprise customers is in the pale blue of the Express Logon form, and the one for Express customers is in the dark blue of the Enterprise Logon form. The contrasting colors are visually appealing, but they contribute to the confusion users experience over which option to select.

Take, for example, the common situation of users forgetting their passwords. As the site is currently set up, users must first remember what kind of customers they are (Enterprise or Express) and then click the corresponding "Trouble Logging On?" button to request a password reminder be e-mailed to them. If by chance an Express customer enters his or her e-mail address under the Enterprise prompt, he or she will get a message stating "You either mistyped your e-mail or we are having trouble locating your password in our database. Please contact our <u>support team</u> for further assistance." For the converse situation, no message appears immediately; users must wait to receive a similar message via e-mail.

Horizontal Scrolling

Finally, let's turn to the issue of the horizontal scrolling required on this site. If users do not have their browser windows opened to a full 1024×768 monitor resolution, the right-hand side of the site is cut off. In fact, on my laptop, even with the browser opened to maximum width, a small part of the text is still cut off in the Netscape browser (see Figure 13-6). This is avoided in Explorer (see Figure 13-7), although a tiny bit of the middle section, the "available now," is cut off. Obviously, having any of the text cut off at maximum browser width impairs usability, but this is a relatively minor issue and could be easily remedied.

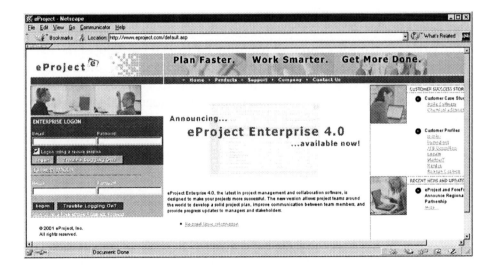

13

Figure 13-6 | eProject home page at full width in Netscape (1024×768 resolution)

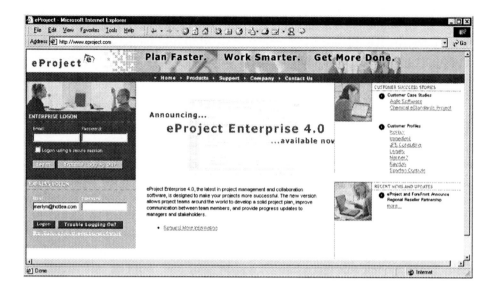

Figure 13-7 eProject home page at full width in Explorer (1024×768 resolution)

The larger issue revolves around requiring horizontal scrolling of the user. In general, horizontal scrolling on the Web is frowned upon. In some design schools, it is outright condemned. But before leaping to a conclusion, consider for yourself the pros and cons of this design and determine what you would advise this client. Consider the following questions:

1. What, if any, are the benefits of including the material on the right-hand side of the page?

_____

_____

2. How would you rank the right-hand material in terms of importance, compared to the other information on the page?

_____

_____

3. What would be the effect of moving the right-hand material beneath the left-hand material?

_____

_____

4. Do you suppose the audience of this site will have their monitors set to 640×480, 800×600, 1024×768, or higher?

5. What would your overall recommendations be to the client, regarding this and all the other aspects we have discussed? (Try sketching some examples of a home page redesign on a separate sheet of paper.)

Although it would preclude the site from earning the highest usability marks possible, I would not outright condemn the horizontal scrolling on the eProject site for two primary reasons:

● The site may well be targeted at professionals using higher-end equipment with large monitors or laptops set to 800×600 or higher resolution. It would, however, be necessary to confirm this before making any design decisions.

● The information included on the right-hand side of the page is not vital—with the exception of the "Get more done" headline that is cut off. All of the other vital information is visible within an 800×600 resolution setting; in fact, it appears as though the bulk of the site was designed for that resolution. The majority of the most vital information is also visible within a 640×480 resolution.

Additionally, the site is designed with an appreciable economy, and so in a sense it can afford this one indulgence. I like how clean and simple each of the pages is. That the logon box is present by itself on the left-hand side of every page gives a strong and consistent emphasis for users to take the action of logging on and beginning to use the eProject software. Moving the customer success and news material beneath this box, a logical place for sitewide material, would likely take some of the emphasis away from this action and increase the emphasis on this less-than-vital information.

13

I would, however, recommend that the site be created in a more flexible format (such as using relative-width tables) so that it would better adapt to whatever resolution users' monitors are set to. At the very least, the site should be adjusted to fit without any scrolling at all on all browsers and monitors set to 1024×768 resolution, and preferably on those set to the more common 800×600. It would also be relatively easy to add a better visual clue to indicate that there is, indeed, content on the right-hand side. This is particularly true of the Customer Stories section of the site, which describes the kinds of success stories that are available. With the current design, users may not realize that they can see actual stories by scrolling to the right.

Additional Recommendations

As for the larger issue of logon confusion, there are a couple key remedies to consider:

- The best solution from a Web usability perspective would be to present a single logon form. The distinction between Enterprise and Express users would, thus, have to be made further down the line by a system that could check both databases and determine which path to send the user request for access. This would, of course, require consultation with the database programmers to determine if it is a viable option.

- A brief textual clarification between the Enterprise and Express applications needs to be presented on the home page, along with links to more details and links to sign up for each of them. Ideally, the links to sign up should be combined with the logon forms, as the Express form currently allows. The emphasis can still be placed on the Enterprise package, the company's flagship product, through visual treatment (graphics, colors, and placement on the page) as well as the text description.

- If the database programmers require separate logon forms, each one would best be paired with its corresponding text blurb. This could be as simple as placing the logon form for the Enterprise package in the upper left, next to an Enterprise blurb, and then placing the Express logon form beneath it, with the Express text blurb beneath the Enterprise blurb.

─┤*Caution*─────────────────────────

It can be easy to focus entirely on the flaws of a site, and generally speaking, the more closely you analyze a site, the more little flaws you will find. None of the sites in this module, however, are unusually bad examples. They represent common, real-world sites and have many strengths. It just so happens that the Web as a whole has a great deal of room for improvement in terms of usability, and these sites are no exception.

The Audubon Site

Unlike the eProject site, Audubon's site does not have an isolated usability issue driving its redesign. Rather, it is in need of overall general improvement and rethinking. The site is considerably older and larger than the eProject site and, not surprisingly, has undergone a number of minor revisions and additions that have started to impact the integrity and functionality of its original design.

The site has garnered a number of accolades, but if you look closely at them (see Figures 13-8 and 13-9), it is evident that the highest and most frequent praise is also the oldest. Dates are not included for all of the accolades, but at least 12 were given to the site in 1997, at least four in 1998, and then the number severely drops off. No date beyond 1998 is mentioned, although the site is featured in a book that was published in September 2000, so that author was still favorably reviewing the site in late 1999 or early 2000. Note that Audubon pulled this page off the Web site before the redesign was undertaken because it was felt to be too dated.

As we discussed in Module 3, the Audubon Web redesign is starting with a user-centric design process and, at the time of this writing, is collecting user feedback through a pop-up survey on the Audubon.org Web site. See Module 3 for screen grabs showing the complete survey. As a quick reminder, however, their stated purpose is: "Audubon would like to make its Web site more user-friendly, informative, and effective." The survey is roughly divided between

13

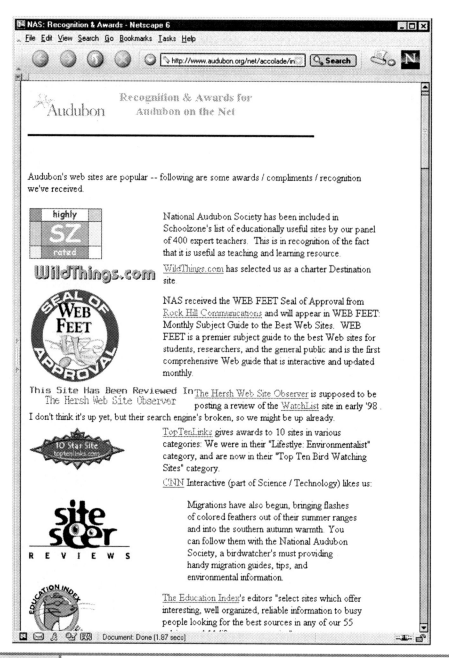

Figure 13-8   Top part of Audubon's accolades page

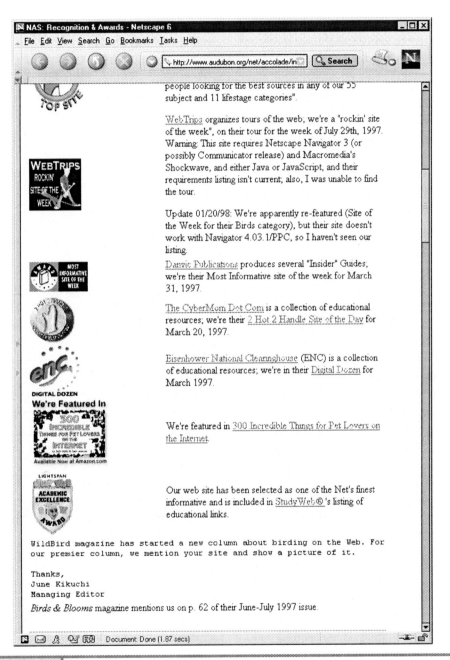

people looking for the best sources in any of our 55 subject and 11 lifestage categories".

WebTrips organizes tours of the web; we're a "rockin' site of the week", on their tour for the week of July 29th, 1997. Warning: This site requires Netscape Navigator 3 (or possibly Communicator release) and Macromedia's Shockwave, and either Java or JavaScript, and their requirements listing isn't current; also, I was unable to find the tour.

Update 01/20/98: We're apparently re-featured (Site of the Week for their Birds category), but their site doesn't work with Navigator 4.03.1/PPC, so I haven't seen our listing.

Danvic Publications produces several "Insider" Guides; we're their Most Informative site of the week for March 31, 1997.

The CyberMom Dot Com is a collection of educational resources; we're their 2 Hot 2 Handle Site of the Day for March 20, 1997.

Eisenhower National Clearinghouse (ENC) is a collection of educational resources; we're in their Digital Dozen for March 1997.

We're featured in 300 Incredible Things for Pet Lovers on the Internet.

Our web site has been selected as one of the Net's finest informative and is included in StudyWeb®'s listing of educational links.

WildBird magazine has started a new column about birding on the Web. For our premier column, we mention your site and show a picture of it.

Thanks,
June Kikuchi
Managing Editor
Birds & Blooms magazine mentions us on p. 62 of their June-July 1997 issue.

| Figure 13-9 | Second part of Audubon's accolades page |

13

questions on Web site usage and demographics to determine how their current
Web site is being used, how it could be better used, and by whom.

Some of the key Web site usage questions include:

- Why are you visiting the Audubon site today?

- Have you ever given a donation or made a purchase or other financial
  transaction online?

- How likely would you be to give a donation online to Audubon?

- How often do you contact public or elected officials about issues of
  concern to you?

- How interested are you in using the Internet to contact public or elected
  officials about issues of concern to you?

It is evident from these questions that the Web team is considering a couple
of ways to better take advantage of the medium of the Web. A number of other
nonprofit Web sites are currently using the Web to solicit two things: online
donations and political activism in support of their cause. Instead of just mindlessly
following suit, however, Audubon is taking those suggestions to the users and
asking them for their feedback first.

The survey also provides two opportunities for users to make suggestions in
their own words for improving the site—yet another sign that Audubon is serious
about redesigning its site following a user-centric design process. Providing
such opportunities takes into account that some of the best user feedback may
not be anticipated by a specific (often unintentionally leading) question.

So let's take a closer look at the Web site from a user's perspective. Study
each of the screen grabs that follow and try to determine your own opinions
about how to improve the site's usability. Take into consideration each of the
major topics we have discussed so far in this book, including:

- Usage scenarios

- Providing the content that's needed

- Information architecture

- Navigation design

- Screen design

- Providing user-friendly content

Note

The layers of a Web site are often referred to as *first-tier* (also called top level or home page), *second-tier*, *third tier*, and so on in conjunction with the number of clicks needed if you were to drill straight down.

Figures 13-10 through 13-16 show the home page and a couple of the second-tier pages. Make a list of your suggested improvements to these pages either here or on a separate sheet of paper.

_____

_____

_____

_____

_____

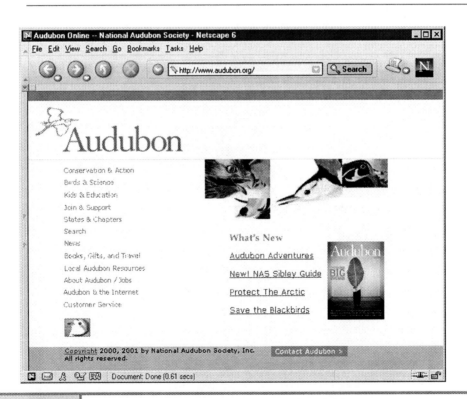

Figure 13-10   The Audubon home page (http://www.audubon.org)

13

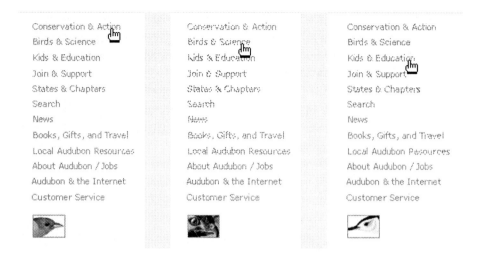

Figure 13-11   As users roll their cursor over each topic on the home page, the picture of the bird at the bottom of the topic list changes

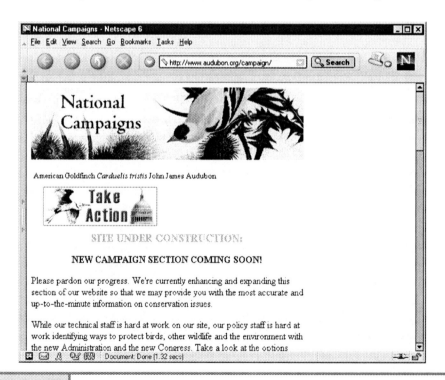

Figure 13-12   Clicking the "Conservation & Action" link on the home page takes users to this page (http://www.audubon.org/campaign/)

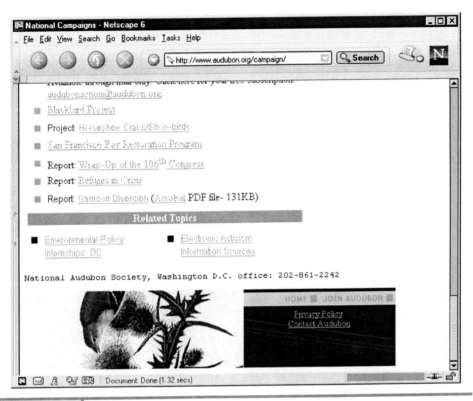

Figure 13-13   The bottom of Audubon's "Conservation & Action" page provides some navigation options

Home and Second-Tier Page Analysis

The home page has a lovely look and feel. It is simple, clean, and elegant, and it has an attractive display of bird images that are entirely appropriate to the Audubon Society, whose primary focus is on protecting birds. Although it does not take up space on the home page, the mission statement is included in the Meta tags, making it easy for users to find the site through search engines: "The mission of the National Audubon Society is to conserve and restore natural ecosystems, focusing on birds and other wildlife for the benefit of humanity and the earth's biological diversity."

The title, which appears at the very top of the browser, is also crystal clear: "Audubon Online -- National Audubon Society," although you could quibble that it is not necessary to point out that this is the organization's "online" presence; "National Audubon Society" would be adequate.

13

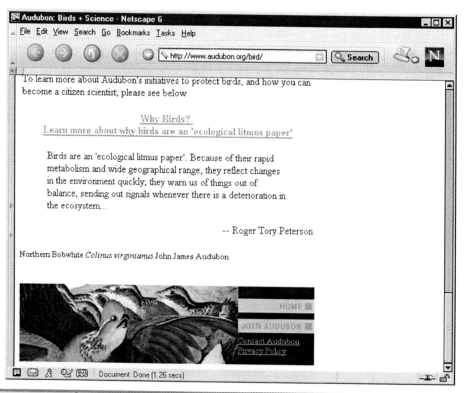

Figure 13-14   The bottom of Audubon's "Birds & Science" page provides the same navigation options in a slightly different format

Navigation Aids

The images on the home page are all small and, thus, are quick to download, making the home page suitable for users with low-bandwidth connections such as many home users, likely visitors of this site, would have. However, the associations of a specific bird icon with each topic, depicted by the rollovers in Figure 13-11, have a rather limited functionality. There may be an aesthetic benefit of having this little design accent beneath the list of Web site sections, but it serves poorly as a navigation aid for the following two reasons:

- First off, the icon is located too far away from each section head for users to immediately grasp that an icon is associated with each topic. Instead, most users form a general impression that "things are moving on the page" in response to their cursor movements.

Figure 13-15 The top of Audubon's "Bird & Science" page
(http://www.audubon.org/bird/)

- Second, there is no visible thematic connection between the choice of bird and topic. In fact, the choice of bird even changes in some cases from the home page to the top of the subject page and then again to the bottom of the subject page. For example, the "Conservation & Action" representative bird on the home page (see Figure 13-11) is a red-headed bird, perhaps a Cardinal; the corresponding bird at the top of the Conservation & Action page (see Figure 13-12) is an American Goldfinch; and the bird at the bottom of that page (see Figure 13-13) appears to be a third kind of bird, but unfortunately it is not labeled.

The current site thus employs a device that *appears* to be in keeping with a growing convention on the Web, namely, creating unique identities to distinguish between sections of a Web site and assist users in navigating the site and

13

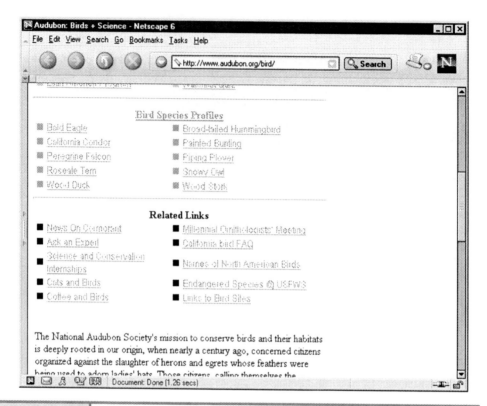

Figure 13-16 The middle of Audubon's "Birds & Science" page

recognizing at a glance where they are in a site. In reality, however, the current use of birds does none of these things and, at best, only adds pretty graphics to the Web site.

Information Architecture

In terms of information architecture, the site has some interesting traits. The appearance of the information architecture on the home page is very neat and tidy. There are two groupings of content: the main topic list on the left-hand side and a clutch of four new topics under a "What's New" heading.

The "What's New" topics include two features that can be reached through the main navigation (the first and last options) and two that launch completely different Web sites (the second and third options). Additionally, the image to the right of these options is also a link—to a fifth topic, the *Audubon* magazine

Web site. It is the only image on the home page that is a link, so it took me a bit by surprise—as it would, presumably, other users.

The text labels appear to be pretty clear, although the rationale behind the order of the main topic list is not so obvious to me. Particularly confusing is the placement of the "Search" option smack in the middle of the list. A more useful place for that would be at either the very top or the very bottom of the list. Typically, either users are looking for something specific and want to use a search capability immediately, or they review the navigation options and use the search capability only if it is not obvious to them where they could logically find the information they seek through the navigational system.

More egregious, though, is the lack of consistency between the information labels on the home page and the actual labels *and* content of the second-tier pages they link to. As you may have noticed in Figure 13-12, for example, when users click "Conservation & Action" on the home page, they are taken to "National Campaigns." Or in Figure 13-15, when users click "Birds & Science" on the home page, they are taken to "Bird Conservation Initiatives." In these cases, the labels are pretty similar, and you might think that an easy fix would just be to decide which one indeed best represents the contents and then to use it consistently throughout the site.

Unfortunately, however, the content on many of the pages doesn't completely fit under any one label at the moment. This is not an uncommon problem for sites that have grown over time. Sites tend to outgrow their information architecture, and while you can periodically clean up stray bits of information on Web sites, eventually it is usually necessary to start over from scratch. Take a small example on the "National Campaigns" page (see Figure 13-12). Clicking the "Take Action" text links to another site altogether, at http://www .capitolconnect.com/audubon. Thus, that material would need to be moved back to the same section if, indeed, the title remained "Conservation & Action."

In another example, the content of the "Birds & Science" page that appears above the fold (see Figure 13-15) supports the title "Bird Conservation Initiatives" completely. The additional content below the fold, however, is broader in scope; it includes "Bird Species Profiles," "Related Links," and a text statement on the National Audubon Society's mission regarding birds (see Figure 13-16).

The "Kids & Education" link from the home page continues this trend. It takes users to a page labeled "Educate Yourself" that includes a number of educational programs for kids, as you would expect from a "Kids and Education" link, but it also includes the Audubon Expedition Institute, which caters to undergraduate and graduate college students—who hardly qualify as "kids" these days. This page, however, also randomly includes links to material that is only tangentially related to education at all, such as a list of Audubon centers and a list of state birds.

Vertical Versus Horizontal Alignment

A couple other key aspects of the second-tier pages, such as "Conservation & Action" and "Birds & Science," could benefit from usability improvements. An easy one to fix is the strong vertical alignment. These pages appear to be designed for the print medium, which is generally vertical in nature like the pages of this book. The Web pages are not taking advantage of the largely horizontal alignment of computer monitors. With the current design, users need to scroll down a great deal more than necessary, even to see the navigation options available to them—which leads us directly to the second area in need of improvement: navigation.

Navigation Design of Interior Pages

You may well have noticed straight off the bat in Figures 13-12 through 13-16 that there is very little global (sitewide) navigation. There is none, in fact, above the fold at the top of the pages. The Audubon logo—which does not appear consistently on each page, a failing in its own right—is not even a live link directing users back to the home page, as has become conventional in Web design. The only navigation options available to the user are the text links within each page to various sections of the site, the skimpy navigation at the very bottom of the page—sometimes available only after paging down three or more times, and the browser Back button.

Another minor criticism: the format of the global navigation at the bottom of the page is not even consistent in appearance. Compare Figures 13-13 and 13-14 to see the differences. Although this navigation box includes the same links, namely "Home," "Join Audubon," "Privacy Policy," and "Contact Audubon," the position and spacing of each of these elements vary. Inconsistencies like this throughout the site can easily be fixed by using templates and sticking to them. It also helps to have someone in charge of quality control on the Web team.

Third-Tier Pages

If we had world enough and time, we could go through each of the second-tier pages in this manner and find other minor ways in which each one could be improved for its users, but I think you get the general idea by now. Let's take a quick look at one of the third-tier pages that touches on another component of usability. Take a look at one of the "Bird Species Profiles" in Figure 13-17 and jot down your thoughts on how that page could best be improved for users.

_____

_____

_____

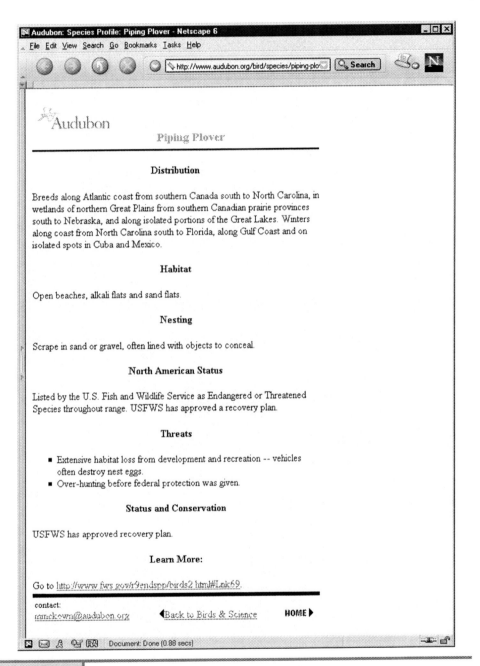

Figure 13-17   Bird Species Profile of the Piping Plover
(http://www.audubon.org/bird/species/piping-plover.html)

As with the other pages in the Web site, the profile of the Piping Plover lacks any navigation whatsoever, other than the minimal navigation provided at the bottom of the page, but we've already discussed that. It is not the most beautiful page, but to its credit, it contains good information on just the kinds of things users might be looking for in a "Bird Species Profile," including distribution, habitat, nesting, North American status, threats, and conservation, and even a link to learn more elsewhere on the Web. The page, however, lacks what I would think might be one of the most interesting features—an image of the bird. There isn't an illustration, a photograph, or even a sketch.

Ironically, I did stumble across an illustration of a Piping Plover on the Web site. It graces the head of the "Local Audubon Resources" page, seen in Figure 13-18. If users are looking specifically for this image, however, there is nothing on the site to direct them to its location. Thus, the images of the birds are used primarily as decoration instead of information—which seems contrary to Audubon's mission.

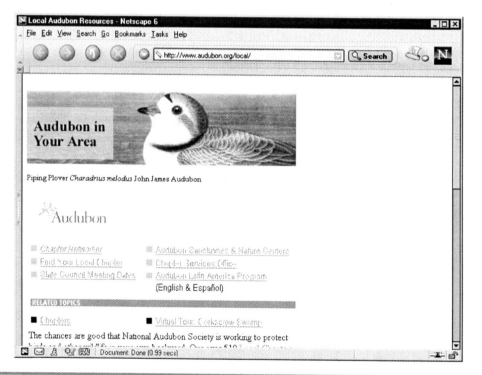

Figure 13-18 The Piping Plover portrayed in the Local Audubon Resources header (http://www.audubon.org/local/)

Audubon Watch List Subsite

Another way to analyze the user's experience of a Web site is to drill down through the site in a linear fashion. Figures 13-19 through 13-24 show the sequence of screens users might see as they investigate endangered North American bird species through Audubon's "Watch List." To get to the first of these screens, users would need to click the "Birds & Science" link on the home page, and then select "WatchList," the second option appearing under "Bird Conservation Initiatives." You can see each of these options in Figures 13-10 and 13-15.

Evaluate the following sequence of pages and identify ways in which they could be improved for the benefit of the user.

_____
_____
_____
_____
_____
_____

You may well have noted many possible areas for improvement. Three of the most important ones include:

- **Inconsistent look and feel**   From just glancing at the screen shots on this page, it would be difficult to guess they were all from the same Web site. The site does little to build and promote Audubon's identity or even the WatchList's identity.

- **Lack of global navigation**   There is a link to the WatchList home page somewhere on most of these pages, but it is a small text-only link. Links to the Audubon home page or any other sections of the site are few and far between and are not presented with any consistency.

- **Lack of interior navigation**   An example is the absence of any links within the "What the Statistics Mean" page depicted in Figures 13-23 and 13-24.

13

Figure 13-19   This is the first page users see after clicking the "WatchList" link on the "Bird Conservation Initiatives" page (http://www.audubon.org/bird/watch/)

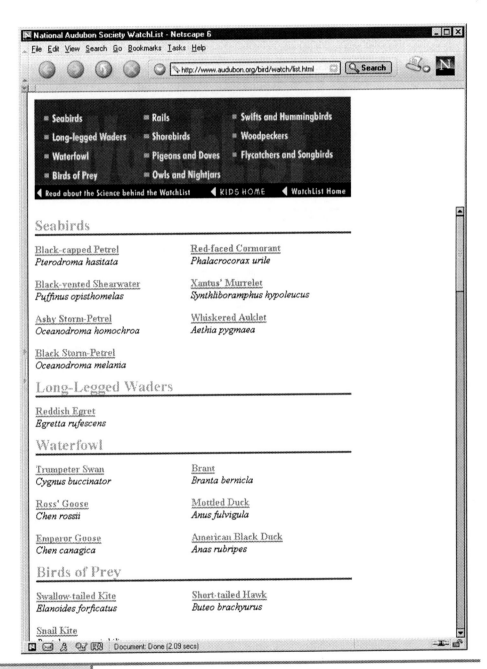

Figure 13-20   Clicking "GO to the WatchList" yields this page
(http://www.audubon.org/bird/watch/list.html)

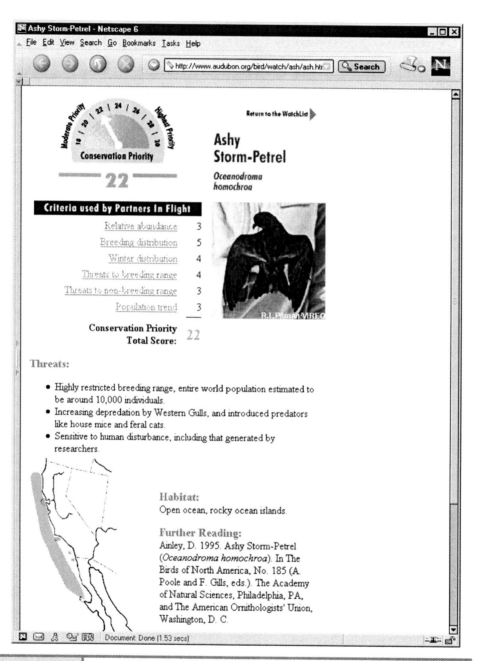

Figure 13-21 Clicking "Ashy Storm-Petrel" takes users to this page. Note that there is, indeed, a photograph of the bird included on this page (http://www.audubon.org/bird/watch/ash/ash.html)

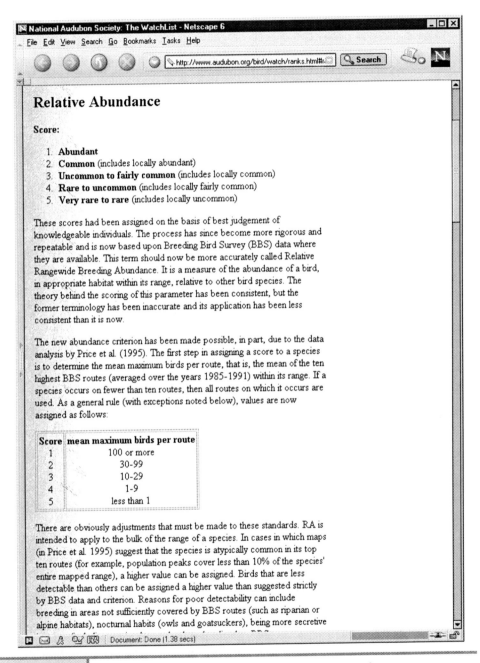

Figure 13-22   Clicking "Relative Abundance" takes users to this page
(http://www.audubon.org/bird/watch/ranks.html#ra)

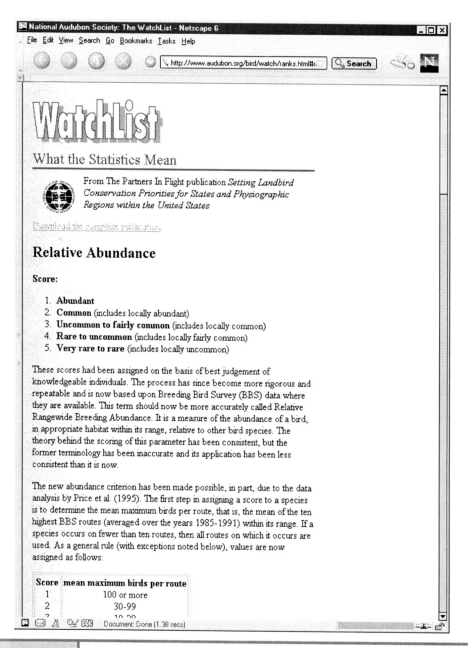

Figure 13-23 By scrolling up the page with the "Relative Abundance" information, we learn that all of the criteria listed on the Storm-Petrel's page are detailed on this very lengthy page

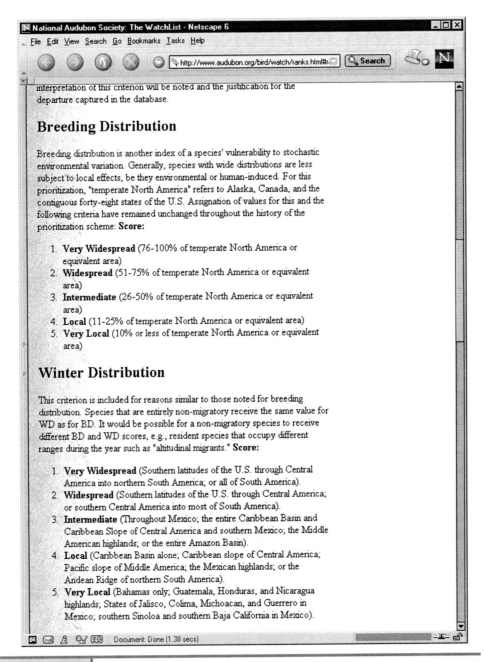

Breeding distribution is another index of a species' vulnerability to stochastic environmental variation. Generally, species with wide distributions are less subject to local effects, be they environmental or human-induced. For this prioritization, "temperate North America" refers to Alaska, Canada, and the contiguous forty-eight states of the U.S. Assignation of values for this and the following criteria have remained unchanged throughout the history of the prioritization scheme: **Score:**

1. **Very Widespread** (76-100% of temperate North America or equivalent area)
2. **Widespread** (51-75% of temperate North America or equivalent area)
3. **Intermediate** (26-50% of temperate North America or equivalent area)
4. **Local** (11-25% of temperate North America or equivalent area)
5. **Very Local** (10% or less of temperate North America or equivalent area)

Winter Distribution

This criterion is included for reasons similar to those noted for breeding distribution. Species that are entirely non-migratory receive the same value for WD as for BD. It would be possible for a non-migratory species to receive different BD and WD scores, e.g., resident species that occupy different ranges during the year such as "altitudinal migrants." **Score:**

1. **Very Widespread** (Southern latitudes of the U.S. through Central America into northern South America; or all of South America).
2. **Widespread** (Southern latitudes of the U.S. through Central America; or southern Central America into most of South America).
3. **Intermediate** (Throughout Mexico; the entire Caribbean Basin and Caribbean Slope of Central America and southern Mexico; the Middle American highlands; or the entire Amazon Basin).
4. **Local** (Caribbean Basin alone; Caribbean slope of Central America; Pacific slope of Middle America; the Mexican highlands; or the Andean Ridge of northern South America).
5. **Very Local** (Bahamas only; Guatemala, Honduras, and Nicaragua highlands; States of Jalisco, Colima, Michoacan, and Guerrero in Mexico; southern Sinoloa and southern Baja California in Mexico).

13

Figure 13-24   More criteria are unveiled by scrolling down this lengthy page; there are more than 1700 words on this page, but no internal navigation

Comparison to Revised Site

After analyzing the screen grabs we've discussed so far in this module, I'd recommend comparing those screen grabs to the current, redesigned sites that will likely be live on the Web by the time you are reading this book, or soon thereafter.

Consider for each one the following questions:

- What changes were made?

- How have the changes addressed the usability problems identified in this module?

- Can you think of better ways of improving the usability?

- Have any new usability problems been introduced?

The URLs for the Web sites are

- eProject at http://www.eproject.com

- Audubon Society at http://www.audubon.org

Project 13-1: Evaluating Live Sites

So far, it's been pretty easy to spot some areas where usability could be easily improved. At least in part that's because the sites we've looked at so far in this module are in the early stages of planning a site redesign; the Web teams are already aware that there are some usability issues to address. Here we'll look at a few sites developed by the Canadian Broadcasting Corporation that are not currently scheduled for a redesign; so far as the Web team knows, they're working pretty well. Each one, however, presented a set of challenges during the design and development stages.

Step-by-Step

1. Visit the live versions of the following sites so that you can see them in full color and full action. If you do not have access to the Web, review instead the screen shots of their home pages in Figures 13-25 through 13-28.

- http://www.newmusiccanada.com
- http://www.justconcerts.com
- http://www.cbc.ca/belgrade2001
- http://www.artscanada.cbc.ca

Figure 13-25   Home page of the New Music Canada site
(http://www.newmusiccanada.com)

2. Evaluate each of the sites in terms of usability. If, at first glance, you don't
notice any usability issues, keep looking and keep exploring the site until you
can identify at least one area that caused you momentary confusion, or a link
that takes you someplace you hadn't expected, etc.

3. Consider the following description provided by the site producer of the
audience and goals for the Arts Canada site, which is similar for the audience
of all the CBC sites, and evaluate how it might affect your preliminary
thoughts about the site:

> "The site was designed for a target audience of over-35-year-olds, who
> are in an upper middle income bracket and university educated. They have
> good computers at home and many of them have high-speed connections.
> They use their computers mostly for information and e-mail. We wanted

13

to give them something else to do. Still, we couldn't frighten them away with a lot of eye candy and fancy hidden buttons, so the navigation was made fairly transparent, and The Guide was designed to give them something they are likely more used to: an annotated index, complete with a simple sort feature. We aimed for 'elegant' as our prime expression."

4. Write a list of recommendations that could improve the usability for each site.

(Figures 13-25 through 13-28 are used with permission, all rights reserved. Copyright Canadian Broadcasting Corporation, 2001.)

Project Summary

It's sometimes surprising how many improvements you can find for sites that appear at first glance to be in pretty good shape. The New Music Canada and Just Concerts sites, for example, are very straightforward projects. They are

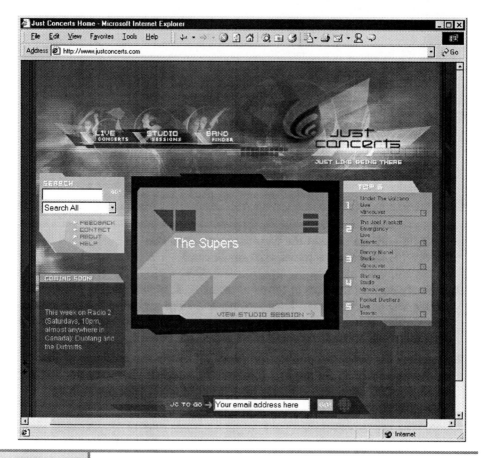

Figure 13-26 Home page of the Just Concerts site (http://www.justconcerts.com)

Figure 13-27 Home page of the Belgrade 2001 site (http://www.cbc.ca/belgrade2001)

essentially databases of material that the Web designers needed to make
available to the public in an interesting format, and they succeeded to a large
degree. The look and feel of both sites is fresh, and the graphic design goes a
long way to establish a mood and identity for each site. The (usability) devil is
in the details, though. On the bottom half of the New Music site, for example,
users have to position their cursors over the very small print "Get Some" in
order to link to the material. It would be so much easier for our hands and
wrists if the entire block of text and image were hot. Additionally, I almost
missed the link to "Latest Songs" next to the "Top 5" because it is grayed
out (or screened back) so well. And then the boxes and links for "Just Concerts"
and "Soundbytes" confused me a bit. I didn't realize until after clicking them
that they would take me to entirely different sites. There was plenty of room
in those boxes; why didn't they tell me more about what I was clicking?

13

Figure 13-28 Home page of the Arts Canada site (http://www.artscanada.cbc.ca)

Belgrade 2001

The Belgrade 2001 site is probably the most problematic of this clutch of sites. It is clearly attempting to do something quite different from ordinary Web sites. It is more of a documentary feature on the Web than a straight information source, and as such, I believe it conveys atmosphere and impressions over clarity and fact. The designer and producer of the site, Rob McLaughlin, disagrees a bit with this assessment. As he says, "Television is far better able to give the viewer a sense of place and time with sound and moving images than say a newspaper is, but no one would argue that television does that at the expense of clarity and fact."

As a designer, I am drawn into exploring what the designer is experimenting with. As a user, however, I find that this Web site initially requires a high learning curve. Just getting to the navigation is a learning process, much less using it, although once you figure it out, it is pretty straightforward—arguably more straightforward than many sites that use more common navigational devices and load up on the hypertext links. Much of this play with the navigation is deliberate and an integral part of the experience design. As McLaughlin says, "In a sense, there is the constant play of making it clear to the users where to click, and at the same time, keeping a little back and building on the notion that they are never completely sure what might come next. It's really using navigation as content, rather than a way of simply getting to the content. How you move through the content is as important as the content itself."

Fortunately, some of the details are explained to the user right off the bat, like the text blurb that instructs users on how to close out of the site and regain control over their desktop and the forthright label "Site Navigation." Unfortunately, some of the instructions, like telling users to adjust their volume, aren't very helpful. In this particular case, the instruction comes after the Web site has commandeered the desktop—a big usability issue in itself—so the only way users without speaker controls can adjust their volume is to quit out of the Web site to access their control panel. A better solution would be to provide the information earlier (before the site takes over the full screen) or to provide a mechanism for adjusting the volume right within the Web site. Also, it would be very helpful if audio were playing at the time the prompt is given so that users are able to adjust the levels appropriately.

Note

One caveat to the Belgrade 2001 site: The entire site was designed and built by a single individual in a short three weeks after coming back from a visit to Belgrade. Thus, a lot of the design decisions were made very quickly; still, they resulted in a remarkable creative and technical product.

Arts Canada

The Arts Canada Web site is the newest of these four; it just launched at the end of October 2001. It makes good use of Flash—which by itself provokes a usability dilemma, as we discussed in Module 10. There are many strong aspects to the site, and I feel that it does accomplish an elegant look and feel that the Web team was aiming for. My biggest criticism of it in terms of usability, though, is that it over-abbreviates the navigation options. This is most evident in the topic list on the left-hand side where, quite literally, each topic is abbreviated and ends with an ellipsis. There's no way for the users—no matter how well educated—to know without following the "Author" link through, for instance, that it will lead them to a news story about how a particular author was honored by a new typeface. It's anybody's guess what the next topic "Toronto…" will lead to. At least these news teasers change frequently, so it would be a relatively easy matter to insist that the link labels be crafted more carefully.

The icons in the lower right-hand corner also do not convey their meaning well enough by themselves, and the lack of labels forces the user to roll over each one of them to see what function it serves. This is perhaps a lesser flaw,

13

though, since the labels *can* be easily obtained without clicking them (by rolling one's cursor over them); they are also clear and to the point. The icons also provide some added functionality, such as the "make bookmark" option that helps overcome some of the usability limitations of Flash.

Module Conclusion

Analyzing Web sites for usability issues can be a real challenge—and a lot of fun. Despite all the criticisms you may unearth, however, it's always a positive task: the goal is to make things better, one way or another. As you may well have discovered by now, there are always ways to improve Web sites; sometimes you just have to study them longer than at other times. And, in fact, there are almost always multiple good solutions as well.

In the next module, we will address the more formal side of usability testing and how you can ensure that all of your planning, design, analysis, and revision have indeed created a site that serves the users' needs.

☑ *Mastery Check*

1. If 15 percent of a site's users complain that they don't understand how a navigation feature works, which of the following can you safely assume?

   A. Those individuals are the lowest common denominator and can, thus, be ignored.

   B. You have a serious usability issue with that one feature.

   C. The entire site needs to be redesigned to address the needs of these users.

   D. The navigation feature should be eliminated.

2. True or False: As a designer, if something confuses you when you visit a site, you should first try to figure it out, and only if you do not succeed, should you analyze what might be making the site fail.

3. True or False: It is best to first evaluate a Web site as a user and then as a designer instead of the other way around.

4. True or False: Horizontal scrolling should never be permitted on a Web site.

5. Which of the following are the most typical traits of older Web sites?

   A. They generally improve with age.

   B. They generally decay with age.

   C. They generally grow in scope from the original plan.

   D. They generally deviate from the original design decisions.

6. True or False: As a general rule, if you do not discover any usability issues in your first, cursory review, you will not find any upon more detailed review.

Module 14

Testing, Testing

The Goals of This Module

- Understand the purpose of usability tests
- Identify the basic components of any usability test
- Discern differences between "quick and easy" and "more thorough" usability tests
- Identify the roles and responsibilities of everyone involved in a usability test
- Identify the components of a usability lab and the purpose each serves
- Understand the general process of conducting a usability test
- Participate in a usability test

As you may recall from Module 3, there are a number of pre- and postlaunch methods of analyzing the way audiences use a Web site. For ease of reference, Table 14-1 supplies a quick summary of the most common methods; see Module 3 for a fuller discussion of each one. As we discussed in Module 3, the final item, usability testing, is a complex enough topic that it merits its own module: this is it.

Don't be misled by the placement of the modules within this book, though. Remember, Web site design is an iterative process. You could feasibly employ all of these user-analysis methods at different points throughout the design cycle. When outlining this book, I chose to place the introduction to usage analysis near the beginning of the book to clearly establish that the analysis process should start early on in the design phase. I felt this module on testing was better placed at the end of the process, since the final usability test is, perhaps, the ultimate method of analyzing Web site usage and should be conducted *after* the final design tweaks and *before* the site is launched. On real-world Web site projects, however, you should employ some kind of usability testing periodically throughout the design and development process.

Don't fall into the trap that some of your predecessors may have set. Many Web teams in the past have taken a short cut and conducted the launch of a site concurrently as a usability test. Granted, this can work fine if your Web site is, indeed, flawless. But in this business, first impressions make a huge impact. If you drive away your audience because the site is unusable when it is first launched, it is next to impossible to get them to come back. It's a much more solid business principle to conduct a usability test, identify any problems, and fix them *before* exposing the site to public scrutiny. The good news is that if you employ a user-centric design process from the beginning, including usability tests as needed, than the final usability test should serve mostly to confirm you have succeeded.

Prelaunch Methods	Postlaunch Methods
Market research	Web site feedback prompts
Focus groups	Web forms
Questionnaires	Web usage analyses
Interviews	Observation
Heuristic evaluation	Usability testing
Observation	
Usability testing	

Table 14-1   Web Site User-Analysis Methods

Setting up and conducting usability tests are not inherently difficult, although they can be time and resource intensive. You may see the process outlined in a number of different ways by different usability experts, but essentially, any usability test requires three steps:

1. Plan the test.

2. Conduct the test.

3. Interpret and implement the results of the test.

This process can, of course, be manifested in a wide variety of ways. We'll look here at a quick and easy way and then spend much more time detailing a more thorough approach.

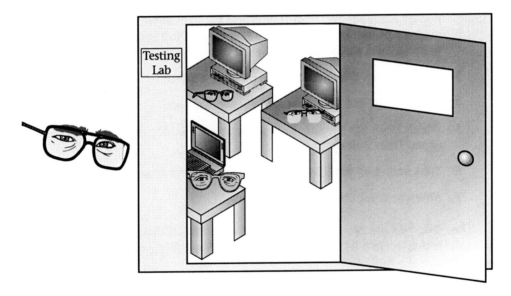

Note

Making sure your Web site actually works properly is another important part of ensuring the usability of your Web site. Broken links, missing images, and other problems with the code can degrade the usability instantaneously. For a description of how to test your Web site for basic functionality, see Appendix C.

Quick and Easy Usability Tests

There are two quick and easy ways to conduct usability tests. Pedrito (a.k.a. Peter van Dijck) summarizes the first very well in an Evolt.org article at http://www.evolt.org/article/Getting_Started_with_Usability_Testing/4090/1604. As Pedrito says so elegantly:

There are a few important rules and steps to follow when doing user testing:

1. Get a person who fits the user profile for the site. Don't get someone who has worked on it, don't get a geek. Get a real person (off the streets if you have to). Try to get someone that's as close as possible to the intended users of the site.

2. Sit them down in front of a computer, give them the URL, and tell them a small scenario, like: "I'm testing this CV [curriculum vitae] site, imagine you're a person looking for a job and try to enter your CV." Also, tell them to think aloud, especially when they're wondering about something.

3. Then shut up. Don't speak. Do not utter a word!

4. Sounds easy, but see if you actually can shut up.

5. Watch them use the site. If they ask you something, tell them you're not there. Then shut up again.

6. Start noting all the things you're gonna have to change.

7. Afterwards ask them what they thought.

The National Cancer Institute presents a variation on this theme that they call an "informal test," in a four point list (see http://usability.gov/methods/same_way.html for the full article):

In an informal test, which can be conducted in any space, with or without tape recording equipment, you:

- Sit with the user and may have another note-taker sitting nearby
- Let the user do the work, but in addition to encouraging the user to think aloud, you may also ask clarifying questions while the user is working
- May probe how users interpret a screen or what they would expect to happen if they click a particular item
- Collect primarily qualitative data

See, that's not so difficult, is it? Usability testing can be a piece of cake, and you should never let any aspect of the process daunt you to the point of skipping this vital step. One way or another, find a way to conduct usability tests on your site before launching it.

The second quick and easy method is to let somebody else do it for you by outsourcing the task to experienced professionals. If you want to hire someone to conduct the usability testing, a good starting point is the Usability Professionals' Association. Their Web site, at http://www.upassoc.org, has a directory of usability consultants.

Do not mistake this as a "cheap and fast" option, however. (The bill of sale reads "quick and easy" not "cheap and fast.") Hiring a firm to conduct the usability testing can start at $30,000 (and go upward) and can take several weeks.

If you've read this far, however, chances are that you're at least interested in knowing what needs to be done to properly conduct usability tests yourself, so hang on to your wallet and read on!

More Thorough Usability Tests

As mentioned, even the most thorough usability tests require only three steps:

1. Plan the test.

2. Conduct the test.

3. Interpret and implement the results of the test.

The steps can get a little involved, particularly the planning stage.

Plan the Test

Not unlike the Web design process itself, the planning stage of usability tests can be much more involved than any test participants might be aware of. There is a wide range of factors to take into consideration, including logistics, scope of test, content of test, participants, location, lab equipment, and, of course, budget. These can roughly be broken down into the five W's: who, what, where, when, and why.

14

Who

You need three groups of people to conduct a usability test:

- Test participants

- Test facilitator

- Test observers

Test Participants   As with the quick and easy usability tests and all the user-analysis methods discussed in Module 3, the success of the test is utterly dependent on who takes the test. The best test participants are by far and away the Web site's current or potential users. Surrogates don't even come in a close second, and fellow Web designers or other members of the team are sure to give you skewed results, although they will unearth some usability problems. If you do not have ready access to users that fit the profile of your target audience, consider hiring a recruitment firm to find them for you.

Tip

With each usability test that you conduct, add the names and profiles of test participants to a database to make the selection and recruitment process easier for future tests.

How many users should be recruited for a usability test has been a matter of some discussion within the usability community. It used to be thought "the more, the merrier," but some key usability gurus have made a good case for needing only five good users for the final usability test—if other, adequate testing has been conducted throughout the design process. In his alertbox column on the Web, Jakob Nielsen posted a mathematical model that shows the number of test-takers correlating to the percentage of usability problems found during the test. His conclusion was that you reach the point of diminishing returns by employing any more than five good users on the final test.

In his words: "The curve clearly shows that you need to test with at least 15 users to discover all the usability problems in the design. So why do I recommend testing with a much smaller number of users? The main reason is that it is better to distribute your budget for user testing across many small tests instead of blowing everything on a single, elaborate study. Let us say that you do have the funding to recruit 15 representative customers and have them test your design. Great. Spend this budget on three tests with five users each!" (Note, these three tests should be of sequential versions of the site, not all viewing the same version.) See http://www.useit.com/alertbox/20000319.html for more details.

Consider this rule of the "perfect 5" to be a good guideline for typical sites with fairly uniform audiences and that have the leisure during the development process to employ good usability analysis and revision. The exceptions to the rule may include the following:

- Particularly complex sites.

- Sites with strongly diverging target audiences. (In testing a children's game site with sections for educators and potential investors, for example, the target audience may be hard to represent with just five test participants.)

- Sites that have followed a chaotic development process with lots of changes. (The benefits of prior usability tests may have been lost on the site that makes it to the final test.)

- Sites that depend utterly on the quality of their usability.

In these cases, you may wish to employ a few additional test participants. In general, however, it is not necessary to test more than 15 people.

Tip

Most users are not willing to participate in usability studies for free. Be sure to include in your budget the cost of some user incentives. Cash is always a good option, as are company products, T-shirts, hats, and gift certificates.

Test Facilitator   The test facilitator is, in many ways, the interface between the test and the test participant. Chief among his or her tasks is putting the test participants at ease so that they can concentrate on the Web site and not feel self-conscious. As such, it's imperative that the test facilitator has good people skills. Additionally, the facilitator needs to be familiar with the Web site, the test, the testing environment, and, of course, the usability test process.

14

You may well be able to conduct usability tests if you have the requisite people skills. It is best, however, to observe a few usability tests and participate in as many as possible before taking on the role of the facilitator. Make sure you are entirely comfortable with the process before taking on a role in which you need to make others feel comfortable.

Test Observers   Ideally, every usability test should have a few observers. There are many subjective qualities to usability tests, such as the expression on a participant's face or the intonation behind comments. Multiple observers can help to both record all of the findings in the test and to add their interpretations to these subjective factors.

The number of observers can be somewhat limited by the size of the testing facility and the comfort level of the test participant. If the test is being conducted in a lab with a mirrored window, for example, then any number of observers can stand behind that mirror—depending on how large the window is, of course. If the test is conducted in a small cubicle, however, any more than one or two observers crammed in with the test participant and the facilitator will seem overcrowded and the participants may literally feel as though the staff are breathing down their necks. This is not going to serve the purpose of making them feel comfortable.

One way to circumvent both of these limitations is to videotape the test and play it back to as many observers as you like. You miss out on the real-time experience a bit and the opportunity to pose additional questions at the end of the test, but it gives you a tremendous advantage to be able to replay actions that you either missed or weren't sure how to interpret the first time around.

Observers do not need to be as experienced as test facilitators. They need only understand the testing process and their role in it as silent observers.

For the benefit of the Web team as much as for the benefit of the usability test, encourage as many members of the Web team as logistically workable to participate in the role of observers. There's nothing quite like watching users struggling with a Web site to further anyone's understanding of the importance of creating usable Web sites. Directly observing the user's interactions with any stumbling blocks also has the added benefit of validating the subsequent changes that will need to be made to the site. No longer will the change requests seem to come out of nowhere from the top down. The team members can see the cause of them straight from the user.

1-Minute Drill

● True or False: It is not necessary to do any preparation ahead of time in conducting a quick and easy usability test.

● What three roles need to be filled in order to conduct a usability test?

Where

The choices of where to conduct a usability test range from a single desk in a corner to a full-blown usability lab. Oftentimes conference rooms are converted for the period needed, or portable labs are set up by a Web team on a client's site. Budget often plays a big role in this decision-making process, but as designer Constance Petersen has said, "People often assume that usability testing costs a great deal of money. Building a permanent usability-testing lab can cost tens or even hundreds of thousands of dollars, and even a portable lab can cost many thousands of dollars. But if cost is an issue, skip the technology and focus on what's important: a representative set of testers, some carefully crafted test scenarios, and a watchful, objective observer or two." (See Petersen's other thoughts on usability testing at http://www.smartisans.com/usability_testing.htm.)

Tip

Do not let the excuse of not having a formal usability testing lab prevent you from doing usability testing. One desk with paper printouts can serve pretty well in a pinch.

Usability Labs   Usability labs commonly offer the following features:

● A pleasant facility that the test participants can be comfortable in

● Computer equipment necessary for displaying the Web site for the user

● Computer equipment for the test facilitator or observers to record their findings on

● Viewing windows, most typically mirrored windows, through which observers can silently watch the test being conducted

---

● False. It is necessary to identify ahead of time what you want to test and to create sample usage scenarios to ask the test participant to complete.

● Test participants, facilitator, and observers

14

● Recording devices such as a video recorder or Web cams to capture the test participants' reactions and speech and a scan converter to record the computer screen

Additional equipment in high-end facilities can include microphones, audio mixers, video editing facilities with a video mixer to place the video of the participant and the monitor side by side, and display monitors and speakers for reviewing the final video.

Note

To see the facility specifications and photos of one usability testing lab, take the "Virtual Lab Tour" at the Lotus Notes site at http://www.notes.net/usability.

Although the costs of recording equipment add a substantial amount to the total budget for building a usability lab, videos of the tests can prove invaluable. They make it possible to review an event that may have been unclear at the time or that two or more observers may have conflicting interpretations of. Also, they can help justify budgets needed to make the corrections. We talk about "a picture conveying a thousand words." Well, replaying video scenes with users having trouble with particular Web site features can convey to CEOs and decision makers better than any paper report that the site has a problem that needs to be fixed.

Tip

When looking for temporary space for conducting simple usability tests, consider renting a computer classroom at a local school or university. Sometimes even public libraries have adequate facilities that they may allow you to use.

Remote Testing   Remote usability testing allows the test participants to stay in the most comfortable environs of all—their normal workspace; it can more closely approximate a real-world usage scenario than the artificial environs of a usability-testing lab. It is accomplished by computer networking, with the "observers" at the other end of the network, reviewing data sent in by the user's machine. This process favors the collection of objective data over subjective data, for the observers cannot see the user's facial expressions or reactions, the best sources of subjective data. Thus, it is more appropriate for testing specific tasks or functions than for testing overall impressions. It also relies on the participants recognizing when they have encountered a usability problem and reporting on it.

The Usability Methods Research Laboratory at Virginia Tech has made some significant contributions in developing this method and technology, including a software tool that resides on the users' computers and enables them to report errors at the time that they occur. It is currently employed more for software development than Web site design. However, with the mechanisms in place, it would be relatively easy to adapt this for Web usability testing, for it already uses a Web-based reporting tool.

Note

An additional benefit of this method is the cost savings by not having to transport participants or the usability testing team to remote locations, an expense that can be prohibitive.

They have established the following criteria for this system:

- Users self-report own critical incidents through a Web-based reporting tool.

- Tasks are performed by real users.

- Users are located in normal working environments.

- Data are captured in day-to-day task situations.

- Incidents are augmented by screen-sequence video clips.

- No direct interaction is needed between user and evaluator during an evaluation session.

- Data capture is cost-effective.

- Data are high quality and therefore relatively easy to convert into usability problems.

Tip

For more information on remote usability testing, visit the Usability Methods Research Laboratory at Virginia Tech Web site at http://miso.cs.vt.edu/~usab or their collaborative remote usability evaluation site at http://miso.cs.vt.edu/~usab /remote.

14

When

The timing of usability tests takes on a couple of dimensions. The most important, of course, is to administer the tests at the most appropriate times during the design and development phases. These will vary from project to project, but a good rule of thumb is to administer one near the end of the design phase before the development has actually begun, to confirm that the design ideas are, indeed, inline with the target audience's probable use of the site. Additionally, mini- usability tests can be administered when particular problems are identified to help find the best solution. And, as we discussed earlier, the final usability test should be conducted after the final design tweaks and before the Web site's launch.

Scheduling all the participants to be in the right place at the right time is a second facet of the question of "When?" It is one of the most persistent logistical challenges of usability testing, but it is not insurmountable.

Tip

Phone calls to each of the participants on the day before the test can have remarkable results in ensuring attendance.

Why

This question hardly needs to be asked at this point in the book. Why conduct a usability test? To gauge and correct a site's usability, silly.

On the more serious side, however, for each test you should identify which aspects of the site most need to be tested for usability. In some cases, you may well want to conduct a site-wide usability study, but with the constraints of schedules and budgets, you will also often have to prioritize your questions and focus the test within a smaller sphere. This leads us directly to the last but not least element, the "What are you going to test?" question.

What

So, what are you going to test for in any given usability test? The first question to ask yourself in this decision-making process is "What about the site are you most unsure of or worried about?" You'll want to test every item on that list.

The second consideration is "What are the most vital functions of this Web site?" If you are working on an e-commerce site, for example, making sure that users can easily buy products is a pretty vital function.

To prepare the test, it can be very helpful to develop a number of specific usage scenarios for the test participants to engage in. Even in the "quick and easy usability test," Pedrito had a scenario that he proposed pitching to the test participant: "Tell them a small scenario, like: "I'm testing this CV site, imagine you're a person looking for a job and try to enter your CV." As off-the-cuff as he makes this sound, it's crucial to identify the scenarios *prior* to the moment you are facing the test participants. A couple of guidelines for you:

- Identify relevant tasks to be tested. You want to test on how the site will actually be used.

- Cull from your own usage scenarios that you developed to aid in the site design if they are still relevant.

- Develop scenarios with the same care that you apply to the Web site design. Write them, review them, revise them, and by all means try them out yourself—within the time constraints that you will place on the test participants.

Note

See Appendix D for a number of common things to test for covering a Web site's content, information architecture, navigation design, and site design.

Conduct the Test

Conducting the test is generally a more straightforward process than the planning stage. It has three core phases:

- The set-up

- The test

- The wrap-up

Following are some guidelines for each of them.

The Set-up

The testing environment, facilitator, and observers should be fully prepared prior to the arrival of the first test participant. Ideally, each test participant should walk into a clean, pleasant room with a relaxed atmosphere.

14

In greeting the participant, the facilitator should strive to do the following:

● Put the test participant at ease.

● Explain the purpose and methodology of the test, including the expected duration and incentives.

● Clarify what the participants' role is in the test—and that *they* are not being tested; the Web site is.

● Inform them of your role and that of the observers and that you will be taking notes, videotaping, or otherwise recording the session.

● Clarify what level of interchange you will be able to provide during the test, for example whether or not you will answer any questions or what kinds of questions you would address, etc.

● Encourage the participants to think out loud throughout the test, explaining what they are thinking, what they are trying to do, what options they are considering, what seems to be an obstacle or what is just confusing, what they like and don't like, etc.

● In cases where the facilitator is not going to introduce each task but instead give a list of tasks to the participant, ask the participant to read each task out loud before trying to complete it.

The Test

Conducting usability tests is inherently a rather paradoxical situation; it is necessary to go to a lot of effort to create a controlled environment in which the unexpected can be revealed. Although tests are never entirely predictable, the goal is to conduct the test according to plan and schedule.

● The facilitator and observers should watch, listen, take notes, and/or videotape or otherwise record the testing session. Note the Web site features utilized in each task, the time needed to complete it, any difficulties that were encountered, and what kind of assistance (if any) was needed to be given in order to successfully complete the task. It is not, however, necessary for participants to successfully complete each task. In some cases, it is sufficient to note that they were not able to complete the task in the allotted time.

- The facilitator and observers should adopt a neutral stance in body language and speech and should avoid expressing reactions to the test participant's interaction with the Web site.

- While trying to stick to your original schedule, if something unusual comes up ask the participants if they would mind staying longer to more fully explore it, but respect their wishes if they cannot oblige.

- Periodically encourage participants to think out loud as they work if they begin to fall silent.

- Encourage participants to express their emotional as well as intellectual reactions.

Ask the Expert

Question: Is there anything that you should *avoid* doing while conducting a usability test?

Answer: Yes, there are. Software and Web designer Constance Petersen makes an excellent point in her discussion of usability tests when she says, "Usability tests do a great job of showing what's not working in a design, but don't get caught in the trap of asking testers to suggest design improvements. Testers are not designers, and their answers will be wrong. Use the test results to expose bugs, but don't go overboard. If you derive the design from testing, you'll see small improvements, but these amendments will come at the expense of innovation and creativity." For her additional comments on usability testing, see http://www.smartisans.com/usability_testing.htm.

A few additional pointers are

- The facilitator and observers should not direct the participant's behavior in any leading way. For example, it would be inappropriate to ask leading questions that imply what answer you would like to hear or to offer unasked for assistance.

- Do not, in any way, defend the Web site design or blame the user for failing to accomplish the assigned tasks.

- Do not keep participants any longer than is absolutely necessary.

14

The Wrap-up

At the end of the testing session, debrief each participant and ask for general feedback. This often takes the form of an end-of-test survey that each participant is asked to complete, but encourage the participants to express their thoughts orally if they are more comfortable doing that.

Also, feel free to ask any additional questions that you or the observers may have thought of during the test.

Interpret and Implement Test Results

Immediacy is key to accurately collecting the data and impressions from each test. Before doing anything else—going to lunch, breaking for the day, starting another test—consolidate notes from the facilitator and all observers. If you don't get the immediate impressions down on paper, chances are those involved will forget them or they will start to blur with the impressions from other tests.

Interpreting Test Results

Once you have accomplished that, you can review and assess the results in a more leisurely fashion. This includes the following tasks:

- Compile the data from all test participants.

- Review video recordings of test as needed (and if available) to clarify issues.

- List the difficulties that participants encountered and rank them by priority and frequency.

- Keep an eye out for the unexpected. Test participants may, for instance, reveal a method of using the site that the design team had not anticipated yet may be able to capitalize on for providing even better service.

- Explore the problematic areas in terms of the original site goals. In some cases you may find that contradictory site goals are contributing to the problems. In others, you may find that the problem has occurred because the site has deviated from the site goals.

● Determine solutions for the problems. Consult with members of the Web team, the client, or other potential users as needed in identifying the best solution.

Tip

Jakob Nielsen, et al, offered this advice in a January 2001 ZDNet article: "Evaluate the data. Pay close attention to areas where users were frustrated, took a long time, or couldn't complete tasks. Respect the data and users' responses, and don't make excuses for designs that failed. Also, note designs that worked and make sure they're incorporated in the final product" (http://www.zdnet.com/ecommerce/stories/main/0,10475,2679774,00.html).

Implement Test Results

This final stage is relatively easy (in theory, at least). You need only do two things:

● Fix the problems on the Web site per the solutions you determined in the previous phase.

● Test the revised site to ensure you made the right design decisions and that the implementation is successful.

1-Minute Drill

● True or False: It is necessary to have a usability lab in order to conduct a usability test.

● What are the three phases of conducting a usability test?

● False
● Set-up, actually conducting the test, and wrap-up

Ask the Expert

Question: What are some other good sources of information on usability testing?

Answer: There are lots of them. Some good ones that I've referred to in writing this module include:

- Kelly Goto's presentation on usability testing at http://www.gotomedia.com/seattle00/usability/intro/intro1.html

- Keith Instone's presentation on usability testing at http://instone.org/keith/howtotest/index.html

- The National Cancer Institute's guide for usability testing guide at http://usability.gov/methods/usability_testing.html

- User Interface Engineering's Web site at http://www.uie.com

(You can find additional links from the Usable Web site at http://www.usableweb.com.)

Example Web Site Usability Tests

Here are two real-world examples of Web site usability tests that are available on the Web. As you will see in examining them, there are many variations on how to approach and conduct usability tests. The goals are the same, however —to identify ways to improve the usability of a site by drawing on feedback collected from potential users.

MIT Libraries

The libraries at the Massachusetts Institute of Technology (MIT) conducted a usability test of their Web site in March 1999 and have posted an outline of that process on the Web in the following format:

The Test

- Introduction
- Testing process (including schedule, questions, observers, and testers)
- Testing materials

The Results

● Overview (including who was tested, their fields of study or department, whether or not they had used the site previously, primary language, and where the test was conducted)

● Success rate

● Observed problems

● User survey summary

Note

For the full details of the MIT Libraries usability test, see http://macfadden .mit.edu:9500/webgroup/usability/results/materials.html. For a chart specifically on the observed problems and proposed solutions, see http://macfadden .mit.edu:9500/webgroup/usability/results/solutions.html.

Abeleto

Abeleto, a usability and Web site (re)design company based in Scotland and Holland, has outlined the elements of their generic user test as follows:

Part 1: User Expectations

● Task 1: A first glimpse of the home page

● Task 2: Second thoughts about the home page

● Task 3: Expected destinations of links

● Task 4: Finding one's bearings at three random pages

Part 2: Monitoring User Behavior

● Task 5: Actual tasks

Part 3: Evaluation

● Task 6: What users expected earlier

● Task 7: What users did not expect earlier

14

Note

For a full discussion of each of these components, see Abeleto's Web site at http://www.abeleto.com/resources/articles/usertest.html.

Project 14-1: Participate in an Armchair Usability Test

Ideally, at this point I would organize a good, real-world usability test for you readers to participate in. The medium of a printed book, however, makes that a bit difficult, logistically. I can just hear myself asking, "So Angelina, Fred, and Marie-Claire, would you be available at 2:30 P.M. on April 19, 2002—or perhaps 2003—for a usability test to take place in Boulder, Colorado, U.S.A.?" Not a very workable scenario, is it?

Note

I'd encourage anyone using this book in a group or classroom setting to set up a real-world usability test to try out what you've learned!

I figure the next best thing to conducting a real usability test is to participate in an armchair test from the comfort of your own home or office, and Macromedia and Girlzilla have kindly (although perhaps inadvertently) provided just such a venue. As luck would have it, Girlzilla, Inc., ran an independent study evaluating the effectiveness of Macromedia's Top 10 Usability Tips for Flash Web Sites. As they report, "The study was built around the creation of two identical Web site specifications; the only difference was the second site was built with the guidance of the 'tips' [Macromedia's "Top 10 Usability Tips" for Flash sites]. The goal of Girlzilla and testing guru Tina Miletich was to determine if the second site would prove to be substantially more usable than the first."

To compare the usability of the two sites, Girlzilla conducted a usability test with 28 users (14 for each version of the site). They each undertook a five-part test, including the following components:

1. Two factual questions

2. Two task-oriented questions

3. Observation/interview questions

4. A post-test survey about the overall experience

5. A feedback question for expert users

Those are the steps that we will follow in this activity as well.

Step-by-Step

1. Locate a stopwatch, or at least a watch or clock with a second hand, so that you can time how long it takes you to complete some of the tasks.

2. Visit the SnugWear T-shirt sites at http://www.girlzilla.com/test/index.html and pick one (without looking at the other) on which to conduct a usability test. (If you cannot visit the live Web sites, see Figures 14-1 and 14-2 for screen grabs of the home pages.) Record which site you have chosen (Site 1 or Site 2): _____

Tip

If you are working with a group or in a classroom environment, split the group up into two halves, one for each site.

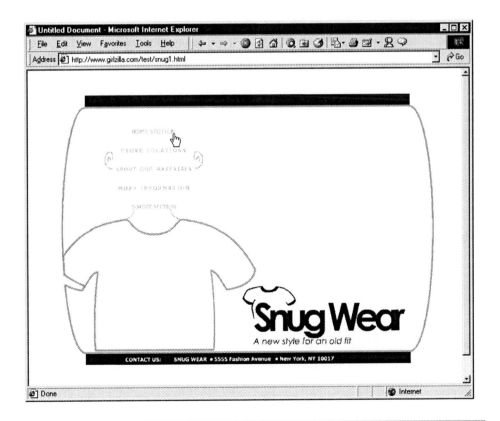

Figure 14-1   Home page of the first version of the SnugWear site (Site 1)

14

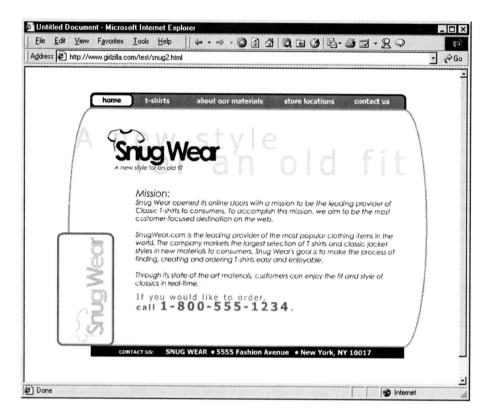

Figure 14-2   Home page of the second version of the SnugWear site (Site 2)

3. Read and respond to the following usability questions in the order they are presented for your chosen site. Record the time it takes you to answer each one in the blank provided.

Factual Questions

1. Snug Wear T-shirts come in different materials. Which material has the most colors? _____ Time: _____

2. How much is a Pink breathable plastic woman's medium T-shirt? _____ Time: _____

Task-Oriented Questions

1. Where is the store nearest you that carries Snug Wear T-shirts?
_____ Time: _____

2. You need to order six large T-shirts for a volunteer organization but only have $75.00, which T-shirt could you afford?
_____ Time: _____

Observation/Interview Questions

1. Your hip tech company needs T-shirts for an upcoming conference. Which type of material would you buy to give your team that cutting edge look?

_____

2. What was your impression of the ease of use of the site when looking to answer the above question?

_____

_____

3. Complete the following post-test survey by ranking the site that you tested on a 7-point satisfaction scale.

Unsatisfactory	Very Poor	Poor	Adequate	Good	Very Good	Excellent
1	2	3	4	5	6	7

- Ease of finding specific information _____
- Readability of content _____
- Logic of navigation _____
- Appearance of site _____
- Quality of graphics _____
- Reinforcement of Snug Wear Brand _____
- Speed of site _____
- Fun to use? _____
- Explanations of how to use site _____
- Overall ease of use _____
- Your overall productivity with the site _____
- A cool site? _____

14

4. Compare your results with those of the original test. See the following screen shots or visit the Macromedia Web site at http://www.macromedia.com/software/flash/productinfo/usability/usability_test.

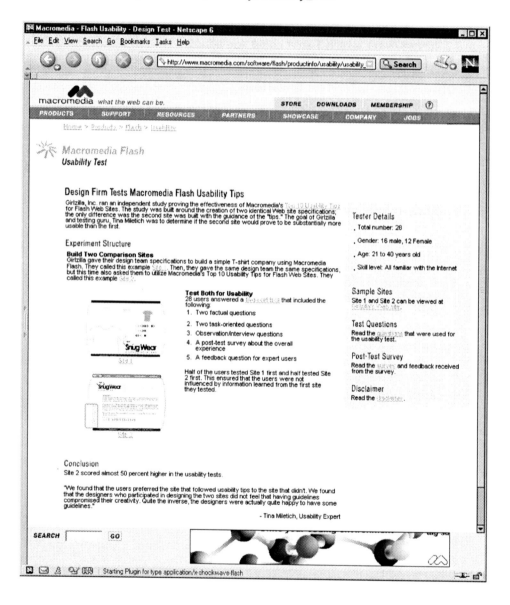

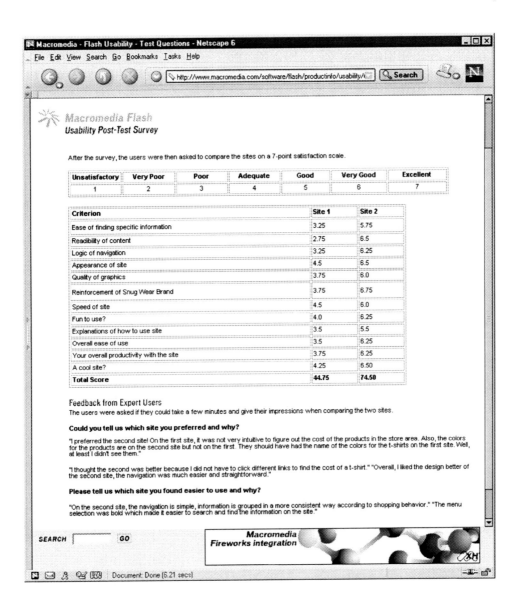

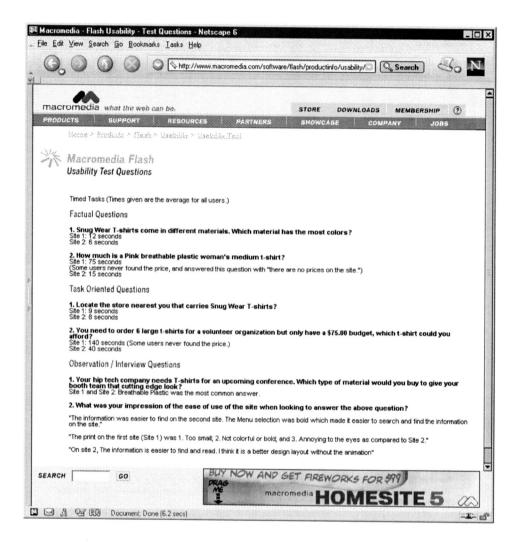

5. Review the partner site of the one you tested and evaluate the changes made.

6. Jot down any additional improvements you think could be made to improve the usability of Site #2.

_____

_____

Project Summary

That should give you a good idea of what a usability test is like. Your results and opinions regarding the site may well vary from the averages reported by Girlzilla, but that wouldn't be surprising. After all, you may or may not fit the target audience profile for that particular site, and you probably know a whole lot more now about usability issues than the typical users. You may also be able to identify other good ways to further improve the site's usability. That's good!

Module Conclusion

At this point, you have enough knowledge to be able to make a significant contribution as a team member to the planning and conduction of Web site usability tests. Some hands-on practice with actual Web sites will help fill in the corners. Congratulations!

14

☑Mastery Check

1. True or False: The requirements for test participants are exactly the same for quick and easy or more thorough usability tests.

2. In general, a Web site usability test needs how many test participants?

   A. 2

   B. 5

   C. 10

   D. As many as possible

3. Which of the following tasks are the responsibility of a usability test facilitator? (Select as many as apply.)

   A. Putting the test participant at ease

   B. Correcting the participants when they make a mistake

   C. Implementing the changes identified by the test

   D. Debriefing the test participant at the end of the test

4. What are the advantages and disadvantages to videotaping a usability test instead of having observers present?

   _____

   _____

5. What is the range in possible costs in constructing a usability lab?

   _____

   _____

6. What is the chief advantage of conducting remote usability tests over conducting tests in a formal usability lab?

   _____

   _____

7. Which two of the following places in the development cycle are generally the most appropriate for usability testing?

   A. In the idea-generation stage

   B. Near the end of the design phase

☑ *Mastery Check*

    C. Midway through development

    D. After the final design tweaks and before the launch

    E. Concurrent with the launch of the Web site

8. Which two of the following questions can be most helpful in identifying what to test for in a usability test?

    A. What about the site is the Web team most unsure of or worried about?

    B. What is the age range of the test participants?

    C. What operating system will the users be likely to have?

    D. What are the most vital functions of this Web site?

9. Which of the following tasks are *not* appropriate for the facilitator while administering the test? (Select all that apply.)

    A. Watch the test participant conduct the test.

    B. Listen to the test participant's comments during the test.

    C. Interject instructions when the participant seems confused.

    D. Take notes about the participant's actions during the test.

10. What is the most important task to conduct immediately after completing a usability test?

    A. Compile the data from all test participants.

    B. Consolidate notes from the facilitator and all observers.

    C. Review video recordings of test as needed (and if available) to clarify issues.

    D. List the difficulties that participants encountered and rank them by priority and frequency.

    E. Identify possible solutions to the difficulties test participants experienced.

14

Module 15

Looking Ahead: Through the Users' Eyes

The Goals of This Module

- Understand two key trends in the future of the Web
- Understand how Web technologies are evolving
- Understand how Web design is evolving
- Understand how Web users are evolving
- Practice envisioning the future of the Web
- Identify your role in the evolution of the Web

In discussing the future in any context, it's easy to get caught up in envisioning all sorts of things that may or may not even be possible. This free flow of ideas can be a useful and important part of innovation; in fact, you could make a good argument for it playing an *essential* role. However, when you get down to the practical side of needing to create something this year that will serve a useful purpose in the world, you naturally have to establish criteria to hone in on those ideas that have the most real-world potential.

In thinking about the future of the Web in this context, I would highly recommend that you consider it from the perspective of the user. Not only will such an approach help make the Web more user-friendly, which is an inherently good thing to do, but it will also likely lead to the most *successful* ideas. True to the metaphor of a "web," the greatest potential of this medium lies in its ability to interconnect. And the users are the linchpins; without them, our "world wide web" would float away in the breeze. A bunch of stuff interconnected to itself has no real use in the world; its value comes when it connects to human beings (a.k.a. users). And it's our job as Web designers to figure out how to best facilitate that point of connection.

In the simplest terms, you could compare the Web to a good strawberry milkshake on a summer's day. It's a yummy combination of key ingredients that has absolutely no value without being connected, typically through a straw, to an enthusiastic user. As a designer of this strawberry web, your primary tasks are two-fold. First, you need to create the content that the user wants (mmm, a tasty strawberry shake), and then you need to provide an interface through which the user can get to it with the greatest ease and enjoyment.

Sealing that milkshake in a glass bottle and providing the user with a dozen straws and plastic spoons of all shapes and sizes is not going to do much good. Nor would it help much to cut a hole that is one-tenth of an inch in diameter and then provide a straw that is a quarter of an inch. As you can imagine, such faulty interfaces can create some very frustrated strawberry milkshake users. Users all over the Web are bellying up to the bar, so to speak, in search of sustenance in the forms of information, entertainment, communication, and so on. All too often, however, their experience is more akin to a carnival game than the simple operation of drinking a milkshake through a straw.

In the early days of the Web, users *would* engage in it with a carnival-like enthusiasm. In some ways, the challenge of the technology and the interface designs as well as the race to become one of the "in" crowd were part of the appeal. But the appeal of the Web as a carnival game has passed, right along with its novelty. It serves far too important a purpose in our lives.

Just in case you were wondering, let me dispel some rumors that have emerged about the future of the Web from the recent dot-com fallout:

- **The Web is *not* dissipating with the dot-com industry.** Yes, many companies have folded, and many Web sites, good and bad, have disappeared. But the Web is here to stay. It has proved to be a useful component of our lives—despite the many failings in technology and design that we have discussed in this book. Users buy books and other retail goods over the Web, they research topics using resources that far exceed many local libraries, they communicate with other users through e-mail and chat rooms; they play games, visit art exhibits…. They also engage in activities of more questionable value, such as viewing pornography or gambling—often things many of us would rather they not do but nonetheless fuel the success of the Web. And sometimes users still just plain surf; they go out into the Web and explore the world through it.

- **The Web is *not* at a standstill.** The use of the Web is growing daily. As Nielsen//NetRatings reported, nearly 15 million people worldwide gained Internet access in the third quarter of 2001. And companies and designers are continuing to create and revise Web sites, as you may have observed from comparing the screen grabs in this book to the current live sites on the Web. The pace has admittedly slowed, and in general companies are looking for lower-risk, more conservative design solutions. This is not all bad, however, and the economic downturn has in fact contributed a great deal to boosting the importance of functionality in Web design. E-commerce companies, for example, have emphasized the need for users to be able to easily buy their products. There is still room, however, for innovation and improvement in Web design. After a decade of splashing paint on the canvas and experimenting wildly with everything, we simply need to change tactics and provide more thoughtful designs.

- **Changes for the Web are *not* unidirectional.** Unidirectional changes would make our lives as designers far too easy. Bandwidth is not, for example, only getting broader. It is broadening and narrowing at the same time, depending

15

on whether users have desktop computers or the slew of other Internet devices that are coming on the market such as handheld and wearable computers. Support for Web technologies and languages is becoming more widespread at the same time it is becoming less widespread, again depending upon the kind of computer or Internet device being used. And the reach and focus of Web sites are not all becoming more global; some are becoming more global; some are becoming more local.

I find it useful to break up the discussion of the future of the Web into three key components:

- Evolving technologies
- Evolving designs
- Evolving users

We will examine each one of them in more detail later in this module, but first I'd like to couch them in two broad trends:

- The Web is becoming more integrated with our daily lives.
- The reach of the Web is expanding and deepening.

Integration of the Web with Our Daily Lives

Keep an eye out for an increasing use of the terms *integration, confluence, interoperability,* and so on in terms of the future of the Web. The Internet is reaching a point in development where it is becoming so ubiquitous and so handy that it no longer needs to exist as a thing apart, and it certainly needs to rise above its perceived connection with desktop computers. Most of the soothsayers are predicting that the Internet in various forms, including the Web, will continue to become more fully integrated with our lives, and I can only agree. In a similar vein, consider how often we talk about the atmospheric conditions of our planet; it is so natural to us that we just breathe without giving it a second thought.

Kunitake Ando, Sony president and chief operating officer, put this very well. He said, "Technology needs to drive people out of the PC-centric world and into one in which information and data can be accessed anywhere, using any type of personal device." He called this concept the "ubiquitous value network" and predicted that one day all devices will have an Internet protocol (IP) address. This day may be sooner rather than later, and such products are already available in the marketplace. For example, at Comdex Fall 2001, one of the biggest industry trade shows, Ando demonstrated a combination digital camera, telephone, and Web-based wristwatch that uploads images simply by moving it close to a VAIO laptop. Ando referred to the name of this technology as "feel." (See the full story at http://www.cnn.com/2001/TECH/ptech/11/12/comdex.sony.keynote/index.html.)

Note

The quickly increasing number of Internet devices, all requiring a unique IP address, will likely necessitate some changes to the IP addressing system because we will simply run out of numbers. Already, there is talk of expanding the current 12-digit numbering system (for example, 123.456.789.012) to a 16-digit system.

At the same trade show, CNN reporter Richard Richtmyer asked Dave Nagel, chief executive for the Palm platform group, about the future of PDAs (personal digital assistants) and wireless network communications. Nagel's response was, "They'll all have some kind of communications capabilities. It will vary whether they are focused principally on data, voice, or some combination of the two. Everybody uses a telephone, everybody communicates. And my expectation is that that's what's going to blow the industry wide open." (For a full interview with Dave Nagel, see http://money.cnn.com/2001/11/13/technology/comdex_palm.)

One of the forerunners of this whole trend was introduced in Japan in February 1999 and has racked up the success points (and profits—an unusual phenomenon in this industry) as if there were no technology downturn at all. It's a little, hand-held device called the i-mode, recently dubbed the "Pocket Monster" by *Wired* magazine. It was introduced with modest expectations, but at the time of this writing it has 28 million subscribers—and growing—in Japan. As its Web site (http://www.nttdocomo.com) claims, the i-mode has "revolutionized the way nearly one-fifth of the people in Japan live and work…. With i-mode, cellular phone users get easy access to more than 40,000 Internet sites, as well as specialized services such as e-mail, online shopping and banking, ticket reservations, and restaurant advice. Users can access sites from anywhere in Japan, and at unusually low rates, because their charges are based on the volume of data transmitted, not the amount of time spent connected."

Tip

In the U.S., keep an eye on AT&T Wireless in the coming months. They have just formed a partnership with DoCoMo, the inventor of the i-mode. Also, keep an eye out on what kids and teenagers in your local area are using. AOL's Instant Messaging and ICQ ("I Seek You") services are already wildly popular in many areas. Both of these serve to inform users which of their friends are online at any given moment and enable them to contact those friends and chat. Additionally with ICQ, users can send files, exchange Web page addresses, play games, and create their own homepages.

Key to the i-mode's success is its design team's user-centric focus. Integrating the capabilities of the Web into a handy, usable Internet appliance was only the means (not the motivation) through which they were able to add value to their customer's lives. Representative of this shift in thinking is the fact that the "i" in i-mode does not stand for "Internet," as many of us in the Web industry tend to assume. No, it stands for "information" instead; even the logo draws from the worldwide symbol for information with a small "i" surrounded by a red circle. When the design team asked themselves what their customers (or users) wanted, it was clear to them the answer was information. Whether or not it came via the Internet was beside the point. Nowhere in the marketing materials is the Internet even mentioned. As i-mode's manager of domestic operations and global partnerships Takeshi Natsuno says, "We never mention 'Internet' or 'protocol' or 'wireless something,' because content is everything."

Note

For more information on the i-mode "pocket monster," see the DoCoMo Web site at http://www.nttdocomo.com and the September 2001 issue of *Wired* magazine. (Ironically, the Web site has received some criticism for not being nearly as well designed or tested as the i-mode product. See http://www.japon.net/imode for one such critique.)

Ask the Expert

Question: Where do "Web services" fit into this tendency toward integration? And what exactly are they, anyway?

Answer: It's easy to get confused over this terminology. Many Web designers and developers, for instance, feel they have been offering "Web services" to clients for several years now in creating Web sites. What are commonly being referred to today as "Web services," however, are essentially a form of personal information management. These services are intended to facilitate the integration of all the information technology sources in our lives, including the Web, PDAs, cell phones, and so on. I see them becoming a good transitional step toward full integration.

It might help to think about them as an electronic form of wallet. All of the data from your regular wallet—name, address, phone number, credit card numbers, discount coupon codes, bank information, combined with other data you may have collected like contact information for all your associates—will be available in one central place in a format that could communicate with whatever digital device you wanted. There are some built-in safety features to try and make sure that only the information that you want to share with any given source is permitted. Just as with your regular wallet, though, there is always the chance that someone can break through the system and steal it from you.

Thomas Powers discusses Web services in more detail in a Web Review article at http://click.webreview.email-publisher.com/ maaaerXaaQDMTa2vsatb. As he says, "Web Services are oriented around us, instead of around a specific device, application, service, or network. We, as the user, are in control of our own data and information, protecting personal information and providing a new level of ease of use and personalization. Web services make our personal consent the basis for who can access our information, what they can do with it, and for how long they have that permission."

> You can also listen to Tim Berners-Lee, the founder of the Web, discuss Web services and the future of the Web through DDJ's TechNetCast at http://click.webreview.email-publisher.com/maaaerXaaQDMWa2vsatb.
>
> **Question:** Who is developing these Web service systems?
>
> **Answer:** A number of the major companies are well into the research and development phases, such as Microsoft Passport, AOL's Magic Carpet and ICQ, and Sun's Project Liberty Alliance initiative. Check out any of their Web sites for more information.

1-Minute Drill

- What is the greatest potential of the Web as a medium?
- True or False: Bandwidth for the Web is getting simultaneously better and worse.

The Expanding and Deepening Reach of the Web

You could say the early days of the Web were farsighted in vision. Most of the discussion revolved around its potential as a *far*-reaching medium, and the terms most commonly bandied about were of *global* reach and *virtual* dimension. If you put on your reading glasses, however, and examine how the Web is being increasingly used closer to home, you can see that the Web also has considerable reach on a local level and impacts the physical dimension as well. Have you ever bought movie tickets over the Web? Looked up what's happening in your local community? Checked out an online map for directions of how to get from your home to that new pizza parlor? Those are all tasks that have an immediate physical tie-in to the world around you.

- Its ability to interconnect
- True

Regardless of the ups and downs of the dot-com industry, the Web has infiltrated the daily lives of millions of people. It is not just a virtual phenomenon that we can hold at arm's length. It is, sometimes quite literally, in our face.

When you think about the future of the Web, it might help to consider a paradigm with two axes: one ranging from local to global and one from physical to virtual, as in the following illustration. Most Web sites can be mapped somewhere along these axes.

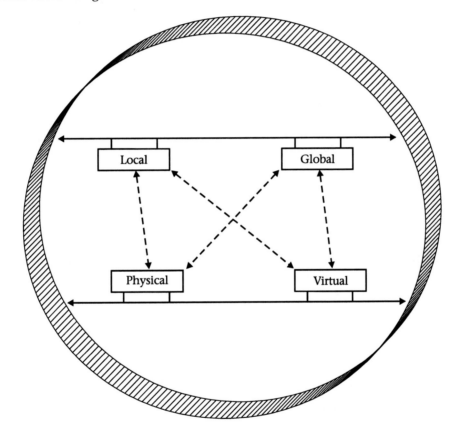

There are four kinds of Web sites that mark the perimeters of this model, although in reality the vast majority of Web sites fall somewhere in between:

● **Global-virtual Web site**   Many information sites fall into this category, as well as promotional sites and personal sites. Chat rooms and game sites may perhaps be the easiest to recognize, though. They often have a global

15

reach (anyone from anywhere can participate at any time), and they offer an experience clearly out in "cyberspace"; one that is not possible in the physical world (due to such physical things as distances separating the participants and the nonphysical aspects of the play space itself, such as teleportation).

● **Global-physical Web site**   Many e-commerce sites fall into this category where you can order a product from anywhere in the world and have it delivered to your physical address. I would classify any site that enables users anywhere in the world to change their physical environs in some way as a global-physical Web site.

● **Local-virtual Web site**   Community organizations and businesses are increasingly using the Web to connect with their members or employees and expand their services. Hand-in-hand with the traditional reliance of such organizations on physically meeting in town halls, churches, classrooms, members' homes, boardrooms, and so on, they have also frequently experienced a common problem in scheduling. As many committee organizers can attest, just finding a day, a time, and a place where every member can meet can consume an enormous part of their time. With local-virtual Web sites, however, it is not essential for every member to be in the same place at the same time. Organizations can host events, lectures, self-study courses, even planning meetings that the members can log into from the comfort of their home or office at a time that is convenient for them. One caveat: There's a fine line here between local-virtual and global-virtual Web sites. There is no reason, for example, that members or employees who are traveling (or living) overseas cannot participate as well. The defining factor is a fairly loose construction of membership base. If a Web site's users are all live within a defined regional area, I would classify it as a local-virtual Web site.

● **Local-physical Web site**   Web sites that provide maps and driving directions, reports on traffic conditions, and weather all fall into this category. They provide something of immediate, tangible benefit to how their users interact with the physical world around them. The integration of Internet appliances with global positioning systems will spur the development of this kind of Web site. Imagine being out on a trail selected from the OneDayHikes Web site. If you come to an unexpected fork in the trail, you could whip out your i-mode-like device and key in to discover which path you should take, or when that lightning storm is supposed to strike, or even perhaps where your buddies are further along the trail.

Tip

Use these axes as guidelines for envisioning a Web site's key function in the world, and design it accordingly.

Ask the Expert

Question: Are there any current examples of local-physical Web sites being integrated with handheld devices?

Answer: Yes, there are an increasing number of them. The content providers for i-mode were probably at the start of that trend in Japan over the past two years. One good example in the United States, however, is Vindigo. Dubbed as a "personal navigation tool," Vindigo is a downloadable (and updatable) information system that currently caters to Pocket PC, mobile phone, and Palm users living in or visiting a number of major cities in the U.S. You can download and install it from the Web to your handheld device. You then tell it where you are or where you're going and what you are looking for (in terms of eat, shop, or play), and it will give you a selection to choose from and directions to get there.

The staff members at Vindigo are constantly updating their database and in turn are tracking the numbers and kinds of requests for information, which then aids them in securing advertisers.

For more information, see the Vindigo Web site at http://www.vindigo.com.

15

1-Minute Drill

● What percentage of the population of Japan has subscribed to the i-mode handheld device?

● What does the *i* in i-mode stand for?

Evolving Technologies

The path that Web technologies are evolving along makes much more sense in the context of the trends toward integration into our daily lives and the broadening and deepening reach of the Web. That context may help to explain some of the seemingly contradictory paths of evolution and the lack of unidirectional change.

The Bandwidth Tides

In the early 1990s, all the talk was about increasing bandwidth. The only question people asked was when, not if, and nobody every thought to ask about how bandwidth might decrease for select groups of users, or ebb and flow like the ocean's tide depending on what device they were using.

This perspective was based on the assumption that the Web was largely a phenomenon of desktop, and then, grudgingly, laptop computers, a perspective that is no longer valid in light of the trend toward integration. The minute somebody thought a user might like to carry around a device that was capable of accessing the Web at any given moment from any given location, we kissed that perspective goodbye. Wireless technologies are not, currently, broadband in any shape or form, so designers who are creating Web sites must in some cases cater to both super-high-bandwidth and super-low-bandwidth Internet devices. In the most extreme cases, this means creating multiple Web sites, using different technologies.

The Wireless Access Protocol (WAP), for example, was developed just for mobile Internet devices, although it has not caught on as quickly as expected. Ironically, for example, the most successful wireless device at this time, the i-mode, does *not* follow the WAP. Instead, it uses a condensed form of HTML.

● Nearly one-fifth of the people in Japan
● Information

Tip

For details on the Wireless Access Protocol (WAP) specifications, visit the WAP Forum Web site at http://www.wapforum.org/what/technical.htm.

At the same time, access from desktop and laptop computers is slowly increasing in speed, and there are always new theories of connecting to the Internet at vastly increased speeds from these traditional platforms. One of the latest theories is for Internet data packets to piggyback on the electromagnetic field of our electric lines. There are no working prototypes at this time, but if researchers are able to make this work, we could theoretically have gigabit speeds just by plugging our computer in to normal electrical sockets instead of phone lines or television cables.

For more information, see William Luke Stewart's statement of October 5, 2000, to the U.S. House of Representatives at http://www.house.gov/science/stewart_100500.htm. The company he founded to pursue this idea, Media Fusion, has experienced managerial and financial difficulties during the dot-com fallout, but it may be resurrected at some point in the future.

Note

Hand-in-hand with the limitations in bandwidth for these handheld devices are limitations or just differences in screen size, color, and multimedia capabilities.

Circumventing the Bandwidth Problem with CURL

One avenue is being pursued that could simply bypass some of the bandwidth limitations. It is a new Web development software called CURL that is being developed by a team from MIT including Tim Berners-Lee, the founder of the Web.

As David Aponovich clearly puts it in an article on Internet.com, "In plainest terms, Curl software speeds Web page downloads. It does so by allowing the Web page source code (the HTML, Java, JavaScript, Flash, etc., that comprises text, photos, graphics and animation) to be compiled on a user's computer, not on far-flung servers…. Since Curl moves the work of turning code into viewable Web pages onto a client machine, smaller files get sent, faster downloads occur, and less bandwidth is used." (See http://boston.internet.com/news/article/0,,2001_729671,00.html for Aponovich's full article.)

15

The downside is that, although the software is free for users, they are required to download and install a plug-in. Curl also charges fees to businesses based on the amount of "Curled" data their users download, so it is likely to be appealing only to content providers that have a heavy server load. This is, however, in a state of flux as they continue to define their business model.

Tip

For more information, visit the Curl Web site at http://www.curl.com.

Internet Thingamabobs

Internet appliances, cell phones with Internet access, PDAs, wearable computers, tiny computers fixed to pairs of glasses or headsets, i-mode "pocket monsters"... other shapes and sizes that we haven't even imagined yet are headed our way, and they all need Web sites—or something akin to Web sites—designed for them or modified for display on them.

For some of the latest ideas and products, check out Xybernaut's Web site at http://www.xybernaut.com for descriptions of wearable computers that are already available, as well as a keyboardless keyboard in the works. Called Scurry, this hand-wearable device uses sensors to detect the positioning and motion of the human hand and then interprets them as keystrokes. Currently in prototype form, the first Scurry device is expected to be released in Korea in October 2002, and in the United States sometime afterward.

See also Handspring's Web site at http://www.handspring.com. Its Treo communicator, voted best of Comdex 2001, promises to combine the technologies of Web services, a cell phone, and personal digital assistant (PDA). It is expected to be available in the early part of 2002 in monochrome and later in the year in color.

One of the biggest limitations to the development of such Internet devices has traditionally been monitors. The prospect of carrying around a heavy, bulky cathode ray tube quelled many early developments. LCD panels have made possible all sorts of smaller devices (including laptops), but even more exciting are the possibilities for *flexible* monitors, which may contest one of the longest standing criticisms of computers that you can't fold them up and put them in your back pocket. To wit, the December 6, 2001, issue of *Nature* magazine reported that Dutch researchers from Royal Philips Electronics have taken an important step in the race for a video screen with the properties of a piece of paper. They are striving to combine the best qualities of paper—lightness, flexibility, and a sharp contrast—with the refresh capabilities of video. See an online synopsis at http://dailynews.yahoo.com/h/ap/20011205/tc/electronic_paper_race.html.

Beyond the Browser

Even the Web as we know it from comfortably sitting at our desks is undergoing technological changes. One of the most visible changes will likely be what Jakob Nielsen termed the "death of Web browsers." Once again, this is a natural development of the trend toward integration. Why in the world would we as users want to open a separate application to access the Web? This might be logical if the material available on the Web were substantially different from that on our desktops or CD-ROMs or DVDs or floppy disks—just as you might store lettuce in the refrigerator, cookies in the cupboard, and antifreeze in the garage. But it makes no sense to store different pieces of information in different venues and to need different tools to access them.

As Jakob Nielsen says in his book *Designing Web Usability,* "A better design will unify the treatment of all information objects, no matter where they live. Local hard disks, local area networks, corporate intranets, and the Internet will all have the same user interface, and users will move seamlessly between various storage locations."

A note of caution, however: this development will likely increase privacy and security concerns, since users may not know as easily where they are sending or storing data within such a seamless environment.

Products are already available that are heading in this direction, although they are not widespread. The Konqueror application, developed for Unix and Linux boxes, is one such example. It is a file management program, universal viewing application, and Web browser all rolled into one that can be easily customized for personal needs to boot.

Tip

Check out the multipurpose Konqueror application at http://www.konqueror.org.

15

Evolving Designs

The evolution of designs for the Web tends to be less heralded than the evolution of Web technologies. All the same, designs have been steadily improving since the first Web page was posted to the Internet. If you have any doubts about this, contrast the original Web Pages That Suck sites at http://www.websitesthatsuck.com/begin.htm with the latest Cool Home Pages sites at http://www.coolhomepages.com. Never fear, Web design has come—and is continuing to go—a long way.

The key to being part of the evolution, instead of riding on the coattails of it, is to remember your beginnings: Leave your assumptions at the door, and try to experience the Web (1) as a user and (2) as though you had never seen it before. Constantly ask yourself the questions, "How could this be most useful to me?" and "How could this site be easier to use for those purposes?"

Also, keep an eye on what other designers are doing—good and bad, usable and unusable, cool and boring—and analyze why the sites make each of those impressions on you. The Web itself is a constant source of inspiration for me, and I never know when I am going to come across a nugget of gold. Sometimes it just takes recognizing the germ of an idea to realize how that idea could really come to fruition. And sometimes, you need to sit with the idea for a long while before you will see its potential.

Tip

Continuing your Web Site Library can be a great tool in remembering what thought-provoking Web sites you have seen and where you can find them.

There are a number of sites that I periodically revisit even though I wouldn't necessarily rank them highly in terms of usability or learnability or good aesthetic design or any of the things that I've tried to convince you in this book to emulate. I am drawn to them because I find their designs thought provoking. I've mentioned a number of them previously, but just in case you haven't yet visited them, now might be a good time to take a look at these three sites:

- http://www.lessrain.com, the "Fish" section (or directly at the more lengthy URL: http://www.lessrain.com/web/main/shock/index.htm) (see Figure 15-1)

- http://www.thebrain.com, talk about far-out navigation (see Figure 15-2)

- http://www.egomedia.com, particularly the user options (see Figure 15-3)

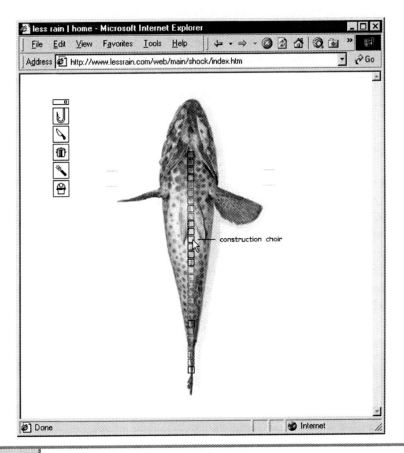

Figure 15-1   LessRain's "Fish" version of their Web site

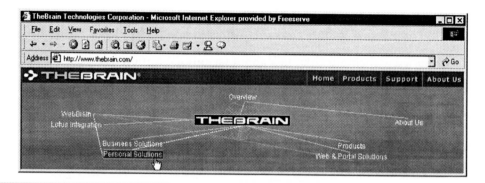

Figure 15-2 The Brain's navigation is quite thought provoking

There are three design avenues that may be particularly worth exploring:

● **Experience design** NewMedia.com published an article by Sean Carton in November 2001 heralding the advent of what he calls "experience design." In his words, "The nascent field of experience design comes from a realization that the Web is about a lot more than graphic identity. A Web site is the place where all the elements of a company—graphic identity, customer service, products, services, and structure—come together in one place. And interacting with a Web site conveys much more than the graphic brand identity of the company—it's all about the experience of moving through

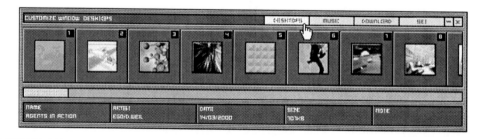

Figure 15-3 EgoMedia gives its users some real options in terms of tailoring their own experience of the site

the site and interacting with all of its various parts." (See the full article at http://www.newmedia.com/nm-ns.asp?articleID=3210.) This is not actually a new idea. Since the beginning of the Web, a number of designers have been seriously undertaking the same tasks under the label of "interactivity design" and have criticized the heavy emphasis on graphic design within the field of Web design. But, hey, "experience design" is a good label, too, and if it can help spur more efforts in this direction, then more power to it.

- **Possibilities for a "global visual language"**   I believe motion graphics guru Hillman Curtis coined the term "global visual language," or G.V.L. If he did not coin it, then he has certainly contributed a great deal to bringing it to the forefront of Web design discussions. The concept stems from the early perception of the Web as a global medium and provides one answer to the serious problem of communicating with a global audience. As we discussed earlier in the book, the current heavy emphasis on the use of the English language on the Web is a serious impairment to the globalization of the Web. As Curtis says in his book *Flash Web Design: The Art of Motion Graphics* (New Riders, 2001), "The challenge, then, for designers is to move toward a global visual language—that is, a language comprised of simple symbology and motion. The symbology is currently and constantly being created. A few obvious examples are the letter 'e' and the '@' symbol…. The development of this language is an organic process, an evolution that we all have a part in."

- **Beyond the visual: interface design for the other senses**   In contrast to the need to strive for a global visual language, we also need to strive toward communicating through the other senses. With the trend toward portable devices, the opportunities to find ways of designing for touch and audio are particularly promising because users on the go often need their eyes for other purposes. BotFighters, a game currently being played on the streets of Sweden with the use of mobile positioning and standard GSM phones, could be a budding example. As described by the BotFighter Web site at http://www.botfighters.com, "In the game, the players locate and shoot at each other with their mobile phones out on the streets, and mobile positioning is used to determine whether the users are close enough to each other to be able to hit…. The phone then becomes the player's radar and weapon device."

Note
The BotFighters game is another example of a local and physical congruence.

Project 15-1: Envision a Far-Out Usage Scenario

Okay, so here's your chance to peer into the future. Combining the possibilities we've discussed so far in this module with other ideas that you have read about or imagined yourself, give yourself some time and a sheet of paper to envision how the Web could be used in a unique way.

Step-by-Step

1. Secure one or more sheets of paper, or even better, a blank white board.

2. Secure a block of time in which you will not be interrupted.

3. If possible, secure two or three friends or colleagues who are also interested in the future of the Web.

4. Brainstorm some wacky ideas about how the Web could be used in the future. No holds barred; the wackier the better.

Tip

Revisit the brainstorming guidelines in Module 6 if you need to.

Project Summary

You may have come up with some great ideas that could make you a million bucks, or you may have only touched on any ideas that seemed remotely feasible. Both of them are worthwhile results. Perhaps I should have warned you that this is a life-long endeavor, and there is cumulative benefit to pondering the questions, "Just what does the future hold for the Web, and how can we harness it to good purpose?" So keep brainstorming.

1-Minute Drill

● What is the chief advantage of Curl?

● What are the differences between experience design and interactivity design?

● It speeds up the download time needed for Web pages.
● There are not any apparent differences.

Evolving Users

The last item in the equation of what the future holds for the Web is perhaps the most ignored. I don't believe I have ever heard anybody mention that all of us users evolve right along with the Web technologies and the designs, and that the technologies and designs need to adapt accordingly. We do evolve. We learn, we form habits, we break habits as we learn some more. Some tasks become so habitual that we stop thinking about them and they become intuitive. And we do demand that the technologies and designs adapt to our needs. If they don't, we stop using them, and they die. We are, in fact, an intrinsic part of the Web—lifelines so to speak. Doesn't that give you a wonderful sense of power as a user?

Tip

With the Web as with most mediums, kids can be a terrific bellwether for predicting user trends. They have proved to be some of the most technologically advanced adopters and adapters for the Web so far and will likely continue to be so.

A key challenge in designing Web sites, however, is that whenever you are designing general-interest Web sites that aspire to a global reach, you are designing for an incredibly broad base of users, from Web neophytes to skilled users. This will continue to be true as new users come on board from across the globe, which will certainly continue for some years to come.

But as we discussed earlier in this module, not all Web sites cater to an ever-broadening global audience. With the increasing trend toward broadening and deepening the reach of the Web, many sites that cater to a local or otherwise restricted user base have the opportunity to evolve along with their users. This happens naturally as an organic process, but it can also take the form of a more conscious and directed evolution. Staying in touch with your users, asking them questions, bouncing ideas off them (before implementing them on the Web site), and listening to their spontaneous suggestions can speed the process up immensely.

Neither as designers nor as users are we pawns of this system. Far too often people seem to feel as though they have no control over the Web. There may be many human-engineered systems in the world that we do not realistically have much control over (political arenas, free-market capitalism, religious ideologies, to name a few), but the Web is not one of them.

Tip

We have the opportunity to participate in a conscious evolution of the Web.

Project 15-2: Usability Mantra: Repeat After Me...

This is the easiest project in the whole book. All you have to do is repeat a few words a few times over a few times every day for the rest of your life. (I've really been doing this quite a bit throughout the book, but I thought I'd bring it to the forefront so that you could see what you've gotten yourself into!)

Step-by-Step

1. Pick one of the following usability mantras. You can base your selection on one that you most agree with, most disagree with, or even would most like to agree with.

   - The user reigns supreme.
   - There are no wrong users.
   - This Web site's primary goal is to serve its users.
   - I can organize the content of this site from the user's perspective.
   - I can make this Web site's interface easily learnable.
   - I can cater to all sorts of learners through the Web site's design.
   - I can find a way to improve the Web today.
   - I can find a way to make this Web site more usable.
   - I can find a way to help the Web evolve.
   - I am a user of the Web first and a designer second.

2. Read it out loud.

3. Read it out loud nine more times.

4. Memorize it.

5. Repeat it in your mind (or out loud) ten more times before going to bed, or when you stop for lunch, or at some other convenient time during the day.

6. When you get up tomorrow, start over with Step 1.

7. Feel free to write your own usability mantras to add to the list at any time.

Project Summary

Okay, I realize that there's no way you are going to do this every day for the rest of your life. If you do it a few times every now and again I'll be happy. More importantly, if you just integrate the mantras into your design style, the Web will be a better place.

Module Conclusion

Congratulations. You are on your way to making the Web more user-friendly. With the knowledge and the skills that you have learned in this book, you can be a valuable resource for any Web development team or just create better sites on your own.

The future of the Web lies in your hands. Take care of it, and good luck!

15

☑Mastery Check

1. What are the key advantages of thinking about the future of the Web from the perspective of the user?

_____

_____

2. As a Web designer, what are your two primary tasks?

_____

_____

3. Which of the following statements are true? (You may select more than one.)

   A. The bandwidth of the Web is *not* improving in any way.

   B. Changes for the Web are *not* unidirectional.

   C. The Web is *not* dissipating with the dot-com industry.

   D. The Web is *not* at a standstill.

   E. Color issues on the Web are no longer a problem.

4. In what way has the assumption that bandwidth for the Web would gradually improve over time been proved wrong?

_____

_____

5. What role was the Internet envisioned as playing in the development of Japan's i-mode "pocket monster"?

_____

_____

6. In what way does Curl speed up the download process of Web sites?

   A. It expands the bandwidth of particular user's systems.

   B. It reduces the size of the elements on each Web page.

☑ Mastery Check

C. It allows the Web page source code to be compiled on a user's computer.

D. It uncurls the network path from the Web server to the user's computer.

7. What is the inherent flaw in having Web-only browsers on our computers?

_____

_____

8. What is the key to being part of the evolution of the Web in terms of design, instead of riding on the coattails of it?

_____

_____

9. What are the two key components of global visual language according to Hillman Curtis?

A. Motion

B. Graphics

C. Simple symbology

D. Effective translation programs

E. Logos

10. True or False: We have the opportunity to participate in a conscious evolution of the Web.

15

Part III

Appendices

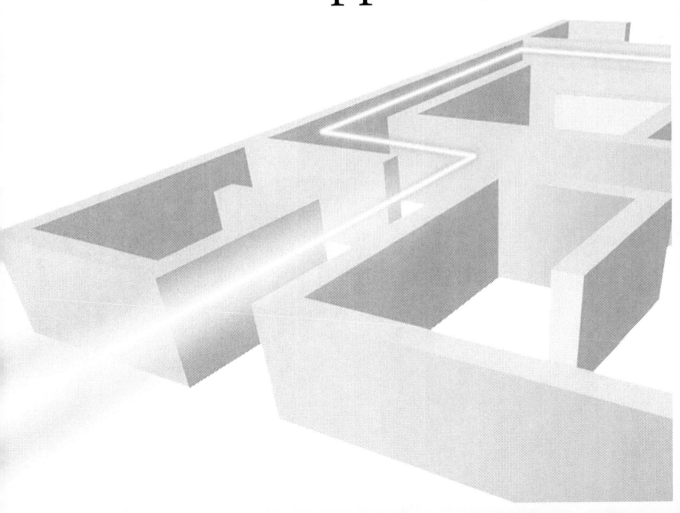

Appendix A

Mastery Check
Answers

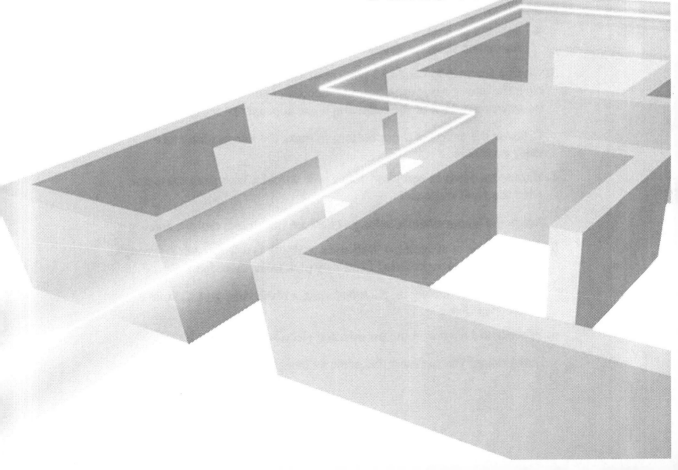

Module 1: You as a Preeminent User: Put on Your Usability Spectacles

1. To get the most value from your experience of the Web as a user, what two things are necessary to do?

Observe your own thoughts and behaviors, and record the thought processes and behaviors that have to do with the functionality of the site.

2. List four common Web site usability flaws.

There are many more than four Web site usability flaws, but a few of them include:

- Interfaces that assume the user knows how to use them
- Inconsistent interfaces
- Labels that use the language, or jargon, of the site's creators, not the users
- Meaningless visual icons.
- Reliance on a single navigation mode and/or the lack of alternative navigation styles for alternative users *and* uses

3. Given a scenario in which 15 percent of a Web site's users accidentally click the wrong navigation button when asked to find a specific piece of information, which of the following is the appropriate action to take?

C. Revise the design of those buttons to make the information more easily accessible.

4. If someone starts to complain about how stupid a Web site's users are, what is a good response?

Assign the blame where it belongs. Users are not stupid; designs are.

5. The first step in assessing a Web site's usability is to approach it through which of these perspectives? (You may pick more than one.)

A. As a babe in the woods; **B.** *Tabula rasa,* a blank slate; and **C.** From a fresh perspective

6. Who should have won the presidential election of the year 2000?

(Just kidding! You can have this point for free.)

7. Define "Web usability."

In its simplest definition, a usable Web site is one that its audience can effectively *use*. Users should be able to find the information they are looking for and make transactions or be involved in their desired interactions *effortlessly*.

8. Which of the following should you do while reviewing the Web as a user (with your usability spectacles on)? (You may select more than one.)

A. Observe your own thoughts and behaviors; **C.** Record the thought processes and behaviors that have to do with the functionality of the site; and **D.** Pay particular attention to the navigation path that you follow.

9. Once we learn how to do something, what do we usually assume about how easily others will learn how to do it?

We tend to assume that it's easy for everybody else, and we forget just how difficult it was for ourselves.

Module 2: Swap Out Your Spectacles: Seeing from Other Perspectives

1. The two types of Web usage scenarios are _____ and _____.

Real-world and imaginary

2. What percentage of the male population worldwide suffers from some form of color blindness?

Between 5 and 10 percent

3. Which statement is true about the relationship between the power of imagination and the power of observation in terms of establishing Web site usability?

C. They are complementary.

4. How many different learning styles are there?

There is no fixed number of learning styles; a number of different theories exist.

5. Which of the following pairs of learning styles are essentially the same?

D. Active and kinesthetic

6. True or False: The technology now exists that makes it possible to include smell and touch in Web site design.

True. It does exist, but that does not mean that we can use it willy-nilly in Web site design. The rate of adoption is quite slow, so not many users could actually take advantage of it.

7. Why should we avoid the use of the color blue in Web site design?

D. Our ability to perceive blues decreases with age.

8. True or False: We should make a practice of designing all Web sites for complete Web beginners, since they will always be the lowest common denominator.

False. They are only the lowest *common* denominator if they share skills and tools "in common" with the majority of your user base. Otherwise, they are just the lowest denominator. Always determine who your user base is, or who you want them to be, and then design the site accordingly.

Module 3: Get to Know Your Users: Creating User Profiles

1. Which of the following format(s) can a Web user profile take? (You may select more than one.)

B. Text; **C.** Tables; and **D.** Diagrams

2. List at least six prelaunch user analysis methods that are available to you.

Here are seven of the most common methods. There are, of course, others as well.

- Market research
- Focus groups
- Questionnaires

- Interviews
- Usability testing
- Heuristic evaluations
- Plain old observation

3. Which of the following user analysis methods are available to you only after you launch a Web site? (You may select more than one.)

B. Web usage analyses; and **C.** Web forms

4. What are two reasons why you can't always rely on what users tell you, instead of what they show you?

Users will often try to give you the answer that they think you want. And sometimes they don't actually know how they would use a Web site. There can be too much room for conjecture in talking about things instead of doing them.

5. What is one of the most inexpensive, powerful tools available to you in assessing a Web site's usability?

The power of observation

6. Why is it a good idea to mentally separate the process of getting to know your users from that of getting to know their hardware and software constraints?

To remind ourselves that the users are, indeed, separate from the technologies. The former requires a life-long study, while the latter changes consistently.

7. Which of the following are likely to suffer if you make assumptions without asking questions and find out months into a project that you were wrong? (You may select more than one.)

E. All of the above

8. Which of the following statements are true in regards to conducting field studies for usability purposes?

A. You visit users in their natural environments; and **C.** They are one of the most effective ways to observe users.

9. What is a "click stream analysis"?

A. An analysis of what users clicked on while visiting a site.

Module 4: Get to Know Your Users' Computer Constraints

1. What are the four primary hardware and software constraints that are most likely to affect the user's experience?

Bandwidth, browsers, operating systems, and monitor screen resolution

2. Which of the following lag times in a Web site will allow the user's stream of thought to remain uninterrupted?

A. One second

3. For typical users with 56 K modem Web access, which of the following page sizes will download quickly enough that you will not have lost the user's focus? (You may select more than one.)

A. 25 K; and **B.** 50 K

4. True or False: Broadband connectivity is gaining acceptance quickly enough that we can soon stop designing Web sites for regular modem users.

False. Broadband acceptance is occurring at a much slower rate than most people projected.

5. Which of the following browsers is the de facto design standard for most general-interest Web sites?

H. None of the above. There is no single Web browser that has a large enough user base that it can be considered a de facto design standard.

6. True or False: A number of Web authoring tools have the capability to thoroughly test for cross-browser compatibility, thereby eliminating the need to test browsers individually.

False. None of the current Web authoring tools is sophisticated enough to catch all the bugs in all the different browsers. Real-world testing is still vitally important.

7. Which of the following guidelines will help ensure that your Web sites will work in future browsers? (You may select more than one.)

B. Write all your code in lowercase. As for tags, you should avoid the deprecated tags in the XHTML 1.0 standard such as the <font> tag in favor of the CSS counterparts.

8. What audiences are you likely to lose users from if you choose not to design your site to work on the Macintosh operating system?

Schools, desktop publishers, and graphics professionals

9. Which of the following guidelines should you follow in naming files for optimal cross-platform compatibility? (You may select more than one answer.)

B. Use no more than a three-letter extension; and **C.** Use only lower case letters. As for length, filenames may be up to 31 characters long (although that is a bit excessive!). Also, in addition to using the letters of the alphabet, it is OK to use the numbers 1–9 plus the hyphen (-) and the underscore (_).

10. True or False: Designing Web sites for 640×480 screen resolutions is the de facto design standard.

False. The predominant screen resolution now typically in use is 800×600. However, it is still better to design relative-width screens than fixed-width ones for that specific resolution, since usage varies so much.

Module 5: Know the Web Even Better Than Your Users Do

1. True or False: You don't need to know more than your users do in order to design effective Web sites.

False. In order to truly take advantage of the medium of the Web, you will likely need to know it much better than your users do, unless they are a particularly knowledgeable bunch of users.

2. True or False. You should not participate in creating Web sites until you can gain a full, comprehensive knowledge of how the Web works and what its potential and limitations are.

False. It's not really possible to attain "full, comprehensive knowledge" about this new medium. The more knowledge you can gain, however, the better sites you'll be able to create.

3. If you know the Web better than your users do, how can you rely on them to tell you what to design to meet their needs?

You can't exclusively rely on the users, or at least not on their ability to express themselves. Oftentimes, they may not even realize that their needs could be met in a better way. But that does not mean that you can ever ignore the users. This is the part of "seeing through the users' eyes" where you need to train yourself to see what they *will* be able to see but may not even be able to imagine yet.

4. Which of the following are limitations imposed by the computer environment? (You may select more than one.)

B. Monitor quality; **D.** Repetitive motion injuries; and **E.** Computer ambiance

5. Which of the following are true statements about the limitations and potential of the Web as a medium?

B. and **C.** Multimedia is both one of the limitations and potentials of the Web.

6. What are five common uses of the Web?

Informational resource, business sites, community sites, educational sites, games/entertainment

7. What are the two key benefits of creating your own Web Site Library?

To keep you consistently analyzing the same types of things and to provide a useful document that you can easily skim or search to find good examples of any particular issue you'd like to explore.

Module 6: Stick to a User-Centric Design Process

1. What is the underlying *modus operandi* of designing usable Web sites?

Sticking to a user-centric design process.

2. What can enable you to fine-tune a Web site during production so that by the time you launch it, it is in perfect harmony with the users' needs?

Constantly checking in with the users, to get their opinions and observe their reactions to each step of the planning and implementation of your design ideas. This enables you to fine-tune the usability aspects of the Web site during production.

3. In a user-centric design process, what role do the users play in relation to the Web team?

The users are considered a part of the Web team.

4. Which of the following is the correct definition for a "Web team composite" in terms of a user-centric design process?

C. A team that includes members who represent the creative, technical, and usability perspectives.

5. What is the client's role in a user-centric Web design process?

The client's role is to inform the team along the lines of any of the perspectives included in the Web team composite. In general, the client can contribute the most within the usability or investment perspectives.

6. In general, to serve the best interests of the client, do you need to create a site that gives preeminence to the client's ideas for a Web site or those of the client's target audience?

Those of the client's target audience

7. Which phase of the Web development process is fairly unique to the Web industry and why?

Maintenance and updating. Unlike so many of its counterparts, no Web site is a final product that can be shipped out the door and forgotten more or less until the next version goes into design. Part of the magic of the Web is its currency and capacity to change practically moment to moment.

8. Which of the following decisions need to be made during the planning phase?

A. What is the target audience?; **B.** What purpose will the Web site serve?; and **E.** Who is the target audience?

9. What two things can you do to best ensure the success of a brainstorming planning session?

   Choose your planning environment carefully, and use proven brainstorming techniques.

10. Which of the following is an appropriate level of user involvement during the design phase?

    C. To provide feedback as to whether the comps will work for them

Module 7: Site Design, First Steps: Getting Users to Your Site

1. Which of the following are techniques for creating good domain names? (You may select more than one.)

   E. All of the above

2. Which of the following are domain names and which are URLs?

   A. hottea.com and **D.** excite.com are domain names; **B.** http://bn.com and **C.** http://go.yahoo.com are URLs.

3. Why should you generally avoid using the number 2 in your domain name?

   When spoken, it can be interpreted as a number of different things, including "two," "2," "too," or "to."

4. Above all, what is the most important thing to do in selecting a domain name?

   Make sure your domain name is logical and guessable.

5. What two tags can you use within the <head> tag to make your Web pages findable?

   A. <title>; and **C.** <meta>

6. What can you do with each of the two correct tags to question #5?

   Give every page a good title using the <title> tag, and include a description and list of keywords used in your site by using the <meta> tag.

7. What roles do the core and supplemental content fulfill on a Web site?

The core content is the information or material that the users may seek, and the supplemental content is all the Web paraphernalia that is needed to support those efforts, such as navigation bars.

8. True or False: The core content provided by a site should tie in directly to the site goals and should be established during the planning stages of the site design process.

True

9. True or False: The media other than text to be included on a Web site are considered part of the supplemental content.

False. They can be part of the core content.

10. Which of the following can be accomplished through the use of supplemental content? (You may choose more than one.)

A. Provide a means of navigating the site; **C.** Provide a sense of security for the user; and **D.** Produce advertising revenue

Module 8: Information Architecture: Organizing Your Web Site

1. What are the two stages in establishing a Web site's information architecture?

Organizing the information from the users' point of view, and determining how to best present those clusters of information on the Web site for your particular users.

2. What is information architecture?

The term "information architecture" is a fancy way of saying the way information is organized. Like the traditional field of architecture, it encompasses the planning stage and focuses on establishing a sound structure. The end result is some kind of model on paper, often called a "blueprint" although it looks more like a flowchart, which can then be followed during the construction or development phase.

3. What trait is essential to good information architecture?

It must be self-explanatory to enable users to easily learn how to use that system to find what information they need.

4. List the four common kinds of exact organizational systems.

Alphabetic, Numeric, Chronological, and Geographic

5. List the four common kinds of inexact organizational systems.

Topic, Task, Audience, and Metaphor

6. What is the greatest benefit from following an exact organizational system?

An exact organizational system follows a set of well-defined rules that can assign every single piece of content a precise position within its scheme.

7. True or False: Exact systems are the most efficient and surest means of organizing information.

False. While exact systems may appear to be the surest means of organizing information, they are not necessarily the most efficient. Imagine, for example, what a nightmare it would be if your local grocery store arranged all its contents in alphabetical order instead of by type.

8. What is the chief challenge in organizing a site's content by topic?

Clustering groups of content together by topic is the method that is most open to interpretation and debate by Web users. Primarily this is because topics often tend to overlap.

9. Under what circumstances is organizing a site's content by audience most effective?

Dividing a site by audience works best if the target audiences are clearly distinct. It does not work well if much of the content overlaps between them.

10. What two things can determine how successful a metaphor-driven site will be?

A metaphor-driven site's success depends heavily on how thoroughly the content can be aligned within the chosen metaphor as well as how responsive the audience is to the metaphor.

11. What purpose does a site diagram serve?

D. To give a visual representation of the placement of and relationship of the site's contents

Module 9: Navigation Design

1. At its most fundamental level, what is navigation design?

A manifestation of information architecture

2. What is the role of graphic design within navigation design?

Graphic design is a key skill employed during this phase, but it is not the only skill needed. Just as the Web differs from print, navigation design for the Web requires skills in developing motion graphics, audio production, and interactivity design in addition to graphic design.

3. What is meant by "making every page feel like home"?

B. Make every page present the site's navigation options

4. What are "bread crumbs" in the context of navigation design?

Bread crumbs are a device used to show a user where the page is within the site's overall structure.

5. True or False: It is not necessary to provide descriptive text throughout the site explaining the navigation functions if this has been carefully explained on the home page.

False. Each page should be able to stand on its own.

6. What is the difference between navigation controls and navigation aids? And what are some examples of both?

Navigation controls are the actual devices that transport the user from one page or section to another, such as a hypertext link. Navigation aids help guide the users around the Web sites and indicate what elements are navigation controls, such as the underlining and blue color used with hypertext links.

7. True or False: The button states that indicate when a button is active, depressed, or released are navigation aids.

True. The buttons themselves are navigation controls, but these indicators are aids.

8. Where does convention indicate the navigation bar should be placed on a Web site? You may select more than one answer.

A. The top of each page; or **D.** The upper left-hand corner

9. What are the limitations when using color-coding of different sections of a Web site?

There is a natural limitation to the number of colors that can be effectively used to color-code sections. Once you start using similar shades of orange, for example, users will have a very difficult time differentiating the sections. Also between if you are using text labels, you cannot use colors with widely varying contrast and be able to ensure the readability of the type.

10. What two things benefit from having a consistent navigation design?

A. Site identity; and **B.** Usability

Module 10: Site Design Usability Dilemmas

1. Which of the following are valid components of the "plug-in conundrum"?

A. Version of plug-ins; and **D.** User adoption of plug-ins

2. Which of the following is the common abbreviation for Flash files?

A. swf

3. Which of the following is the common abbreviation for Shockwave files?

E. swd

4. Which of the following concerns should be the first one addressed whenever you are considering making any part of your site dependent on browser plug-ins?

D. Consider alternative ways to present the content.

5. True or False: In the early days of the Web, building Web sites to work on specific browsers made some sort of sense from a usability perspective.

False. It made some sort of sense from a development perspective, but never from a user perspective.

6. True or False: In designing a Web site with Cascading Style Sheets, it is best to optimize it for one version of one browser, but it is also important to test it on other browsers.

True

7. Which of the following is a surefire solution for the splash page dilemma?

B. Always include a link to bypass the splash page.

8. Which of the following statements are *not* true about frames?

A. Frames always link from one to the other. They are never self-referential; **C.** There is a limit of six frames per Web page; **E.** You can always determine whether a site uses frames by observing its behavior.

9. True or False: Bookmarking a section of a site contained within a frame is problematic.

True

10. Which of the following approaches will help ensure a large Web site is also usable?

C. Treat every page as though it is some user's entry point; and **D.** Establish a consistent, site-wide global navigation system.

Module 11: Screen Design for Usability

1. If you know your users have a screen resolution of 640×480, why shouldn't you design your Web site to fill that space?

If you design a Web site for the full screen resolution, you will guarantee that some of the contents will be cut off because of all the space taken up on computer monitors by the browser and operating system paraphernalia.

2. What is the generic formula for determining an appropriate screen size to design for?

User screen resolution, 640×480, etc.
    – Operating system space
                    – Browser space
    _____
                    Viewable screen size

3. What is the correct definition of the term "browser offset"?

C. The pad between the edge of the browser and the content of a Web page

4. Which of the following permit you to adjust the browser offsets in versions 4 and above of Netscape and Explorer? (Select all that apply.)

A. Topmargin; **B.** Marginheight; **E.** Marginwidth; and **F.** Leftmargin

5. Why should you use caution in specifying that the scroll bars of frames be invisible?

Making the scroll bars invisible will mean users who are looking at your site in a smaller viewable screen area than you have designed for may not be able to access all the information within the frame. This would also be the case for visually impaired users who increase the default type size for easier readability.

6. What two limiting factors should influence the guideline that suggests in determining how much content to include on each page, you should include as much related content as possible that can be displayed within the viewable screen area?

You should include as much related content as possible *without* cluttering the page up and *without* overwhelming your user's bandwidth limitations.

7. Since it's the information architect's role to determine how the content of a site is organized, why are some decisions about how much content should go on any given page left to the screen design stage?

In many cases, the information architects do not have all the content at hand in the early stages of planning a Web site. They may know only, for example, that there needs to be a section on a company's history, not whether or not there's one paragraph's worth of material or ten pages. Thus, many of these decisions are left until the screen design stage.

8. True or False: Most users generally prefer scrolling over linking.

False. About the only case where users prefer scrolling to linking is in reading lengthy documents.

9. What would be a key difference achieved in a Web site design by using a color palette of highly contrasting colors as opposed to a set of earth tones?

There would likely be differences in energy level. Highly contrasting colors can evoke a sense of high-energy, while earth tones can be calming and relaxing.

10. How many colors are in the truly Web-safe palette?

A mere 22

11. List four key factors that may impact readability.

Type size, font face, level of contrast against background, and whether or not the background pattern "gets in the way" or conflicts with the text

Module 12: Preparing User-Friendly Content

1. Why can it be helpful, during the content preparation stage, for every member of a Web team to have at least a rudimentary understanding of a user-centric design process?

Usability issues come into play even at the content preparation stage.

2. Which of the following are benefits of a good content management system? (Select all that apply.)

All but **D**. It creates a more usable Web site. A good content management system's greatest impact is on the production process, not the design, although it may indirectly benefit the implementation of the design.

3. True or False: Approval stages should be integrated into an effective content management system.

True

4. In the creation of user-friendly text for a Web site, what aspect is even more important than the presentation of text and its readability on a Web site?

The content of the text itself

5. True or False: On the Web, the text can just be fast and dirty.

False

6. Why doesn't it usually work to just lift copy developed for print publications and slot it into a Web site?

The medium of the Web is significantly different than the print medium— different enough that the same company, the same message, and the same audience will produce a significantly different experience on the Web. For starters, the basic experience of reading online *is* different than that of reading printed material.

7. In what way could a document that has the following types of information be effectively reordered for presentation on the Web: preamble, supporting arguments, and conclusion?

The conclusion should be presented first, followed by the supporting arguments. Chances are the preamble will best be omitted.

8. Which of the following is/are *not* appropriate guidelines on writing for the Web?

B. Explain every point in full detail.

9. What is meant by the phrase "chunk your text"?

Chunking is breaking material down into bite-sized portions.

10. True or False: If you find a piece of art on the Web that does not have a stated copyright or digital watermark, it is okay to reproduce it on your Web site.

False. The absence of a copyright indication does not mean that the art is free to use. It is always best to ask for permission from its creator.

11. In preparing user-friendly media files for a Web site, what aspect is even more important than the presentation and delivery of the files across the Web?

It is important to identify which media files will be most appropriate for your users.

Module 13: Case Studies: Analyzing Web Sites

1. If 15 percent of a site's users complain that they don't understand how a navigation feature works, which of the following can you safely assume?

B. You have a serious usability issue with that one feature.

2. True or False: As a designer, if something confuses you when you visit a site, you should first try to figure it out, and only if you do not succeed, should you analyze what might be making the site fail.

False. That first impression may be your biggest clue that something about the site may well confuse other users.

3. True or False: It is best to first evaluate a Web site as a user and then as a designer instead of the other way around.

True

4. True or False: Horizontal scrolling should never be permitted on a Web site.

False. In general, horizontal scrolling should be avoided, but there are almost always exceptions to every rule.

5. Which of the following are the most typical traits of older Web sites?

B. They generally decay with age; **C.** They generally grow in scope from the original plan; and **D.** They generally deviate from the original design decisions.

6. True or False: As a general rule, if you do not discover any usability issues in your first, cursory review, you will not find any upon more detailed review.

False

Module 14: Testing, Testing

1. True or False: The requirements for test participants are exactly the same for quick and easy or more thorough usability tests.

True. They need to match the audience profile for the site.

2. In general, a Web site usability test needs how many test participants?

B. 5

3. Which of the following tasks are the responsibility of a usability test facilitator? (Select as many as apply.)

A. Putting the test participant at ease; and **D.** Debriefing the test participant at the end of the test

4. What are the advantages and disadvantages to videotaping a usability test instead of having observers present?

You miss out on the real-time experience a bit and the opportunity to pose additional questions at the end of the test, but it gives you a tremendous advantage to be able to replay actions that you either missed or weren't sure how to interpret the first time around.

5. What is the range in possible costs in constructing a usability lab?

It can range from tens to hundreds of thousands of dollars.

6. What is the chief advantage of conducting remote usability tests over conducting tests in a formal usability lab?

Remote usability testing allows the test participants to stay in the most comfortable environs of all—their normal workspace. Thus, it can more closely approximate a real-world usage scenario than the artificial environs of a usability-testing lab.

7. Which two of the following places in the development cycle are generally the most appropriate for usability testing?

B. Near the end of the design phase; and **D.** After the final design tweaks and before the launch. **C.** is also a strong contender.

8. Which two of the following questions can be most helpful in identifying what to test for in a usability test?

A. What about the site are you most unsure of or worried about?; and **D.** What are the most vital functions of this Web site?

9. Which of the following tasks are *not* appropriate for the facilitator while administering the test? (Select all that apply.)

C. Interject instructions when the participant seems confused.

10. What is the most important task to conduct immediately after completing a usability test?

B. Consolidate notes from the facilitator and all observers.

Module 15: Looking Ahead: Through the Users' Eyes

1. What are the key advantages of thinking about the future of the Web from the perspective of the user?

Not only will such an approach help make the Web more user-friendly, which is an inherently good thing to do, but it will also likely lead to the most *successful* ideas.

2. As a Web designer, what are your two primary tasks?

First, you need to create the content that the user wants; then you need to provide an interface through which the user can get to it with the greatest ease and enjoyment.

3. Which of the following statements are true? (You may select more than one.)

B. Changes for the Web are *not* unidirectional; **C.** The Web is *not* dissipating with the dot-com industry; **D.** The Web is *not* at a standstill.

4. In what way has the assumption that bandwidth for the Web would gradually improve over time been proved wrong?

This perspective was based on the assumption that the Web was largely a phenomenon of desktop computers, a perspective that is no longer valid in light of the trend toward integration and the development of mobile devices.

5. What role was the Internet envisioned as playing in the development of Japan's i-mode "pocket monster"?

Integrating the capabilities of the Web into a handy, usable Internet appliance was only the means (not the motivation) through which DoMoCo was able to add value to their customer's lives.

6. In what way does Curl speed up the download process of Web sites?

C. It allows the Web page source code to be compiled on a user's computer.

7. What is the inherent flaw in having Web-only browsers on our computers?

It makes no sense to store different pieces of information in different venues and to need different tools to access them.

8. What is the key to being part of the evolution of the Web in terms of design, instead of riding on the coattails of it?

The key is to remember your beginnings: Leave your assumptions at the door, and try to experience the Web (1) as a user and (2) as though you had never seen it before.

9. What are the two key components of global visual language according to Hillman Curtis?

   A. Motion; and **C.** Simple symbology

10. True or False: We have the opportunity to participate in a conscious evolution of the Web.

   True!

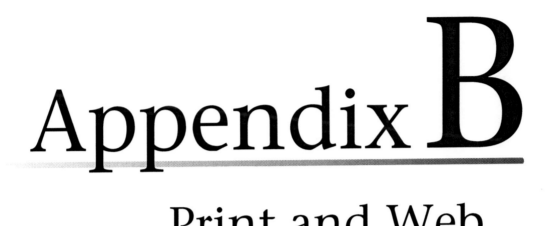

Appendix B

Print and Web Resources

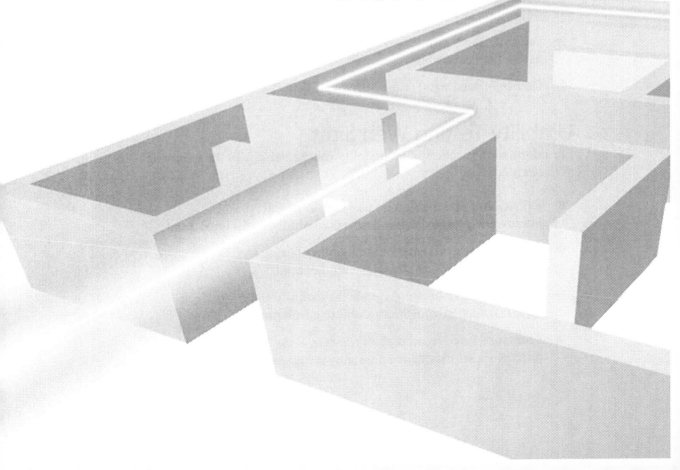

Web Usability Resources

The most extensive online resource for anything to do with Web site usability issues is indubitably Keith Instone's Usable Web (http://usableweb.com). This is a vast collection of links (at the time of this writing numbering 1,423) to current information on Web usability issues.

A handful of other useful sites include:

- Section 508: http://www.section508.gov (with details on the U.S. government's requirements for making Web sites accessible); The final technical requirements are available at http://www.access-board.gov/news/508-final.htm

- Society for Technical Communication (STC) Usability Special Interest Group: http://www.stcsig.org/usability

- Usability Methods Research Laboratory at Virginia Tech: http://miso.cs.vt.edu/~usab (part of the Human Computer Interaction Department)

- UseIt Alertbox: http://www.useit.com/alertbox (A free biweekly newsletter is available.)

- User Interface Engineering: http://world.std.com/~uieweb

Usability Testing Web Sites

For information specifically on usability testing, see any of the following Web sites:

- Kelly Goto's presentation on usability testing at http://www.gotomedia.com/seattle00/usability/intro/intro1.html

- Keith Instone's presentation on usability testing at http://instone.org/keith/howtotest/index.html

- National Cancer Institute's guide for usability testing guide at http://usability.gov/methods/usability_testing.html

- Constance Petersen on usability tests at http://www.smartisans.com/usability_testing.htm

Books and Related Web Sites

These books and their related Web sites are good usability resources:

- Alexander, Janet E., and Marsha Ann Tate, *Web Wisdom: How to Evaluate and Create Information Quality on the Web* (Lawrence Erlbaum Associates, 1999). Related Web site on "Evaluating Web Resources": http://www.widener.edu/libraries.html.

- Nielsen, Jakob, *Designing Web Usability* (New Riders, 2000). Related Web site at http://www.useit.com/alertbox.

- Pearrow, Mark, *Web Site Usability Handbook* (Charles River Media, 2000), and *The Wireless Web Usability Handbook* (Charles River Media, 2001/2002).

Web Design and Development Resources

The following Web sites are good general design and development resources:

- Bandwidth Place: http://bandwidthplace.com

- Browser.com: http://www.browser.com (Note: This is now a CNET Topic Center with a direct URL of http://www.cnet.com/internet/0-3773.html—not nearly as memorable as "browser.com," is it? Fortunately, for the time being at least, you can type in **http://www.browser.com**, and it will forward you to the more cumbersome URL.)

- BrowserWatch: http://browserwatch.internet.com (See the Browser Boulevard section for details on most of the available browsers. It's so long that it's broken into two parts—it includes more than 100 browsers, with information on the developer, cost, platform, operating system requirements, hard drive space needed, and whether it supports Java, CSS, and plug-ins.)

- Cool Home Pages: http://www.coolhomepages.com

- Curl: http://www.curl.com

- Digimarc: http://digimarc.com (digital watermarking)

- Ewatermark: http://www.ewatermark.com (also digital watermarking)

- Inform IT: http://www.informit.com

- Internet Week: http://www.internetweek.com (A free print version is also available.)

- InterNIC's Accredited Registrar Directory: http://www.internic.com (domain name registration)

- Network Solutions: http://www.networksolutions.com (domain name registration)

- NewMedia: http://www.newmedia.com (A free online newsletter is available.)

- Nielsen//NetRatings: http://www.nielsen-netratings.com (A free online newsletter is available.)

- Search Engine Watch: http://www.searchenginewatch.com

- Silicon Valley Localization Forum: http://www.tgpconsulting.com/translators.htm

- StatMarket: http://statmarket.com

- Web Review: http://webreview.com (A great Web development resource. A free online newsletter is available.)

- Web Sites That Suck: http://www.websitesthatsuck.com

- Webby Awards: http://www.webbyawards.com

- WebMonkey: http://hotwired.lycos.com/webmonkey (Another great Web development resource.)

- WebTechniques:http://www.webtechniques.com (Free magazine available as well.) (Note: This magazine and Web site are going to change into New Architect Magazine at http://www.newarchitectmag.com in early 2002.)

- WebTV Development: http://developer.webtv.net

- World Wide Web Consortium: http://www.w3.org

Of special note: Internet.com (http://internet.com) is a growing umbrella organization for a number of Internet technology and news sites. It now includes BrowserWatch, Server Watch, Internet Product Watch, and Internet

News among about 100 other subsites. It organizes all the sites into the following 16 channels:

- ASP Resources http://www.internet.com/asp

- Careers http://www.internet.com/careers

- Downloads http://www.internet.com/downloads

- Earthweb http://www.earthweb.com

- E-Commerce/Marketing http://www.internet.com/marketing

- International http://www.internet.com/international

- Internet Investing http://www.internet.com/stocks

- Internet Lists http://www.internet.com/lists

- Internet News http://www.internet.com/news

- Internet Resources http://www.internet.com/resources

- Internet Technology http://www.internet.com/it

- ISP Resources http://www.internet.com/isp

- Linux/Open Source http://www.internet.com/linux

- Web Developer http://www.internet.com/webdev

- Windows Internet Technology http://www.internet.com/win

- Wireless Internet http://www.internet.com/wireless

Books and Related Web Sites

Following are some good books and their related Web sites on Web design and development.

- Curtis, Hillman, *Flash Web Design: The Art of Motion Graphics* (New Riders, 2001). Related Web site at http://www.hillmancurtis.com.

- Honeywill, Paul, *Visual Language for the World Wide Web* (Intellect Books, 1999).

● Lynch, Patrick J., and Sarah Horton, *Web Style Guide: Basic Design Principles for Creating Web Sites* (Yale University Press, 1999). Related Web site at http://info.med.yale.edu/caim/manual.

Useful Resources Beyond the Topic of the Web

Here is a list of great books that can help inform your design sense for the Web or any other medium:

● Kelly, Tom, *The Art of Innovation: Lessons in Creativity from IDEO* (Doubleday, 2001).

● Norman, Donald A., *Learning and Memory* (W.H. Freeman and Company, 1982).

● Norman, Donald A., *The Design of Everyday Things* (Doubleday, 1990).

● Raskin, Jef, *The Humane Interface: New Directions for Designing Interactive Systems* (Addison-Wesley, 2000).

● Tufte, Edward, *The Visual Display of Quantitative Information*, Second Edition (Graphics Press, 2001).

● Wilde, Judith and Richard, *Visual Literacy: A Conceptual Approach to Graphic Problem Solving* (Watson-Guptill Publishing, 2000).

● Williams, Robin, *The Non-Designer's Design Book* (Peachpit Press, 1994).

● Wurman, Richard Saul, *Information Anxiety* (Doubleday, 1989). A second edition was released in 2001.

Learning Styles Web Sites

Four sites specifically about learning styles are

● Canfield's Learning Style Inventory: http://www.tecweb.org/styles/stylesframe.html

● Howard Gardner's Multiple Intelligence Inventory: http://surfaquarium.com/MIinvent.htm

- Richard M. Felder's Index of Learning Styles:
  http://www2.ncsu.edu/unity/lockers/users/f/felder/public/ILSdir/
  ilsweb.html

- TecWeb: http://www.tecweb.org

B

Appendix C

Web Site
Functionality
Testing

There's nothing quite like broken links, missing images, funny characters, or other malfunctioning elements to get in the way of a user trying to accomplish something on a Web site. A key underpinning to a Web site's usability is that it needs to actually work as it was intended. Thus, functionality testing goes hand in hand with usability testing.

Functionality testing is not something that should be left entirely to the end of the project. As is the case for much of Web development, testing is an iterative process. You test a little here, a little there, make some changes, and test again; you then conduct one final, big test at the very end of development, prior to publicly launching the site. Large Web teams often have a dedicated testing staff, but this never takes the HTML developer off the hook. Each member of the team is responsible for conducting preliminary tests of his or her pages to make sure that they work like they're supposed to.

Before diving in to the functionality testing, we'll take into consideration two key elements that can make sure you run the most effective and efficient test:

- Testing equipment
- Testing tools

In general, it's a good idea to start every testing session with broad, site-wide issues and then narrow your focus down to the nitty-gritty details on each page. It's far too easy to get caught up in the little details and miss something big—far too easy and with far too serious consequences as well. Most project managers don't like to hear excuses along the lines of "Oops, wasn't that content supposed to be on this page?" And yet such stupid mistakes as mixing the content up, or using old versions of documents, happen far too frequently. As such, we will analyze the kinds of things to test for, according to:

- Site-wide testing issues
- Specific page testing

Finally, these site-wide and specific page issues are summarized in a handy form that you should feel free to photocopy and employ on any Web site functionality tests:

- Web site functionality testing checklist

Testing Equipment

Keep in mind that your typical work computer may well not be what the Web site visitors will be using to view your site. Ideally, you should test on all the browsers, operating systems, screen resolutions, and bandwidths your visitors are likely to have. Now, it may be unlikely that you'll just happen to have that full range of equipment to hand, unless you're a very rare bird. Some Web development companies have testing rooms set up for this purpose with a broad range of computer hardware and software or even rent such facilities on an as-needed basis.

Tip

Due to the wide variations between different versions of browsers, be sure and test on as many versions as possible; the 3.x, 4.x, 5.x, and 6.x versions of Netscape and Explorer cover a fairly wide range of user systems. Actually, Netscape skipped the 5.x version of its browser, so you need only test on 3.x, 4.x, and 6.x for it!

If you're on your own, however, or with a very small team, it may be necessary to scrounge around a bit. Some good places to look for this variety of equipment are with your friends and family, of course—don't you just love them?!—as well as at public Internet access points such as libraries, Internet cafes, sometimes even shopping malls. And then, of course, a really valuable source is with your users themselves. This way you can combine getting user feedback with the technical side of testing.

With every testing situation, however, it's a good idea to follow the pattern of testing broad to specific issues.

Testing Tools

You may be glad to hear that it is not necessary to conduct *all* of the Web site testing by hand. There are a number of free services, as well as some fee-based services, that can do a lot of the legwork for you. Code validators, for example, have saved millions of hours of tedious review and probably caught more mistakes than most human effort, especially those little mistakes that may actually not cause a problem in some browsers, such as forgetting to close all your tags.

The validators are designed in such a way that they can identify any aspect of your code that does not fully comply with the latest standard. A number of Web authoring tools have built-in validators. The W3C also offers two key validators for free:

- HTML validator at http://validator.w3.org

- CSS validator at http://jigsaw.w3.org/css-validator

There are also a number of Web site diagnostic services that usually charge some kind of fees, such as the following:

- Web site "tune up" at http://www.websitegarage.com

A number of Web development tools, such as Macromedia's DreamWeaver, offer a browser check as well, which will check your site performance on whichever browsers (and versions of browsers) you specify that your target audience will be using. Take advantage of these tools. They can provide very valuable information and help you spot trouble areas for your site to a considerable degree. However, do not rely exclusively on them. They are still no substitute for actually testing on the operating systems and platforms of your intended audience.

Site-wide Testing Issues

Some key areas to test for on a site-wide basis are consistency and performance. Ask yourself each of the questions that appears throughout this module.

Does the site appear consistently in target browsers and operating systems? Sometimes, if you've developed a site exclusively in one browser such as Internet Explorer, it will look terrific in that browser and just awful in another, such as Netscape. This can be in part because the browser vendors have frequently developed proprietary tags—tags that will only work in their browser and that have not been adopted by other browsers or included in the HTML standards issues by the World Wide Web Consortium (W3C). Additionally, support for Cascading Style Sheets (CSS) was very slow to be implemented, so you can see a wide variation of results of CSS pages displayed in different versions of different browsers. Fortunately, this problem is lessening as the W3C standards are becoming stronger and the competing browser companies are agreeing to increase their support of those standards with each new release. This does not solve the problem, however, for older browsers, which are still very commonplace among users.

A few Web authoring tools also occasionally have a bias toward one browser over another. This has been particularly true in the past for Microsoft's products, such as FrontPage and MSWord, having a bias in favor of Microsoft's Internet Explorer.

If you run into this problem, there are three things you can do:

- Determine whether the Web site features that you want are supported by all targeted browsers. In general, avoid any markup that is not cross-browser compatible. In some cases, however, you may decide to leave the feature in for users with one browser if it will not hurt the display for other browsers.

- Check code for browser proprietary tags, and delete them or replace them with fully supported tags whenever possible.

- Confirm that your code conforms to the latest standard—with the XHTML 1.1 standard, for example, all tags need to be closed. Don't be sloppy; stay up to date with the latest standards. Adhering to them will ensure that Web sites you build today will still work tomorrow.

Tip

See Module 4 for a discussion of the wide range of user hardware and software constraints as well as a summary of the key differences between the new XHTML standard and the old HTML standard.

Is the navigation consistent throughout the site?   A Web site's navigation design should have logic and structure that is upheld throughout the site, so that at any point users can identify where they are on the site and what their options are. If you have global navigation (such as a nav bar with links to each of the major sections of the Web site) on some pages but not on others, or if you change the global navigation options available to the users, you will be bound to confuse and frustrate the user. Having to use the browser's Back button or go to the home page every time you want to explore a new area are signs of poor navigation.

Subsections of the site may certainly add a secondary navigation scheme so that users can easily decide between the options available to them in that section. This should not, however, replace the global scheme.

It can be very helpful even on small sites—and is fairly essential on large sites—to develop HTML templates for coding each page. HTML templates are similar in principle to word processing or spreadsheet templates. If you are going to write a bunch of letters, for example, you would probably find it useful to create a word processing template that included your company logo and return address so that you would not have to re-input that information on each new letter. In the same vein, when you are creating a Web site, there are often many elements shared in common with each page, such as the global navigation bar. Thus, it can save you a lot of time to create a template with those elements already in place, which you then use to build out each page. On large sites with a number of different sections, you may also find it helpful to create a new template for each section: for example, a blue one for the section that had a blue tab, a red one for the section with the red tab, and so on. In addition to streamlining the production, templates help you build the Web site correctly in the first place because they ensure consistency. They also give you a standard to check against during the testing phase, in which case, you need to do two things:

● Confirm that each section follows the site template.

● Confirm that each page follows the section template.

Tip
See Module 9 for more guidelines on navigation design.

Is the look and feel consistent and appropriate for the audience?

No matter how large a Web site is, it should have a consistent look and feel throughout all its sections if it is to establish a strong identity. This is not to say that each sub-section may not also have distinct identifiers, such as the use of colors or icons that are unique to that section, but they should be integrated with the overall site design. This is best secured by creating HTML templates and writing down a set of design guidelines for the site, often called a style guide, before the HTML development process begins. The style guide may include such things as the typefaces, sizes, and styles to be used in the heads, the colors chosen for each section, and specifications on how the company logo can or can not be used. By spelling the details of the design out ahead of time, all members of the Web development team can refer to and check their work against it throughout the production process.

Tip

See Modules 9 and 11 for more information on this topic.

C

The look and feel of a site also needs to be appropriate for the content and audience. A conservative business such as a bank, for instance, that needs to convey a sense of trustworthiness and security to its consumers would not be served very well by highly-saturated neon colors with fast-moving animations that promote excitement and surprise. Those design elements might be more appropriate for an adventure sports site targeted at youth. See the following sections for more information.

Thus, the first step of this review stage is to confirm that each page conforms to the style guide and templates

If there are variations in the site's look and feel between testing systems, consider the following:

- Check the monitor bit depth, or color settings, to confirm that it matches your target audience. For example, in designing a site for users who have their monitors set to thousands of colors, the colors may appear differently on monitors set to 256 colors or millions of colors.

- Confirm that you are using only truly Web-safe colors, particularly if your site needs to appear the same at all three common bit depths.

- Check monitor gamma settings if images appear darker or lighter. The gamma settings of Macs, for example, are typically darker than Windows or Unix machines

Is the background color consistent?   If the background color in particular varies between testing machines, check the following:

- Confirm that background color is specified in the HTML. Relying on the browsers' default background colors may produce variations. For example, Explorer's typical default for the background color is white, while Netscape's is gray.

- Confirm that code is correct and that all tags have been closed.

Is the correct content in each section? Step back from the close work you have been doing in programming the pages and look at each one from a user's perspective to make sure the right material actually appears under the right heads:

● Review content list to confirm that each page has correct information in the correct place.

● Verify nothing is missing altogether from the Web site.

Does the site map correctly reflect the structure of the site?
Site maps, which give a visual overview of the entire site, can change a lot during the course of production. Before launching a site, it's essential to confirm that the final, published site map does indeed correctly reflect the structure of the final version of the site and all documentation. It is, thus, necessary to do two things at this stage:

● Check the site map against the actual site.

● Check the site map against the final information architecture plans or flow-charts, just in case the site has been built incorrectly.

Do all pages load? This is a good test to conduct while you are confirming the site map since it involves clicking through to every single page:

● Confirm that links to each page work.

● Confirm that pages are located in intended location per information architecture and site plan.

● Confirm that no pages are missing.

Specific Page Testing

To test for some key areas on a page-by-page basis, ask yourself each of the following questions:

Do the titles appear correctly at the top of the browser? An often overlooked piece of the coding, especially the deeper you go into a site, titles are one of the very first things that users see in their browser. They rely on them to provide valuable information about where they are in a site, so be sure to check the following three aspects:

● Confirm that a title tag is completed for each page.

● Confirm that code is correct so that title displays properly.

● Confirm that text for each title accurately and succinctly describes the contents of the page.

Are the meta tags complete?   Unlike titles, users never even see the meta tags, but they can inadvertently be influenced by them nonetheless. Whenever a user conducts a search on the Web, many search engines use whatever you include in your meta tags to determine whether or not to recommend that site to the user and how high to rank it. Many developers include appropriate meta tags on the home page document but then forget to include them when new material is introduced on subsequent pages. You don't want to make that mistake.

● Confirm that code is present.

● Confirm that code is correct.

● Confirm that key words are an accurate reflection of the Web site content.

Does the page download quickly?   Ideally, each page should download in *less than* 10 seconds on your target user's systems. Any longer and you risk losing the user's attention and causing frustration. (Ten seconds gives users a lot of opportunity to click away to another site.) Too often Web site developers conduct all their work on computers that have high-bandwidth connections, so they may never even notice if particular pages are performing sluggishly. There's nothing quite like actually trying to use your own site on the lowest bandwidth that your users will have to drive home what that actual experience of the Web site will be like.

If you find that any pages are loading slowly, take care of the following three items:

● Minimize the size of graphics and other media.

● Clean up the code.

● Optimize the server. Sometimes the problem is not with the Web site at all but with the server. You may need to discuss this possibility and its solutions with the system administrator.

Tip

For more information and guidance on optimizing your Web site, see Jason Cook's "Site Optimization Tutorial" on the WebMonkey site at http://hotwired.lycos.com/webmonkey/design/site_building/tutorials/tutorial2.html.

Are the most important elements on each page visible before scrolling?

Test this on the lowest screen resolution that your user-base will have, commonly 640×480 or 800×600, with the browsers set to their default preference settings. All of the primary navigation and contents of your Web page should be readily visible at this setting. Users tend not to scroll to see what other information or options may be available on a page, particularly the home page. They strongly prefer to be able to assess the site and make their decision about where they'd like to go at a glance.

Consider each of the following:

● Review layout of elements on the page to ensure optimum presentation.

● Confirm that table widths accommodate this lowest common denominator.

● Confirm that image heights and widths are appropriate for this page size.

● Replace fixed-width tables with relative-width ones whenever possible to provide maximum flexibility for users who drag the corners of their browser windows to make them even smaller than the default settings.

Does resizing the browser window adversely affect the page or individual elements?

Have you ever been looking at a Web site and decided to resize the window on your desktop only to find that the page goes haywire? That's what this check is for. This is an interactive medium, and users may do all sorts of things to your site that you haven't planned for, like resizing the browser window. Fortunately, for the most part, this is not a problem with HTML-only pages. It is more frequently a problem with pages that use the positioning capabilities of CSS coupled with JavaScript to create dynamic content, also referred to as Dynamic HTML (DHTML), so it only needs to be tested on sites that use more advanced technologies.

C

Does the correct version of the page display in the browser?
Ah, this is the dreaded "version control" monster. Web pages go through many iterations during the development process, and, if you're not careful, it can be easy to lose track of which one is, indeed, the most current one. This is largely just a management issue, and you just need to cross-check files.

Sometimes, however, you can make changes to a file, then look at it again in the browser and find yourself staring at an old version. If you run into this problem, take the following steps:

- Double-check that you saved the corrected file.

- Try reloading the file into the browser using, the browser button.

- If that does not work, clear the browser cache and reload the page or even just restart the browser.

Is the source code well commented in preparation for maintenance?   This aspect of Web development may have no impact on the user experience, but it can have a huge impact on the maintenance and revision of a Web site. Well-commented code can save hours of tedious, eye-straining labor trying to find which bit of code needs to be updated. This is particularly true of complex tables or frames. If nothing else, label all your tables and frames with descriptive titles such as "main navigation" or "lower right-hand frame."

Even if you will be the one doing all the maintenance on a site, you may forget over time just how you set something up. That's how our memories work. A detail may be crystal clear one day and then need to be completely rediscovered another.

You need only do two things:

- Confirm that comments are present.

- Confirm that comments are informative and correct.

Is the text content readable?   This is a major usability issue for the Web. Requiring users to read off monitors is already a liability because it can induce such eye-strain. Presenting them with unreadable type, however, can be a sure way to lose them. First off, it's necessary to design the site so that the text will be readable. Designating all the type, for example, to be 6 point Times may look cool, but many of your users will just not be able to read the words. See what I mean? It's essential to design the site from the ground up to be easily readable.

I recommend you change the text settings a couple of times in your own browser to see how the text might look if a user changed the settings (which they sometimes do).

Note

See Module 11 for more information on making your text readable on a Web site.

If the site is fully readable on one system, but not on another, there are several things to check:

- **Check monitor bit depth.** A shift in colors between, say, using 256 colors or thousands of colors may reduce the contrast between type and its backgrounds, making it hard to distinguish the letters.

- **Check monitor gamma settings.** Gamma controls the range of mid-tones on a monitor, so different gamma settings can alter the contrast, making grays fade into blacks, etc. and thus making it hard to distinguish the letters. Unfortunately, Macintosh monitors out of the box typically have a darker gamma setting (1.8) than Windows and Unix machines (2.2-2.5), so it's best to design your site to work within a gamma range of 1.8 to 2.5. Some image editing programs such as Photoshop include a gamma control panel and enable you to toggle between Mac and PC gamma settings. Alternatively, you can reset the monitor to its default settings, which will reset a Mac monitor to 1.8 and a PC to somewhere in the range of 2.2-2.5. Check your monitor reference guide for individual instructions.

- **Check browser's font settings.** Some users change the default font preferences on their browsers. It's best to test each site using default settings since most users do *not* alter them.

- **Check specified font settings in Web page.** When designating any font other than the fonts automatically installed with an operating system, it is impossible to confirm that every user will have your preferred fonts installed on his or her system. It is best to always include one of the default fonts in your list of font choices and to test the appearance of the site with each font you've suggested.

Does text appear in desired font?   If you know the computer you are testing on has your designated font installed but the Web page is still not using it, check these two things:

● Confirm that code is correct.

● Confirm that font name is spelled correctly.

Does unwanted content (such as code) appear on any page?
"@o!pfthhhth!!!" Have you ever seen bizarre bits of text appear on your Web page that you just wanted to curse back at? It happens to the best of us, but of course the very best of us make sure that it is put back in its proper place before the Web page goes live. To find and destroy such invaders, do the following:

● For whole pages that have gone nuts, confirm that the document has been saved with an .htm or .html extension.

● Confirm that the document is saved as text-only. Some programs that can nominally convert files to HTML, such as MSWord, save all sorts of other strange directions within the file, which can be the source of all sorts of problems, including this one. You can get rid of all that information, just by saving it as text-only.

● Check for unclosed tags. In most other cases, this is the source of the problem. One thing to watch out for in particular are tags that appear to be closed but that are missing the final backslash, such as <p> <p> instead of <p> </p>.

Do all special characters appear properly?   If you've specified a special character such as a copyright symbol or accent, but it is not appearing correctly on the page (often they appear as a string of strange characters), check these two things:

● Confirm that the entity begins with an ampersand (&) and ends with a semicolon (;).

● Confirm browser support.

Do any unwanted characters appear in the text?   Unwanted characters (such as § or Ü) often appear in the text if you have typed a special character into the code, such as ©, without coding it as a special character.

- Confirm that desired special characters are designated correctly in code.

- Confirm that document has .html or .htm extension.

- Confirm that document is saved as text-only.

Do all page elements load?   Broken image icons never add much beauty to a page. If graphic or multimedia files fail to load properly, look into the following:

- Confirm that code is correct.

- Confirm that paths are correct, particularly when dealing with relative paths.

- Confirm that files are in correct place indicated by path.

- Confirm that filenames are consistent.

- Confirm that file types are Web viewable (e.g., GIF, JPEG).

- Confirm that necessary plug-ins are installed.

Do page elements load in the appropriate order?   One sure way to slow down the performance of a Web page is to have each of the elements load inconsistently so that the browser has to load all the pieces and then redraw the page to fit. This is what is happening when you just think a Web page has loaded and suddenly the whole page disappears and then, eventually, reappears. There's one key culprit for this problem:

- Verify all element sizes are specified in HTML. If you omit the height and width attributes, the browser does not know how much space to reserve on the page for that element, so it has to load everything, analyze the dimensions of the file, and then redraw the page accordingly, slowing the process way down.

C

Do unwanted dashes appear by linked images?   This is a simple problem with a simple fix:

- Delete all carriage returns within image tags so that the code is on a single line. For some unknown reason, the carriage returns cause unwanted dashes in some browsers.

Are the alt attributes for each element working?   The chief culprit for this problem is usually the developer forgetting to code alternative text for each graphic or media element. Providing alternative text is becoming ever-increasingly important. Visually-impaired users, in particular, rely on these descriptions (which are often read to them through smart browsers) to understand what is included on a page. But they are not the only ones; anyone who has graphics turned off can also at least read the text so they know what is supposed to be in that spot. And, of course, if there are ever any problems with a file, alternative text provides any user with that information.

- Confirm that code is present.

- Confirm that code is correct.

Are all the links working properly?   This is one area that needs constant checking on even *after* a Web site is launched. A Web site's internal links are unlikely to change unless someone on your team intentionally changes them while updating a site, but external links can frequently change. You have no control over Web sites other than your own, but you do have an obligation to your users to make sure that your links stay current. Occasionally, of course, a server will go down, and a Web site will disappear for a period of hours or even days, so there may be no way to avoid having a dead-end link for that period. However, to have a page full of dead-end links simply because you have not maintained your site will detract from the sense of reliability for the whole Web site. Fortunately, much of this task can be automated, at least the identification of broken links. You, however, need to supply the information to correct any broken links.

- Confirm that code is correct.

- Confirm that linked pages exist in place where you have linked to.

Do all scripts work? If your site includes scripts such as rollovers or scripts to process forms, it is necessary to confirm that each one of them works as intended. Even if you do not have the knowledge to program such scripts, you can still help determine whether they are working properly:

● Check browser settings to confirm that the scripting language has been enabled.

● Confirm that the script works as intended.

Are the pages printable? Finally, are all pages that users will likely want to print out adequately printable? There's nothing quite like trying to print a Web page and getting a band of solid black where the text should be. Not every single Web page needs to be able to be completely captured in print form; that would, in fact, be impossible just due to the differences between the media. Animations, video, and audio, for example, are inherently antithetical to print. But if there are text or graphics within any Web page that users might want to print out, make sure that they can do so successfully.

● Confirm that backgrounds do not interfere with the content of the page when printed on a black and white or color printer.

● Confirm that the use of color for text, particularly light colors such as white or yellow, are readable when printed out on white sheets of paper.

● Confirm that the use of Cascading Style Sheets for layout does not interfere with the readability of any of the text when printed. The line-height property when used to create cool-looking overlapping lines of text can be particularly problematic when printed out.

● Consider providing printable versions of Web pages that are problematic.

Functionality Testing Checklist

Here is a testing checklist to use whenever you get to the testing stage of the Web site development process. Feel free to photocopy it and keep a stack handy for your personal use.

C

		Testing System Specs. Operating System: _____ Browser: _____ Screen Resolution: _____ Bandwidth: _____	Testing System Specs. Operating System: _____ Browser: _____ Screen Resolution: _____ Bandwidth: _____	Testing System Specs. Operating System: _____ Browser: _____ Screen Resolution: _____ Bandwidth: _____
Site-wide Checks	Does the site appear consistently in target browsers and operating systems?			
	Is the navigation consistent throughout the site?			
	Is the look and feel consistent and appropriate for the audience?			
	Is the background color consistent?			
	Is the correct content in each section?			
	Does the site map correctly reflect the structure of the site?			
	Do all pages load?			
Page-by-Page Checks	Do the titles appear correctly at the top of the browser?			
	Are the meta tags complete?			
	Does the page download quickly? (Ideally in less than 10 seconds on your target user's system.)			
	Are the most important elements on each page visible before scrolling?			
	Does resizing the browser window adversely affect the page or individual elements?			
	Does the correct version of the page display in the browser?			
	Is the source code well commented in preparation for maintenance?			
	Is the text content readable?			
	Does text appear in desired font?			
	Does unwanted content (such as code) appear on any page?			
	Do all special characters appear properly?			
	Do any unwanted characters appear in the text (such as § or Ü)?			

Table C-1 Web Site Functionality Testing Checklist

		Testing System Specs. Operating System: _____ Browser: _____ Screen Resolution: _____ Bandwidth: _____	Testing System Specs. Operating System: _____ Browser: _____ Screen Resolution: _____ Bandwidth: _____	Testing System Specs. Operating System: _____ Browser: _____ Screen Resolution: _____ Bandwidth: _____
	Do all page elements load? (including any multimedia)			
	Do page elements load in the appropriate order?			
	Do unwanted dashes appear by linked images?			
	Are the alt attribute tags for each element working?			
	Are all the links working properly?			
	Do all scripts work?			
	Are the pages printable?			

Table C-1   Web Site Functionality Testing Checklist (continued)

Appendix D
Web Site Usability Checklists

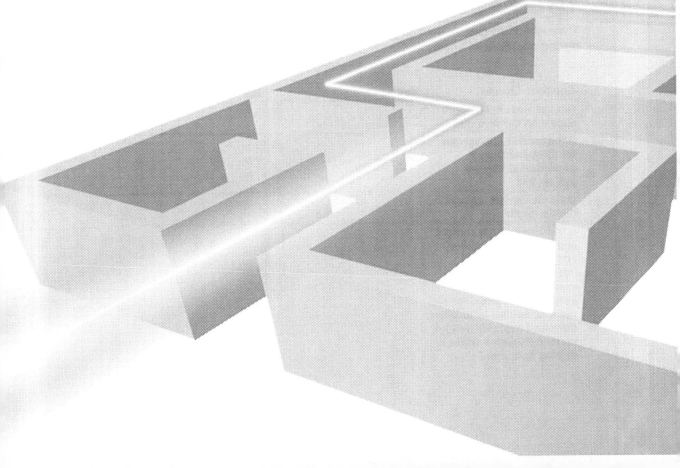

Periodically asking yourself the questions in the following checklists can help you identify some common usability problems throughout the Web site design and development process. The checklists are by necessity generic and as such cannot be comprehensive; every Web site is unique and requires careful thought about how it may be made more usable. Nor are these checklists intended to be a replacement for actual usability testing with people who are representative of the Web site's user base. In my mind, there is *no* effective substitution for placing real users in front of a computer with your Web site on it and asking them to perform a set of tasks or just to explore the Web site however they want.

As per the book, the checklists are broken down in terms of

- Content

- Information architecture

- Navigation design

- Screen design

Tip

These checklists can be used to good effect in conjunction with the functionality testing questions in Appendix C.

Content Checks	Yes	No
Does all intended content appear on the Web site?		
Is the content appropriate for the users? Does it provide what they are looking for?		
Does the content support the site goals?		
Is the format of the content appropriate for the users' computer systems and Internet connections? For example, if the content includes multimedia, will the users' computers be able to download it quickly enough for them to view it without causing frustration?		

Content Checks	Yes	No
Is the domain name easy to memorize, pronounce, and spell?		
Are the URLs helpful in identifying the content?		
Are the page titles helpful in identifying the content?		
Do the meta tags give an accurate summary of the content in a format that can be easily used by search engines?		
Does supplemental content adequately secure user trust, e.g., privacy statements, security notices, real-world context, contact info, and so on?		
Does supplemental content adequately secure your own or your client's protection, e.g., copyright notices, disclaimers, and so on?		
Is the text written in the users' language? For example, does it avoid unnecessary jargon?		
Is the text well-written and grammatically correct?		
Is the text written in such a way as to help users achieve a task?		
Is the text written to be easily scanned for online reading? For example, is it concisely written, and does it have a clearly visible structure that takes full advantage of headings, bullet point lists, and so on?		

D

Content Checks	Yes	No
Are the headlines and titles short, sweet, and communicative?		
Are the fonts used on the site likely to be installed on the users' computers?		
Is the point size of the text large enough to be easily read by the users?		
Are the graphics and multimedia elements optimized for presentation on the Web? This would apply to file size, file format, compression, and image or audio quality.		
Are alt attributes provided for each graphic or multimedia element?		
Will users find the media files appealing and informative instead of annoying or irrelevant?		
If users are not able to access any media files, will the Web site's content, message, and navigation be adversely affected?		
Do the media files convey information more effectively than just using plain text or lower-bandwidth media files, such as graphics instead of animations?		
Are users provided with the means to disable any multimedia elements?		

Tip

See Modules 7 and 12 for more information on selecting and developing the content for a Web site.

Information Architecture Checks	Yes	No
Is all the content placed where it is supposed to be?		
Is the information organized from the users' point of view?		
Is the information organized in a way that will make it easy for users to accomplish tasks on the Web site in accord with the site goals, such as researching and buying a product?		
Is the information organized in a coherent fashion, following an identifiable classification system?		
Is the information organized in a consistent manner throughout the site?		
If the information architecture relies on any metaphors, are they appropriate for the content as well as the audience?		
If the information architecture uses any metaphors, are they followed consistently throughout the site?		
Can users find important pieces of information within three clicks from the home page?		
Is the content of the Web site grouped according to the seven, plus or minus two guideline, to present clusters of between 5 and 9 sets of information?		
Is the information architecture presented clearly on the Web site?		
Are the content labels used to present the information architecture on the Web site short, sweet, and communicative?		
Does the site map correctly reflect the structure of the site?		

D

Tip

See Module 8 for details on creating a Web site's information architecture.

Navigation Design Checks	Yes	No
Does the navigation design fully support the information architecture?		
Does the navigation design provide the tools that users need to find whatever they may be looking for on a Web site?		
Does the navigation design effectively employ principles of graphic design, audio design, motion graphics design, and/or interactivity design?		
Do the aesthetics of the navigation design fully support its functionality?		
Are the navigation controls and navigation aids appropriate for the content and the users?		
Do the navigation controls work as intended? For example, do all hypertext links actually link to the correct destination?		
Do the navigation aids effectively inform users about the navigation options in a site as well as complement the aesthetic look and feel of the site?		
Can users effectively navigate the site if they enter from pages other than the home page?		
Is the navigation design consistent throughout the site?		
Is the supplemental navigation integrated into the look and feel of the rest of the Web site?		
Does the navigation design of sub-sites complement the site-wide navigation?		
Does the navigation design provide site-wide context so that users can easily answer each of the following questions from any point in the site: "Where am I?" "Where have I been?" "Where can I go?"		
Does the navigation design provide descriptive text as needed for each navigational element, ranging from page titles to icon labels?		
Are alt attributes assigned for every graphical piece of the navigation design?		
Will users still be able to navigate the site if they have disabled JavaScript (and the resulting support of JavaScript rollovers)?		
Will users still be able to navigate the site if they do not have the "correct" plug-ins installed, such as for Flash animation?		

Tip

See Module 9 for more information on navigation design.

D

Screen Design Checks	Yes	No
Is the screen design appropriate for both the content and the users?		
Does the screen design fully support the navigation design?		
Is the screen design consistent throughout the site?		
Does the screen design effectively employ principles of graphic design, audio design, motion graphics design, and/or interactivity design?		
Does the screen design effectively direct the user's eye to tell a story with each page and reveal the priority of content?		
Does the screen design appear consistently on all the identified user systems?		
Does each Web page download quickly on your users' systems?		
Is all the vital information, including navigation, for each Web page visible without scrolling?		
Is the targeted screen size appropriate for the users' systems?		
Is the screen design's color palette fully supported by the users' systems?		
Is an appropriate amount of content included on each screen?		
Does the screen design fully support on-screen readability of the text?		
Are the fonts specified by the HTML and CSS code likely to be installed on the users' computers?		
Are the screens printable, or are alternative printable versions made available?		

Tip

See Module 11 for more information on screen design for usability.

Index

INTERNATIONAL CONTACT INFORMATION

AUSTRALIA
McGraw-Hill Book Company Australia Pty. Ltd.
TEL +61-2-9417-9899
FAX +61-2-9417-5687
http://www.mcgraw-hill.com.au
books-it_sydney@mcgraw-hill.com

CANADA
McGraw-Hill Ryerson Ltd.
TEL +905-430-5000
FAX +905-430-5020
http://www.mcgrawhill.ca

GREECE, MIDDLE EAST,
NORTHERN AFRICA
McGraw-Hill Hellas
TEL +30-1-656-0990-3-4
FAX +30-1-654-5525

MEXICO (Also serving Latin America)
McGraw-Hill Interamericana Editores S.A. de C.V.
TEL +525-117-1583
FAX +525-117-1589
http://www.mcgraw-hill.com.mx
fernando_castellanos@mcgraw-hill.com

SINGAPORE (Serving Asia)
McGraw-Hill Book Company
TEL +65-863-1580
FAX +65-862-3354
http://www.mcgraw-hill.com.sg
mghasia@mcgraw-hill.com

SOUTH AFRICA
McGraw-Hill South Africa
TEL +27-11-622-7512
FAX +27-11-622-9045
robyn_swanepoel@mcgraw-hill.com

UNITED KINGDOM & EUROPE
(Excluding Southern Europe)
McGraw-Hill Education Europe
TEL +44-1-628-502500
FAX +44-1-628-770224
http://www.mcgraw-hill.co.uk
computing_neurope@mcgraw-hill.com

ALL OTHER INQUIRIES Contact:
Osborne/McGraw-Hill
TEL +1-510-549-6600
FAX +1-510-883-7600
http://www.osborne.com
omg_international@mcgraw-hill.com

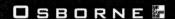

...ng Source UK Ltd.
...eynes UK
...RUK00003B/11/A

9 780072 192612